LAUREL
&
HARDY

When they weren't being Stan & Ollie . . .

LAUREL & HARDY

A Bio-Bibliography

Wes D. Gehring

Popular Culture Bio-Bibliographies
M. Thomas Inge, Series Editor

Greenwood Press
New York • Westport, Connecticut • London

Library of Congress Cataloging-in-Publication Data

Gehring, Wes D.
    Laurel and Hardy : a bio-bibliography / Wes D. Gehring.
      p. cm. — (Popular culture bio-bibliographies, ISSN
0193–6891)
    Includes bibliographical references.
    ISBN 0–313–25172–X (lib. bdg. : alk. paper)
    1. Laurel, Stan. 2. Hardy, Oliver, 1892–1957. 3. Laurel, Stan—
Bibliography. 4. Hardy, Oliver, 1892–1957—Bibliography.
5. Comedians—United States—Biography. 6. Motion picture actors
and actresses—United States—Biography. I. Title. II. Series.
PN2287.L285G4   1990
791.43′028′0922—dc20
   [B]   89–25708

British Library Cataloguing in Publication Data is available.

Copyright © 1990 by Wes D. Gehring

Library of Congress Catalog Card Number: 89–25708
ISBN: 0–313–25172–X
ISSN: 0193–6891

First published in 1990

Greenwood Press, 88 Post Road West, Westport, CT 06881
An imprint of Greenwood Publishing Group, Inc.

Printed in the United States of America

The paper used in this book complies with the
Permanent Paper Standard issued by the National
Information Standards Organization (Z39.48–1984).

10 9 8 7 6 5 4 3 2 1

Copyright Acknowledgments

The frontispiece and Figures 6 and 11 were provided by the Lester Glassner Collection (New York).
Figures 1, 7, 10, 13, and 14 came courtesy of the National Film Archive (London). Figures 2, 5,
7, 9, 12, and 14 were furnished by the Museum of Modern Art/Film Stills archive (New York).
Used with permission. The poems "Laurel at a Hundred: Never One to Stan Around (1980–1990)"
and "Stan & Ollie: two minds without a single thought," originally appeared in the Scottish journal
Bowler Dessert, issues 39 and 40.

To Eileen, Sarah, and Emily;
and my original threesome—
Mom, Dad, and Sue.

LAUREL AT A HUNDRED:
NEVER ONE TO STAN
AROUND
(1890–1990)*

Laurel's twin passions in
Life were film & fishing—
Both being reel sports.

The key to success in
Each depended on knowing
When to give the line.

Less lucky in love, his many
Marriages were like seasickness—
He couldn't contain himself.

A true romantic, he forever
Believed there were ''more
Fish in the sea'' but like

The screen Stanley, these fishwives
Put the hooks to him, often
Reducing Laurel to chicken-of-the-sea.

Even his teaming with Ollie
Was like fishing—slapstick
Jerks on either end of a line.

Their love of tit-for-tat
Humor also matched the
Fisherman's Logo—bait & sea.

Thus, we celebrate them
As high watermarks of
Humor—eternal *Saps at Sea*.

> With best fishes,
> L & Hardally yours

---

*Dedicated to a pun loving duo named Laurel & Hardy.

                    stan & ollie:
                "two minds without
                a single thought"*

Stan seldom rested
On his Laurels
Even though he was
Never less than Hardy.

Because Ollie always
Thought he was right
Stan forever got
What was left.

As henpecked husbands,
Marriage was not a word,
It was a sentence, proving the
Advantage of adieu to I do.

Their logic was forever
Looney—"You can lead
A horse to water but a
Pencil must be lead."

Well-intentioned chuckleheads,
They never thought
Of wrong; Indeed they
never thought at all.

For silly Stan & Ollie, William
Shakespeare could be any play*bill*,
Or Hamlet any plate of
Eggs with cheese.

Forever fated to "another fine mess,"
They were a good comic investment—
Guaranteed laughing*stocks*, whose films
Were like a funny fortuneteller—
                    A happy medium.

*Courtesy of the skinny one.

Contents

Illustrations   xi

Preface and Acknowledgments   xiii

1.   Laurel & Hardy Biography   1

2.   stan & ollie: *the* comic antiheroes   125

3.   Laurel & Hardy: PERIOD REFLECTIONS   143

    "Those Two Goofy Guys"   145

    "Ka-Plop and Ka-Bloop: Laurel and Hardy Reveal What Makes You Hear Such Funny Things"   147

    "Encore: An Interview/Article Collage"   151

4.   A Laurel & Hardy Bibliographical Essay   155

    Books   156

    Shorter Works   169

    Laurel & Hardy Archival Holdings   246

5.   Bibliographical Checklist of Key Laurel & Hardy Sources   247

Chronology   259

Filmography   273

Selected Discography   289

Index   291

Illustrations

When they weren't being Stan & Ollie . . . frontispiece

1. Ollie's tie-twiddling routine   11

2. "Little Lois" (age 2) with father and friend   39

3. Stan & Ollie as Sons of the Desert   43

4. "Obliging Oliver"—the newspaper comic strip (1914)   49

5. Leo McCarey on the set of *The Awful Truth*   52

6. Oscar night 1932 (with Walt Disney)—the duo wins for *The Music Box*   53

7. *The Flying Deuces* (1939)—Ollie returns as a horse   71

8. The Ulverston (England) tombstone "lighthouse"   78

9. On the set of *Babes in Toyland* (1934), with Virginia Karns   80

10. Stan showing his age as early as 1937—a nonretouched publicity still from *Way Out West*   100

11. Another London tour exit—October 8, 1952   112

12. Stan & Ollie seem to be footnoting their status as comedy icons in *The Flying Deuces*   126

13. Posed antiheroic violence for *Block-Heads'* garage door scene   177

14. Stan's "white magic"—about to light his thumb   201

Preface and Acknowledgments

The goal of this work is to present a combined biographical, critical, and bibliographical estimate of Laurel & Hardy's significance in film comedy, the arts in general, and as popular culture icons. The book is divided into five chapters. Chapter 1 is a biography of Laurel & Hardy, exploring the public and private sides of their lives.

Of the two, Laurel emerges as the central player scrutinized in this duo biography for four reasons. First, in later years Laurel forever made himself available to the team's adoring public, while Hardy tended to be the more private individual. Consequently, pioneer team chronicles, such as John McCabe's watershed *Mr. Laurel & Mr. Hardy* (1961) could not help but have a Laurel slant.

Second, Laurel's late-life accessibility was consistent with his earlier role as team spokesman. Because Laurel was the creatively dominant duo member (though Hardy's artistic input is currently being given a revisionist upgrading), the skinny one often acted as the key and/or sole speaker in team literature from their glory days. Thus, Laurel & Hardy period material often has more of a Laurel stamp to it.

Third, just as Hardy was a more private person, he exercised greater control over his personal life than Laurel did over his. Put another way, Hardy was better at keeping his private difficulties out of the news. While both men had problems (especially in relationships with women), Laurel seemed always to be the one living his life in newspaper headlines. While this is hardly pleasant for the victim, it provides added insight for the biographer and added interest for the reader. Indeed, I am reminded of one definition of the perfect biographical subject—a success who has paid a great price for that position; indeed, this subject's audience can fluctuate between jealousy and sympathy. And Laurel, the wonderfully gifted comedian but often troubled man-child, certainly matches this interpretation of the ideal biographical subject.

Fourth, Laurel outlived Hardy by eight years (1957 to 1965) and was able to take part in the ever-burgeoning public fascination with the team—a fascination that reached new and unique proportions in the 1960s. Thus, Laurel lived to be honored with a special Oscar in 1961 for his groundbreaking work in comic cinema, to see the warm critical and commercial response to McCabe's 1961 book, and the founding shortly before his death of the still-growing Laurel & Hardy fan club, the Sons of the Desert. In fact, Laurel contributed the idea for the club logo, two derbies, and slogan, "Two Minds Without a Single Thought." Moreover, he comically blessed the organization, only hoping it would have "a half-assed dignity" about it. For these reasons Laurel has more visibility than Hardy does in Chapter 1.

Chapter 2 is a critique of four broad influences of Laurel & Hardy—as special icons of comic frustrations; as developers of a change in film comedy pacing (which also eased their transition from silent to sound film); as movie pioneers in the innovative early use of comic sound; and, most important, as valuable participants in the evolution of the comic antihero into mainstream American humor.

Because no examination of artists would be complete without some of their own observations, Chapter 3 is composed of two very early reprinted Laurel & Hardy articles and a special "Encore" collection. The first two pieces are a *Motion Picture Classic* interview, "Ka-Plop and Ka-Bloop: Laurel and Hardy Reveal What Makes You Hear Such Funny Things" (1930) and a *Photoplay* article/interview, "Those Two Goofy Guys" (1930). The third piece, "Encore: An Interview/Article Collage," is a sampling of team spokesman Laurel's observations drawn from various early career sources.

The reprints represent a balancing act. Appearing nearly concurrently, one is a big picture overview of the team, while the other addresses a more narrow focus (the comic use of film sound). An added bonus for the latter article is that Hardy assumes a more active part than is often the case in team interviews. And lastly, the "Encore" selections tie the chapter together by offering a final showcase for a broad assortment of pivotal and/or provocative early Laurel observations drawn from sources that are often now obscure.

Chapter 4 is a Laurel & Hardy bibliographical essay, assessing key reference materials and locating research collections open to students and scholars. The majority of the chapter is allocated to reference works and is divided into two sections. The first is devoted to book-length sources written about the comedians. These materials are subdivided into four categories: Laurel & Hardy viewed by an insider (an author who knew the subject firsthand), general biographies, critical studies, and references. The second section of Chapter 4 is made up of shorter works and includes articles, interviews, book chapters, and monographs. It is subdivided further into two parts: Laurel & Hardy critical essays and print interviews/reminiscences with the comedians, colleagues, or families. To facilitate the use of both sections as a reference guide, Chapter 5 is a bibliographical checklist of all sources recommended in Chapter 4. The checklist is meant to be a research guide, not an all-encompassing bibliography of the team (although it is more detailed than any other such listing currently on the market).

There is always a temptation to note every source of related interest, but this can open such a floodgate of material that key works are shortchanged. Thus, chapters 4 and 5 maintain the most disciplined of configurations. The reader/ researcher who must have additional related sources can study the notes that close the other chapters.

The pivotal research collections examined in Chapter 4 are found in the Laurel & Hardy Museum (Ulverston, England); the British Film Institute (London-BFI); the New York Public Library system, especially the Lincoln Center branch, which houses the Billy Rose Theatre Collection; the Margaret Herrick Library at the Academy of Motion Picture Arts and Sciences (Beverly Hills); the American Film Institute (Beverly Hills—AFI); the Cinémathèque Francaise (Paris); the University of Iowa's (Iowa City) main library and its audiovisual center; UCLA's (Los Angeles) Theatre Arts Library within its University Research Library; and the Museum of Modern Art (New York City).

The appendixes contain a chronological biography, a filmography, and a selected discography.

Few books are solely the result of one person, and special thanks are in order for David Gill, archivist, Academy of Motion Picture Arts and Sciences; Pat Perilli, library services, British Film Institute; Dorothy Swerdlove, curator, the Billy Rose Theatre Collection; Mary Corliss, stills archivist, Museum of Modern Art; Charles Silver, Film Study Center Director, Museum of Modern Art; Bill Blackbeard, archivist, San Francisco Academy of Comic Art; Marla Y. Muse, bibliographer, Library of Congress; and stills collector Lester Glassner.

There is a worldwide army of Laurel & Hardy aficionados, and several of them made major contributions to the book. Laurel & Hardy researcher, essayist, and editor Leo Brooks, Jr. was most helpful, from his team writing to his supportive correspondence. Bill Cubin, curator of the Laurel & Hardy Museum in Ulverston (the English town in which Laurel was born) was very accommodating during my research visit and provided a wealth of additional Laurel & Hardy contacts. *Pratfall* editor Lori Jones (Universal City, California) could always be counted upon to answer questions or provide additional reference sources. William McIntyre (Renfrewshire, Scotland), editor of *Bowler Dessert*, was able to provide back issues of his journal, just as Laurence Reardon (Cheshire, England) furnished a copy of his informative monograph on Laurel & Hardy's tour visits to Coventry, England. Additional assistance was provided by Nancy Wardell (England—a second cousin of Stan Laurel), Mabel Radcliff (the present owner of Laurel's birthplace), and team author A. J. Marriot (Tilbury, England). All journals cited herein focus on the team.

Additional thanks are in order for my department chairperson, John Kurtz, for his ongoing support of my writing projects; Maria and Joe Pacino and Mandi

Summers for their translation assistance; Janet Warrner, my typist and general troubleshooter; and Veva McCoskey, interlibrary loan librarian at Ball State University's Bracken Library.

This volume has generated a great deal of travel research funded in part by a National Endowment for the Humanities ''Travel to Collections'' grant and the assistance of Ball State University.

This was also a family project, with my wife, Eileen, often assisting on the archival work, while my daughters, Sarah and Emily, never missed a chance to sit in on a Laurel & Hardy screening—especially *Them Thar Hills* (1934).

Finally, I thank both Dr. M. Thomas Inge, series editor for Greenwood Press's Popular Culture Bio-Bibliographies, and Marilyn Brownstein, humanities editor at Greenwood, for making this project possible, and my family for their patience and understanding in seeing me through both the extensive research and the eventual writing. None of this would have been possible without their support.

1

Laurel & Hardy Biography

A rare backlash (*Helpmates*, 1932) by Stan over his Ollie-assigned chores still has the traditional ending:

Stan: "Say, who do you think I am, Cinderella? You know, if I had any sense, I'd leave!"
Ollie: "Well, it's a good thing you haven't!"

Laurel & Hardy, film comedy's definitive skinny man/fat man (respectively) combination, were figuratively and literally *miles apart* in their backgrounds, as well as their pants size. Stan Laurel was born in Ulverston, Lancaster County, England on June 16, 1890 (the same year as comedy contemporary Groucho Marx). The surname Laurel was, however, not acquired until after he became a comedian. At birth he was christened Arthur Stanley Jefferson. Hardy was born Norvell Hardy on January 18, 1892, in Harlem (near Augusta), Georgia. And even at birth his size was *the* distinguishing factor: "Hardy" (such an appropriate name) weighed in at fourteen pounds!

For the sake of familiarity and simplicity, the two comedians will be referred to as Laurel & Hardy throughout this work when their behind-the-screen activities are being examined. Their on-screen personae will be designated Stan & Ollie, as they often referred to each other in their comic antiheroic adventures.

Laurel was born into a theatrical background. His father was a struggling comedian, actor, and writer named Arthur J. ("A.J.") Jefferson, and his mother was actress Madge Metcalfe. Her speciality was the type of vamp roles for which silent film actress Theda Bara later became famous. A.J. found his most lucrative accomplishments, though, as a theatre manager and the author/stage producer of a number of melodramas which frequently featured his wife.

As if in anticipation of Laurel's future success in the United States, he was also a descendant of the famous British-born American actor Joseph Jefferson (1774–1832). Indeed, this ancestor's even more celebrated thespian grandson, Joseph Jefferson III (1829–1905) was still very prominent in American theatre circles during Laurel's boyhood. And, fittingly for future silent comedy star Laurel, the central role in Jefferson III's long career was both comedic (Rip Van Winkle) and famous for his attention to physical detail in a long silent passage of this stage adaptation of Washington Irving's work. Appropriately, an early Laurel & Hardy biographical piece observed, "Stanley Jefferson made his stage debut in a carried-on part. Dressing-rooms were his nursery, theater alleys his playground."[1] (Possibly drawn from a creatively whimsical Laurel, since his early boyhood was spent with his maternal grandparents—examined later in the chapter.)

While Laurel's family was rich in entertainment background, Hardy's ancestry was completely devoid of any footlights tradition. His jack-of-all-trades father, Oliver Hardy, died when the future comedian was only a baby. While still young (prior to his film career) he adopted the name Oliver Norvell Hardy in honor of his father. But despite later accounts by Hardy, there is neither record of his father being a lawyer nor the comedian having once studied law.

From early childhood Laurel's career goal was to be a comedian. And like many other comedians before and since, he was the class clown in and out of school. Indeed, one of his boarding school teachers, Mr. Bates, frequently used Laurel as a court jester in off hours. The boy would successfully perform comic material for the teacher and his drinking companions in Bates's quarters. This support first proved to Laurel that he had comic talents, and well it might, since class clowns seldom have their teachers for fans. And, while Laurel's boarding-school entertainment repertoire was largely recycled comedy sketch material culled from his theatrical haunts, he did show signs of individual creativity. Ironically, one of his most inspired bits of comic authorship, a devastating parody of an unpopular pencil-chewing German instructor, got him into trouble. Bates so enjoyed the performance he kept having Laurel repeat it. But the dreaded teacher was also present on one occasion and he showed none of Bates's enthusiasm.

Laurel's childhood idol was Dan Leno (1860–1904), the most honored comedian of the age. As revealed later in the chapter, this music hall performer influenced both the public and the private Stan Laurel.

Hardy's early show-business tendencies were toward music. While there had never been professional entertainers in his family, they all (mother, half brothers Sam and Henry, and half sisters Elizabeth and Emily) enjoyed singing and the theatre. Indeed, Hardy was so fond of music he delighted in telling how at eight years of age he had briefly toured the South as a boy soprano in "Coburn's Minstrels." But evidence now suggests this was a Hardy fabrication. (His mother forever denied the story, suggesting she would have been a poor parent to let such a young son tour.) The comedian was sometimes inventive with his background. Still, his singing voice would, on occasion, grace the team's films, including his "The Trail of the Lonesome Pine" (also known as "In the Blue Ridge Mountains of Virginia") duet with Stan in *Way Out West* (1937).

Ironically, the death of Hardy's father indirectly contributed to his interest in show business. His widowed, financially pinched mother, M. Emmie (whose maiden name, Norvell, was given to Hardy, seemingly because of its regional importance), eventually derived her income from operating hotels, first in Madison and later in Milledgeville, Georgia. (The elder Hardy had been managing a hotel at the time of his death.) Hardy's childhood thus created both a fascination with entertainers (via the colorful stories and/or characteristics of performing hotel guests) and an ongoing interest in the habits and idiosyncracies of people in general. The latter development was especially significant due to the great importance later placed upon Laurel & Hardy believability by the man who teamed and helped mold them, Leo McCarey, as well as by the comedians themselves. Thus, late in Hardy's life he observed that the pivotal event of his childhood was acquiring a "lobby watching" habit. "Whenever I travel, I still am in the habit of sitting in the lobby and watching the people walk by—and I tell you I see many Laurels and Hardys."[2] Hardy's third wife, Lucille, later revealed (in the 1974 BBC documentary, *Cuckoo: A Celebration of Stan Laurel and Oliver Hardy*) that Ollie's florid writing of his signature (as when he signs into the hotel in *Any Old Port*, 1932) was drawn from his memories of guests at both his mother's establishment and other hotels.

While both Laurel & Hardy were indifferent students in boyhood (something over which the former later expressed regret[3]), their parents' approaches to education were decidedly dissimilar. Since young Laurel was forever preoccupied with show business, from mimicking the comics in his father's theatre to having his own miniature theatre at home where he produced plays for and with friends, he was allowed to drop out of school in his mid-teens. Not surprisingly, his father then gave him a position in his theatre, which at this time was in Glasgow, Scotland's impressive Metropole.

In contrast, twice during Hardy's childhood school received increased emphasis when his interest in the theatre hurt his studies. The first time resulted in a Milledgeville boarding school placement. And later, when he neglected his classes at the Atlanta Conservatory of Music, Hardy was enrolled in the Georgia Military Academy of Milledgeville.

Yet, while both Laurel & Hardy were apathetic students, this period still represents a fascinating microcosm of their adult worlds. For instance, Laurel's total fascination with the theatre, to the detriment of all else was a sneak preview of a future artist who totally immersed himself in every aspect of filmmaking (from the initial gag brainstorming to uncredited assisting in the editing) to the detriment of his private life. And work invariably followed Laurel home. Indeed, his daughter, Lois, remembers the house as always littered with yellow paper pads for convenience if an idea occurred to Laurel.[4]

In contrast, while Hardy was seemingly no more contented with school than

Laurel, he still managed to find related diversions. At Georgia Military School he blossomed as an athlete, playing football and baseball, and showed comic stage presence in a school sketch called "Who Killed Cock Robin?" As a young man Hardy and three equally "hardy" friends formed a musical quartet with the tongue-in-cheek name of "Half-a-Ton of Harmony." In the spirit of this comic self-consciousness one is tempted to describe Hardy as more "well-rounded" than Laurel. Consistently in their years as a team, Hardy left much of the creative decision making to single-minded workaholic Laurel while he pursued various interests including gourmet cooking, card games, sports, and golf. Indeed, sports rivaled his comedy career, from his later obsessional golfing to his weakness for gambling, especially at the racetrack. (Hardy was a friend and sometimes betting companion of compulsive gambler and rival comedy team member Chico Marx.)

Interestingly enough, school itself also seems to have had a direct impact on Hardy's future screen persona. He credited a school teacher as the model for his character's renowned expression of exasperation at Stan's stupidity.[5] (This was the visual equivalent of his famous refrain at Stan's sap-headedness: "Well, here's another nice mess you've gotten me into.") To extrapolate on this revelation is to reveal how teacher-like Hardy's screen character is in relation to Laurel's. Ollie is forever trying to teach simpleton Stan the most basic of tasks, such as how to light a gas stove in the ironically titled short subject *Helpmates* (1932, and later repeated in the 1938 feature *Block-Heads*), only to have it literally blow up in Ollie's face. And though teachers always grimace at that hoary axiom—"Those who can't, teach"—Ollie's character quite nicely fits its expression.

A now legendary footnote to Ollie's patented look of exasperation and the real Hardy's golfing obsession is that comedy team leader Laurel used to save shooting those "inserts" (close-ups of that Ollie expression that could be "inserted" wherever appropriate in the film) until late afternoon. By this time Hardy was more than a little anxious to put whatever sun time remained to golfing use. Thus, those screen looks of Ollie frustration were often assisted by some very real Hardy exasperation. And Stan Laurel was still the culprit! (While no doubt true some of the time, late afternoons also frequently found *both* comedians and others discussing comedy ideas for the next day. Still, Hardy was bewitched by golf.)

The "why" behind his fascination with the sport also says much about the gregariously competitive, yet ever graceful, real man. In John McCabe's biography of Hardy, the comedian observes, "I love it [golf] because it's social . . . —nothing is quite like a good foursome of nice guys enjoying each other's company. And it's challenging . . . without a whole lot of fuss."

Laurel's behind-the-screen domination of the team also reveals the most basic difference between the two, beyond the agelessly fundamental comedy contrast of fat man/skinny man. Unlike many Laurel & Hardy comedy contemporaries whose film personae often seemed close to their real-life identities[6] the behind-the-screen Laurel & Hardy were commonly just the opposite of Stan and Ollie. Laurel was a bright comedy mind to whom a talented but modest Hardy looked for team leadership.

There is no question Laurel was the creatively dominant team member, especially during the early days when Hardy was very much the junior partner (Laurel was so driven that he continued to write team material late in life, after Hardy's death!). But Hardy was not without some input. For example, though not the norm, an occasional interview showcases a seemingly production-involved Hardy (see the Helen Louise Walker piece reprinted in Chapter 3).

Hardy's standard position regarding comedy differences was the "don't rock the boat" belief that inferior material would show up in the rushes and eventually be cut. Otherwise, he was often on record as acquiescing to the decisions of Laurel, though he was capable of subtly planting the occasional idea during production. Moreover, the sometimes apparent connection between team material and Hardy's background (see this chapter's later discussion of *Pardon Us*, 1931) suggests the creative input was not completely Laurel's. Consequently, while Laurel is still to be considered the dominant behind the scenes partner and team spokesman, it was not a complete one-man show.

At the beginnings of their solo careers in entertainment, minor hometown business opportunities surfaced. Laurel's position was of a managerial trainee nature in his father's Glasgow theatre. Hardy was a film projectionist in Milledgeville. As might be expected, their responses differed.

Stan could not wait to perform. (Technically, his stage debut came in May 1900, when the 9-year-old found himself blowing a horn in celebration of a British battle victory in the Boer War.) Very early in Laurel's business tenure, unbeknownst to his father, he arranged an audition at a modest Glasgow theatre/penny arcade called Pickard's Museum. Thus, in May 1906 a sixteen-year-old Laurel found himself on stage. Though his material was largely "borrowed" from his favorite comedians, as in his "command" performances for his teacher, Laurel's comic enthusiasm put the act over.

In fact, it was one of those magic evenings when even the mistakes were successful. Laurel completely lost his composure when he spotted his father in the audience at the close of the routine. Quite by chance earlier in the evening A. J. had been walking by the museum when its owner (Albert E. Pickard), a friend of the well-known theatrical father, invited him in, assuming he had come to see his son's debut. Father played along and was soon treated to Laurel's well-received opening. But when his son spotted him, Laurel gave a completely unintended comic encore. A. J. later recalled that first Laurel let out a muffled scream and then promptly dropped his top hat, which belonged to his father:

Stan pursued it, tried to grab it and in so doing kicked it accidently into the orchestra [where it was soon squashed] ... As he ran off he came in contact with a [trapeze] ... and the hook ripped off half the skirt of my beautiful frock coat. Exit ... loud applause![7]

Assuming it was a nicely polished comedy encore, the audience, including the owner, was impressed. But besides being an entertaining Laurel slice of life, it anticipates a pivotal comedy development in the future screen world of Stan and Ollie—comic destruction. Of course, the team's trademark approach to comedy violence is of the methodical tit-for-tat nature, where the team patiently takes turns with some comedy antagonist in the destruction of each other's property. An example is the classic short subject *Big Business* (1929), where Stan and Ollie are Model-T driving, door-to-door Christmas tree salesmen who get into a comic row with home owner James Finlayson, resulting in a destroyed vehicle and a heavily damaged house. But Stan and Ollie are just as effective wreaking comic destruction by accident. Indeed, a good case can be made for their being more lethal this way. Witness the total destruction of Ollie's house in *Helpmates*, as he and Stan paradoxically attempt to clean up the place, or the major comic damage Ollie's home suffers in the team's attempt to put a radio aerial on his roof in the short subject *Hog Wild* (1930). Regardless, their definitive incompetence is forever played out in comic violence, whether methodical or just plain muddleheaded. While this chapter eventually addresses the apparent impact McCarey's antiheroic personal life had on comic destructiveness in the world of Stan & Ollie, the highlight of Laurel's stage debut anticipates a cornerstone of the future team.

Moreover, Laurel now had an ally in his father, though A. J. thought his son needed more comic seasoning in a company of performers. Consequently, through the assistance of his father, Laurel became a member (1907–1909) of the Levy and Cardwell Juvenile Pantomimes Company (ages six to eighteen). An important career was underway.

Unlike Laurel, Hardy's early business connection on the outskirts of the entertainment world working in a pioneering movie theatre did not immediately propel him into a professional comedy apprenticeship. Still, it was equally as important as Laurel's catalyst, and it put him into the movies ahead of his partner-to-be. Hardy spent three years as a film projectionist (1910–1913). At the beginning his goal was still to be a singer, some time earlier he had been musically re-inspired by attending an Enrico Caruso performance in Atlanta. But as he watched the various comedians convulsing across his screen in those pre-Chaplin movies, he was not impressed. Eventually, this projectionist/"student" of film decided he could improve upon these early screen comedians. Again, this methodical Hardy decision (both in terms of its practical nature and its three-year incubation period) differentiates him from his more singleminded future partner.

The year Hardy started working (1910) was also a significant one for Laurel. After literally outgrowing Levy and Cardwell's troupe (Laurel turned nineteen in 1909), he tried his luck as a vaudeville solo in small English variety houses, writing his own material. But his father gave him another career break. Laurel was hired to replace a comedian in the A. J.-authored major vaudeville house comedy *Home from the Honeymoon*. (The sketch became the foundation for the later Laurel & Hardy short subjects *Duck Soup* 1927, and *Another Fine Mess* 1930—the latter version introducing Ollie's memorable lament.)

Home from the Honeymoon led to other Laurel work, such as a major role in a second hit production—*Gentleman Jockey*. Thus, in 1910 Laurel was "discovered" (despite being a longtime aficionado of comedy, with a sizeable amount of experience) by the legendary Fred Karno—*the* name in British music hall comedy. Karno was a talented comedy starmaker whose troupes were then the toast of Britain. His music-hall reputation might be likened to that of Mack Sennett in American film comedy during the same period. Moreover, both Karno's and Sennett's biggest discovery (for their respective mediums) was Chaplin, to whom Laurel would for a time be both understudy and roommate (when employed by Karno).

Laurel biographer Fred Lawrence Guiles, in noting the affectionately salty verses World War I British soldiers sang when linking themselves to a Karno cast—"We are Fred Karno's Army"—likened the broader crazy comedy meaning of Karno to World War II American soldier's good-natured use of the term SNAFU (Situation Normal, All Fucked Up).[8] In a sense, Karno troupes were the Monty Python's Flying Circuses of their day. Regardless, this would be a comedy finishing school for both Laurel and Chaplin. In fact, Laurel later said, "Fred Karno didn't teach Charlie [Chaplin] and me all we know about comedy. He just taught us most of it."[9] Though an overstatement, it still provides a sense of the high comedy regard in which Karno was held.

Laurel's ties with Karno included tours of the United States in 1910 and 1912. During the first trip Laurel was Chaplin's roommate and understudy in the *Mumming Birds*, with the title soon changed to the more descriptive *A Night in an English Music Hall*. The sketch followed the comic rudeness of a wealthy, drunken audience member (played by Chaplin) as he disrupts the evening's entertainment. It was much more successful than the production with which the company originally opened—a satire of secret organizations entitled *The Wow-Wows*. The durability of *A Night in an English Music Hall* was later underlined by Chaplin when he used it as the basis for his popular film short subject *A Night in the Show* (1915).

Unfortunately for Karno's performers, the prestige associated with his troupes did not include generous salaries. And Laurel was not then, nor for a long time, a good manager of money. Thus, badly needing cash, he asked Karno tour manager Alf Reeves (later Chaplin's studio manager) for a raise, but Karno said no. Laurel consequently left the tour, with his father providing the fare home. He was soon appearing in a sketch he had written entitled *The Rum 'Uns from Rome*. He played a dull-witted (shades of the future Stan) Roman soldier who engages in the black comedy action of planting an ax in someone's head. The initial audience reception was good, and Laurel was hired for what was to be a more lucrative role in an act called *Fun on the Tyrol*. But because of booking problems it was not a success for Laurel. The young comedian went through some hard financial times, which he tried to keep from his family.

Providentially, he was then again hired as Chaplin's understudy for the 1912 Karno troupe tour of the United States. Once more the sketch was *A Night in an English Music Hall*. Most important, Laurel received his previously requested raise, but the tour would be a mixed blessing. While very successful with Chaplin as the drunken theatre patron, when Chaplin (who Carl Sandburg later described as the man with the "east-and-west feet"[10]) left the company for a more lucrative film contract with Mack Sennett, the Karno tour quickly failed. This represented a double whammy for Stan; not only did this failure reflect poorly on the complete membership of the company (had Chaplin been carrying them?), now former understudy Laurel was the sketch star the public did *not* want to see. It was to be Chaplin or nothing, and even the eventual importation of Karno's number-one homefront comedian, Dan Raynor, would not humor the American audiences. The year was 1913, and Laurel decided to stay on in the United States. He did not see his homeland again until 1927, when he returned quietly, on the verge of fame, but five years before the triumphant 1932 visit of Laurel & Hardy.

As for Laurel, 1913 was also a new adventure for Hardy. He left his position as a film projectionist and journeyed to Jacksonville, Florida, then an active but minor-league film production center. At this time the industry was largely located in New York City, though the gradual migration to California had already begun. (California was where Chaplin reported to Sennett in 1913.) Hardy's entrance into Jacksonville filmmaking was assisted by his 1913 marriage to film pianist and first wife Madelyn Saloshin. This union, to a much older woman, seems to have ended soon after he found early Florida film success.

Between 1913 and 1917 Hardy went through the most extensive of film apprenticeships. Like many other movie pioneers in the years before strict union craft lines, Hardy wore many production hats, from prop man to, if necessary, director. (The latter was a role he would have liked to return to later in his career.) More important, he started earning bit parts early on, a development no doubt assisted by his enthusiastic and ever-present attendance on the set. This speaks highly of his growing interest in film, since Hardy spent his evenings singing in local nightclubs—both out of love and a need for expense money.

Jacksonville was also where Hardy received the nickname he would forever after go by: "Babe." The story behind it, though brief, represents one of the few surviving anecdotes from Hardy's little-documented early life. Hardy's heavily accented Italian barber especially liked the comedian and enjoyed patting powder on the comedian's face after a shave, saying, "Nice-a bab-ee. Nice-a bab-ee." Through the kidding of friends it evolved from "Baby" to "Babe." Moreover, "Babe" might have gained later reinforcement for one-time baseball umpire and still occasional player Hardy from the coincidence that the start of the good-sized Southerner Babe Ruth's celebrated career parallels the comedian's Jacksonville period.

Hardy's use of the nickname (for a time he even billed himself as "Babe" in his Florida film credits) is rather ironic. The term "Babe" is generally based, as it was in Hardy's case, on fat men having baby faces. And Hardy had always been heavy and sensitive to being kidded about it, despite the name of his college quartet or a later cabaret billing as "The Ton of Jollity."

A comment Hardy later made on television's "This Is Your Life" (a 1954 team tribute) helps explain the apparent contradiction between the quartet's name of "Half-a-Ton-of-Harmony" and the comedian's sensitivity to his weight. When program host Ralph Edwards asked the group's name, Hardy responded, "The 20th Century Four." When Edwards pressed him about the other billing, the comedian quietly responded they were also known by that name, but he was obviously not fond of it.

His sister, Elizabeth, remembered that at fourteen he weighed 250 pounds. Coinciding with his entry into the Milledgeville military school, he was a victim of fat jokes from classmates. Though possibly out of defense, he was also considered a very entertaining and amusing student. And an earlier childhood friend appearing on "This Is Your Life" remembered carrying Hardy's school books so that the future comedian might sing and dance them to and from class.

On the dark side, Hardy's widow, Lucille, observed on the BBC documentary that he would sometimes ask her, "How could you love a great big fat man like me?" And though the comedian seemed to accept the weight with his more public friends, "he hated being fat." (One is reminded of how Laurel & Hardy's comedy team contemporary Curly Howard of the Three Stooges hated part of his persona—the shaved head. Indeed, though incongruous with their comedy characters, both Hardy and Howard were considered ladies' men in private.)

Recent writing by authors, such as Leo M. Brooks, past editor of various Laurel & Hardy journals and newsletters and a researcher on John McCabe's Hardy biography, suggests the comedian was a much more complex individual than is usually suggested in team literature. The subject of weight might be considered one of the Hardy ambiguities. Certainly, as this chapter will demonstrate, there were times when he was the first to draw attention to his weight when interacting with the press.

Regardless, at the "Babe" stage of Hardy's career, weight was finally becoming something positive; those extra pounds were giving him a corner on the characterization often based on a pun: playing the "heavy" or villain. In truth, Hardy could make money per pound. A 1917 King Bee production contract, when he played heavy to Chaplin impersonator Billy West (a series that began in Jacksonville) had financial incentives for him to gain 50 pounds (Hardy then weighed 265). His contract would pay an extra two dollars for every extra pound added, plus a $250 bonus if all 50 pounds appeared in six months.[11] Fittingly, his first film appearance ever had been for a "fat boy" bit in a Lubin film. His weight evidently fluctuated greatly at this time, because newspaper articles on the young Hardy had him weighing 350 pounds.

Working for Jacksonville's Lubin Motion Pictures and later Vim Studios (which had bought out Lubin in November 1915), he worked his way up to minor-league star performer by 1917. A February 20, 1916 newspaper article from the *Florida Metropolis* (Jacksonville) chronicles part of Hardy's rise as well as its tie-in with his weight. In fact, the punning title is an excellent encapsulation of this combination—"Babe Hardy, The Fat Boy with the Vim." And even then, the essay was praising what would become an ongoing career compliment—his great agility despite his size (besides his weight, he was six feet-one or -two, depending on the source).

A November 25, 1916 article in *Motography: Exploiting Motion Pictures* also jointly handles Hardy's success and his size. Entitled "Story of a Fat Boy," it raves about the "originality and intelligence" of his early film work. And there are fleeting but fascinating personal observations, such as the comedian came by his huge size naturally, because both his mother and father "were exceptionally large people."

Jordan R. Young's 1975 *Pratfall* article, "Early Ollie: The Plump and Runt Films" (see Chapter 4) suggested Hardy's most significant early work, with relationship to his later pairing with Laurel, was his 1916 Vim teaming with Billy Ruge. They made thirty-five one-reelers (film shorts approximately ten minutes long) comically known as the "Plump and Runt" series. Though I am not alone in finding this connection tenuous (see my Chapter 4 commentary on Young's essay), the mere act of teaming—with anyone—would certainly be important preparation for the wonderful pairing with Laurel. And for that reason one should also note Hardy was later paired at Vim with comedienne Kate Price in fourteen films. And this says nothing of the comic heavies he would play to Billy West, Jimmy Aubrey, and Larry Semon, which will soon be examined.

Hardy himself pinpointed a specific film that anticipated his later pairing with Laurel—*The Paperhanger's Helper* (1925, an abridged retitled version of the 1925 *Stick Around*), where Hardy is teamed with the physically slight (à la Laurel) comedian Bobby Ray. Hardy observed that his physically larger character was also the eventual victim (which Ollie invariably was). "Still, I [Hardy] think of that picture once in a while as being the start of the Laurel and Hardy idea as far as I was concerned."[12] I only mention a 1925 film now because Hardy wrongly remembered *The Paperhanger's Helper* production date as 1915. Unfortunately, many filmographies of Hardy's solo work continue to list the 1915 date. Thus, what for Hardy was a seminal pre-Laurel film actually appeared on the verge of the 1927 teaming.

An important development during Hardy's 1910s period, though not something that can be isolated to one film, is the often overlooked fact that he learned the comedy ropes as a *screen* performer. Such later classic Ollie gestures as the embarrassed fumbling with the tie, or the disgusted stare at the camera (in effect, the viewer) when Stan is especially dumb—are the subtle work of a *movie* actor. Even the wonderful mime of Laurel's Stan, polished on the British music hall *stage*, is often much broader.

Hardy's exit from Jacksonville had a Chaplin catalyst. Billy West, the best of many Chaplin impersonators, began his King Bee productions in Jacksonville during early 1917. Hardy, as an Eric Campbell-like heavy (Chaplin's then-current large, comically fierce villain), won the nod to play opposite Billy West. (Vim had gone under in 1917, and Hardy was then the manager/featured singer at a Jacksonville cabaret that was a favorite with area entertainment figures. His wife directed its orchestra!)

Ollie's tie-twiddling routine

Regardless, Chaplin's popularity was such that numerous Tramp imitators made a living playing his famous character, on stage and in movies, with the films often made to be passed off as the genuine article. West made this trick on the less-sophisticated viewer easier by being both very good and physically similar (in size and coloring) to Chaplin. Other prominent Chaplin film imitators included Billie Richie (another former Karno member) and Mexican actor Charles Amander, who even changed his name to Charles Aplin. (Chaplin sued and eventually won a judgement against Aplin in 1925 that decreed Chaplin's tramp suit and shuffle to be Chaplin's own.[13])

Production of the Billy West films soon moved to New York City in late spring 1917, with no doubt a reluctant Hardy in tow. He had briefly visited there in 1915. However Hardy, with more than a little of the stereotypical southern gentleman in his makeup (something he also, of course, later carried over to his Ollie character), had found New York less than pleasant, from the colder weather to the more hurried pace. Still singing on the side, Hardy also found New York competition for such positions intense. The New York topper came, however, when the United States entered World War I in April 1917 and patriotic Hardy tried to enlist. The recruiter just stared at Hardy and yelled, "Hey, Sarge, come look at what wants to enlist!"[14] More Hardy-as-victim insults followed, and the weight-sensitive comedian was devastated. The best measure of his ongoing pain is the fact that the source of that quote was Hardy's widowed third wife, Lucille, someone the comedian did not even meet until more than twenty years later.

Regardless, Hardy's second professional stay in New York City was brief. The West comedies soon moved to production facilities in Bayonne, New Jersey, and then to Hollywood's fledgling film industry (October 1917). One would assume that the small-town southern Hardy found the still-modest Hollywood and its warm climate to his liking. And while the King Bee—Billy West comedies continued only into 1918, Hardy was finally in the new film capital, the eventual site of that memorable future teaming with Laurel.

Like Hardy, Laurel landed in 1917 Hollywood, too. But for the skinny half of the future duo it was a brief stay. While Hardy had been serving an on-the-job total film apprenticeship since 1913 (primarily in Jacksonville), Laurel challenged himself to survival in American vaudeville after Chaplin's 1913 exit from Karno. This was difficult for Laurel since he hardly excelled at money matters or his personal life in general. Unlike the tight-fisted Chaplin, whose impoverished, often on-the-street childhood made him rather money conscious, Laurel's more-affluent, cared-for background (reflected by his father's financial assistance on different occasions early in Laurel's stage career) tended to be a liability when it came to his finances. Yet a "live for today" attitude was hardly something rare on the 1913 vaudeville circuits. However, Chaplin would probably have paid more attention to a popular syndicated newspaper humorist of the day, Frank "Kin" Hubbard, whose aphorisms appeared under the name of Abe Martin, when he observed, also in 1913, "Opportunity only knocks once but th' wolf is liable t' drop around any ole time."[15]

Laurel, however, soon found vaudeville success with an act he authored called *The Nutty Burglars*, which also starred Edgar and Wren Hurley, close friends and former colleagues from the disbanded Karno company. Mainly a string of gags, what "plot" did exist centered on two less-than-competent house burglars running into a maid and other distractions while on the job.

The sketch was popular enough to attract the attention of major talent agent Gordon Bostock, who led them to better bookings largely by repackaging their act. While Bostock kept their basic sketch premise, he decided to cash in on the then-current (1914) phenomenal success of Chaplin's screen character by having Laurel play his *The Nutty Burglars* role as Chaplin's Tramp, with Edgar and Wren Hurley emulating Chaplin's sometime costars at Sennett's Keystone— Chester Conklin and Mabel Normand. And as if the change was not obvious enough, Bostock switched the group's name from "The Three Comiques" to "The Keystone Trio."

Not surprisingly, the act was very successful. After all, Chaplin and Laurel not only had had similar English music hall backgrounds, they had roomed together on tour with the Karno company. No one was better qualified to mirror the Chaplin screen persona than Laurel.

While most people prefer to have entertainment favorites (such as Laurel) completely original, the Chaplinitis that swept the world after the early appearances (1914) of The Tramp was unique. One of the first world media stars, Chaplin enjoyed a popularity limited neither by language (the universality of silent films) nor age. Moreover, his popularity touched off marketing schemes that are still with us. There were Chaplin lapel pins, hats, socks, ties, complete costumes, spoons, Christmas decorations, statuettes, buttons, paper dolls, games, playing cards, squirt guns, comics, dolls, and anything else on which his likeness could be reproduced.

The world even started to take on a certain "trampish" look. His mustache became *the* fad. Adults grew them, and children pasted them on or smudged charcoal on their upper lips. "His clothes, his boots, his postures and gait were imitated by would-be humorists."[16] Even theatres were capitalizing on the craze by having Charlie Chaplin look-alike contests; the winner of one such Cleveland competition was a youngster named Leslie T. Hope—better known today as Bob Hope. As a lark, Chaplin himself is said to have entered one of these contests and finished third. The saturation level of early Chaplinitis is nicely articulated in one of several Charlie the Tramp jokes then making the rounds:

"You appear worried."
"Well, you see I have two invitations to dinner. At one home the young daughter is learning to play the piano and at the other the son gives imitations of Charlie Chaplin."[17]

An analogy exists between the early career "borrowing" of a solo Laurel and a solo Hardy from Chaplin with the beginning screen work of another great film comedian—Harold Lloyd. Like Laurel & Hardy, Lloyd took years to reach the character for which he is now famous: the energetic, bespectacled, boy-next-door who frequently was sidetracked by thrill comedy, especially his hanging from the face of the skyscraper clock in *Safety Last* (1923). But Lloyd first established himself in film playing a figure named "Lonesome Luke" (1915–1917), whom comedy historian Kalton C. Lahue has labeled "a sort of hayseed copy of Chaplin's [Tramp] character."[18] (This also parallels the Chaplin "assisted" solo careers of the future duo.) Lloyd did not actually perform a literal imitation of Chaplin, as did Billy West and so many others, but his costume (which attempted to reverse The Tramp's baggy attire with tightness) and story situations were often reminiscent of Chaplin's rough-and-tumble Keystone comedies. While Lloyd eventually evolved his own distinctive comedy identity so closely tied to the American success story, it is an excellent gauge of Chaplin's influence that one of silent comedy's traditional pantheon of four (Chaplin, Keaton, Langdon, and Lloyd) toiled so long in Chaplin's shadow. Thus, the solo careers of Laurel and Hardy and their early ties to Chaplin were in good company.

The involvement, consequently, of Laurel in this Chaplinitis or that of Hardy via the Billy West comedies was almost a "natural" response to an unprecedented time when a new medium and a new shuffling comedian collaborated to turn the entertainment world on its ear.

Despite the success of the Chaplin-inspired "The Keystone Trio," the team broke up when friction developed between Laurel and the Hurleys. Accounts of why differ. Laurel's next partners, Alice and Baldwin "Baldy" Cooke, credit Laurel with wanting to drop the Hurleys by 1915 because they did not meet his performance standards.[19] Laurel's memory of the events had the breakup being caused by Edgar Hurley wanting to play the Tramp part in their act. After Laurel refused, thinking Hurley could handle it, the latter copyrighted "The Keystone Trio" sketch out from under Laurel. Thus, from Laurel's viewpoint, it was he who was bounced from the act.

Quite possibly the Hurleys saw it all coming and acted first to get what they could—rights to a meal-ticket sketch. Regardless, Laurel's comments on comparative skills seem to hold up, because the Hurleys and their replacement for Laurel soon disbanded. Conversely, Stan formed a successful new team, "The Stan Jefferson Trio" (with the Cookes), performing an act very similar to "The Nutty Burglars" entitled "The Crazy Cracksman." Once again there would be burglars surprising a lone young woman and Laurel dressed as Chaplin's Tramp. The difference between this sketch and the earlier version was that "The Crazy Cracksman" involved a fake burglar (Baldy Cooke) staging a robbery for the publicity of an actress (Alice Cooke), and a real burglar (Laurel) pursuing his vocation. Needless to say, mistaken identity contributed to the comedy, just as it was necessary for all three characters to meet eventually. The thin plot was bolstered by Laurel's physical comedy, though the comic premise of a real burglar being mistaken for a hired one has continued to appear. For instance, it was the basis for a Jackie Gleason *Honeymooners* sketch on mid-1950s television.

Laurel and the Cookes spent two seemingly idyllic years together touring with "The Crazy Cracksman." They lived for the moment, spending money as quickly as it came. When necessary their agent, Claude Bostock (often assisted by his brother Gordon) would give them an advance. Eventually Laurel and the Cookes "decided that this [an advance] was even astute on their part as it gave [Claude] Bostock an incentive to get them a better booking in order to get his money back."[20]

Finally, as all "parties" must, this one ended—at least for the Cookes. In 1917 Laurel fell hard for an older woman, Mae Dahlberg, half of vaudeville's singing and dancing Hayden Sisters act. Soon after the most messy and unstable of relationships began. Mae was Laurel's common-law wife until 1925, as well as teaming intermittently with him on stage. (As if describing the instability of their pairing, the act was called "No Mother to Guide Them"!) But just as Mae's former partner had not actually been her sister, the "marriage" of Laurel and Mae also had a false billing. It seems that Mae was already married to an actor from her native Australia.

This would be the documented beginning of a merry-go-round of relationships for Laurel. Not including Mae, Laurel married four different women a total of eight times! Ironically, this was another and most blatant difference between the heart-on-the-sleeve Laurel and his eventual screen persona Stan. Indeed, Stan was either asexual or a virginal shrinking violet male.

Laurel's major weakness was women. As he was often later reported to say, when the subject of hobbies came up: "I married all of mine." Only these self-destructive relationships seemed capable of periodically derailing his single-mindedness toward comedy. In fact, they would seemingly even be the cause of the most unprofessional of actions. For instance, when he broke with the Cookes after establishing his liaison with Mae, he gallantly gave his former partners the rights to the act, "The Crazy Cracksman." But then he usurped their bookings by going on the road with Mae in the same act. Yet, such was the inherent goodliness of the man, save for his Cupid weakness, that Alice Cooke "saw nothing caddish about Stan's behavior and never blamed him for their humiliation. 'He was hooked on Mae,' she explained."[21]

These, then, were some of the mini-melodramas Laurel experienced between Chaplin's 1913 Karno exit and Laurel's 1917 entry into Hollywood filmmaking.

Stan and Mae were playing the Los Angeles Hippodrome Theatre with a slapstick act that now frequently had Laurel in drag, and dominated by Mae (the Cookes having legally wrested back "The Crazy Cracksman"). Hippodrome owner Adolph Ramish was impressed with Laurel and financed his first film—*Nuts in May.*

Once again Chaplin entered Laurel's life, having been invited to the preview of the short subject. The creator of The Tramp liked this film about an insane asylum escapee who had a penchant for wearing Napoleon hats. Briefly it looked like Laurel might come under the Chaplin production umbrella. But just as, much later, Chaplin somehow never got around to mentioning Laurel in his epic-sized memoir, the redundantly titled *My Autobiography* (1964), no real arrangements for a Chaplin-funded Laurel career were ever forthcoming.

Luckily for Laurel, the head of Universal, Carl Laemmle, also had been impressed by *Nuts in May*, and a one-year contract was signed. But this, too, soured; the country yokel screen character Laurel assumed, Hickory Hiram, clicked with neither the public nor the comedian. In later years Laurel could not even remember whether he had done three or four of the films. He just recalled they were bad, forever adding that they were released ''to all the very best comfort stations [toilets].''

Joe Rock, a comedy contemporary of the 1910s and later a producer/advisor of Laurel's, cited an additional problem with the Hickory Hiram films: they included Mae. As Laurel's partner on stage and off, she felt justified in carrying this role over to films, even if she was not right as the ingenue. This later became a major issue when Laurel did a series of films for Rock. Mae's presence in a film package with Laurel was seemingly driving away potential film producers.

Mae's one claim to fame, besides nearly aborting Laurel's film career before it really began, was in giving the comedian the name Laurel. It is appropriate that a comedian whose future screen persona would sometimes be threatened by wives (with frequently similar roots in real life), should be christened by a woman.

On the eve of *Nuts in May*, Laurel, still using the family surname Jefferson, was interested in a name change. One explanation had the comedian saying there were too many letters in Jefferson, thus necessitating the use of smaller-sized lettering (than his colleagues') in professional credits. But a more frequently cited reason was superstition: the billing ''Stan Jefferson'' contained thirteen letters. Living up to the age-old superstitious thespian ''break a leg'' tradition, Stan felt a change was necessary. And Mae, while killing time leafing through an old discarded history book left in their vaudeville dressing room, came up with the name Laurel.

The selection had been triggered by a picture of a famous Roman general wearing a wreath of laurel. First Mae and then Stan simply liked the sound of the word. But it is ironically fitting that half of what became cinema's most comically antiheroic team should be named for the foliage the ancient Greeks and Romans wove into wreaths to crown battlefield and playing field victors—and in this case a Roman general, no less. Thus, one might truly call Laurel & Hardy ''leading'' incompetents.

Appropriately, superstition was also responsible for the large one's eventual marquee billing—Oliver Hardy. Born Norvell Hardy, he had long gone by the name of his deceased father Oliver. For a time in his early film career he preferred the nickname billing ''Babe.'' But unlike Laurel, Hardy opted for additional letters, returning to Oliver Hardy when informed that a longer name would result in success by a numerologist (possibly a heritage from his mother's interest in fortune tellers).[22]

Though superstitions born of show-business lore seem to have been key factors in their name selections, the choices are also consistent with what one knows about their family relationships. Hardy's family ties were close, as already demonstrated by his honoring of his father's name. Moreover, what few early Hardy stories exist are usually of an upbeat nature—family sings, or his prodigious appetite—even as a child—once eating twenty of his mother's baking powder biscuits at one sitting.

In the John McCabe interview with Hardy, the comedian doubly underlined the importance to him of his family name, from an illustrious background (a Hardy ancestor was claimed as an aide to British Admiral Nelson), to the pleasantly impressive sound of his full name—Oliver Norvell Hardy. (Use of the mother's maiden name, Norvell, for her youngest child also suggests family closeness, as well as being prophetic, since the early death of the father literally made her *the* parent.) While the name Oliver Norvell Hardy was not used in billings, it did surface on occasion in the team's film dialogue, when Ollie wanted to appear imposing.

Interestingly, Hardy emphasized that pride more when he became almost testy over a question concerning his sometime cinema use of what he called a "three-barreled name."[23] Ironically, he was adamant about never having made cinematic fun of his name. But since both Laurel & Hardy used their own names on screen and off (so their rights to the characters could not be usurped by a studio), the names Laurel and Hardy are forever equated with delightful blockheadedness (as in the later title of one of their films—*The Block-Heads*). Thus, when antiheroic Ollie attempts to assume a dignified air by using Oliver Norvell Hardy, it is comic incongruity at its best, like Chaplin's tattered Tramp swinging his aristocratic cane. Add the fact that "Norvell" meets the most fundamental rule of verbal comedy—it sounds funny—and one most definitely has comic fun being made of a full name, though in an inoffensive manner.

Hardy returned to a family name, but Laurel dropped his (Jefferson). Guiles's detailed personal biography of Laurel, with research assistance from lifelong Laurel & Hardy aficionado and author John McCabe, draws a picture of a father-son relationship that was ambivalent at best. Laurel's preschool years were spent largely with his maternal grandparents (the Metcalfes), with some accounts crediting this to his parents' theatrical touring. (Jenny Owen-Pawson and Bill Mouland's fascinating though obscure biography *Laurel Before Hardy*, 1984, also adds that "because Stan had such a shakey [sickly] beginning . . . [he] was the only one of the Jefferson children to stay in Ulverston while the rest of the [touring] family travelled."[24]) When the Jeffersons were more affluent, Stan was often away at boarding school. And while he both admired and utilized his father's theatre and comedy connections, Laurel was bothered by A.J.'s womanizing ways and the pain it caused his mother. This special concern for his mother's feelings was further heightened by her early death (September 1, 1908). Though she had been in poor health for several years, he in part blamed A.J.

While he always cherished those early years at his grandparents', it does not seem surprising that a few years later the second Karno trip (1912) found Laurel absenting himself from Britain and his family for fifteen years.

Ironically, A.J.'s casual approach to amours, especially after he became a producer and his wife's poor health kept her from a once-active theatre involvement, later surfaced in Stan's much married life. Of course, sexual dalliances were hardly rare among Laurel's entertainment contemporaries, including Charlie Chaplin, W. C. Fields, and the Marx Brothers. Yet Laurel suffered the most damaging publicity from such relationships, excepting Chaplin, who like Laurel would eventually marry four women but with no repeat "engagements."[25] Paradoxically, Laurel later winced through this increased negative attention because he was more open about his relationships—to the point of marrying them several times.

Hardy's early Hollywood years were spent methodically playing the comic heavy to Billy West, Jimmy Aubrey, and Larry Semon. Aubrey, as if anticipating Hardy's future involvement with Laurel, had also been in Karno's English music hall company. Like Hardy, Aubrey free-lanced with different Hollywood film companies. This minor comedian probably had his greatest success at Vitagraph, where Larry Semon was *the* resident comedian. Indeed, Semon had directed some of Aubrey's early Vitagraph work. And it is quite possible that this is how Hardy graduated to being Semon's comic villain. And "graduating" is not a loosely used term. Today most people would find comedians Semon and Aubrey equally obscure, but there was a time during the 1920s when Semon was sometimes considered in the same lofty comedy stratosphere as the silent pantheon greats.

Though more an eclectic collection of gags (stories about Semon invariably mention the little black book of comic notes he always carried for easy consultation and additions), his films were well known for the elaborate and expensive lengths to which he went in the name of slapstick. His were the special-effects comedies of the period. Semon's jerky, speeded-up movements, frequently on tiptoe, were that of a marionette on diet pills, while his pasty white face and beak nose comically yet paradoxically anticipate F. W. Murnau's spookiest of all Draculas in *Nosferatu* (1922-German). More fittingly, since Semon was also a former cartoonist for several New York newspapers, his film character is best described as cartoon-like, especially that other-worldly face and balloon pants pulled up to his chest. But all his special gags and/or stunts did not allow the viewer time to get to know his character. Indeed, the comic gags were sometimes so dangerously elaborate that one did not even see Semon; he had been replaced by a stuntman in long shot.

Interestingly, a still solo Laurel predated Hardy in working for Semon at Vitagraph. In 1918 Laurel supported Semon in three films: *Huns and Hyphens*, *Bears and Bad Men*, and *Frauds and Frenzies*. Popular legend has Semon editing down Laurel's footage because Laurel was comically topping the boss/star.

Regardless, he did not stay long at Semon's Vitagraph. But then he did not have any lengthy film company ties for some time.

Consistent with the ongoing noted differences of Laurel and Hardy, the pre-duo Hardy enjoyed working with Semon and unwound with him off the lot. But then, that too was company policy, indirectly contributing to the comedy. As Semon observed in a 1922 interview:

"I've a great company. Most of them have been with me four or five years and we're just chums working together. You must have harmony and be happy if you would make good comedy.

It isn't all work for us, for we bowl, play golf every Saturday and have the best baseball team in these parts. We've won eleven out of the last thirteen games we have played," and the crack pitcher of the Semon Nine grinned with pride.[26]

Appropriately, Semon introduced Hardy to golf and acted as his instructor, with the large one becoming one of Hollywood's premier players. Besides providing Hardy with a lifelong passion for golf, the company camaraderie that Semon describes sounds a great deal like Hardy's Jacksonville film group—a cinema family that worked and played together. Just as Hardy initially had difficulty upon leaving the friendly Jacksonville company for his first free-lance work in New York City, it is easy to see how he would have enjoyed the Semon group.

Another Laurel-Hardy contrast with relationship to Semon concerns show-casing. There are those (such as team author Jack Scagnetti) who suggest that Hardy was not allowed his full comedic range in his Semon roles due to the alleged editing reductions of Laurel's work. Yet, in the Semon films featuring Hardy as the heavy, such as the celebrated short subjects *The Sawmill* (1922) or *Golf* (1922), the amount of comic business given to Hardy is impressive. The comedian himself observed, "he [Semon] gave me every opportunity to shine, and that wasn't usually Larry's way with other comics and supporting people."[27]

Unlike Chaplin's Mutual comic villain Eric Campbell or, to a lesser extent, Harry Langdon's later heavy for Sennett, Vernon Dent, Semon really accented the comic in Hardy's *comic* villain. That is, while all the heroes eventually won out over their burly antagonists (for such is, or at least was, the order of comedy), the comic personae of Chaplin and Langdon were more likely to have a few rough spots along the way. Not so with Semon, this bouncing leprechaun from Mars who was rarely bettered, despite his comically ludicrous grin. (The grin was made possible by not putting makeup on his upper lip and whitening it with the rest of his now hello-boob clown face). Yet, this is slapstick; someone has to get buffeted about. Thus, in Semon films like *Golf* and *The Sawmill* one practically needs a pocket calculator to keep up with all of Hardy's "accidents" as he tries to be the bad guy. For example, he somehow manages to whip himself in the rump, get bumped by a huge log, have a board drop onto his foot, have the posterior section of his pants catch on fire, get showered with paint several times, and survive the dynamiting of a house cartoon-style—with the required tattered and smoking clothes. Truly, it is a part on which Wile E. Coyote, the Road Runner's nemesis, could not have improved. Consequently, one tends to like, or at least feel for, Hardy's comic villain more than for the average stock bad guy. Besides, in the special effects world of the other worldly Semon, what kind of damage could even an unhindered Hardy do, anyway?

That Hardy also had a following by way of his work with Semon is nicely documented in the British comic strip "The Artful Antics of Babe Hardy," which appeared briefly in early 1920. (This also, of course, reflects the period box office of Semon, even outside the United States.)

After Semon broke with Vitagraph due to his elaborate, overbudgeted productions, Semon remembered Hardy in other works, including the 1925 feature-length adaptation of *The Wizard of Oz*. Though largely reviewed as a children's film (*Variety* called it "one of the best pictures of all times to take the kids to see"[28]), it was a critical and commercial success. Semon directed and also starred as the Scarecrow, with Hardy playing the Tin Woodsman, though the latter role was not as central to the story as it was in the more well-known 1939 adaptation of *The Wizard of Oz*. (During 1924–1926 Hardy also appeared in three other Semon features: *The Girl in the Limousine*, *The Perfect Clown*, and *Stop, Look and Listen*.)

Hardy's ties with Semon were significant for four reasons. First and most obvious, it provided Hardy with a great deal of screen exposure, especially when one considers Semon's period popularity. Moreover, he allowed Hardy to be a more refreshingly comic heavy than the norm. Second, these ties gave Hardy contact, on and off the set, with one of early film's great gag men. Indeed, as Hardy fondly remembered his days with Semon in 1954, he observed that no one other than Laurel, put more effort into making a gag work than Semon.[29] Third, though Hardy was only a supporting player to Semon, his work anticipated Hardy's later working relationship with Laurel. Both Laurel and Semon were obsessive in their pursuit of gags, while it was not a top priority with Hardy. Of course, a number of other people besides Laurel had major input on the future of Laurel & Hardy films, especially Leo McCarey. In contrast, Semon attempted to go the total auteur filmmaker route of a Chaplin; he ultimately lost. Fourth, Hardy's Wile E. Coyote heavy is at least a step in the direction of the future Ollie. He constantly tries to dominate—actually bully—but is forever the victim. While Ollie is hardly a heavy (metaphorically, anyway), he does attempt to act the teacher/parent (occasionally even a bit of the bully) but invariably ends up the victim.

Even prior to their Larry Semon connection, Laurel and Hardy were acquainted in those pre-team Hollywood days. (Actually it would have been hard not to, since Hollywood was, literally, a small town.) But no light bulbs of inspiration went on about what later seemed so obvious—that here was a comedy pair of pairs. Besides their coincidental 1917 arrivals in the film capital, they had even shared screen time briefly in 1918. The film, as if prophesying great things, was entitled *A Lucky Dog*, with Laurel starring and Hardy having merely a minor supporting role as, appropriately for that stage of his career, the heavy. Hardy is a crook who has mistakenly stuffed stolen money into Laurel's pocket instead of his own. When he realizes the mistake only a film comedy burglar could make, he commands Laurel, via a title card, "Put 'em both up, insect, before I comb your hair with lead."

While funny, it is not exactly what one might expect of their first screen communication. Fittingly, in terms of their future team inner action, Laurel gets the better of Hardy. But it is a much more animated Laurel than the methodically restrained Stan who audiences eventually come to expect. Still, the real teaming would not take place for years (1927) after the chance film encounter of *A Lucky Dog*. (In 1926 they both appeared in *45 Minutes from Hollywood* but had no shared scenes.)

Something might have possibly developed earlier if Laurel had spent all his time in Hollywood. But a lack of steady film work kept him and Mae (still teaming on and off stage) busy in vaudeville until the early 1920s. Ironically, he had had a great opportunity to establish himself with the man who would become *the* film comedy producer of the 1920s—Hal Roach, the same one who later produced the Laurel & Hardy films. But in 1918 Roach needed someone to replace Toto the Clown (Arnold Nobello), the famous circus clown. Missing the big top interaction of clown and audience, an unhappy Toto had left Roach in mid-contract (1918) in order to return to the circus. Roach was anxious to sign a replacement and finish shooting the remaining five-picture obligation that Toto's exit had created. Laurel was equally anxious for any and all film work, though the stage was still his first love. (Leo Brooks contends in correspondence that Laurel initially only took film jobs when there were no vaudeville bookings.) In 1918 Laurel divided his time between vaudeville and the Semon films. Thus, Laurel shot five short subjects (one-reelers) before the end of that year. Two were released late in 1918 (November and December), and the rest appeared monthly in early 1919.

Unfortunately, the shorts did not send Laurel's film stock soaring. In fact, just the opposite occurred. Laurel had yet to discover a comfortable film persona. Consequently, his screen character frequently changed and no audience "hook" (attraction) developed, like Chaplin's underdog Charlie the Tramp—still one of cinema's most alluring personalities. And Chaplin's Charlie represents more than a random comparison, because Laurel's screen persona in those pre-team days often flirted with the quick graceful movements of Chaplin's Tramp. This is nicely exemplified in Laurel's *White Wings* (1923) and *Oranges and Lemons* (1923), both from an even later comedy tour of duty for Hal Roach. In fairness to Laurel, Chaplin's popularity was still so great that theatre owners had only to display a cardboard image of The Tramp with the simple statement "I am here today" to draw a large audience. Certainly, it would be a difficult influence to avoid, even if one did not have both the parallels between Chaplin's and

Laurel's professional (Karno) training and the fact that Laurel had had considerable past success in vaudeville imitating The Tramp.

Besides this professional problem over identity, Laurel evidently encountered something of a similar problem at home. At least Roach's termination of Laurel's contract after the completion of the series was in part based on Laurel's personal instability. Roach not only believed in family entertainment (this was the man who in 1922 brought viewers "Our Gang," a longtime goal of his), he also believed in family values. And while this predated the Fatty Arbuckle scandal (1921–22) that led to Hollywood's Hays (censorship) Office, it would be naive to think Roach was not sensitive to the danger of scandal. Add to this the fact it was a small family-oriented comedy company, without job castes or secrets. Moreover, it was still little enough that the head man was involving himself in film direction. Thus, Roach was all the more cognizant of the everyday lives and times of his workers. Consequently, when the Toto obligation had been fulfilled, "the stories and telltale evidence of his [Laurel's] bouts with the bottle and with Mae had made his position with Roach untenable."[30]

Laurel's fun time recreational drinking of the early vaudeville days, such as with his former team mates and friends Alice and "Baldy" Cooke, was a thing of the past. The stormy relationship with Mae had made alcohol an escape. The drinking problem and his volatile relationships with women resurfaced periodically during the 1920s and 1930s. This frequently threatened his career, or in the case of Roach and another pre-team Laurel producer, Joe Rock, it endangered the very establishing of a film career. And though it might seem like a darkly comic anticipation of Stan & Ollie's future film fears of thrashings from frequently large homicidal-looking wives (often accented with opening titles like the 1928 *Their Purple Moment*: "Dedicated to husbands who hold out part of the pay envelope on their wives—and live to tell about it."), Laurel sometimes had reason to feel physically threatened by the women in his life. Unfortunately this was one place where his life and art were similar.

Regardless, after his first exit from Roach, Laurel's film activity went from little to the proverbial nothing. He made no films in 1919 (though three of the 1918 substitutes for Toto were released) and repeated the shutout in 1920. In 1921 there was a single film for Vitagraph. Finally, in 1922, Laurel's luck, or maybe his thoughts towards film, began to change. And it was the gift of seemingly the most unlikely of comedy producers—Gilbert M. Anderson, though better known as early western comedy star Broncho Billy. He was not new, however, to the world of comedy. George K. *S*poor and Anderson, co-founders of Essanay (S & A) films, had stolen Chaplin away from Mack Sennett during the mid-teens. Anderson himself had both produced Laurel's first film and maintained a long-term interest in Laurel's potential.

Anderson's patience paid off. The six Laurel short subjects he produced and directed for Amalgamated and Quality-Metro were well received. Especially popular was their parody of Rudolph Valentino's *Blood and Sand* (1922), which became *Mud and Sand* (1922), with Laurel playing Rudolph Vaselino. Not only was it a subject ripe for spoofing, it was an inspired idea to utilize Laurel's talent for mimicry upon someone other than Chaplin's Tramp.

The catalyst for Anderson's decision to do a spoof might have come from Buster Keaton's *The Frozen North* (1922), a takeoff of western film star William S. Hart, which appeared three months before *Mud and Sand*. *The Frozen North* was both popular and, within the film community, mildly controversial, since Hart was upset with being a comedy target. Moreover, since Gilbert ''Broncho Billy'' Anderson had been a western star who, in part, was usurped by Hart, he certainly would have had an added incentive to be interested in the production and eventual success of *The Frozen North*.

Interestingly, the following year Keaton made his transition to feature-length films with a parody of D. W. Griffith's 1916 epic *Intolerance*, entitled *Three Ages*. Since parody has a built-in structure (whatever genre and/or star persona one is comically self-destructing), there is usually an adaptation-like wealth of material to skewer comically. Thus, Keaton used a spoof for his feature debut, while the Anderson-Laurel *Mud and Sand*, at three reels (approximately thirty minutes), was the comedian's longest film thus far.

A lesser but unique aspect of *Mud and Sand*, noted by Laurel biographer Guiles, was that Stan played the handsome individual he was—appropriate in a parody of a good-looking leading man.[31] Laurel, like most comedians, was generally made to look funny. This was especially true in the Laurel & Hardy years, when his short red hair was combed straight up, his eye makeup was applied to give him smaller, comically dullard peepers, and his patented comic response to problems was a face-elongating cry that he further accented by scratching the top of his spiked-hair head. Together this comic formula said: ''I am less than bright.''

Of course, utilizing Laurel's natural good looks in this sendup of Valentino was only one way of doing it. The following year (1923) cross-eyed comic Ben Turpin also scored high marks in the Valentino spoof *The Shriek of Araby* (Valentino having played *The Sheik* in 1921). Indeed, utilizing the funny-looking comic is more apt to be the norm in parody. The visually amusing persona is doubly funny when cast as a romantic and/or traditional handsome hero of serious drama.

This is important to keep in mind, as later parodies by Laurel & Hardy derived much of their humor from just such a comic incongruity. For instance, *Way Out West*, one of their best features, is a delightful spoof if for no other reason than seeing them in their traditional modern garb (right down to their derbies) comically interacting within this other world of cowboys and six-shooters. Like Keaton, Laurel & Hardy used a parody for their first feature film (again, a ready genre structure waiting to be comically collapsed at length). The film was a prison movie spoof with the punning title *Pardon Us* (1931). The target was the classic father of prison films *The Big House* (1930), as well as others that had quickly followed. And again, the general comic contrast of Laurel & Hardy in the land of hardened convicts makes this sometimes uneven film worth seeing.

Moreover, the comic incongruity of seeing these two pussycats in piranha land is intensified all the more by the fact that unlike most comedy teams, Laurel & Hardy's enduring popularity is largely based in friendship and love. Despite countless variations of "Well, here's another *nice* mess you've gotten me into," Stan & Ollie genuinely liked each other, and it showed. Most film teams, such as the Marx Brothers, Abbott & Costello, Hope & Crosby, Martin & Lewis, the Three Stooges . . . have comic relationships based on open hostility. This could be the tootsie fruitsie ice cream scene of *A Day at the Races* (1937), where Chico sells Groucho a library of unnecessary betting books, or Crosby actually *selling Hope* to slave traders in *The Road to Morocco* (1942). Neither activity was imaginable for Laurel & Hardy.

This was, however, to be sometime in the future. In 1922 and 1923 Anderson was just starting to give a still-solo Laurel a modest taste of film success. After completing the series of Anderson shorts, including *When Knights Were Cold* (1923), a spoof of Marion Davies's epic *When Knighthood Was in Flower* (1922), Laurel went back to vaudeville while the ex-cowboy attempted to raise capital for a new Laurel series.

Unfortunately for Anderson, Roach decided to re-hire Laurel. He had been impressed by Laurel's work for Anderson, and was in a position of expanded production, thanks mainly to the phenomenal success of his "Our Gang" series and the profits from his former studio star Harold Lloyd. During 1923 and 1924 Laurel did over twenty films for Roach. These were important for six reasons.

First, the sheer volume of films provided Laurel with something new—a sustained period in filmland. Second, it demonstrated that he was finally receiving some film comedy recognition. Third, while this expanded time allowed for additional film comedy persona experimentation, it underlined the ongoing importance of parody in Laurel's career, as the majority of his Roach films this time were of a spoof nature. For instance, *Under Two Jags* (1923) was a send-up of *Under Two Flags* (1922), while *The Soilers* (1923) parodied *The Spoilers* (1923). (Of course, Laurel did not have a corner on the parody approach at Roach. For example, Will Rogers, who also signed in 1923, was being utilized in spoofs.) Fourth, Laurel first began to work with James Finlayson, a central character to the future Laurel & Hardy films. Indeed, as a catalyst for comedy he was to the team what Margaret Dumont was to the Marx Brothers. Fifth, the more prominent Laurel became, the greater the threat Mae became to his film career by her ongoing demands to co-star with him, the late-night drinking bouts she provoked, and simply her status as Laurel's mistress. If Stan was to have a major film career, something had to change. Sixth, once again Roach let Laurel go, and their on-again, off-again relationship continued into the Laurel & Hardy years, though not always resulting in an actual firing.

A real-life guardian angel, masquerading behind tough-guy moxie, soon entered Laurel's life and temporarily brought it some stability, both personally and professionally. Comedian-turned-producer Joe Rock offered to star Laurel in a series of short subjects—but not with Mae as ingenue. Laurel, who was in financial straits because the studios wanted nothing to do with the Laurel and Mae package, readily accepted.

Rock had taken a chance with Laurel after being approached by their common friend, director Percy Pembroke. Things had become so tight for Stan and Mae that they were then living with Pembroke and his wife. But Rock was not running a comedy welfare office; he had admired Laurel's earlier work. Still, getting funding for a projected series of Laurel films was not easy.

It proved impossible, with the money men (potential distributors) concerned over Laurel's drinking problem. But a stubborn Rock decided to go ahead with the project, at least through a pilot film. All went smoothly during a three-week preparation, but problems arose just as shooting began. As if anticipating the battle-scarred husbands of future Stan & Ollie films, Laurel appeared with deep scratches in his face and what amounted to a picture-appearing ultimatum from Mae (after Laurel had stopped trying to convince Rock that the scratches were from his cat!).

Needless to say, Rock was not receptive to this old argument, even when Laurel threatened to walk himself. But Rock did offer to talk with Mae, under cover of an acceptance of her demand. Once there, however, the producer read her the proverbial riot act, and all was once again calm on the comedy front— at least temporarily. Several films were then completed with Laurel demonstrating the most professional of behavior.

Strangely enough, as if Laurel film titles were becoming prophecies, during the production of *Somewhere in Wrong* (1925) Laurel began to show signs of domestic stress, including a tired physical appearance and a short-tempered attitude. This situation continued through *Twins* (1925) and *Pie-eyed* (1925), coming to a head on *Snow Hawk* (1925). Because *Snow Hawk* involved shooting on location, a situation necessitating close cast living conditions, Mae was encouraged to play one last selfish card for herself—she accused Rock of having made sexual advances. It was a ploy she had used before with other film rivals. And while the accusation was quickly proven false, Mae did not come out of the proceedings empty handed. She had been disruptive enough to make her offer (presented through Stan) palatable: Mae would return to her native Australia if someone paid her passage, bought her new clothes, gave her some cash, and got her jewels out of hock (pawning jewelry was a popular way for vaudevillans to raise money).

Rock considered the offer a bargain and an agreement was made. But as a safeguard, the producer also made an arrangement with the ship's purser that Mae had to be on board at sea one day before receiving the money and the jewels. Also, in the week before Mae's exit Rock had his brother babysit Laurel to help guarantee everything went smoothly. Rock, who was proving to be quite the ''producer'' in real life, even played matchmaker for a happy Laurel on the day Mae was officially gone (via a one-day-out cable from the ship's purser).

In the main, this too worked out, since the blind date in question, actress Lois Neilson, became Laurel's first wife. (They married August 13, 1926, following that choreographed 1925 first meeting.)

With Neilson, personal stability for a time entered Laurel's life. Paradoxically, the engineer of this calm, Rock, did not long benefit. Laurel metaphorically did what Rock had planned against Mae doing—he jumped ship. Receiving a better salary, Laurel once again signed with Roach, though the second half of 1926 was taken up with a legal battle between the two comedy producers. In fairness to this sought-after comedian, who comes off sounding less than loyal, Laurel had been on an unpaid production hiatus from Rock. Inasmuch as Laurel had finished a contracted series of films ahead of schedule, no money would be forthcoming until the next Rock production began. Conversely, Rock would have permitted Laurel to assume temporary film work elsewhere, as long as Laurel did not star in any picture that would compete on screen with Rock's Laurel films. But there was no reversal; the case was eventually dismissed, and Laurel was again working for Roach.

Before addressing the birth and heyday years of Stan & Ollie at Roach studios, it is important to note three ongoing personal and professional Laurel patterns emerging strongly with Rock. First, though Mae was gone, Stan had not learned from this relationship, and there were other volatile women and messy relationships in the future. At times this triggered an alcohol problem, an affliction from which his maternal grandfather had suffered while Laurel spent his early childhood there.

As with any great artist, however, the personal pain and problems eventually became material for his work—the domestic frustration of the antiheroic Stan and Ollie. Witness the sometimes threat of cinema wives who might have doubled as linebackers for the Chicago Bears, or the nights when the boys try to slip out for a drink. But as will be shown, it seemed to take a Leo McCarey to really bring Laurel & Hardy's antiheroic comic possibilities into perspective, though the ingredients had been dogging Laurel for years.

Second, though Laurel was normally the most dedicated of film comedians, his self-destructive personal life was the one thing to threaten his film career, especially late in the 1930s (not unlike so many of the other gifted but not otherwise worldly wise film pioneers). Laurel's friend Buster Keaton, a prime period example of a brilliant but overly comic-focused mind, later paid dearly, personally and professionally, for this narrowness (allowing a loss of his production control to take place at M-G-M, made more complex by the coming of sound, a traumatic divorce, and alcoholism). Laurel, however, generally seemed able to bounce back. Ironically, the eventual exception also included a Laurel & Hardy 1940s loss of production control at M-G-M (a graveyard for film comedians of the period[32]) and 20th Century-Fox. Yet even here, Laurel was able personally to weather this frustrating close of an otherwise comically inspired career, something that would not have seemed very likely in his problematic mid-1920s.

Third, despite the problems, Laurel was a "comer." While still without a consistent screen persona, his general comedic abilities were receiving more and more attention; Roach was just one of several producers interested in stealing him away from Rock. While still successful in parodies (his 1924 spoofs for Rock included the *West of Hot Dog* takeoff of *West of Pecos*, 1922, and the *Monsieur Don't Care* parody of Valentino's *Monsieur Beaucaire*, 1924), he could now generate excellent reviews in a straight comedy like *Half a Man* (1925), even though his character was somewhat derivative of Harry Langdon's baby-like persona. Moreover, as if fate were determined to team Laurel & Hardy some day (based upon their past professional contacts and near contacts), Rock had even suggested utilizing Hardy the comic villain in a similar capacity for the Laurel films (though with no thought yet of *teaming*). Stan had vetoed the supporting character idea, however, not wanting to compete with someone who had expanded the range of the stock comic villain. Laurel had been aware of Hardy's scene-stealing abilities for some time, especially from his appearances in the Semon comedies. But destiny received its reward (the teaming) once it had the foresight to include Leo McCarey in the process.

Appropriately, both Laurel and Hardy worked at the Roach studio in 1925, though Hardy was free-lancing there in 1924. His pre-team work included minor supporting roles in some of the McCarey-directed Charley Chase films. While there is no record of McCarey and Hardy initially palling around, the director had much in common with this half of his future comedy duo. Both very much enjoyed golf, music, and singing. McCarey sets would later become famous for his piano playing both between takes and when he was brainstorming for comic ideas. During his years with the team both Laurel & Hardy and others joined him in song around the on-the-set piano.

But unlike Hardy's claims of family law ties, McCarey had flirted with a career in law. Indeed, McCarey had completed his studies and briefly played at being a lawyer before entering the film world. And the sports-loving Hardy no doubt would have appreciated a director whose father was a prominent West Coast boxing promoter. It also suggests how the famous Jack Dempsey–Gene Tunney "long count" fight became the basis for the later Laurel & Hardy short subject *The Battle of the Century* (1927, supervised by McCarey), which comically even borrows the title from the advertising hype for the boxing match (of course, the "reel" battle for Laurel & Hardy in this film is an epic pie fight).

Going beyond any specific McCarey and Hardy ties is simply the talented and charismatic nature of this man behind the team. But McCarey's storytelling and on-the-set seeding of an improvisational setting went well beyond just being fun to work with. He seems to have been pleasantly overpowering with his story-telling mix of both verbal and mime skills:

McCarey had a habit of dominating every film he directed [and/or supervised], in ways that were spontaneous, graceful and various . . . Sometimes his constant pantomimes in the course of his conversation were infectious enough to show up on film being performed by the actors. (Many of Stan Laurel's familiar mannerisms, in fact, were originally familiar mannerisms of McCarey's. The director [and/or supervisor] had a "Let's go have a beer" gesture and an "Anybody want to play tennis?" gesture that friends and associates haven't shaken yet.)[33]

Celebrated antiheroic humorist and close McCarey friend H. Allen Smith (author of such books as *Low Man on a Totem Pole* and *Life in a Putty Knife Factory*) remembers one visit with McCarey when the storytelling was so diverting that the identity of another visitor was hardly noted. Later Smith was told he had missed talking to Ingrid Bergman.[34]

Laurel and Hardy as a team did not surface until 1927. As team biographer Randy Skretvedt has observed, for part of that Roach pre-1927 period "they did a remarkable job of avoiding each other."[35] Still, a number of important things were going on. Laurel directed Hardy in three short subjects: *Yes, Yes, Nanette* (1925), *Wandering Papas* (1925), and *Madame Mystery* (1926, co-directed by Richard Wallace). Because of the contract dispute with Rock, Laurel was keeping busy behind the camera (working on gags and directing) and enjoying it immensely. And Hardy's pre-team tenure at Roach studio was opening up a wider range of supporting roles. Privately, things had also changed. Besides Laurel's new bride, Hardy too had changed romantic partners. In 1925 he married Myrtle Lee Reeves. His second wife was an actress originally from Georgia. But the Georgia-born Hardy had *not* known her since childhood, as was claimed in a Roach Studio press release. The latter assertion, however, did make for a romantic story, and is still sometimes noted as fact. (Hardy was attracted to Southern women.) This would turn into a volatile relationship more in the tradition of Stan and Mae, with publicized breakups and reconciliations. In part, these were fueled by Myrtle's alcoholism. But initially, all was quiet on the Hardy homefront, as it was on Laurel's.

Fittingly, Hardy accidently caused Laurel's return to the screen in a matter suitable for any of their future antiheroic storylines. According to a July 24, 1926, Los Angeles newspaper article, Myrtle injured her leg in a hiking accident and Oliver later suffered burns at home trying to prepare supper.[36] (The injury caused Laurel to replace Hardy in the film *Get 'em Young*, 1926, which Laurel had been directing.) But with the comic hindsight of a Laurel & Hardy armchair quarterback, the article seems to brim with details comically anticipating the later duo. For instance, Hardy, though with good reason, was playing servant to his wife Myrtle—the basic henpecked storyline of so many Laurel & Hardy films. With antiheroic consistency, he messed up in the kitchen, always a danger zone for the team—especially Ollie. Moreover, Hardy suffered a burn using comedy's favorite kitchen utensil—the frying pan. But in order not to disturb his wife, he attempted a quick back-door exit. (This was reasoning right up there with Stan & Ollie deciding to take the piano back down the mountainous flight of steps in *The Music Box*, 1932, as well as the duo's general tendency to attempt to keep secrets from their wives). And Hardy managed to top this real misadventure just as the future Ollie might have: he took a painful accidental fall. Slapstick by any other name . . . Herein, truth was not stranger than fiction but merely its equal . . . Oh, and where did the initial accident (to Myrtle) occur, which triggered this whole affair? It was in a place called "Laurel" Canyon! Certainly, the gods of comedy were having some fun at the expense of Oliver and Myrtle.

If it took a "Hardy" accident to put Laurel back on the screen, the impetus for the teaming came from McCarey. This director/producer originally established himself at Roach studios with an apprenticeship of sorts as first a gag writer on the "Our Gang" series, then by direction of Charley Chase in a series of inventive, popular short subjects (with McCarey later crediting Chase as his comedy mentor). McCarey's work with Laurel & Hardy was then the launching pad for an extremely successful career, commercially and critically, in feature length films. Moreover, McCarey displayed a great comedy genre range. For example, he became a pivotal screwball comedy director, winning an Academy Award for direction of one of the genre's central works—*The Awful Truth* (1937).[37] Yet, he proved even more capable in the populist comedy track, especially with *Going My Way* (1944). Besides setting box-office records, the film won for McCarey directing and original story Academy Awards. And as was befitting such a comedy master so important to the birth of Laurel & Hardy, McCarey was also most capable of directing other cinema clowns in the genre of personality comedian. Indeed, McCarey was the only director to put an auteur stamp on a Marx Brothers film—*Duck Soup* (1933). As well as being the team's greatest film, with such McCarey-inspired material as the classic mirror sequence (where Harpo plays at being the reflection of Groucho), *Duck Soup* is sometimes cited as the greatest sound film comedy of all time. While these many comedy achievements were ahead of McCarey, they nicely demonstrate the sizable talents of the man so bound up with the birth of Stan & Ollie.

To a large degree, the Stan & Ollie the world know today were born in 1927. Roach gagman Frank Butler, who was working with the team at its inception, is most adamant about crediting McCarey's significance:

It was Leo McCarey, and no one else, who created the team of Laurel and Hardy [Roach has sometimes appropriated credit for the teaming] . . . Leo was the first among us to notice that putting the skinny fellow in juxtaposition with the fat fellow was not only nice contrast but very funny contrast . . . At the time Leo first thought of giving the boys the biggest roles . . . Roach was on an around-the-world tour.[38]

That is, McCarey not only teamed them, he also made the duo the focus rather than the supporting players they had played originally. Biographies on and/or related to the team also grant McCarey a special status. John McCabe's *Laurel & Hardy* called "brilliant director and producer" McCarey the "catalyst for the joining," while McCabe's *Mr. Laurel and Mr. Hardy* (done in close collaboration with Laurel) credits McCarey with being a frequent "starting point for

[Stan & Ollie] ideas . . . a natural idea man for Laurel and Hardy."[39] And McCabe's *Babe: The Life of Oliver Hardy* includes several McCarey accolades, including the comment that Laurel "revered" him. The significance to the team of his comedy ideas is best demonstrated by noting that McCarey was still occasionally receiving Laurel & Hardy story credits a year after he left the Roach studio.

Fred Guiles's Laurel biography states that: "the formula for their films had been codified by McCarey."[40] This meant that from an early date McCarey was able to see a larger Laurel & Hardy world and worked towards maintaining that always-important comic consistency of character and story. (For more on McCarey, see my book on the director.[41])

One must be quick to add, however, that Laurel was a giant comedy talent who worked closely with McCarey. Indeed, at one point in the American Film Institute's unpublished "Leo McCarey Oral History," the director observes, "Stan and I shaped all those things [the character traits of the duo]."[42] Thus, according to Frank Butler (see n. 38), Laurel was responsible for developing the team's "invincible dumbness" characteristic. Appropriately, McCarey and Laurel seem to have had a close friendship, with the comedian having "adored" McCarey.

Regardless, the unique characteristic of the new duo—slower pacing, something that would literally change silent comedy—is generally attributed to McCarey.[43] (For a Laurel perspective on slower pacing see "Encore: An Interview/Article Collage" in Chapter 3.) The director observed:

At the time, comics had a tendency to do too much. With Laurel & Hardy we introduced nearly the opposite. We tried to direct them so that they showed nothing, expressed nothing [in a drawn-out manner] and the audience, waiting for the opposite, laughed because we remained serious.[44]

The inspiration for this change in comedy pacing was something that had come to McCarey suddenly, and he presented it (as recorded in his unpublished "Oral History") to his crew in an amusingly earthy style:

I came in one morning and I said, "We're all working too fast. We've got to get away from these jerky movements and work at a normal speed." I said, "I'll give you an example of what I mean. There's a royal dinner. All the royalty is seated around the table and somebody lets out a fart. Now everybody exchanges a *glance*, that's all." Everybody died laughing, but I got my point over.[45]

This deliberate McCarey pacing gave Laurel & Hardy a fresh approach to visual comedy late in the silent period, enabling them to, as critic/historian Walter Kerr observed, "alter silent film comedy in a way that made it possible for them [Laurel & Hardy], alone among their [speedier] contemporaries, to pass over into sound films [where sound technology required a slower pace] with scarcely a hitch of their philosophical shoulders."[46]

A slow pace was also most appropriate for the slow-thinking Stan & Ollie.

The best demonstration of this leisurely deliberate approach to screen life is the way Stan & Ollie calmly proceed through what in other people would quickly become uncontrollable rage. An example is the celebrated destruction of cars in the McCarey-written and supervised *Two Tars* (1928). Stan & Ollie are sailors caught in a traffic jam. When Ollie tries to back out, he crunches Edgar Kennedy's radiator—twice. Edgar is thus moved to kick the Stan & Ollie car. Stan retaliates by ripping off one of Edgar's headlights and proudly displays what he has done to Ollie and their dates. Stan then boots the light, but it goes through another driver's windshield. This man then pops one of the girls' balloons. Stan methodically returns the favor by calmly covering this driver's head with some wet cement from nearby. (The combatants always patiently and politely take turns.) The driver with the cement bonnet next slashes the tires of Stan & Ollie's car. Never to be outdone, the comic duo proceed to remove all of his tires. This polite and orderly "tit-for-tat" violence gradually spreads to include all the drivers and cars stuck in the traffic jam.

When a traffic cop finally arrives and restores some order to the situation, one views what appears to be the final contestants in a world cup demolition derby, anticipating the ultimate destructive traffic jam aftermath in Jean-Luc Godard's black comedy, *Weekend* (1967). But in the *Two Tars* world of Stan & Ollie, all of these junkyard jalopies miraculously and comically wobble by the traffic cop, and the jam is over.

Fittingly, the tit-for-tat routine was another Stan & Ollie technique introduced by McCarey. The inspiration for this phenomenon ranks with any of the team's later comically restrained acts of shared violence. McCarey was in New York City with a number of comedy colleagues, including Mabel Normand, Hal Roach, and Charley Chase. One evening they plan to visit a nightclub. But McCarey has always had difficulty tying a bow tie, and when his designated tie-tier (Normand) leaves him at the hotel, apparently as a prank, McCarey is thrown into a tizzy. However, with highball in hand and the circular logic of his Stan & Ollie, he remembers a West Coast friend whose wife ties a beautiful tie. She is also a professional skater presently performing somewhere in New York. Thus, he calls California and then numerous places in New York. With uncharacteristically good luck, the antiheroic McCarey (a tendency that will be explored further), both contacts this tie-tier extraordinaire and extrapolates a promise she will come to his rescue:

Well, sure enough, she came by and tied a beautiful bow tie and I went out to this night club [sic] and told the whole story to the gang, and no sooner had I finished than Mabel grabbed my tie and pulled it. I said, "You little son of a bitch!" Well, everybody laughed, so I pulled Roach's tie. Somebody else laughed, so Roach pulled *his* tie. It began to spread to other tables and everybody started pulling each other's ties and, running out of ties to pull—it was too much fun to stop—they started ripping collars off—rrriiip— until everybody's collar was off. Then somebody got an idea that if you took a knife you could start up the seam of a tuxedo, then grab ahold and tear it, and this was very effective. Pretty soon the nightclub was a shambles. Well, *that* was the basis for at least a dozen Laurel and Hardy pictures.[47]

Another Laurel & Hardy basic with McCarey roots is the importance of realistic humor. He always aimed for the human factor, something in which both co-medians saw the inherent wisdom. In fact, throughout Hardy's life he enjoyed quoting McCarey's axiom on the subject: "In your fundamentals, you've always got to be real—no matter how far-fetched you get. . . . " (See Chapter 4 for even more pointed hosannas to realism by the comedians and several critics/historians.)

A rough facsimile of the team surfaced immediately with *Duck Soup* (1927). But after that Laurel & Hardy's roles together fluctuated between being teamlike and merely being cast in the same film. Examples of the latter included *Slipping Wives* (1927) and *With Love and Hisses* (1927), where they are unteamed and on the comic outs with each other. (*Slipping Wives* even has Hardy's character plotting to kill Laurel's—hardly Stan/Ollie fare.)

McCarey was the one who turned this around. As Laurel & Hardy biographer Randy Skretvedt noted: the early "films themselves indicate that McCarey—the Roach staffer who was most enthusiastic about L & H—began decisively guiding the construction of the films in June 1927, with *The Second Hundred Years*" [story by McCarey].[48]

The opening title for the film is both funny and an axiom to be broken: "Will Rogers says—'Being in jail has one big advantage—a man doesn't have to worry about wearing his tuxedo.' " Well, being the most perfect of antiheroes, Stan & Ollie are prisoners who *do* have to worry about tuxedos. Their luckless prison escapees (referred to as Little Goofy and Oliver Hardy) manage to accidently waylay two French police chiefs who are going to, of all places, the governor's mansion on the prison grounds. (It makes more sense to think of this as the warden's home.) "Borrowing" their tuxedos from the Frenchmen, Stan & Ollie have to watch their tuxedo-attired social graces, Will Rogers notwithstanding. Predictably, these two less than competent "misfits" fail and find themselves once again as true "guests" of the state, and thus the title—*The Second Hundred Years*.

In addition to the starting-point significance of this film, it also generated an unexpected comedy bonus for future Laurel & Hardy films. They had had their hair cut short to look the part of prisoners. But when Laurel's hair grew back it would not lie down when he tried to comb it back. Receiving unsolicited laughs on the set for his now standing-on-end hair, it did not take long for this singleminded comedian to incorporate it into his screen persona.

Appropriately, McCarey's importance to the team was soon rewarded by his being made supervisor. McCarey later explained to interviewer Peter Bogda-novich what this title meant:

Supervisor meant being responsible for practically everything on the film: story, gags, screening the rushes, working on the editing, sending out the prints, cutting again when the previews weren't good enough. But in those days, your name wasn't mentioned in the credits; the industry knew who'd do what.[49]

In keeping with that industry awareness, Frank Capra later observed about his early days in film: "the man I watched and admired most was . . . Leo McCarey. The ease and speed with which this young genius cooked up laughs on the spot for Laurel and Hardy made my mouth water."[50] And despite the great populist comedy significance of Capra's film work, he also noted: "At comedy, no one was better than Leo McCarey."[51]

There is little that could top such high comedy praise except, possibly, an accolade from Charlie Chaplin. And McCarey had this, too. In his unpublished American Film Institute's Oral History, McCarey confessed that "one of the most precious souvenirs I have is a fan letter Chaplin sent me in which he congratulates me on my work with Laurel & Hardy and predicts a beautiful future for me."[52]

For many film historians, including myself, Laurel & Hardy's work after McCarey's 1929 exit for feature films (though he received story credit for several Laurel & Hardy shorts in 1930) is generally not on a par with the greatness that preceded it. As film scholar Charles Barr observed in his book-length critical analysis of the team, Laurel & Hardy's "only time of unbroken inspiration was 1928–1929, on either side of the introduction of sound, working under McCarey's supervision. [Moreover] after 1930 . . . fewer shorts [were made] from year to year and . . . the quality becomes on the whole less consistent."[53] Film comedy historian Gerald Mast echoes this while also referring to George Stevens, the team's principal cameraman, who would later move on to major success as a director of feature films: "With sound and without McCarey or Stevens, Laurel and Hardy were not what they had been."[54]

In the 1969 *Take One* essay, "The Crazy World of Laurel," film historian and Laurel & Hardy author William Everson found the team's "really creative work" to have been done in the silent era. Moreover, he labeled their later films "largely reworkings" of these early classics. When *Films in Review* had queried the comedian in the 1959 interview "Laurel Without Hardy," he also gave the nod to the silents. Though as with the Everson reference, McCarey was not noted. (For more on these articles, see Chapter 4.)

This position on McCarey, which is not a unanimous critical stance among students of Laurel & Hardy, should neither obscure the team's creative use of sound during the transition to "talkies" (see chapters 2 and 3) nor distract from the team's occasional later great films, such as *The Music Box*.

Praise of McCarey was not limited, however, to mere verbal niceties from colleagues and critics. In late December 1927 he was made a Roach corporation vice-president. In February 1928, after the last quarter figures of 1927 showed it to be the most profitable Roach period to date, McCarey was given a new contract in which he received a percentage of the Laurel & Hardy film profits.[55]

Roach himself had already felt secure enough to leave for Hong Kong in January, on the first leg of a five-month, around-the-world tour.

Stan Laurel and Oliver Hardy, two solo film veterans who had, as the stereotype goes, toiled for years in the business with only so-so success, became another one of those always misleading "overnight successes" once they were teamed and supervised by McCarey. Before the pairing, Laurel had been the more successful of the two. And this was reflected in their initial responses to the idea of being teamed. Hardy was euphoric; he correctly saw this as a unique opportunity. Laurel initially was adamantly opposed. It seemed like a professional regression, and he was not even sure performing was a career to which he wanted to return, since he was then enjoying success writing and directing.

Once the teaming took place, it was quite natural that Laurel would be the more dominant of the two. Moreover, Laurel's continued behind-the-scenes activities in gag construction and general filmmaking activities further encouraged this dichotomy. McCarey later noted that early in the teaming Laurel was not beyond flaunting his position in Hardy's presence: "Right in front of him, Laurel would say, 'I'm doing twice as much as he is, and whatever he gets, I want to get twice as much money.' "[56] (E. R. Moak's June 1933 *Photoplay* article, "Tear-Stained Laughter," had Laurel receiving $500 more per week than Hardy, but with seemingly no hard feelings on either side.)

McCarey's reminiscences on the subject are even more pointedly controversial in the *Cahiers* interview, where Laurel is alleged to have said, "Hardy was really incapable of creating anything at all—it was astonishing that he could even find his way to the studio."[57] Laurel biographer McCabe, in a special "McCarey Appendix" (from his *The Comedy World of Stan Laurel*, strongly questioned the latter statement, refusing to believe "either that Stan said it, or that Leo McCarey said he said it."[58] Yet, there seems to be a tacit acceptance that Laurel could be blunt about salaries in Hardy's presence. But McCarey's professional ties with the team were at its inception when Laurel was initially only lukewarm about the idea. Any question about the early Laurel & Hardy relationship merely complements the loving one that evolved, and one that an adoring public is always quick to defend—since any negatives seem so out of character. Reframed another way: they got along remarkably well for a long-term teaming. After all, even the Marxes had differences—and they were brothers! Moreover, Laurel & Hardy (in their later tours) became progressively closer, whereas the normal team pattern moved toward a split—as with Abbott & Costello or Martin & Lewis.

The McCabe comments are understandable, moreover, since the vast majority of reminiscences about the team paint a much more harmonious relationship (see Chapter 4), though it is invariably observed that Laurel, not Hardy, worked behind the screen, and the two did not generally socialize. However, sympathetic detractions about the younger Laurel are not limited to McCarey. A 1971 issue of *Pratfall*, a journal devoted to Laurel & Hardy, has a pertinent interview with

Ruth Laurel, whom the comedian married on three separate occasions. In an otherwise very pro-Laurel piece, she observes:

Stan *was* temperamental, but he was always sweet about it. If he did anything that hurt you, he'd always make up for it in a very quick way. But Babe [Hardy] had plenty of cause to get mad at Stan. He [Hardy] would sometimes tell me, "You know, Stan is kind of difficult." And I'd say, "I know it."[59]

Ruth did not, however, remember cross words between the two.

In all fairness to Laurel, possibly McCarey was not fully crediting the comedian's comments with a tongue-in-cheek comic cynicism. Because Laurel did have a dark sense of humor, which is examined later in the chapter. Still, Laurel's comments would not necessarily have been painless. For instance, a Lakeside Country Club golfing friend of Hardy's said he found Laurel & Hardy very compatible, that "the nearest Stan and Babe came to a quarrel would be when Stan would show up at the club, and he'd look at Babe and say something like, 'Well, I've been over at the studio doing your work.' "[60]

Comments Laurel made during the team's 1932 visit to Europe are also not inconsistent with the McCarey position. When a London *Daily Herald* reporter visited a Laurel family reunion, the comedian observed:

"Oli [sic], the great old scout, has shuffled off and left us to it [the reunion].

"He went to see the changing of the Guard this morning. They must have heard he was coming and were afraid he might get up to something cos [sic] they didn't have it.

"And that peal of [Laurel's] laughter bounced off the ceiling [a possible link to the alleged Laurel comment about Hardy having a hard time getting around?].

"So he's [Hardy] gone to the Cheshire Cheese to have a few cheeses. Reckon he's pretty well full of—er—cheese by now . . ."[61]

Four days after the London *Daily Herald* visit with Laurel, British *Film Weekly* humorist Ian Fox's article "Laurel High-hats Hardy" manages to further cloud the issue. Here is a comic piece that reverses the Stan & Ollie stereotypes, with Ollie playing dumb (as a first-time English tourist) to a dominating (now back home) Stan. Thus, the fat one's every comment and action are the nonstop target of the thin one's retorts, with the ongoing put-down refrain, "Oh, Ollie!" Though obviously a gimmick for the press, does it reflect any minor but real irritation? Or, was Laurel's sarcastic tone in the London *Daily Herald* interview merely a comic warmup for the *Film Weekly* switch of their personae?

Ironically, years later, when there was no questioning Laurel & Hardy's fondness for one another, it was the skinny one who desired an added closeness. It seems Laurel remembered Hardy's birthday and other special occasions with cards and modest gifts, something not reciprocated by Hardy. (This is consistent with Laurel's drive to answer all his fan mail.) There was nothing personal in Hardy's neglect to respond—it was just his nature. Along similar lines, late in their joint career Laurel would have spent more personal time with Hardy if his partner had been more available. But Hardy had an active circle of friends whose interests did not mesh with the simpler tastes of Laurel. Thus, the tours not only helped make them real friends, it necessitated their spending more time together.

If any early Laurel air of superiority towards Hardy existed, even of a tongue-in-cheek nature, it would also clash with the thin one's democratic reputation for being blind to any type of studio caste system. Of course, for the family-oriented Roach studio, a more intimate environment was the norm anyway. But Laurel seems to have genuinely placed little importance on position in most of his contacts, which also helps to explain his herculean attempt to answer all his fan mail during his old age.

Conversely, like his Karno colleague Charlie Chaplin, Laurel was a demanding perfectionist. Comedian/author Steve Allen noted, in his foreword to Randy Skretvedt's *Laurel and Hardy* that he (Allen) had met a former Laurel & Hardy film crew member who had decidedly preferred Hardy. When asked why, he replied, "Oh, he [Laurel] just seemed stuck-up. He was too much of a perfectionist. He always wanted everything to be just right and if it wasn't he could be kind of a son-of-a-bitch about it." But then as Steve Allen fittingly added, "The same might be said, I suppose, of every talented perfectionist who ever lived."

Comments such as these are added not to distract from Laurel but rather to present a more complete view of the man as well as possibly shedding more light on his art. Testimonies to his kindness, especially in his retirement years, should forever document the inherent goodness of the man. But just as this chapter will also further explore his sometime macabre sense of humor and his frequently volatile relationships with women, it should be recognized that he was a much more complex man than the portrait of congeniality established in his final years.

Interestingly enough, the question of salaries eventually generated another type of contract tension. Since Laurel & Hardy were already employed at Roach when the team was established, they were still under separate solo contracts. Now, the magnanimous thing would have been for Roach to tear these up and offer the team a new joint contract. But Roach the businessman recognized the added negotiating power the individual contracts gave him. By maintaining them (and their different expiration dates), he guarded against Laurel & Hardy staging a shared walkout. This will be expanded upon later in the chapter, when Laurel has his own one-man strike.

In the late 1920s, however, Laurel & Hardy were too busy making short subject after celebrated short subject. Indeed, 1928 and 1929 were one long hosanna. This is best demonstrated by leafing through the period issues of the *Motion Picture Exhibitors Herald-World*. As its title suggests, this was a publication geared to the theatre owner, offering marketing tips, general theatre information, and feedback from other exhibitors.

Of particular interest to this project was the *Herald-World* section entitled

"What the Picture Did for Me." It was composed of numerous mini-reviews (approximately a paragraph in length) written by theatre owners across the country. Unlike most publications, it gave equal time to film short subjects.

By 1928 reviews of Laurel & Hardy were a regular part of "What the Picture Did for Me," because the team was now both firmly established and prolific (approximately one short subject per month). Moreover, their popularity seemed to be keeping the titles before the public for longer-than-normal periods. And the reviews all read like something the team's mothers might have written. Thus, a Dayton theatre owner's comments on the duo's epic pie fight of a film, *The Battle of the Century*: "Absolutely the best comedy I have ever played and I don't mean maybe. Hal Roach comedies are in a class all by themselves."[62] When the team explored the world of high-rise thrill comedy, such as Harold Lloyd's, a Canadian exhibitor wrote: "Boy, oh, boy, what a comedy! You remember how [Lloyd's] *Safety Last* left them gasping? [where Lloyd climbs a skyscraper, including the famous scene of him hanging from the face of a clock.] This [film—*Liberty*] will do the same. Be sure and feature it. It's chock full of laughs."[63] The same *Herald-World* issue that had the *Liberty* review included several other Laurel & Hardy rave mini-reviews. These might best be exemplified by the one simply listed under the entry "Laurel-Hardy Comedies": "All these are good. My people [patrons] often ask for them to be repeated"—another Canadian theatre owner.

The reviews were not only nonstop high praise, they could become comically aggressive in their support—*Soup to Nuts* (1928), where Stan & Ollie are the most comically incompetent of domestic help, produced the response: "Here are the best two rough-house comedy artists in pictures today. If they [the audience] won't laugh at this one, throw 'em to the lions!"[64] And this was from little Paoli, Indiana—hardly a place known for big-city aggressive marketing, the "throw 'em to the lions" notwithstanding. This *Soup to Nuts* piece appeared in a lengthy Laurel & Hardy "What the Picture Did for Me" segment of the May 4, 1929 *Herald-World*.

A typical sampling of this issue's Laurel & Hardy wave of homage included the Louisville, Nebraska, exhibitor's comments on *Finishing Touches* (1928), in which the team are the world's worst carpenters: "Another scream from these boys. If only we could show a comedy every night as good as this one. [Today this is hardly considered one of their classics.] Many good [patron] comments, and a few folks asked us when we were going to show another of this pair." A Florida theatre owner said of the legendary tit-for-tat *Two Tars*: "This is what you call real comedy. This is in all probability one of the best ever released. Playing with Clara Bow in *Three Week Ends* [1928] and it created more comment than the feature."

One might best sum up this lauding of Laurel & Hardy with the *Big Business* comments of a Nevada exhibitor in still another issue of *Herald-World*: "Getting so that I'm running out of good adjectives in reporting on these Laurel-Hardy wows, so I'll merely say that the boys start out in the Xmas tree business and end up as house-wreckers. Imagine the complications."[65] This theatre owner might also have used the title of the film as an economic metaphor for the state of their success—Laurel & Hardy were truly "Big Business"!

Naturally, Roach did not miss an opportunity to capitalize on the duo's phenomenal popularity. In a March 9, 1929, *Herald-World* ad, under the Roach-quoted heading "There is no substitute for laughter," acclaim is paid "The Amazing Success of M-G-M Short Subjects! [Roach's new, 1929, distributor]." And while photos of Laurel & Hardy, Charley Chase, and Our Gang (Roach's key series) are featured, the best excerpted reviews clearly belonged to the team: "Laurel-Hardy prove best comics since Lloyd" (*Detroit Times*); "Laurel-Hardy comedies are stealing the shows quite frequently" (*Los Angeles Record*); and "We had a big feature on bill [as well as Laurel & Hardy] and truthfully cannot say which was biggest draw" (Linton, Indiana, theatre owner).[66] (M-G-M's large chain of studio-owned theatres and its powerful publicity department helped the Laurel & Hardy bandwagon along all the more.)

Still, the key to this early critical and commercial success was tied to the talents of all involved, on both sides of the screen, with special asterisks by the names Laurel & Hardy and McCarey. This devotion to comedy and the matching gift for comic antiheroic humor, often of an improvisational nature, was truly inspired.

The hard work often intensified *after* a film was initially finished. Sneak previews meant a crash course in statistics, be it the duration of a laugh or the total number of them in the film (to be compared with the tallies of other sneak audiences and the original number of laughs the filmmakers felt were in the picture). The end result, naturally, of all this survey work was often more work—reshooting and/or re-editing. Like most great comedy, it eventually looks easy, but the procedure for getting there is seldom that.

On the Laurel & Hardy homefronts, things would seem as upbeat as their late 1920s film success, especially for Laurel. He and wife Lois had had a daughter on December 10, 1927. They named her Lois, Jr., though wife and daughter also went by "Big Lois" and "Little Lois." (A premature son, Stanley Robert Jefferson, lived little more than a week after his May 7, 1930 birth. Laurel's numerous future relationships were childless.) On June 16, 1928, Laurel's 38th birthday, he bought a new Beverly Hills home. On Bedford Drive, it was not far from the new Beverly Hills home (North Alta Drive) of Hardy and his wife—though the families rarely socialized. It was becoming a comic neighborhood, especially with Marie Dressler, of later *Min and Bill* (1930) and *Tugboat Annie* (1933) fame, across from the Laurels.

Big Lois gave Laurel the most stable of existences, even acting for a time as the comedian's financial manager. But for the comedian it seems to have been claustrophobic. For instance, he loved his daughter but he was not particularly patient with or comfortable around children. This was possibly a reflection of the limited contact he had had with his parents as a child, though his workaholic nature was certainly also a factor. And like many talented but self-destructive

"Little Lois" (age 2) with father and friend

artists, he eventually resented any guidance, even from a level-headed wife. And with live-in friend/handyman Pete Gordon (with whom he had worked at Larry Semon's Vitagraph), Laurel had a natural distraction and drinking companion.

In fact, drinking itself was no doubt another separator, because Big Lois eventually gave up drinking when she realized what a problem it was for Laurel. A number of key Roach people besides Laurel knew their way around a bottle, including McCarey (a later drinking companion of W. C. Fields, no less!), or the Parrott brothers—Charles (better known as Charley Chase) and James (a frequent later Laurel & Hardy director). Indeed, the early 1940s deaths of both Parrotts were alcohol related.

A studio entourage also gradually surfaced around Laurel, and in 1928 he took Alyce Ardell as a mistress. Besides being beautiful and bright, her French accent further fascinated Laurel; women with European accents were a special weakness of the comedian.[67] (A Freudian biographer might ponder the fact that Laurel's actress mother specialized in Theda Bara-like vamp roles.) Ardell was a central character in Laurel's life into the 1940s, outlasting numerous other concurrent relationships. Laurel biographer Guiles has described her as an ongoing "refuge" from the problems he always seemed to have with other women.[68] Because of Laurel's fickleness in love, the Ardell relationship was unique if for no other reason than its length. His ongoing interest might also have been from the fact that Ardell maintained relationships with a number of other important Hollywood men simultaneously. However, at least in his case, she was not a fortune hunter, since Laurel's antiheroic connections with wives frequently left him in a poor financial state during much of this time—the 1930s and early 1940s.

Hardy also took a mistress in the late 1920s, though he preferred the term "close companion." Viola Morse was an attractive young divorcee with a little boy, though like Hardy the child, he was frequently away at a military school. Unfortunately, Hardy's wife seems to have chosen to cope with this affair through alcohol, with a drinking problem developing at the same time. As has been documented so often before, being married to a comedian hardly seems the joy one would expect.

Quite possibly, the near 1929 divorce of Hardy and Myrtle was also precipitated by his gambling. The comedian, and presumably Viola (who shared this interest), were said to have lost $35,000 in a single day of betting at a Tijuana racetrack.[69] In addition, Myrtle had charged Hardy with frequently remaining away from home (he kept a separate hotel residence) and often being drunk when he did return.[70] First separated in July 1929, they reconciled before the end of the year.[71] However, the union remained volatile. Hardy filed for divorce in June 1933, only to be reconciled again in October. At that time a widely disseminated, ever-so-diplomatic statement from the comedian was released through Roach business manager and later team lawyer Ben Shipman. Authored by Shipman, it read, in part: "We are making a new start realizing that we owe to

each other the duty of taking our just share of blame for any past misunderstandings.''[72] (Hardy disliked writing anything.)

Regardless, a permanent reconciliation just did not seem possible. In November 1936 Myrtle sued Hardy for separate maintenance. "She accused him of
drinking, gambling and associating with other women, and once causing her to
be confined in a sanitarium against her will [besides being an alcoholic she was
later diagnosed as having a nervous disorder].''[73] While the separate maintenance
suit was eventually dismissed, the rotund half of the comic duo was granted a
divorce from Myrtle in May 1937. Paradoxically, the divorce was based on *her*
frequent disappearances from their home, as related to her drinking and nervous
disorders. Regardless of who was most at fault, Laurel found himself later
affectionately describing his partner as a "playboy" interested in golf, "the
horses, card games, entertaining, and what have you."[74]

Besides these late-1920s personal distractions for Laurel & Hardy (which
continued to surface periodically), the film industry served up its own end of
the decade diversion—the coming of sound movies. But there was no career-
ending threat for Laurel & Hardy. Because of their slower comedy pace and
basic pantomine focus, sound film was not an obstacle. It is no doubt from this
period that McCarey's famous motto—"Do it visually"—was born. And, it
should be stressed, Laurel & Hardy was that rare team created for *silent* film.

The duo's unique silent comedy base becomes most obvious after a study of
films from their transition to sound period. For a short time Laurel & Hardy
films were released simultaneously in both silent and sound versions. This was
because not all theatres had initially converted to sound—cost kept many small
houses from making the switch initially. When I later screened films from this
mixed-bag period, it was very easy inadvertently to leave off the sound on some
sound prints, only to discover later with a "correct" rescreening that no comically
significant material had been missed.

While the team, therefore, did not have to change either their pacing or their
personae for sound, the added bonus was the comic acceptability of their voices.
Hardy's Southern tenor and Laurel's soft English accent which, in times of
stress, could so quickly escalate to a high squeak, perfectly fit these "two minds
without a single thought." What a pleasant irony that two of the most distinctly
comic film voices of the 1930s this side of W. C. Fields and Mae West came
from a team accidently designed to be nearly "soundproof." Indeed, the team
had further played it safe (and silent) late in the transitional 1920s by minimizing
what initial sound-era dialogue they did have.

The early use of sound in Laurel & Hardy films had another pleasant irony.
Despite being clearly secondary to their visual comedy, the team's use of sound,
or, more precisely, sound effects, could at times be innovative. This is best
demonstrated by their first dialogue film, *Unaccustomed As We Are* (1929), with
its delightful tongue-in-cheek title reference to talking pictures not yet being
their norm. In this film, where Ollie courts marital disaster by bringing home

unplanned dinner guest Stan, the thin one is a true disaster victim—taking a horrendous fall down a flight of stairs. Or, at least it sounds like a horrendous fall. The camera stays focused on the point of comic departure—the top of the stairs, allowing the viewer only a secondhand look via Ollie's comically pained expression as he watches the accident in progress. This is a brilliant use of off-screen space, and a truly creative employment of sound at a time when too many "talkie" films were just that—uncinematically talkie. One is also reminded of classic radio's imaginative use of sound, such as the later trademark gag of the "Fibber McGee and Molly" program (1935–1957), where the periodic opening of an overstuffed closet would comically result in a tidal wave of sound effects (for the outpouring of junk). The success of the auditory gag is best demonstrated now by the fact that so many filmmakers went on to use it and/or variations upon it. After all, a cliché is like that old comic definition of plagiarism: the sincerest form of flattery.

The impetus for the noisy but unseen fall was Laurel's desire not to alienate any viewer who might find the actual tumble more painful than funny.[75] Regardless, this excellent use of off-screen space became a norm in Laurel & Hardy films.

Another creative use of sound that often effectively defused the pain factor in their films was the addition of funny noises to the slapstick. This is nicely capsulated in the title of the 1930 interview/article: "Ka-Plop and Ka-Bloop: Laurel & Hardy Reveal What Makes You Hear Such Funny Things." Reprinted in Chapter 3, the piece portrays a team very interested in the discovery of funny sounds. Indeed, Hardy seems so enthusiastically attentive one must question tales of his total non-involvement in the creative process. At the same time Hardy offers one of the piece's most comically entertaining insights of *sound* "research": "We got a good effect the other day when Stan had to swallow a nickel. We dropped an automobile crank into a metal washboiler and it made a good 'plink.' " Comic noises like this, or the now traditional slapstick sound effects for the bonk on the head, the banged or punched nose, the stubbed or stomped toe, the poked eye, the kicked shin . . . all help defuse the pain by slightly distancing the comic violence from reality. This cat-and-mouse game with reality is further reinforced by the simple cartoon character-like survival of the team despite the comic violence that so often engulfs them. (See Chapter 2 for more on their innovative comedy contributions to this period.)

A Laurel & Hardy cartoon connection is also most appropriate given their tradition of tit-for-tat violence. And while it might seem in minor conflict with the McCarey/Laurel policy of staying as close to reality as possible, any and all comedic characters, from Cary Grant to the Three Stooges, allow a certain suspension of belief to exist when it involves surviving bouts of violent slapstick.

Besides, on a general narrative level, the early Laurel & Hardy—which means the *best* Laurel & Hardy—seldom veers from the world of everyday reality, whether conflicts with wives and/or problems with the mechanical. Fittingly, this is also true of their greatest feature, *The Sons of the Desert* (1933), where

Stan & Ollie as Sons of the Desert

the team attempts to sneak off to a convention without their wives' knowledge . . . or permission. In contrast, comedy contemporaries like the Marx Brothers are at their best when placed in the most unlikely of settings—the national government in *Duck Soup* (1933, with Groucho as president, no less!) or friends of high art in the 1935 *A Night at the Opera*. An interesting corollary to this Laurel & Hardy connection with realism is that their highest initial critical praise often came from reviewers now most synonymous with documentary film, people like John Grierson and Alberto Cavalcanti. (But comic exceptions to a Laurel & Hardy setting do occur, such as the duo popping up *Way Out West*.)

For Laurel & Hardy a more problematic aspect of early sound was the now often forgotten policy of making numerous foreign language versions of each film. After a short subject was shot, previewed, and edited, four additional versions were often prepared in French, German, Italian, and Spanish. The foreign dialogue would then be spelled out phonetically on cue cards for the team, with each scene of the original film shot four more times, once for each language version.

It was an expensive process, both in terms of expanded production costs and additional people, from translators to supporting casts fluent in the focus language. Of course, by first finishing the English language version, which might have had a high shooting ratio (much more film shot than what was used), the foreign renditions could closely follow the English plot—minimizing any further wasted footage.

Use of this process was not limited to the team. "Other comedians of the time used a similar process, but it does appear that Laurel and Hardy were the most successful at it."[76] Fittingly, the duo was more popular abroad, something Laurel himself noted in a 1959 interview with Boyd Verb.[77] This *global* popularity was in part a result of their extra foreign-language efforts. While language mistakes were not unheard of, the phonetic "fluency" of these funnymen was effective enough for Laurel to observe: "when we finally went over there [Europe], they were amazed that we couldn't speak their language."[78]

Laurel & Hardy's foreign language efforts were not, however, without detractors. French authors Raymond Borde and Charles Perrin (see the Chapter 4 critique of their *Laurel et Hardy* book) found the duo's accents frightful and the comedians visibly bothered by reading their phonetic cue cards. Incongruously, these authors (whose book is generally a Laurel & Hardy celebration) could still, however, accept the team's artificial diction. They found a certain off-beat charm to the French-speaking supporting cast's attempt to emulate it!

In 1929 Laurel & Hardy had still another adjustment to make, though it had nothing to do with new technology. That was the year McCarey left to pursue a career in feature-length films. However, his influence on the team continued along two levels. First, the duo he had teamed, and whose personae he had worked so hard to help mold, was nicely established. Thus, there was an ongoing general McCarey "touch" to their future work. Second, and more specifically, even after his exit, stockpiled McCarey stories were the short-subject foundations for a number of Laurel & Hardy films, stretching into 1930.

Though no one seems to have been traumatized by the exit, after such an affectionate and creative partnership it could not have been easy for anyone. Thus, decades later McCarey could still observe: "It caused me a lot of pain to leave Laurel & Hardy."[79] After all, here was a man so fascinated by the team that:

I [McCarey] found myself spending almost every waking hour thinking of Laurel and Hardy, those two wonderful *characters*, not the boys who played them, Stan and Babe. Almost everything that happened to me during the day, I'd some way or another tie up with Laurel and Hardy, consciously or unconsciously. Getting into my car I'd think of the boys and what trouble they'd get into with a car. Passing a bus I'd think of them causing a rumpus on the bus. Seeing an advertisement in a newspaper for a cabaret, I'd think of them going there and wreaking havoc . . . [80]

Still, McCarey wanted to direct feature films and his critical and commercial success with Laurel & Hardy made this possible. He found himself in the enviable position of having offers come to him. A popular McCarey anecdote comically links this opportunity to ambition:

Roach was a [physically] powerful man, with a chest furred like a grizzly pelt, and one day Leo found himself sitting in the athletic club steam room, studying his employer thoughtfully. The more he studied, the more thoughtful he grew. Finally he reached a decision. Rising to his feet, he announced, "I quit. A guy hasn't a chance to get to the top around here with a boss as healthy as you."[81]

Though McCarey was missed, the comically gifted Laurel was an excellent idea man as well as performer. Moreover, Laurel & Hardy each had a firm handle on just what was appropriate for their screen characters. In contrast, one thinks of the earlier shooting star comedian Harry Langdon, who briefly reached the silent comedy pantheon only to suffer a quick feature-film demise after the exit of director Frank Capra. Langdon seemed to not fully understand just what his screen persona was about.

Interestingly enough, besides Langdon and his decline being a general counterpoint to Laurel & Hardy's ongoing success (after a break with a mentor), Langdon had more specific ties with the duo. First there is more than a little of the original Langdon persona in Laurel's screen character. Thus, how ironic that the borrower—Laurel—should better respect the confines of a given character. Second, with the Langdon-Laurel persona parallels, it is most fitting that Langdon eventually did some screenwriting for Laurel & Hardy. (His influence is most apparent in *Block-Heads*, 1938, which draws from the Langdon short subjects *All Night Long*, 1924, and *The Soldier Man*, 1926, three reels.) Third, after what appeared to be the permanent 1938 post-*Block-Heads* breakup of Laurel

& Hardy (due to Roach's firing of Laurel), there was an attempt to team Langdon and Hardy. But the one film to come of this experiment—the 1939 *Zenobia*—was not well received. Strangely enough, Langdon and Hardy are given few scenes together, and it is more of a star vehicle for Hardy, who plays an 1870s southern doctor treating a carnival elephant named Zenobia. The thankful pachyderm then loyally follows him everywhere. Langdon is the carnival owner who eventually sues Hardy for alienation of affections!

Such discord was well into the future, however, and the period in question—their early years as a team—found Laurel & Hardy on an incredibly popular roll. But why such a film success, a success that frequently found their short subjects billed *over* the feature film, a success that produced sacks full of fan letters simply addressed to Laurel & Hardy, care of Hollywood? This success which might be said to have peaked during their tumultuous 1932 visit to Great Britain, where the mobs predated Beatlemania by over thirty years.

There can seldom be a single answer to such a popular culture success story. But easily the most significant for the team were their ties with the evolution of the comic antihero in American humor.

In the late 1920s the comic antihero, who tries to create order in a disordered world, was making his presence known in American humor. He was not a new figure to American humor—few comedy types are. But he was now drawing attention because of his advancement to center stage. Previously he often had been relegated to the fringe areas of American humor—an irrational figure in a world still considered to be rational. (See Chapter 2 for an expanded look at Laurel & Hardy as antiheroes.)

The increased visibility of the comic antihero was due in large part to the birth of *The New Yorker* magazine and four writers: Robert Benchley, James Thurber, Clarence Day, and S. J. Perelman.[82]

While the central impetus for the eventual ascension of the comic antihero in American humor took place in the 1920s, there were numerous antiheroic fore-shadowings in a host of mediums. These included the comic strips of George Herriman (''Krazy Kat,'' 1913) and George McManus (''Bringing Up Father,'' 1913), the movie comedies of John Bunny (1910–1915), the earlier writings of Benchley (1910s), and the copyrighted Library of Congress stage sketches of W. C. Fields (late 1910s and 1920s[83]). Indeed, former vaudevillian Fields, whose antiheroic material such as his trademark frustrations at pool, frequently surfaced in his silent and sound films, represents an excellent reminder of the antiheroic roots in America's once-favorite entertainment format: vaudeville. In *American Vaudeville as Ritual*, author Albert McLean notes that again and again after 1900 critics implied that a ''new humor'' had developed in this country.[84]

In twentieth century American humor an antihero tries to create order in a world where order is impossible. He is generally a young urbanite who appears all the younger due to his utter comic incompetency at every task. This childlike nature is further underlined by the fact that work is not of central importance; the figure is more apt to be concerned with the frustrations of leisure time (especially wives and mechanical objects). Moreover, he is so thwarted by domestic daily problems that he never approaches political issues—unless addressing the basic comic absurdity of the world.

While Stan's and Ollie's close ties with the antihero will be examined more closely in Chapter 2, it should be obvious that the team could literally be called the "poster boys" for this new comedy phenomenon. What better showcase for frustration is there than Laurel & Hardy movies, whether domestic battles royal with wives or Model-T Fords. Though predated by other popular culture antiheroes, both the timing of their emergence (concurrent with the full emergence of the comic antihero) and their nearly immediate and astonishing popularity— soon reaching global proportions—underline their significance in this watershed period of transition in American humor.

I hasten to add, however, that Laurel's British music hall comedy heritage also contributed to his antiheroic persona. Laurel seems to have borrowed from his early comedy hero Dan Leno, the first British music hall artist to give a royal command performance (King Edward VII, 1901). Besides bearing a physical resemblance to Leno, Stan's delightfully startled look (so appropriate for a comic victim of the modern world) was a constant in Leno's stage persona. And Stan's periodic nonsense statement (especially after Ollie mistakenly asks him to repeat something which was accidently insightful), was also an element of Leno's character. In his accent on the comic (including misspellings) autobiography, *Dan Leno Hys Booke* (1901), "written by Himself," he makes such observations as, "I had washed my breakfast and swallowed myself" and "She winked at me with her ear—not her eye."

In a larger context, of course, Stan's simpleton character (and Ollie's) draws from a long humor history of "blockhead" types stretching back to Roman comedy. Still, their distinctive 1920s antiheroic characteristics best link them to a pivotal period in American humor.

In terms of the cited antiheroic precursors to Laurel & Hardy, it seems most fitting that Hardy himself should credit part of his Ollie characterization to an obscure comic strip from his Georgia childhood named "Helpful Henry."[85] Henry, like the later Ollie, invariably met frustration in his attempts to be "helpful." After consultations with archivist Bill Blackbeard of the San Francisco Academy of Comic Art, it was revealed that a "Helpful Henry" strip matching Hardy's description did not appear until well after the comedian was an adult (1920s).

If this was Hardy's "Helpful Henry," it does not negate the importance of the character to the comedian. But in exploring the comic-strip world of Georgia's *Atlantic Constitution* (according to Blackbeard, the one Hardy would have been reading, since only large papers could then afford comics) early in the century (when strip sections first appear in the *Constitution*), one cannot help thinking other pre–"Helpful Henry" antiheroic comics might also have influenced Hardy. For example, such still well-known antiheroic strips as Fred Opper's "Happy Hooligan" (1900, Leo Brooks' choice for the mystery strip), or Bud Fisher's *team* of "Mutt and Jeff" (1907). But in examining period back issues of the *Constitution*, I was especially taken with the now obscure "Obliging Oliver."

With a title Oliver Hardy would no doubt have noticed, "Obliging Oliver," like "Helpful Henry," was forever trying to assist people only to be continually frustrated. Besides its antiheroic theme and title, it anticipates the future Ollie in two ways. First, the final cartoon panel frequently has "Obliging Oliver" in direct address with the reader over his current frustration, just as Ollie often shares his comic disgust through camera direct address with the viewer. Second, the character's frustration is generally reinforced by eventually making him the comic victim of some slapstick dishevelment, forever Ollie's plight in his misadventures with Stan.

Though one cannot be sure Hardy ever saw "Obliging Oliver," the influential presence of McCarey is a given. And this is significant, if an antiheroic personal life counts for anything in the creation of antiheroic comedy. All artists, to a certain degree, are influenced by real-life experiences, a maxim to which McCarey adhered.[86]

McCarey's personal biography ranks with the best story of any comic antihero this side of a State Farm Insurance report. McCarey's antiheroic tendencies break into three categories: accidents, failures, and the proverbial battle of the sexes (within a marriage). First, his propensity for accidents later became as famous as the man himself—real-life slapstick. Few available articles on McCarey neglect to deal with this character trait. Thus, the well-known *Saturday Evening Post* biographer Pete Martin later called him "the film industry's leading physical Humpty Dumpty."[87] Author Sidney Carroll wrote a McCarey article for *Esquire* in which the title served as a comic summary: "Everything Happens to McCarey: During those sparse times when he isn't breaking his valuable neck, Leo McCarey does direct some extraordinary pictures."[88] Though his most dangerous accident was a post–Laurel & Hardy car wreck, he seems to have led a life that was "one long chronicle of miraculous escapes from hospital beds."[89] For instance, as a young college student on his way to a law class McCarey walked into what he assumed was an elevator. Wrong. In actuality, it was merely an elevator shaft, and the fall broke his legs. In the spirit of dark comedy, Carroll called this "the beginning of his [McCarey's] experiments in the field of self-destruction [sic]."[90]

This is the very essence of Ollie & Stan's world. The above Carroll phrase could even serve as the title for any number of Laurel & Hardy films. While this McCarey spirit of comedy through destruction is most logically seen as a general influence on the team, a permanent comic aura of sorts, one can even find an apparent correlation between the noted McCarey elevator accident and a McCarey-authored Laurel & Hardy story. In his *Double Whoopee* (1929), Stan & Ollie play two less-than-capable hotel doormen accidently causing a pompous hotel guest—a prince (John Peters,—the double for Eric von Stroheim) periodically to fall down an elevator shaft. Fittingly, the prince, is a white-suited, monocled spoof of Eric von Stroheim (score possible points for Laurel and his

"Obliging Oliver" —the newspaper comic strip (1914)

parody-oriented screen past) forever stopping before the elevator and turning to impart some self-centered comments to the always present celebrity-conscious guests. His comic mistake is in turning away from the door, because each time after his remarks and an about-face, he confidently strides forward into the elevator . . . shaft, having just missed the departed car. Needless to say, the cause of each elevator exit is Stan and/or Ollie, though they are always oblivious to that fact. These repeated comic falls are the heart of the film, though it is more famous now for the brief but sexy appearance of the then-unknown Jean Harlow: Stan accidently closes a taxi door on the train of her dress, soon causing her backside to be revealed provocatively.

Another key antiheroic McCarey trait that coincidently assumes major importance in the Laurel & Hardy films is failure. And without film, McCarey would have been decidedly less celebrated. He failed as a lawyer, a nightclub operator, and as a songwriter. By the 1940s he had "written more than 1000 songs, all of them monumental failures—unless you count one mild success: 'Why Do You Sit on Your Patio?,' which netted him two dollars and fifty cents."[91] McCarey had his share of life's little failures as well, such as his inability to tie a tie or keep it tied, which led to the birth of Laurel & Hardy's honored tit-for-tat.

While most people can demonstrate some examples of failure, McCarey's defeats have become the stuff of Hollywood legends. Thus, director Peter Bogdanovich (who did the McCarey Oral History) used McCarey's permanent exit from law (through a comically failed case) as the opening to his entertaining film on the early days of Hollywood—*Nickelodeon* (1976). Fittingly, the McCarey figure (Ryan O'Neal) is a central character. McCarey was also the uncredited model for the banalities of the nameless film character in a comic essay by James Thurber, no less, entitled "The Man Who Corrupted Moonbaum."[92] Though the piece is not entirely in the antiheroic mold, the linking of McCarey and banalities is significant. Though McCarey would probably not want the analogy on his resume, comic antihero characterizations are based on banalities. The little day-to-day frustrations of modern life are the fate of the everyman antihero. And no one personifies this better than McCarey's Stan & Ollie, whether it is the trial of merely trying to get away for a picnic (*A Perfect Day*, 1929, McCarey story), or taking care of their young sons (*Brats*, 1930, McCarey story). Everyday problems were also, of course, the foundation behind keeping Laurel & Hardy based in reality, or a comically close facsimile.

In terms of failure, the black cloud McCarey's father hung over his son's world when the boy was fresh out of high school is noteworthy. Landing a job on the *Los Angeles Times*, Leo decided *not* to go to college. But Papa McCarey worked out a deal with the editor and close friend Henry Carr that the youngster's world would become forever topsy-turvy until he went back to school. And it was not long before McCarey was attending UCLA, on the path to that father-influenced law degree . . . which he did not use. Such frustration and manipulation were mainstays of that future comedy duo.

The third antiheroic McCarey characteristic of Laurel & Hardy importance is one in which the team needed little instruction—the battle of the sexes. It is quite possible, however, that McCarey first saw the appropriateness of this comic conflict, along henpecked lines, for antiheroic Stan & Ollie. Moreover, McCarey had just finished a series of films with Charley Chase, which the director later described in his "Oral History" as having "dealt with the misadventures of husband and wife."[93] McCarey differentiates between the Chase and Laurel & Hardy films, correctly implying that the former films had more of a romantic comedy subplot, as did television's original *Dick Van Dyke Show*. Still, marital antiheroic roots bind McCarey's ties with Chase and Laurel & Hardy.

Regardless of who receives credit for the *henpecked* nature of Stan & Ollie, McCarey was most sympathetic to this type of character interaction. Though his personal life was without the real-life marital discord of Laurel & Hardy, his longtime marriage to high school sweetheart Stella Martin McCarey (they were married July 29, 1920) still provided the director with battle of the sexes comedy material. His "Oral History" reveals that the idea for the classic screwball comedy marriage of *The Awful Truth* (1937) was based on "misunderstandings" he had had with his own wife: "It told, in a way, the story of my [married] life, though the few scenes about infidelity, I hasten to add, were *not* autobiographical—they were imagination only."[94] And one can link McCarey's own screwball marriage closer to his Laurel & Hardy period by the fact that earlier in his "Oral History" McCarey revealed that several routines in *The Awful Truth* "are paraphrases of identical scenes in [the very successful] *Part-Time Wife* [1930]."[95] The latter film, co-scripted and directed by McCarey, appeared at a time when the former Laurel & Hardy's supervisor's story ideas were still forming the foundation for a number of the duo's films.

Some readers might object here by noting the original screen credit for *The Awful Truth* has it being based on Arthur Richman's 1920s Broadway play of the same name. McCarey, famous for improvising much of his screen material (regardless of how the credits read) indirectly pooh-poohed the notion that his work was merely a film version of the play in his "Oral History." And once this now-obscure Richman play is tracked down in script form (at the Library of Congress), the McCarey autobiographical story is all the more credible because the Richman play bears very little similarity to McCarey's film. Moreover, *Part-Time Wife* is a film with several parallels to *The Awful Truth*. A final note along these lines is that a close reading of Thurber's "Moonbaum" story also suggests that McCarey was an antiheroic husband in his own home.[96] Any way one gauges it, Leo McCarey was the right man at the right time for Stan Laurel & Oliver Hardy—pivotal antiheroic clowns. As Charles Barr later observed in his book critiquing their work, "They were fortunate to have McCarey."

Personally and professionally, the decade of the 1930s would be a roller-coaster ride for Laurel & Hardy. No doubt, their greatest highs came early—both in 1932. In late July and August they received a phenomenal reception throughout Great Britain, in part helped by another film Leo, the logo lion of

Leo McCarey on the set of *The Awful Truth*

Oscar night 1932 (with Walt Disney)—the duo wins for *The Music Box*

M-G-M, which as the Roach distributor made the duo's trip into a marketing event. (M-G-M's British distributors were urged to capitalize on the team's visit by focusing on their films, with July 25 to August 21 becoming "Laurel & Hardy Month.") Yet, the outpouring of fan support was genuine, and Laurel & Hardy, for the first time, were really made aware of the international popularity of Stan & Ollie. Then on November 18 they received an Academy Award for the "Best Live Action Comedy Short Subject of 1931–32"—their crated piano-moving escapade, *The Music Box*. This delightful film, with its epic hike up an endless flight of stairs, perfectly matches their comically epic stupidity. (When it *finally* seems they have accomplished their task, a passing mailman informs them there is an access road to the top of the hill . . . Stan & Ollie could have saved both their backs and their sanity by driving up in their horse-drawn wagon! Then, compounding their comic simplicity, they proceed to carry their cargo back down the steps in order to utilize the labor-saving road!) As good as *The Music Box* is, its selection was quite possibly assisted by the team's triumphant visit to Britain just a few months prior to the Academy Awards ceremony.

The trip had begun as a private family holiday for Laurel, who had not been home since 1927. But the young man who had left as Chaplin's understudy was returning as a major star. Ironically, however, the trip again put Laurel in Chaplin's shadow. The creator of Charlie the Tramp had just returned the previous year (1931) from a rousing visit home to England. (Also in 1931, the Marx Brothers had enjoyed great popularity during their limited engagement run at the London Palace.) Such visits, especially Chaplin's, might just have been an additional catalyst for Laurel's trip. Besides, few people dislike attention, and in Laurel's case, he had realistically to expect a great deal of it on such a trip. Psychologically, moreover, upbeat attention might just have been what Laurel needed, since his marriage was in trouble. Wife Lois did not accompany him on the trip, and they divorced the following year. Thus, the trip also worked on a temporary getaway level.

The travel scenario became more complex when partner Hardy signed on. It seems—at least so the traditional story goes—that Hardy the golfing fanatic became interested in the British trip when he realized that country's rich tradition in the sport, including Scotland's claim as its birthplace. In all fairness to Hardy, he was building a reputation as quite a golfer. A 1930 M-G-M publicity sheet noted: "Hardy is one of the best golfers in California and has twenty-four cups and two medals to show for his skill."[97] He was always the best bet to win Hal Roach's annual studio tournament. In the early 1930s Hardy's golfing abilities, despite his 250–pound weight, were even featured in a "Ripley's Believe It or Not" newspaper panel, with the trophy total now at forty. Golfing great Bobby Jones was his frequent links partner. (On a less public note, Hardy also hoped that his shakey second marriage would be strengthened if Myrtle accompanied them.)

Whether or not M-G-M coached Hardy on the golfing "appropriateness" of accompanying Laurel on a British holiday (Laurel biographer Fred Guiles simply called it a "personal appearance tour," while Laurel himself, shortly after dock-ing, called it a tour and announced planned stops.[98]), the studio was no doubt happy with the marketing potential of the team. But even M-G-M was probably not prepared for the grassroots popularity generated by the duo.

On the eve of their visit England's *Kinematograph* (later *Kine Weekly*) reported that M-G-M's London offices had been "beseiged with inquiries" for weeks concerning the team's visit. This July 21, 1932 article, "Laurel and Hardy: Big European Itinerary," called it a holiday but noted well over a dozen stops. The piece only erred in claiming Laurel had not been home since 1910—still a common mistake in team chronicles. Laurel's 1927 visit, before he became famous, has generally gone unnoticed by team followers. (For a rare passing reference to it, see "Those Two Goofy Guys" in Chapter 3.)

Fittingly, the same issue of *Kinematograph* carried a huge full-page ad exhort-ing theatre owners to "PREPARE for the Coming Laurel & Hardy Boom . . . " by purchasing Stan & Ollie display heads. These famous noggins (reproductions of which also dominated the page 1 ad) were painted and varnished (for possible outside use) and stood five feet tall. Cinema Signs Ltd. claimed to have a corner on this marketing device. Regardless, this and other *Kinematograph* issues pro-vide an excellent ongoing chronicle of the team's tour adventures.

Laurel & Hardy (plus Myrtle) landed at Southhampton on Saturday, July 23, 1932, and were met by Laurel's father and stepmother, Venitia, who traveled to London with them. The team's eventual trip through much of Britain as well as a visit to Paris found them forever treated as comic conquerors. Their plan to make other quiet stops outside Britain was dropped in part because of the frenzy of attention they also generated in Paris, though a blurb in the August 18, 1932 *Kinematograph* also credited their abridged visit to Europe—a "quickie" Paris stop—to their London recording date (which will be addressed shortly).

Though the entourage left Southhampton immediately by train for London, their send-off from fans had one reporter comparing it to the crowds caused by a visiting Chaplin at his zenith—his 1921 return to England.[99] Laurel & Hardy's arrival in London easily topped the Southhampton mob scene. A very well attended press conference followed at the Savoy Hotel, their temporary London residence.

In London the Laurel family was joined by his sister Beatrice and her husband, no doubt as anxious as everyone else to see "the Prodigal Son" (Laurel's tongue-in-cheek description of himself.[100]).

Beatrice, four and one-half years younger than Laurel, had been a talented but not overly successful actress. Or, as her comedian brother later described it, "She never made it big."[101] At this time and for a number of years to come, she and her husband operated a pub in Bottesford, England (near Nottingham). A key feature of the pub was its behind-the-bar pictures of Laurel & Hardy, though history is unclear as to whether this tradition had started in 1932 and the visit of her very famous big brother.

Laurel had a family tea party on July 24, with the London *Daily Herald* carrying a front-page picture of the festivities (Laurel pouring tea for his parents) on July 25, accompanied by a comically insightful article and Laurel interview. Besides Laurel's comments on the tour nature of the trip, the piece gives an idea of the comedian's off-screen sense of humor—a phenomenon sometimes noted but seldom exemplified (see also n. 61). Still, at least on this day, he maintained some ties with his screen character: "We fell in love with the Aquitania [the ship on which they made the voyage]. It was wonderful. We wanted to bring it away, only we didn't have anywhere to put it, and Oli [sic] said I'd lose it before we got to London anyway."[102]

Another London *Daily Herald* article chronicled their mixed media activities while in the British capital, from a rare radio guest spot on the BBC (July 26) to their visits to the "Empire [Theatre of] Leicester-square, where they are appearing on the stage as well as on the screen."[103] Laurel & Hardy were playing in support of their short subject film *Any Old Port* (1932). On the night of July 25 it took seven policemen to keep back the crowds when the team left the Leicester, with the duo's car losing a door to the mob of fans.

Other stops on the trip included Tynemouth, Leeds, Newcastle, Manchester, Liverpool, Glasgow, Edinburgh, and Paris, as well as more-modest towns of Laurel's northern England and Scotland childhood. Everywhere the outpouring of fan attention was amazing, though no other would top the dangerous ramifications of their visit to Glasgow. The front-page account of the London *Daily Herald* was nicely succinct in its heading: "20 Hurt In Laurel and Hardy Stampede: Women Crushed At Midnight Welcome."[104] Eight thousand Laurel & Hardy fans met their idols at Glasgow's Central Station, with the comedians literally being carried off their feet. Of the twenty hurt, nine were seriously injured, while the duo themselves escaped with their coats—enthusiastic fans tried to tear off coat buttons as souvenirs.

Ironically, the incident was made worse by a macabre domino effect that, freakishly, might have come right out of a Laurel & Hardy movie. The extreme pressure of the crowd's weight collapsed an elevated stone handrail and the row of posts that supported it. Two persons were hurt by falling debris, while others were injured when, in trying to miss being struck, they inadvertently entered the path of an approaching streetcar. Naturally, the ultimate result was further stampeding by the crowd. The *New York Times* reported, "Laurel wept with emotion. Each of the comedians said he never had seen such a welcome."[105]

A lengthy August 4, 1932 *Kinematograph* article, "Laurel and Hardy: Enthusiastic Admirers in the North," recorded this and additional scenes of pandemonium in the provinces. The team's initial stop at Newcastle and Tynemouth matched the enthusiastic receptions they had been given in London. Received at the Newcastle Town Hall by the Tynemouth mayor, huge crowds followed the duo around all day.

They managed, however, to put in personal appearances at two theatres as well as take part in a special welfare program for "The Sunshine Kiddies"—

organized for the assistance of poor families. Thus, 600 children had the double bonus of receiving a prize presented by Laurel & Hardy. Again, police had trouble keeping order. Even when Laurel had slipped away earlier for a surprise visit to the family's old Newcastle home, hundreds of people immediately appeared at the site.

At Edinburgh their arrival generated so much excitement that it was likened to a "royal visit." As Laurel & Hardy exited their train, a waiting band played their "Dance of the Cuckoos" theme song. This engulfing crowd was largely composed of journalists and industry representatives.

Besides noting the team's dangerously tumultuous Glasgow reception, the August 4 *Kinematograph* fleshed out Laurel's close ties with the city where his father was once a theatre manager. (Laurel's stepmother was in attendance at a personal appearance by the duo the following evening.)

One of the articles at the Laurel & Hardy Museum in Ulverston, "Film Comedians in Leeds: Whirlwind Tour of the Provinces by Laurel & Hardy" (August 3, 1932—no source cited), provides a more personalized look at the frenzy of their tour. The fishbowl attention had created "just a couple of worn-out guys." So many people met them at the station it was necessary to transport them by car "the few yards" to their hotel. And they did not go outside in Leeds "for fear of being mobbed."

Conditions such as these are hardly conducive to family visits and restful travel, let alone Hardy's golf game (though he somehow managed to play during the Glasgow stop). Regardless, whatever original ties the two had to being a peaceful vacation never developed. But the team had experienced a unique outpouring of love. And late in the trip they hit upon an idea that would not only say "thank you" but possibly also make a few coins. They cut a commercial record at London's Columbia Gramophone Studios on August 18, six days before departing.

This recorded sketch, entitled "Laurel And Hardy Visit London," is a wonderfully funny thank you in which the more verbally florid Ollie tries to express his appreciation, only to be interrupted constantly by Stan, requesting everything from equal air time to foodstuffs, such as nuts and a hardboiled egg. Apparently written by Laurel at the studio shortly before it was recorded, the sketch successfully incorporates and refers to several basic characteristics of their personae, such as Ollie's wiggling of his tie, or Stan's crying. Most importantly, it was a comically effective thank you. This was the only commercial record in which the duo had direct production involvement. (In 1975 a release of the team's *Way Out West* duet, "The Trail of the Lonesome Pine," became a surprise hit record.)

Laurel's tour contacts with his father suggest the comedian's ambivalence towards him—over A. J. Jefferson's earlier womanizing—was fading. (Possibly there was a Laurel mellowing due to his own womanizing ways.) The previously cited London *Daily Herald* family party piece credited the comedian with having anxiously awaited this reunion since his 1927 visit.

Another *Kinematograph* article, "At Laurel's Home Suburb" (August 18,

1932) reported on the team's visit to A. J. Jefferson's neighborhood cinema in the London borough of Ealing. The stop fulfilled a promise made by the father the previous year when he introduced a Laurel & Hardy film at the same theatre (Walpole Cinema).

Since Laurel's 1932 trip home is usually credited to a decision made early in the year, A. J. probably had merely promised a visit the next time his son was in England. Still, the commitment had been honored, with the team also briefly entertaining the Walpole audience. (Fittingly, the antiheroic Laurel & Hardy film then playing at the theatre was *Chickens Come Home*, 1931.)

Interestingly, 1932 had opened with the fatherly "My Lad Laurel by Stan's Father" in the January *Picturegoer Weekly*. (A possible catalyst, or at least a contributing factor for the visit?) While critical of the Americanization of Laurel's work, A. J. praised his son's talent (placing him at parity with Chaplin) and his great potential. Special father-son connections are alluded to when A. J. mentions the sketch he had shared with Laurel (the unnamed "Home from the Honeymoon" being the foundation for *Duck Soup*, 1927, and *Another Fine Mess*, 1930), and a Laurel invitation for him to retire in Hollywood.

Even with an ongoing father-son dialogue, the "My Lad Laurel" piece suggests a vain and contradictory man of the theatre forgetful of his own comedy roots (for more on the article, see Chapter 4). Thus, any thought of an A.J. retirement in the film capital suggests an invitation to a fireworks display. Further evidence is provided by A.J.'s sometimes stormy mid–1930s visit to Hollywood—to be examined shortly.

Returning to America on the French liner *Paris*, Laurel & Hardy docked in New York on August 30, still happily unable to shake the unique acclaim they had received abroad, a comic popularity they had, perhaps naively, never imagined. (The foreign language versions of their films possibly added to this unique European response.) A tongue-in-cheek "Mr. Laurel said the tour was so strenuous that Hardy . . . lost seventy pounds, while he gained twenty."[106] Despite his persistent interest in the team's comedy having a realistic base, Laurel was also drawn to exaggerated and nonsense humor. This explains film lines like: "You can lead a horse to water but a pencil must be lead," or the previous quote.

Coming back, Laurel was also involved in a shipboard romance that did not end in New York. One might call the woman a comedy groupie; as related by Laurel biographer Guiles, a French-accented fan had originally come to Laurel's stateroom door for an autograph.[107] While in no way justifying Laurel's conduct, his womanizing tendencies were no doubt further weakened by the heady stuff of being treated as a comedy god during the previous month.

Needless to say, the problem marriage he left was not strengthened by such a return. But like Betty Marx, womanizing Chico Marx's long-suffering first wife, Lois Laurel had learned to somehow cope with her boy/man husband, becoming more a mother than a wife. Thus, she advised him to find an apartment for the girl and himself (until this fling, too, passed) and to minimize the cost by getting the girlfriend work as an extra at the studio.[108]

Of course this relationship did pass and Laurel was again home. But he had not changed; in May 1933, Lois filed for divorce. Hal Roach later observed, "The tragedy in Laurel's life was that his first wife, Lois, got a divorce."[109] Roach observed that Laurel still loved her and did not believe she would go through with the divorce. As incredulous as this may sound, considering Laurel's history of infidelity, he seems to have genuinely mourned this loss for years.

In addition to Laurel's alleged emotional pain, there was more than a little financial sting, too. Lois retained their large Beverly Hills home, two trust funds worth in excess of $200,000, and ongoing monetary support for both their five-year-old daughter (of whom she was given custody) and herself. From a business standpoint, Roach also had cause to mourn the divorce. Lois Laurel had often represented her husband in his dealing with Roach, helping to keep things relatively stable. But for the rest of the 1930s, there would be a parade of Laurel women, and the comedian and Roach were often at cross-purposes—especially the conflict that resulted in the short-lived team of *Langdon* & Hardy.

In a February 1933 *Movie Classic* article/interview what was then still a Laurel and Laurel separation was treated with the most deceptively civilized manner, nicely summarized in the piece's title: "No Laughs In Laurel Home-Life, So Comedian And Wife Separate."[110] One is reminded of the gag line in Woody Allen's *Play It Again, Sam* (1972), where he comically paraphrases his wife's explanation for their separation as "insufficient laughter." But the Laurel piece was not meant as a joke. It was a seemingly sincere, no fault/no laughter description of two people falling out of love, with no exploration as to why they were now "getting on one another's nerves."

This now provocative 1933 piece deserves attention for three reasons. First, despite its sometimes "creative" and/or neglectful examination of the total situation, it was poignantly on target, both for Laurel and many other funny men, when he observed:

Comedians, the fellows who make laughs for a living, are seldom funny men in private contacts. To the contrary, they are likely to be very serious-minded fellows. Maybe seriousness is a diversion to them after long days of painfully manufacturing "spontaneous" laughter in front of a camera.[111]

Second, the quote also hints of the occasional depressions through which Laurel sometimes suffered, caused by either the suffocating middle-class lifestyle Lois represented or by the guilt he felt when he denied that relationship (through affairs), and ultimately by divorce. One is metaphorically reminded of a passage from Herman Hesse's *Steppenwolf* (published the same year as the teaming of Laurel & Hardy, 1927). The disenchanted 1920s intellectual Harry Haller (Steppenwolf) observes: "I don't know how it comes about, but I, the hater of life's petty conventions, always take up my quarters in . . . these respectable and wearisome and spotless middle-class homes [and I forever repeat] the same old stupid road.''[112] Paradoxically, Haller/Steppenwolf can also state: ''I like the contrast between my lonely, disorderly existence and this middle-class family-life.''[113] In a self-destructive manner, maybe Laurel did, too.

Third, without trying to play the cynically comic commentator, this *Movie Classic* interview/article also represents that rare time when Laurel's wedded woes could still be taken seriously. Later unions, messy divorces, and all the unintended comedy business in-between that accounts for Laurel's ever-changing personal life sometimes seemed to outnumber the more traditional film-focused articles.

Interestingly enough, the subject of divorce is central to Laurel & Hardy's first film after their trip to Britain: *Their First Mistake* (1932). With the opening title, ''Mr. Hardy was married—Mr. Laurel was also unhappy,'' the duo are again in prime Stan & Ollie territory, though their movie marital conflicts seemed to have more and more in common with their private lives each year.

Their First Mistake finds Mrs. Ollie (Mae Busch) more than a little upset with all the time Stan and Ollie spend together. Stan then comes up with an idea— a comic development in and of itself: a baby should be adopted to keep Ollie's wife busy while the ''boys'' go out nights. Ollie is impressed enough with the idea to admit so to Stan—again, comic surprise considering Ollie's more typical direct address (to the camera) expression of total disgust at Stan's stupidity.

Stan's reply to the compliment, ''You bet your life I'm right. You know, I'm not as dumb as you look'' is funny but is not without a problem. It is a comic malapropism that suggests Stan is less a comic idiot than a wise fool, the intelligent character who plays dumb for safety and/or profit, such as Jaroslav Hasek's the Good Soldier Schweik. Yet, it is central to Laurel & Hardy comedy that they be seen as incompetent *victims* in an antiheroic world, or as *The Times* described the team in its obituary of Laurel: ''Together they seemed . . . to become a single unit, an expression of well-intentioned muddle-headedness in a harsh and practical world.''[114] Their being so totally up against it is also a key to the twentieth-century everyman empathy many viewers feel for the team. Thus, even a Stan malapropism should reflect incompetency, which, of course, the majority do. For instance, in *Sons of the Desert*, he refers to the Exalted Ruler of their fraternal organization as the ''exhausted ruler.''

Before proceeding with this analysis of *Their First Mistake* it should be noted that comparable Stan character inconsistencies occasionally occur elsewhere in their films. Though generally in the dialogue, the most blatantly unsuitable concern Stan's periodic acquisition of silly supernatural *visual* powers, such as his ability to ignite his thumb like a lighter in *Way Out West*, or use of his hand as a pipe in *Block-Heads*—complete with exhaled smoke after puffing on his thumb (sometimes referred to as ''white magic'' in past writing on Laurel). Again, while amusing, it is inconsistent with the delightfully dumb persona of Stan. If he really has such magic skills, there is no reason for his comic suffering through all the team's problems; Stan could solve everything with just a little hocus-pocus. Such power both undercuts Stan's normally wonderful incompetency and breaks the McCarey-Laurel rule of staying close to reality. In contrast, such fantasy characteristics would be perfectly in keeping with the mischievous Pan-like persona of Laurel contemporary Harpo Marx, whose surrealistic antics, not to mention his surrealistic pockets, frequently seem otherworldly.

One might better demonstrate the more typical difference between Harpo and Laurel's screen characters by contrasting the manner in which they respond to the same comedy set-up. In *Horse Feathers* (1932) Groucho admonishes Harpo: "Young man, you'll find as you grow older you can't burn the candle at both ends." But Harpo triumphs by producing a candle doing just that—one of the most pleasant examples of the pocket wizardry that is Harpo's ongoing "wardrobe." In *Them Thar Hills* (1934) the Laurel & Hardy stock company figure Billy Gilbert tells Stan: "You can't burn a candle at both ends." The skinny one replies, "We don't. We burn electric lights." In each case the "response" is consistent with the viewer's comedy expectations for the character—the inspired stupidity of Stan, and otherworldly sorcery of Harpo.

Denying Laurel his "white magic" might be comedic blasphemy to some. And one could conceivably link it to his screen persona by arguing, "Stan is so dumb he doesn't even know one can't do that." Coupled to this is the added explanation: Ollie fails and/or quickly withdraws from "white magic" because he knows it should not work. *But* it still seems a problem since it contradicts the basic realism premise Laurel is forever returning to when comedy theory is the subject. For instance, the *Film Weekly* interview (June 28, 1935—also examined in Chapter 4) finds the skinny comic immersed in realism. His ongoing message here and elsewhere was that their comedy could happen. I am also reminded of an anecdote by pioneer documentary filmmaker/critic Basil Wright, whose affection for the team had realistic roots. The Laurel & Hardy "it could happen" premise was further driven home to Wright when he once found himself helping uncrate a piano, as Laurel & Hardy did in *The Music Box*. In fact, he even stepped on a nail, as does Ollie in the film.

Regardless of how one feels about such non-realistic departures, even magic might not have been able to assist Stan & Ollie in *Their First Mistake*. While they are somehow successful in adopting a baby to keep Mrs. Ollie busy, the wife still manages to get the best of them—an old antiheroic tradition. Mrs. Ollie exits before she knows about the baby, but a process server (Billy Gilbert) is there with an update—a divorce summons for Ollie and an alienation of affections summons for Stan.

Not only that, the boys must now care for the new baby! And one need not have too vivid an imagination to visualize the comic havoc this creates for the duo, feeding and pacifying the little tyke. Possibly the best scene comes on the evening of their nursery activities, at which time the two briefly engage in a one-scene parody of melodrama's standard abandoned young-mother routine. When Stan decides to desert, Ollie (alias the besmirched girl) tells him he was the one "that wanted me to have the baby" and now he's going to "leave me flat!" And when Stan tries to alibi out of his responsibilities with other plans, Ollie unloads the hoary but now spoofingly funny: "You should have thought of that before we had the baby!"

The spoof is, simply, funny—something too often forgotten in comedy analysis, yet it also baldly plays with a basic truth of the team—Laurel & Hardy are a couple (see also Chapter 2). Without casting any homosexual suggestions, theirs is an argumentative but forever loyal friendship of two children occupying adult bodies. That essential affection for each other is what makes the duo work. Indeed, this is comically addressed early in *Their First Mistake* when Stan asks Ollie what is bothering the rotund one's wife. Ollie's reply: "She says I think more of you than I do of her!" Stan's matter-of-fact reply says it all: "Well, you do, don't you?"

The parody scene differs from other more self-conscious film "couplings" of Laurel & Hardy only by assigning the male role to Stan, who normally assumed the woman's part in such situations. Examples include the sexual assault-like measuring of kilt-attired Laurel in the first official Laurel & Hardy film, *Putting Pants on Philip* (1927, though the duo also had other movies ready for release), or a number of additional films in which Stan appears in drag. And Laurel's screen persona when contrasted with that of Hardy's is, of course, more in fitting with an older stereotypical image of a woman. That is, Stan is physically smaller and generally submissive to the louder, dominating Ollie, and he is the one more likely to cry (Stan's famous shtick of crying while scratching his head is an integral part of his character). A basic given of the comic antihero world is the emasculation of the male, and Stan frequently takes it to the emotional and/or physical (in costume) extreme.

Possibly one of the most interesting things about *Their First Mistake*, considering the rocky state of Laurel's real-life marriage, is that the original script for the film had Mrs. Ollie's parents talking her out of a divorce.[115] No such optimistic scene appears in the final film. And while the behind-the-screen Hardy reconciled with his wife the following year (1933), newspaper accounts of that time spoke of their "four years of intermittent marital troubles."[116] Thus, while the change in scenario of *Their First Mistake* (to keep the divorce) might have been nothing more than a coincidence, it was probably not too far from the real-life moods of comedians Laurel & Hardy.

Despite this possible parallel between life and art, a volatile personal life is not always the best thing for the productivity of the working comedian. At least that was the case with Laurel. Biographer Guiles is most blatant about the comedian's creative comedy skills being adversely affected by this messy personal life—to the point of even dampening the spirits of Laurel's fellow gag-writers (specifically in the latter half of 1931 and 1932).[117]

What about the 1932 Academy Award–winning *The Music Box*? Guiles posits that film as a prime example of these creative problems: it was a remake proposed at a time of comic impasse.[118] That is, the very popular McCarey-supervised

Hats Off (1927, now lost), served as a model for *The Music Box*, only in the earlier picture Stan & Ollie carried a washing machine up the same flight of stairs instead of the "music box" piano.

Guiles possibly overstates his case, because while *The Music Box* period is not on the same consistently high level as the silents, it did yield some entertaining work, such as *Helpmates*. Regardless, America's celebrated comedy ambassador to the world, Will Rogers, observed at this time that Laurel & Hardy were both "the best of comedians" and "the favorites with all of us movie folks, as well as the audiences."[119]

On a broader level, however, one finds the quality of their films after 1930 less uniform as previously noted by film scholar Charles Barr (see n. 53). Laurel & Hardy are still capable of inspired comedy, but it no longer follows in a seemingly nonstop manner.

McCarey's exit was, of course, examined earlier as a possible factor in this decline. Two lesser but still interesting additional factors might also be noted. First, considering the high number of quality Laurel & Hardy films already produced early in the sound era (see Filmography), it is more than reasonable to assume that genuinely new Laurel & Hardy premises and gags would be progressively more difficult to find. Consistent with this problem, or what might be called the "it's all been done before" dilemma, is the increased tendency for old material or basic comic premises to resurface in "new" Laurel & Hardy films. However, in fairness to the team, at least one Laurel & Hardy author (Bruce Crowther) felt their "re-makes and re-usage generally resulted in an improvement over the original."[120]

A second factor for their 1930s work being less consistent was an ongoing need for a transition from short subjects to feature film—a length with which they were never comfortable. British filmmaker and critic Alberto Cavalcanti, a strong period supporter of the team, metaphorically bemoaned their move to features: "They [Laurel & Hardy] have since cut their hair and gone into long features like the others."[121] The pressure of the Depression marketplace had theatre owners using the double-feature to lure the ever-more bargain-conscious public into the movies. The modest "B" feature, in support of the big-budget, big-star "A" feature, was driving the demand for the normally supporting live-action short subjects into the ground. Unfortunately for Laurel & Hardy, the short subject was their ideal format. Two reels, or approximately twenty minutes, seemed the perfect length for films that were not so much stories as visual essays in frustration. They were frequently focused on a single task of eventual comic defeat, and to expand upon that was, frequently, too much to ask of one's viewers, especially when so much of Laurel & Hardy's best material involved methodical repetition. In fact, it has been my experience in teaching that even the team's classic *The Music Box*, which pokes a great deal of comic repetition into merely three reels, often taxes the student about one reel too many.

Laurel later regretted they ever did any features, but as early as 1929 he seemed to have had a sixth sense about avoiding the phenomenon: "Perhaps we

[Hardy and I] shall do a five-reeler feature eventually. I am not in favor of it myself."[122] The following year both were on record as opposing going into features, "unless they find a sure-fire story" (Dorothy Spensley's *Photoplay* article/interview, "Those Two Goofy Guys"—see Chapter 3 reprint), but as team biographer Randy Skretvedt later ironically related, by the time the piece was in print the duo was involved in the production of what would be their first feature—the prison parody *Pardon Us* (1931).[123]

One could also compound the irony by noting *Pardon Us* was *not* a "sure-fire story." Originally conceived as a two-reeler, the high cost of the elaborate prison sets encouraged Roach to expand it to feature length to earn back its costs. Financially successful but with mixed reviews, the film is very uneven, coming across more as three short subjects edited together rather than a single, unified narrative feature. Laurel himself called it "a three-story building on a one-story base." If broken down, the segments might have been entitled: *Laurel & Hardy at the Big House, On the Lam in Blackface*, and *Back to Prison*, with the last "short" also borrowing heavily from McCarey-supervised Laurel & Hardy dental comedy *Leave 'Em Laughing* (1928).

The film is most dangerously derailed by the short middle segment. The team has escaped to the South and are passing themselves as black field hands picking cotton. Today's social values immediately make the viewer uncomfortable with these blackface scenes, especially the one where Ollie sings "Lazy Moon" while Stan does a comic dance—a compound reinforcement of old racial stereotypes. Of course, within the context of the time it is restrained. For example, *Pardon Us* material is less offensive than Keaton's blackfaced waiter in *College* (1927), or Harpo's Pied Piper number near the close of *A Day at the Races* (1937), where he leads a crowd of blacks as if they were so many children.

Not surprisingly, it is that restraint within this portion of the film that hampers all their comedy. While there are attempted comic bits related to unblackened parts of their body threatening to give them away, this segment of *Pardon Us* (utilizing blacks only as a backdrop) seems to suggest it was merely funny then to just see Stan & Ollie in blackface. And for many it probably was. After all, this was a time when black subject matter was of particular popular culture interest in America. King Vidor's milestone film *Hallelujah* (1929), with its all-black cast and innovative use of sound, was of ongoing interest. It had been paralleled on Broadway by another comparable original production—creative stage and screen director Rouben Mamoulian's all-black production of George Gershwin's rich folk opera *Porgy and Bess*. Of course, the period's most significant Broadway all-black cast story was writer/director Marc Connally's 1930 Pulitzer Prize–winning fable of heaven and the Bible: *Green Pastures*. Thus, just by situating a blackfaced Laurel & Hardy in this cottonfield context, a mild form of parody is produced, no doubt meant to reinforce the film's focus spoofing of the prison film. (One should add that Hardy, as a strong and courtly Southerner, was no doubt more comfortable with such a segment, if not actually recommending it himself. As a young performer he had worked in minstrel shows, and as an adult, this proud son of the south enjoyed telling old Negro dialect stories. In fact, Georgia had been the home of renowned Local Color Humorist Joel Chandler Harris (1848–1908), author of the famous Uncle Remus stories, with characters like Brer Rabbit and Brer Wolf. Hardy had been reared during the heyday of Harris's literary influence, and largely by a black family servant no less. It is the occasional apparent connections between team material and Hardy's background that suggest the fat one had more artistic input than for which he is given credit.)

Fittingly, the best gag of this early sound feature, variations of which occur throughout *Pardon Us*, is dependent upon a comic sound—a raspberry or Bronx-like cheer noise emitted by a bad tooth of Stan's (thus the reason for incorporating a dental sketch). Unless Stan remembers to place a finger on the bad tooth, the razzing sound is forever getting him in trouble—especially with the toughest guy in the cell block (Walter Long, a veteran Stan & Ollie nemesis) and the warden (Wilfred Lucas). And the finger on the razzing tooth is an especially amusing visual compliment to this audio gag, since the comically slow-witted Stan constantly fails at this simple but funny-looking task. For instance, he might put his finger on the wrong tooth, or forget the task entirely until it is too late. And having a finger in his mouth also reinforces his image of being childlike.

The team made a gradual transition from two-reelers to the exclusive production of features from 1931 to 1935. The features made during this period, besides *Pardon Us*, were: *Pack Up Your Troubles* (1932), *The Devil's Brother* (also known as *Fra Diavolo*, 1933), *Sons of the Desert* (1933), *Babes in Toyland* (1934), and *Bonnie Scotland* (1935). There had also been two earlier abridged experiences in features. In 1929 they had done a magic act in M-G-M's all-star *Hollywood Review of 1929*, with their sketch stealing the kudos in this studio variety show. Laurel & Hardy scenes of comic relief were also added to M-G-M's *The Rogue Song* (1930), a showcase for the studio's new star, Lawrence Tibbett, the Metropolitan Opera baritone.

Easily the best of their 1931–1935 features is *Sons of the Desert*, which also maintains that status when measured against their complete feature filmography. It accomplishes this three ways. First, without recycling specific celebrated old Stan & Ollie material, it is the one feature that comes closest to the *spirit* of their early classically antiheroic short subjects.

Once again the duo are childlike husbands trying to put one over on wives (primarily Ollie's) who must act more as mothers than spouses. Particularly memorable is pots and pans-throwing Mae Busch as Mrs. Hardy. Busch appeared in fourteen Laurel & Hardy films. And because of this particular role, as well as her equally lethal Mrs. Hardy in *Their First Mistake*, she represents to this author the definitive domineering Ollie spouse, just as sometimes antiheroic contemporary W. C. Fields was best comically married to Kathleen Howard (see especially Fields's *It's a Gift*, 1934). But Busch also played a wide range of parts in other Laurel & Hardy films (besides Ollie's shrewish wife), from the murdering widow of *Oliver the Eighth* (1934) to the boys' accidental drinking partner in *Them Thar Hills*.

Dorothy Christie, as Mrs. Laurel, is also a most memorable antiheroic wife, frequently seen here with her hunting rifle. In fact, one could credit Christie's role, especially her initial home-from-the-hunt appearance (carrying her rifle and a string of ducks and nicely decked out in hunting attire) as a possible inspiration for Jane Fonda's big game hunter fantasy sequence in *9 to 5* (1980), where she is tracking chauvinist boss Dabney Coleman. Of course, the comic twist in *Sons of the Desert*, as it sometimes is in other Laurel & Hardy films focusing on the domestic scene, is that Stan is eventually babied by Christie because he tearfully tells the truth like a good little boy. In comic contrast, the Hardy wife seldom shows such mercy. Here, Ollie has been so routed by Busch (the viewer has heard the comic off-screen violence while honest Stan has been pampered on screen), that the rotund one is moved to close the film by throwing a pot at Stan.

Even Laurel's weakness for the occasional bit of fantasy and/or the nonrealistic gag is kept consistent with his antiheroic, slow-witted screen persona. The scene in question finds Stan waiting for Ollie and helping himself to an apple . . . a *wax* apple from the Hardy's purely decorative bowl of wax fruit. Now, while most conscious people would not make this mistake, at least beyond the first bite, Stan proceeds happily to munch away. While unlikely, it is a veritable showcase of neorealism compared to that *Way Out West* bit of fantasy where Stan has the igniting thumb. Moreover, unlike the latter example, which goes against type, the wax fruit routine reinforces the comic stupidity of this clown. And like most good comedy, it also comes complete with a topper. After Ollie brings the mistake to Stan's attention, Busch matter-of-factly observes, "That's the third apple I've missed this week."

A second reason for the significance of *Sons of the Desert* is that unlike many personality clown feature films, generally including those of Laurel & Hardy (as in *Pardon Us*), where the plot is merely connecting a helter-skelter line of funny but not necessarily related comedy sketches, *Sons of the Desert* manages to integrate all the comic actions *without* sacrificing any of the rich characterizations. As film comedy historian Donald W. McCaffrey has observed: "Such simplicity [the attempted deception of their wives] within complexity [all that this entails for two antiheroic husbands] makes the work one of the outstanding comedies of the period."[124] However, it should be emphasized that plot cannot be a tradeoff for humor. That is, the team's generally inferior 1940s features, excluding *A Chump at Oxford* and *Saps at Sea* (both 1940), often ploddingly pushed plot to the complete detriment of Laurel & Hardy–style comedy (the team by then having lost most of its production control).

Another plus for *Sons of the Desert*, as related to an integrated storyline, is that Laurel & Hardy did not have to share screen time with singing romantic interests as in the comic opera *The Devil's Brother*, the Laurel & Hardy feature that preceded *Sons of the Desert*. Period tastes often dictated that the duo and other comedians, such as the Marx Brothers, not be totally unleashed on 1930s audiences. Thus, Pulitzer Prize–winning playwright Morrie Ryskind, who co-wrote (with George Kaufman) the Marxes' celebrated *A Night at the Opera*, an excellent example of the era's fragmented approach to comedy presentation, observed: "You have to have a [comedy] break and a change of pace. So the two lovers [enter]...You didn't have ice cream [i.e., comedy] all the way through, you know!"[125] (Consistent with the times, opera singer Walter Woolf King was prominently featured in both the Marxes' *A Night at the Opera* and Laurel & Hardy's *Swiss Miss*.)

Not surprisingly, Hal Roach, who enjoyed casting Laurel & Hardy in comic operas (at their best in *Babes In Toyland*, 1934, to be examined later), also had reservations about unadulterated comedy features:

The greatest comedies that were made by anybody were made in two reels, I don't care who it was. It's a simple damn thing. If you can stop after 20 minutes, you've only got to go up to this peak for your last laugh. But if you've got to go clear to 60 minutes, the last laugh is three times harder. It's that simple. And I don't care how funny a guy is, if you listen to him long enough, you're going to be bored to hell with him.[126]

(Paradoxically, however, Roach found great critical and commercial success later in the decade with his influential unadulterated comedy—*Topper*, 1937, a pivotal screwball fantasy, which also spawned two sequels.) While Laurel pre-ferred the comic operas (among their features) because of the music, exotic backgrounds, and colorful period costumes,[127] Hardy's preference focused on the fragmented comedy. Lucille Hardy, the comedian's widow, said that her husband "always felt that in feature films the comedy should be incidental to the story and over-all production—that the comedian or comedians shouldn't be forced to carry the whole load of the film."[128]

Perhaps if Hardy had lived as long as his comedy contemporary Groucho Marx (who died in 1977; Hardy in 1957), he would have changed his preference, as Groucho did, from fragmented comedy to the unadulterated variety. Regard-less, today's decidedly sold-on-comedy viewer much prefers the latter.

A third reason for the importance of *Sons of the Desert* is its ongoing "con-temporary" appeal. Besides its display of antiheroic humor, there is its gentle yet complex satirizing of man's need for belonging to fraternal organizations. In this case, it is the Shriner-like "Sons of the Desert" from which the film receives its name. It is in order to attend their Chicago convention that the boys (fittingly from "Oasis 13" of Los Angeles) attempt to do the impossible—put one over on their wives.

This affectionate send-up of fraternal associations is accomplished in three imaginatively broad strokes. First, there is the team's late arrival at the lodge's self-important seemingly sacred gathering. Everyone wears uniform sashes and tasseled hats and listens closely to their "Exalted Ruler." Everyone except tardy Stan & Ollie, whose inability to enter quietly and find seats at this solemn occasion is decidedly funny and innocently rebellious. While the Marx Brothers would have openly broken up the meeting with their anarchic style and W. C. Fields would have peppered the air with fifth-columnist asides, Stan & Ollie's incompetent but accidental disruption is ultimately the most comically damning, because these two knuckleheads are actually accepted members of this organization!

The second fraternal jab is dependent upon an excellent but unusual cameo appearance by Charley Chase, *the* Roach comedian after Laurel & Hardy but a talent yet to be fully recognized. Chase's role here, however, is atypical; instead of his normally likable screen persona, he plays a comically abrasive practical joker at the convention. Obviously, this is another legitimate liability of fraternal gatherings everywhere, as well as most national conventions. But it is equally obvious that such behavior was out of character for Stan & Ollie. It is thus farmed out to a supporting character (Chase) but narratively integrated by having the duo be the ones victimized. Moreover, Chase's negative nature is made all the more appropriate when he turns out to be the brother of Ollie's strong-arm wife.

The third side-swiping of fraternal organizations finally implicates Stan & Ollie in another stereotypical activity of such groups—the fun-loving silliness of their public parades, again reminiscent of the Shriners. In this case one follows a "Sons of the Desert" parade as it merrily winds through the streets of Chicago, with Stan & Ollie being two of its most enthusiastic participants—quite literally dancing along in the streets with the amusing progression.

Such childlike fraternal silliness is one characteristic that is an easy yet endearing target for comedy. It is reminiscent of those real parades where miniature cars (frequently piloted by Shriners) produce comic surprise by periodically rearing up on their back wheels and scooting about in the most non-traditional manner. And who better than Stan & Ollie personify the highs and lows of childhood, whether the "stand by me" loyalty of their friendship or its accompanying antiheroic frustrations—so often peppered with comic violence. (See Chapter 2 for more on the childlike nature of the duo.)

The comic artistry of *Sons of the Desert* was also not hurt by the inclusion of the soon-to-be hit song "Honolulu Baby," composed by Roach's talented musical director T. Marvin Hatley, who had composed the team's delightful "The Dance of the Cuckoos" theme song. (Laurel & Hardy literature abounds with title and spelling variations of this song, but "The Dance of the Cuckoos" appears to be the most official.)

Interestingly enough, the unsigned *New York Evening Post* review of *Sons of the Desert* felt the "hummable" "Honolulu Baby" was the best thing about this "all too familiar" Laurel & Hardy film. But while there was no contesting the critic's praise of the tune (which the studio had been high on even during production), this pan was far from the norm. The picture's reviews were generally strong. Moreover, the film was arguably their most commercial feature—landing among the coveted ten top-grossing films of 1934 according to such trade bibles as *Film Daily* and *The Motion Picture Herald*.

For the record, however, the January 9, 1934 *Variety* review (a journal seldom fond of the team) saw *Sons of the Desert* as merely an expansion of the earlier McCarey-directed short subject *We Faw Dawn* (1928), thus representing another complaint about their ability to sustain a feature-length comedy. The review in the January 12, 1934 *New York World-Telegraph* also had trouble with the length of *Sons of the Desert*; something which is punningly reiterated at the critique's close: "It's funny enough for two reels. After that, the Messrs. Laurel and Hardy cease to be sheiks or shrieks." (An immediate period defense, however, was available in Andre Sennwald's *New York Times* high praising review, which found no padding.) And the cigar for the most schizophrenic review went to John S. Cohen Jr., in a January 1, 1934 *New York Sun* piece, who liked the team but found their material hoary with age, the latter subject being the focus of his writing. But despite the "staleness of the material," Cohen still somehow feels Laurel & Hardy have a "brilliant feature" in features.

Sons of the Desert's late 1933 release (reviews generally dating from January 1934) put a close to what must have been a very emotional year for Laurel, from the death of his younger brother Everett (known as Teddy) at thirty-three, to the meeting of still another pivotal woman in his life. Everett, ten years younger, and his family were at that time living with the comedian by Laurel's invitation. Quite possibly this arrangement was an outgrowth of both Laurel's previous year's English reunion with his family and his divorce from Lois, which found Laurel alone, other than a two-person staff, in a rented Beverly Hills house.

Teddy, who was working as a chauffeur at a local hotel, came down with a bad toothache shortly before Christmas 1933. As if in a macabre rewrite of Laurel & Hardy's 1928 laughing gas dental comedy *Leave 'Em Laughing*, Teddy inexplicably died of heart failure at the dentist's office after the administering of nitrous oxide, the drug popularly known as laughing gas. An additional irony, as noted by team biographer Randy Skretvedt, was that Teddy's dental chair death occurred while Laurel & Hardy were shooting a short subject, *Oliver the Eighth* (1934), where Ollie's barber shop chair snooze has him dreaming of death.[129]

Production on the film stopped while Laurel made funeral arrangements. Because of a lifelong difficulty in coping with such events, Laurel did not attend the services, though an informal wake was held at the comedian's home. Paradoxically, the comedian believed in reincarnation. While this helped him handle his brother's death, one might have thought such a belief would have made it easier to attend funerals. (Though Laurel's ties to reincarnation were hardly in a league with actress/author Shirley MacLaine, who has books about her other lives, on at least one occasion *reincarnation* comically surfaced in the film world of Laurel & Hardy—the 1939 close of *The Flying Deuces*, where Ollie dies and comes back as Stan's horse.) Reincarnation also provided Laurel with a personal explanation as to how the occasional young performer could be so brilliant.

Regardless of Laurel's coping skills, the period was made easier by the presence of Virginia Ruth Rogers, who in 1934 became the next Mrs. Laurel. The comedian had met her on a 1933 boating excursion to Catalina Island, just off southern California. Though divorced from Lois by the time of his brother's death, Laurel's decree was not official until October 1934. Unlike his earlier relationships with common-law wife Mae Dahlberg, and Lois, Ruth would not move in with Laurel prior to marriage unless special arrangements were made— in this case, live-in chaperones. Laurel's old friends Alice and Baldy Cooke performed this unusual request, but what they assumed would be only a brief duty stretched into months.

Laurel's relationship with Virginia Ruth took another unusual twist in April 1934, though in the following years the comedian's musical-chairs domestic life became well known for such twists. They were married in Mexico. But acknowledging the fact the marriage would not be recognized in California, it was announced that until his divorce was final, Laurel and Ruth would not live together. Needless to say, this made interesting copy for the newspapers and gave Hal Roach more grey hair.

Laurel's divorce from Lois also produced one of the first occasions when headlines suggested the team of Laurel & Hardy was now over. In February 1934 the word was that Laurel was leaving the country and breaking up the duo to avoid any further divorce-related attachments to his income. The scenario had the comedian fulfilling several requests for European personal appearances. And though this was only a Laurel strategy to safeguard his salary, the overwhelming 1932 response to the team's foreign trip certainly gave credibility to this maneuver. It is an interesting barometer of Laurel's radically changeable emotional state that the Lois-directed travel subterfuge of February could be by the same man who had threatened suicide the previous year upon receiving his initial divorce papers.[130]

Of course, emotional flip-flops seem to have been a given for Laurel during the 1930s and early 1940s. Certainly this was also true of his relationship with Virginia Ruth, whom he would legally marry in September 1935 and divorce in late 1936, only to marry and divorce again in the 1940s.

Besides being an attractive blonde (another Laurel weakness, in addition to foreign accents), Virginia Ruth had a winning sense of humor and the ability to draw the comedian out socially. They were initially very happy, with Virginia Ruth not finding "Stan's temperament difficult with which to live" (see n. 59). With regard to his drinking, she observed, "He drank a lot, but he wasn't an alcoholic; he just drank for fun. He didn't drink at all when he was working."[131]

Though Virginia Ruth's comments are seemingly a bit too roseate (especially since one biographer noted a drunken Laurel once chased Virginia Ruth with a knife even prior to the marriage[132]), this wife did for a time represent a degree of stability in his life. Laurel's daughter, Lois, (who was not quite eight when

The Flying Deuces (1939)—Ollie returns as a horse

her father first legally married Virginia Ruth in 1935) was often a weekend guest at Laurel's Los Angeles home. Lois and Virginia Ruth became close, with Virginia leaving the bulk of her estate to her stepdaughter.

Laurel was married to Virginia Ruth at the time of his father and stepmother Venitia's lengthy 1935–36 visit. Because the California couple did not have a guest room, their visiting family stayed at a nearby hotel—at Stan's expense. (The previous year the comedian had had the remodeling of the master bedroom incorporate the two guest bedrooms—he wanted to discourage overnight guests.)

Though this less-than-hospitable remodeling was not directed at his father's visit, it is not the best of omens for a stay that stretched from summer to the following spring. And this is especially true for a relationship that had not always been harmonious. Still, while there were differences, such as a shouting match over an alleged promise by Laurel to take A. J. to see a Shirley Temple film in the making, all was not discord. Even this disagreement blew over quickly, possibly suggesting Laurel's easily changeable nature was acquired from A. J.

Regardless, a copy of Jefferson's unpublished diary from the trip (courtesy of a team fan) has upbeat, amusing, and revealing entries. For instance, number twenty-eight (specific dates are generally absent) calls: "both of them [Laurel and Ruth] very sweet." A second number twenty-eight (though a decidedly different date) reveals an informal host at home: "Stan grilled chops on barbecue fire—delicious! They [Laurel and Ruth] drove us home [to the hotel] . . . leaving about 1 A.M." (Later in his much-married life Laurel comically attributed his love of barbecues to the fact: "I'm used to them. I've been roasted enough by the women in my life!") Entry five shows the star comedian's democratic side: "Captain Millers, skipper of the Ruth L [Laurel's modest fishing yacht] joined us at dinner."

The diary also offers an amusing look at A. J. as tourist. Entry eight has him taking: "a trip on an alleged glass bottom boat [probably off Catalina Island] to view ocean fish, etc. ghastly experience." Note four records "semi-nudity of the bathers and pedestrians rather embarrassing at first." Entry 23 reveals that A. J.'s accommodations were plagued by ants, first in the bed and then the kitchen.

The diary's dominant subject is Laurel's fascination with the sea—especially fishing. The young boy who loved to fish in the canals of Ulverston continued the hobby for a lifetime. (One has only to walk on Ulverston's commons—a large hill just outside the town, where Laurel played as a child—to appreciate his love of the sea. To the east and south is Morecambe Bay; to the west is the Irish Sea.)

One of A. J.'s more fleshed-out fishing entries documents a similar interest by a Roach comedy colleague as well as a fishing fate appropriate for Laurel's screen persona:

S & R [Stan and Ruth] left about 8 fishing. [Back for supper] phone call . . . that Stan had caught a tuna! . . . went to the Pier big crowd assembled to welcome the fishers. But alas! It was not Stan's catch but Jimmy Parrott's (Charley Chase's brother) [and a frequent Laurel & Hardy director]. Better luck next trip Stan!

The cynic might suggest Laurel's intensified fishing interests merely represented an easy dodge from his father's company. And though possible, it ignores both the fact A. J. occasionally went along and (more to the point) that the comedian was obsessed with fishing. For instance, shortly after the team arrived in England for their 1947 tour a *London Daily Star* reporter asked Laurel about a lapel badge he was wearing. The comedian explained it was to prove he was a qualified deep-sea fisherman. In 1935 he had caught a 256–pound tuna (possibly paralleling his father's visit), and Laurel had worn the badge ever since.

Without taking anything away from his great, ongoing interest in comedy, Laurel's love of the sea and fishing was a lifelong comfort generally given short shrift in team literature. (For more on his fisherman nature, see this chapter's later description of the nautical decor and ocean view of his final home.)

Virginia Ruth's greatest gift to the comedian as well as to comedy disciples everywhere was suggesting that Laurel & Hardy do a parody-western—what eventually became *Way Out West* (1937; ironically, their first marriage had ended by then). After *Sons of the Desert*, this is their best feature film.

Since America's archetypal genre is the western, most major comedians eventually do a cowboy spoof, from Keaton's *Go West* (1925) to Steve Martin's *¡Three Amigos!* (1986). Indeed, other than Keaton's early parody, Laurel & Hardy's six-gun takeoff predates most of those done by their contemporaries. The very active parody western 1940s saw the release of W. C. Fields and Mae West's *My Little Chickadee*, the Marx Brothers' *Go West*, and Jack Benny's *Buck Benny Rides Again*. While the success of *Way Out West* did not hurt this decade-ending tendency, it was more a result of director John Ford's 1939 hit western *Stagecoach* (which also launched John Wayne into A-pictures).

Besides the fundamental parody contrast of *Way Out West*—placing comic antiheroes Laurel & Hardy in western macho land—the film, like all good spoofs, represents a funny, insightful dissecting of a target genre structure. Merely by keeping to a broadly western terrain so familiar to most viewers, *Way Out West* is more of an integrated feature than is often the Laurel & Hardy norm. Thus, the comedy duo find themselves heading to Brushwood Gulch in order to deliver a gold mine to the now orphaned Mary Roberts (Rosina Lawrence)—so virtuously portrayed as to be a send-up of the traditional sickeningly sweet heroine. Like Mark Twain's own western spoof, *Roughing It* (1872), Stan & Ollie find plenty of painfully comic diversions along the way, from hitching a stagecoach ride to confronting the traditional crooked saloon owner Mickey Finn (played by longtime team nemesis James Finlayson). Naturally, good triumphs in the end, though true to comic antihero form, Stan & Ollie's lives never became any easier. The film begins when Ollie is victimized by a shallow stream sinkhole: Stan safely and obliviously walks across, but it closes on Ollie, once again taking another ''bath'' in the stream. For those interested in comic genealogy, the sinkhole is no doubt the forefather of all those wonderful bottomless mud puddles that often turn up in the team's modern setting films.

The beginning and ending symmetry of the sinkhole material makes the repetition work. Moreover, *Way Out West* is generally devoid of the padding that often mars other Laurel & Hardy features, and the two carry the film nicely with no need of a romantic subplot. Any extra footage merely enriches the parody; for instance, most spoofs add additional targets beyond the focus genre or auteur under attack. Consequently, there is the delightful way in which *Way Out West* Stan gets the stagecoach to stop. Playing upon the phenomenal 1934 success and viewer recognition of Frank Capra's *It Happened One Night*, Laurel borrows from the conclusion of that film's famous hitchhiking scene. In *It Happened One Night* Clark Gable has exhausted his supply of hitchhiking hand gestures and the lovely Claudette Colbert offers to give him a "hand," or more precisely, a leg. She pulls up her skirt to expose one of the beautiful limbs for which she was famous on Broadway. Naturally, a car immediately screeches to a halt, with an editing cut to a braking tire for added comedy effect.

In *Way Out West* Stan & Ollie also find themselves hitchhiking, and when it looks like the stagecoach is going to pass them by, Stan, in the spirit of Colbert, pulls up his pant leg and—amazingly—stops the coach. Ever conscious of details, there is also a cut to the braking stagecoach wheel.

Though without the comedy buildup of *It Happened One Night* (Gable initially both fails at numerous hitchhiking techniques and then pooh-poohs novice Colbert's offer of assistance), Stan's exposure of a less-than-lovely limb works for five reasons. First, it is a parody of the earlier film and the comedy contrast of a Colbert limb and Stan's. Second, it is a parody of sexuality in general; this is not something a man would normally do. (Thus, one does not have to be in on the specific parody reference to find it amusing.) Third, it is also, in part, a takeoff on Laurel's screen character, since any sexual awareness (regardless of gender) invariably seems alien to him. Fourth, Stan's feminine action (exposing his leg) is comically consistent with the couple-like nature so often associated with the team, where the bossy Ollie is sometimes seen as the "man" and the often submissive Stan is the stereotypical "woman." Fifth, Stan's success at stopping the coach is a comic affront to Ollie not unlike the one Colbert administered to Gable. An ongoing Laurel & Hardy premise has always been that despite the general comic incompetence of both their screen characters, the seemingly more-dense Stan frequently betters his partner.

It is not necessary, though, to expand at length about brief scenes in order to praise the film. Its comedy richness varies from sexy saloon girl Sharon Lynne's comic seductive stalking of Stan (she eventually tickles a deed out of his possession while reducing him to an audience-contagious laughing fit), to the Stan & Ollie musical interludes, which also vary from a soft shoe number to their crooning of "In the Blue Ridge Mountains of Virginia." They are interludes, however, only in the sense of a Chico Marx piano number, because they are entertainingly comic in and of themselves, as well as representing more parody—

undercutting the musical western. And for all the rich visual humor both expected of the team and to be found here, including the pulley-system approach of breaking into the second floor of the saloon (accidently launching the donkey tied to the other end and giving Hardy a crater-making crash landing), the film also has its verbal moments. For instance, when saloon girl Sharon Lynne poses as the rightful owner of the gold mine, she asks deed messengers Stan & Ollie, "Tell me, tell me about my dear, dear Daddy [from whom the inheritance came]. Is it true he's dead?" Stan replies, "Well, we hope he is; they buried him!"

Way Out West is such an entertaining and integrated Laurel & Hardy feature one is reminded of *New York Times* film critic Frank S. Nugent's amusing opening to his rave review of the film: "Too many books are being written on the anatomy of humor and none on the humor of anatomy."[133]

I do not normally quote disparaging remarks on the subject of comedy theory, even when in jest. But Nugent's review is so unabashedly affectionate about these "anatomical funny men," at a time when many serious critics would never admit to such Laurel & Hardy comedy pleasures, that his insightful criticism merits recognition at any celebration of the film.

Indeed, the reviews for *Way Out West* equaled, if not surpassed, the team's high critical marks for *Sons of the Desert*. The phenomenally positive audience response to this particular Laurel & Hardy picture sometimes became a lead-in for the reviews. For example, Dorothy Masters's (May 4, 1937) *New York Daily News* piece observes one will be "privileged" to see the duo, "if the floorboards hold out under standing-room-only weight and the rafters survive the Vesuvius-rivalling bellows of audience lung power." Archer Winsten's *New York Post* review (May 4, 1937) said of the demonstrably appreciative audience, "You can't pass off that sort of thing lightly even if you fail to share the merriment." And *New York American* critic Robert Garland seemed almost embarrassed in his (May 4, 1937) critique that he so enjoyed *Way Out West* with a "packed" audience who "whoop it up, with Stan and Oliver." Ironically, but not surprisingly, *Variety* (May 5, 1937) panned the film, managing to even turn audience enjoyment into condescension: "For the Laurel-Hardy fans, who howl at anything the pair does, they may appear as comical as ever." *Variety* had this parody western failing on every level.

Matching the disquieting nature of this *Variety* review is a Laurel off-screen prank during the production of the film—providing the best extant example of the comedian's sometimes macabre sense of humor. The story comes from three-time Oscar-nominated Roy Seawright, Roach optical effects man, and close working colleague to the team. "Stan usually expressed humor and warmth, but—I hate to say this—there were times when he could be cruel."[134] Seawright explained that while preparing the pulley system for the elaborate Hardy/donkey scene, Laurel had his double, the young and naive Hamilton Kinsey, hooked into the animal's position and raised to the top of the soundstage. Kinsey was then left there alone as Laurel and his laughing troupe feigned going to lunch. They left the set, closing the stage doors behind them. When a third party responded to Kinsey's hysterical screaming, it was found that he had nearly suffocated from the prank. Naturally, Laurel was very sorry, but as described by Seawright, Laurel had baited his double throughout the production, though in less extreme ways.

In fairness to Laurel and possibly to shed some light on his sense of humor, there were less controversial examples of his comic nature. As a child he once took his Grandpa Metcalfe's leather (disciplinary) strap and later calmly pitched it into Morecambe Bay from a train window—to the shock of an accompanying cousin. In true antiheroic fashion, however, he soon learned there was more than one leather strap in the world, not to mention in his grandfather's possession. Laurel the adult once kidded a pretentious Chaplin habit in the latter's presence. The setting was a ritzy restaurant, where Chaplin was elaborately preparing and tossing a large salad (as was his habit) for some elite dinner guests. Laurel appeared and dragged in a tin bathtub loaded with enough vegetables for the Seventh Cavalry, then proceeded to put on his own salad-preparing performance. While Chaplin's friends were enchanted, the master comedian seemed less than pleased (shades of Laurel the schoolboy imitating a teacher without harmonious results). But, my favorite Laurel story again returns to his Ulverston childhood: for a time, he made punishment in a dark wash house palatable by hiding candles, matches and comic reading material inside!

Obviously, Laurel generally took the comic route, even in the pitch black woodshed. In contrast, it was childhood punishments like this that some critics suggest led to the moody metaphysics of Ingmar Bergman's art house films. (Bergman's father would place him in a dark closet.) Regardless, Laurel examples here and elsewhere demonstrate this lover of the lighter side could take pranks too far. Even close English friend and team editor Bert Jordan suggests (without malice) in an interview by Robert Warwick (see Chapter 4) that Laurel could be tenacious in his kidding if he had a comic weakness upon which to draw. In fact, while it is not addressed that much, a key on-the-set personality difference between Laurel & Hardy was the former's born kidder nature versus the latter's general seriousness.

Since Laurel sometimes had an entourage on the set (seemingly to serve as a comic measuring stick for his otherwise audienceless material), maybe there was also a tendency to be "on" for them. Certainly other Laurel pranks mentioned by Seawright, such as making Kinsey wear a red nose or walk around with a piece of pie on his shoulder, suggest a ready audience.

Of course, there are other darkly comic comments by Laurel that now merely strike one as amusing. For instance, in 1939 Laurel was divorced from yet another wife—Russian cafe singer and dancer Illeanna (Vera Shuvalova). During the divorce proceedings Illeanna (other spellings sometimes surface) accused the gardening lover comedian of threatening to bury her alive.

In describing this . . . alleged episode, she said that one day she found her husband with a shovel, busily digging up the back yard of their home. She asked him what he was doing and charges he replied:

"Digging a hole to bury you in, Shuvalova."[135]

It has already been noted that Laurel had periods of depression, and his dark side observations were hardly limited to any one period as well. But even in the best of times, such as his triumphant 1932 return to England, Laurel could come up with seemingly macabre observations. The example in mind was no doubt heartfelt by the comedian, but at the same time he must have known how startling it would sound. One cannot help wondering if the English night hid any dark mischievousness in his eyes. Regardless, when a London *Daily Herald* reporter joined Laurel in looking at the comedian's name in "letters of fire" at the Leicester-square Empire theatre, where the team was appearing both on stage and screen, Laurel observed:

You should see the lighthouse in the graveyard in Ulverston, in Lancashire, where I was born.

They put it up when I was a kid—a tombstone with a light on top. It was the Eighth Wonder of the world to me.

Ever since then it's been my ambition to have a tombstone like that![136]

This is hardly standard celebrity-reporter light patter. Underlining the added incongruity of this particular comedian making such a statement, the uncredited newsperson closed with: "Yes, that's what Stan Laurel, the laugh-maker, dreams of when he's off duty."[137] (For more on this unusual marker, which a young Laurel probably would have passed on his boyhood fishing trips, see *Laurel Before Hardy*.)[138]

Actually, Laurel did not have to be off duty to uncover his dark sense of humor. The team's standard repertoire often included such violent slapstick as Ollie being dragged down a flight of steps by a crated piano in *The Music Box* or the bandaged foot of the boys's gout-ridden uncle Edgar Kennedy constantly being banged in *A Perfect Day* (1929). In addition, Laurel had a penchant for macabre film endings, though he was not always successful in getting such endings past Roach. There are numerous examples of this tendency.

In the Roach-produced *The Bohemian Girl* (1936), the team find themselves being tortured near the film's conclusion—Ollie on the rack and Stan in a compressing cage. Thus, the film closes with a stretched Ollie and a shrimp Stan strolling by. Granted, this is in the nature of their sometimes cartoon special effects, such as the scene in *Way Out West* where Ollie's head is stretched out to ostrich neck proportions. But still, *The Bohemian Girl* close, following the torture sequence, provides a certain shock effect. Another example of a Laurel & Hardy macabre ending is the close to the post-Roach film *The Bullfighters* (1945), where the duo are reduced to their skeletons. They finally fall victim to both the heavy's ongoing threat: "I'm going to skin them alive," and Stan's fear: "I don't want to walk around in my bones, rattling all over the place."

An interesting shocker that did not make a final print was Laurel's intended ending of *Block-Heads*—the heads of Stan & Ollie were mounted on the wall of hunter Billy Gilbert.[139] Interestingly, James Thurber's antiheroic line drawings during this period also featured at least one mounted husband's head. (*Block-*

The Ulverston (England) tombstone ''lighthouse''

Heads does, of course, include the dark humor gag of Stan sitting in a wheelchair with one leg tucked under him, as if he had lost the limb. Naturally, Ollie assumes the worst, with the humor being drawn from this mistaken belief.)

Other macabre conclusions occur in *Going Bye-Bye!* and *The Live Ghost* (both 1934), two short subjects also liberally sprinkled throughout with dark humor. Appropriately, Raymond Borde and Charles Perrin's *Laurel et Hardy* includes a "Torture" category in the book's "Dictionnaire De Gags" section. This was also the year (1934) of the team's top operetta—the inspired *Babes In Toyland*, with its occasional dark humor, especially the genuinely frightening bogeyman.

Laurel shared and/or possibly borrowed this interest in dark comedy conclusions from one of his film idols and later friend Buster Keaton. For example, Keaton's classic bittersweet short subject *Cops* (1922) closes with "the end" appearing on a tombstone, while his seemingly more upbeat Harold Lloyd-like *College* (1927) finishes with the young hero and heroine going through a rapid series of aging scenes before closing on their final side-by-side grave plots.

While such cinema closes can prove startling, in Laurel & Hardy films they seldom distract from the overall warmly comic nature of their work. Such endings merely seem like a one-joke shock addition. This contrasts with Keaton, where the close of *College* effectively makes the viewer question the whole significance of the hero's comically hard-won romantic victory.

As a black humor footnote, Laurel music hall idol Dan Leno was also adept at the darkly comic. In his tongue-in-cheek autobiography, Leno observes, after an alleged boating accident:

Every one of us was drowned except myself. . . . Of course I did my best for the crew. I pulled out my notebook and took down their last farewells . . . and there wasn't one that I didn't say a kind word to. But I had in my hand a rolling pin . . . and when any of the poor fellows caught hold of my raft, I had the presence of mind to hit them till they let go. You see, I had to be saved, because I was engaged to appear at a Liverpool hall, and I try never to disappoint the public.

In the second half of the 1930s both Laurel's personal problems and his continued conflicts with Roach distracted from the team of Laurel & Hardy while perhaps limiting their independent production possibilities and even briefly teaming Hardy with another partner (Langdon). These events occurred during the second phase of their feature film career (1936–1940), when they were unfortunately no longer making short subjects. The first phase (1931–1935) had fluctuated between features and short subjects; the final period (1941–1945) was composed of their post-Roach features. The feature films made during the sometimes problematic second phase were *The Bohemian Girl, Our Relations* (both 1936), *Way Out West, Pick a Star* (both 1937, the latter only briefly featuring the team), *Swiss Miss, Block-Heads* (both 1938), *The Flying Deuces* (1939), *A Chump at Oxford*, and *Saps at Sea* (both 1940). Some might also include *Bonnie Scotland* (1935), since it was released *after* their final short subject, *Thicker*

On the set of *Babes in Toyland* (1934), with Virginia Karns

Than Water (1935). But *Bonnie Scotland* is not so listed here because, despite its release time, it was actually shot prior to that last short.

The Laurel problems alluded to again involve his musical-chair instability with wives (accent on the plural) and alcohol. Although an ongoing problem for much of his adult life to that point, in the late 1930s it escalated to a level commensurate with the self-destructive Mae Dahlberg relationship of the 1920s. (Fittingly, Dahlberg resurfaced again at this time, suing Laurel for separate maintenance as a past common-law wife.)

To put Laurel's messy late 1930s public image in adequate perspective, one must recognize that it completely usurped his film work. Of course, this was a time when Laurel & Hardy were hardly receiving much serious American critical attention, not that the team is inundated with scholarly research even today. Ironically, when Laurel was compared to Chaplin in the late 1930s, people were generally drawing parallels between their troubled personal relationships with women and *not* between their screen personae. At major research libraries, such as the Billy Rose Theatre Collection of the New York Public Library at Lincoln Center, or the Academy of Motion Picture Arts and Sciences Library (Beverly Hills, California), clipping files for the team fully document this imbalance.

Laurel had suffered public hurts of private matters before, but in the late 1930s it became much more of a public spectacle, as the following headline in the December 10, 1939, *New York Journal-American* demonstrates: "Newest Upheaval in the Not-So-Private Life of Sad-Faced Mr. Laurel."[140] What this headline does not capture is that the press had a comic heyday through the years with the marriage woes of Laurel. For instance, another 1939 article includes a humorously tongue-in-cheek overview of the comedian's single most personally chaotic year (1938):

Screen comedian Stan Laurel has just finished one of the funniest and busiest years [1938] of his life, but the studio which pays him to be funny is fighting with him [Roach fired Laurel in August 1938] because all this fantastic high and low comedy was performed outside [in Laurel's private life] where their camera could not catch it.[141]

Laurel's personal life for 1938 reads very much like the madcap romantic antics of the then-popular film genre—screwball comedy. Certainly, the actions at this time of both former wife Virginia Ruth and the new Mrs. Laurel, Illeanna Shuvalova, could stand comparison with the genre's screwiest 1930s heroine— Carole Lombard.

Laurel married third wife Illeanna on January 1, 1938, five weeks after he auditioned her for a film role. The twenty-eight-year-old bride, nearly twenty years Laurel's junior, and the comedian ran into problems immediately. Second wife Virginia Ruth followed the new couple to Yuma, Arizona, where Laurel and Illeanna had eloped. Virginia Ruth claimed her divorce from the comedian was illegal because they had still lived together sporadically during their separation. Under the comic headline, "Laurel Weds No. 3 as No. 2 Gives Chase," the *New York Daily News* reported that a "bitterly protesting" (but to no avail) Virginia Ruth caught up with the couple just as they were about to board a train back to Los Angeles.[142]

Virginia Ruth continued to harass the couple after their return to Los Angeles. In a January 11 request for a court restraining order against Virginia Ruth (applied in April), Laurel claimed she "kept calling him up at all hours, pounding on his door in the middle of the night and threatening him with 'unfavorable publicity.'"[143] However, to forestall Virginia Ruth's bigamy charges, Laurel and Illeanna repeated their vows in another Yuma civil ceremony on February 27. The two went through still another ceremony (in her Russian Orthodox faith) during April 1938! (Bigamy was then considered a more serious crime, often with an accompanying jail term.)

In a later but very applicable and darkly funny 1941 article, written after Stan exchanged vows for the third time with 1938 troublemaker Virginia Ruth, one uncredited satirist reported, "Stan seems to have reached the point where he could say: 'Let's get married' as easily as another man might remark, 'Let's have a drink and do the town.'"[144] The same imaginatively comic author cited the alleged problems mathematicians everywhere were having coming to grips with the 1941 marriage, since it broke the nice marital progression Laurel had established by 1938. That is, Laurel "was a favorite of theirs [mathematicians] because he was the only man they knew who had wed his first wife [Lois] once, his second wife [Virginia Ruth] twice, and his third wife [Illeanna] thrice."[145] Indeed, these poor mathematicians had even gone to the trouble of considering Laurel's 1938 marital numbers for a school textbook. Two possible story problems might have been:

"If a man marries three women six times, who is he? The correct answer is among the following: King Solomon, Brigham Young, Stan Laurel.: Or, (to make it appropriate for younger children): "Stan Laurel, famous Hollywood comedian, married his first wife once, his second twice, and his third three times. How many times will he marry his fourth?"[146]

Comic commentary aside, Laurel's 1938 marriage to Illeanna was not without danger. After being arrested for drunk driving September 28, 1938, a shirtless and "badly" bleeding Laurel told Officer E. T. Taylor: "I just had a terrible battle at my house. My wife hit me with a frying pan and then she ran out of the house, so I got in my car and I'm trying to find her."[147] But even situations as serious as this seemed peppered with comic irony. Here was a domestic frying pan victim from a comedy team whose duo screen image was also forever endangered by wives who sometimes brandished frying pans! One article on the incident sported a punning title: "Sad Pan, Frying Pan Met, Says Stan Laurel."[148] Another piece inadvertently revealed more information that might have also been borrowed from a Laurel & Hardy slapstick chase: "Police said he [Laurel] was driving fifty-five miles an hour on the wrong side of the highway and narrowly missed colliding with a police car."[149] A near miss and/or total destruction of automobiles and a special ability rarely to escape the hands of the "law" (police or wives) were forever the screen fate of Stan & Ollie.

The drunk-driving charge kept Laurel in jail overnight. When brought to trial the following month (October), a jury failed to agree on a verdict. In December, just before a scheduled retrial, the charges were dropped. By and large, Laurel's drinking problem was to be kept out of the papers. Unfortunately, this was not the case with Illeanna, who would be arrested frequently for public drunkenness. Laurel and Illeanna also enjoyed going the nightclub route, where his Russian bride might burst forth into song at any moment. She was even more intense in private. And like an Ollie screen wife, when quarreling she was loud and prone to breaking glass. While team scholar McCabe amusingly described her as a "one-woman mob scene," Laurel biographer Guiles has hypothesized that Laurel's interest in this eccentric (especially her always unpredictable behavior) was based in his dislike for everyday routine.[150] It is an interesting point, and no doubt true to a degree, since Laurel often seems to have felt suffocated in his marriage to the very stabilizing and domestic-minded Lois, the mother of his only child. Yet, his ongoing attraction to such a volatile and dangerous partner as Illeanna certainly merits repeating the self-destructive label applied earlier. Laurel's masochistic tendency here is reminiscent of his earlier relationship with common-law wife Mae Dahlberg, who was also physically abusive.

As a related footnote to Laurel's stormy lifestyle, including his own rapid mood changes (such as the quick flip-flops between anger and requests for forgiveness), and his sometimes unpleasantly obsessional practical joking, the name Dan Leno could again be evoked. Laurel's music hall idol had nearly identical personality traits, including the habit of going to practical joking extremes. This is not to suggest that Laurel patterned himself after Leno. Yet, given the high esteem Laurel had had for Leno since childhood (not to mention having borrowed some Leno comedy character traits for his own screen persona), such parallels might have reinforced those tendencies in Laurel.

Along similar lines, Laurel had a fear of losing his mind, a fate which befell Leno at the end of his life, and something which Laurel was known to discuss. (Laurel's anxiety on the subject would hardly have been lessened by the mental breakdown Larry Semon suffered shortly before his premature death in 1928). Interestingly enough, during Laurel's especially problematic 1930s, he would have been freshly aware of Leno's often troubled life, since the normally nonbookish Laurel included a Leno volume in an English book order from this period.

Illeanna, who additionally claimed to be a displaced Russian countess (more screwball comedy overtones), did not, however, have a corner on providing the 1938 world of Laurel with unpredictable events. Indeed, the ever-active Virginia Ruth was probably the mystery person behind a number of additional disturbances at the Laurel residence. After Laurel's court action against her, an anonymous person kept calling the police and fire departments, hospital, funeral parlors . . .

and reporting all manner of fictitious mayhem taking place at the Laurel home. Thus, fire trucks, police cars, ambulances, and hearses were forever showing up at all hours. Laurel seemed to take these added Looney Tune disturbances in stride—or maybe he was just pleased the authorities were not there to take someone away. Regardless, his typical polite response to the frequently visiting officials, from firemen to morticians, was: "Not today, thank you."[151] In contrast, the high-strung Russian Illeanna, who was hospitalized twice for nerves during her marriage to Laurel, was greatly bothered by such disturbances, as her entertaining overstatement suggests: "It is a nightmare; one might as well be in Russia."[152]

As later revealed in the drunk-driving incident, however, Laurel was not immune to the stresses of this helter-skelter lifestyle. Thus, after one of Illeanna's nervous breakdowns, *Look* magazine's June 21, 1938 issue carried a disturbing photo of Laurel weeping on the floor as his wife was taken to the hospital. Appearing under the title "The Saddest Man in Hollywood is a Comedian: Stan Laurel," this photo essay also carried pictures of his previous wives.

Revisionist Laurel & Hardy essayist Leo Brooks provocatively suggests in the article "Worth a Thousand Words" (*Shifting Sands*, October 1988) that the picture represents the beginning of the gradual decline in the team's American popularity. His theory is that, besides shocking middle America, this is the first time the public separated Laurel the troubled performer from the simple character of Stan. Moreover, for Brooks, this explains why there was not more public outcry when Langdon temporarily replaced Laurel in the team. Though I would not rate the impact of *Look*'s weeping Laurel as highly as Brooks, it does represent a departure—not since becoming a star had Laurel been revealed as so vulnerable to the personal chaos around him.

Certainly the later drunk-driving incident comes as less a surprise when coupled with the *Look* photo. Still, as the following pages reveal, the media's continuing examination of Laurel's real-life misadventures generally assumed a comic tone—often supplemented by the comedian's own wit. Ironically, even *Look*'s photo essay was not without comic commentary. For instance, one caption repeated Laurel's marital box score—having wed his first wife once, second wife twice, and so on. Another caption includes the comedian's amusing explanation for his three 1938 wedding ceremonies with Illeanna: "It's one way of throwing a party." (Regardless, outside the Brooks article, the *Look* piece is now all but unknown in team literature.)

For a time Illeanna blamed her much-publicized 1938 auto accident on another prank call, which allegedly misinformed her that Laurel was injured, causing her to rush off into a wreck. But in truth the incident seems to have been a case of an inexperienced, unlicensed driver (Illeanna) attempting to drive into downtown Hollywood. Unfortunately, she managed to travel only two blocks from home, striking two parked cars. Booked for reckless driving and not having a license, she later served five days in jail.

As if zany 1938 needed a fuller complement of Laurel ladies, Illeanna later claimed that the comedian's first wife, Lois, and his daughter nearly turned up on their (Laurel and Illeanna's) honeymoon cruise aboard the *Ruth L*. According to Illeanna, Laurel wanted to take his daughter on the trip, "but his first wife wouldn't permit that unless she could go, too. I don't understand all this. I love Stan, but I can't share him with all these ex-wives."[153]

Evidently, Illeanna had given her approval to having Laurel's daughter accompany them *before* a rather shocking "stowaway" (Lois) appeared, explaining "she never let her daughter go anywhere unless she was present to watch over her." When the bride registered extreme horror, the comedian assured her—"It will be alright. We are the best of friends."[154]

These allegations originally came out during the 1939 divorce proceedings of Laurel and Illeanna, but they are in no way inconsistent with either the already established (to borrow from Steve Martin) "wild and crazy" lifestyle of Laurel, or the screwball events of 1938. Moreover, the "best of friends" line is perfectly in keeping with a man who keeps marrying . . . the same women . . . and is continually being pursued by them.

Appropriately, some time in 1938 or early 1939, the comedian had a high wall built around his small estate. Later asked why, he replied he could not live in a normal home "because my ex-wives keep taking it by storm. So I am turning this place into a fort, to be known henceforth as Fort Laurel. All attacking blondes will be repelled on sight."[155] No doubt, he also hoped to repel fire trucks, police cars, ambulances, and hearses. (Laurel even had a "Fort Laurel" sign hanging over the driveway entrance to this "home"!)

Laurel's decision to build Fort Laurel is perfectly in keeping with an individual whose personal life could be every bit as antiheroic as his screen one. In fact, surrounding oneself with a high wall is not unlike the classic James Thurber essay, "A Box to Hide In," whose title so nicely describes one alternative to the antiheroic dilemma.[156] Like a frustrated, henpecked Thurber character, or that movie character named Stan, Laurel was merely looking for a safe haven in out of the insanity. Both Thurber's "Box" and Laurel's walls appeared in the 1930s, a time when the Great Depression began to make antiheroic humor especially palatable to a world gone topsy-turvy.

For the antiheroic artist it never hurts to have a personal mindset also geared to the antiheroic. Tales of a protective wall and box bring to mind a similar story about former Laurel & Hardy soulmate Leo McCarey. The latter's friend and antiheroic humorist H. Allen Smith has chronicled the director's "contemptuous attitude toward New York City" (antiheroic humor frequently uses the frustrating and emasculating modern city for a setting—see Chapter 2).[157] Thus, Smith describes a McCarey who, by utilizing Grand Central Station, underground taxi stands, and basement entrances to his hotel (where he then stayed put), would never be technically outside in New York City. This might have been a premise for a Thurber short story—or a Laurel & Hardy film.

Consistent with the fate of antiheroes everywhere, on screen and off, Laurel's wall failed. Fort Laurel metaphorically surrendered when he remarried Virginia

Ruth in 1941. Asked at the time if he would take down the wall, since she had definitely bested it, Laurel answered most appropriately for a veteran of the battle of the sexes. Referring to France's supposedly impenetrable pre–World War II military defense work, the Maginot Line, which the invading Germans had then so recently (1940) and easily defeated merely by flying over it (not unlike an ex-wife scaling a wall), he answered: "They [the French] didn't tear down the Maginot Line, did they?"[158]

When Laurel expanded further on Virginia Ruth's "defeat" of his fort, he comically revealed another basic characteristic of antiheroes, on screen and off—they contribute to their comic downfall just as much as some amusingly perverse fate:

It [the remarriage to Virginia Ruth] happened suddenly, like heart failure. I invited her out to the fort. We had dinner and talked things over. Making love to an ex-wife isn't like starting in from scratch. You've already been over the preliminaries, so everything goes faster.[159]

Thus, besides providing an entertainingly comic insight, the comedian also admitted playing fifth columnist to himself—"inviting" in the "enemy" (an aggressive ex-wife), which would result in still another failed "collaboration" (marriage).

The fact that Laurel's observations were sometimes funny, too, is equally significant. It covered a great deal of personal pain, and it presented a winsomely vulnerable through humor image to the public—like his polite "Not today, thank you" reply to "visiting" firemen, policemen, ambulance drivers, and morticians. But some of these wisecracks came after the fact, when Laurel had been able to collect himself. In contrast, there were no witty lines the night police arrested him after he had been injured by Illeanna's frying pan. Consequently, setting humor aside, Laurel's true feeling about his messy late 1930s might best be encapsulated in his 1939 observation: "I'm just being persecuted."[160] Though Laurel uttered these remarks after being informed that Illeanna wanted to set aside the divorce he had won by default earlier in the year (yes, another ex-wife wanted him back!), he might just as well have applied it to the cumulative effect of his marriage problems since his first 1938 wedding ceremony with Illeanna. Indeed, Laurel had been concerned about "unfavorable publicity" (see n. 143) since his court action against Virginia Ruth in January 1938. Laurel's concerns were well founded. One is reminded of the much later (1984) flawed musical play based on both the duo's public and private lives—Block-Heads. As at least one prominent critic defined the problem (see Irving Wardle's October 18, 1984 review in The Times), the musical asks you "simultaneously to warm to the memory of two much-loved artists, and to click your tongue over their private lives."

Roach had feared for years that scandal might end Laurel's career, and by association, the team of Laurel & Hardy. Roach fired Laurel in mid-August

1938, replacing him almost immediately with Harry Langdon. The comedian's dismissal was officially the result of his "willful disregard of his obligations in failing to report to the studio for retakes" on *Block-Heads*.[161] The studio also claimed that Laurel had further disregarded his contract by not meeting with his writers to prepare a script for the next Laurel & Hardy film, which was to have started production on August 1.

Laurel stated he had had permission to be absent, and in December 1938 he sued Roach's studio for nearly three-quarters of a million dollars, citing breach of contract. The studio replied in February 1939 by way of elaborating on the causes behind Laurel's firing. While the Roach spokesperson still cited the comedian's uncooperativeness, the real bombshell was that Laurel "violated the morals clause of his contract." Most specifically, this involved claims that Laurel was drinking on the set and that his messy, much publicized, personal life—out of step with public mores—had earned screen audiences' "ridicule and contempt."

Needless to say, the final slam, regarding the public's "ridicule and contempt," found the studio overstepping its bounds, or as *The Music Box* Stan once observed—"bounding over your steps." For instance, a number of the public disturbances referred to (most specifically the frying pan incident) actually occurred during the five months *following* the firing—which probably also contributed to Laurel's instability. Team biographer Skretvedt even goes so far as to claim *all* the incidents took place *after* the August 1938 firing, even though there were disturbances literally from day one—the New Year's Day 1938 marriage to Illeanna.[162] Regardless, Laurel's publicized post-August problems did not exactly detract from the studio accusations.

To say, however, that Laurel had earned the public's "ridicule and contempt" was not true. Had it been, the studio would hardly have rehired such box office poison when it found the public did not respond to the new team of Langdon & Hardy. Thus, in April 1939 all charges were dropped and Laurel was back under contract to Roach.

A more traditional Hollywood reason—though invariably veiled—for such a firing would be management's fear that the public *eventually* would feel "ridicule and contempt" for the accused, which could then threaten to attach itself to the parent company. Hollywood has had a long history of overresponding to possible alienation of its audience, for example, the strict censorship code implemented in 1934, or the widespread blacklisting of alleged communist sympathizers in the late 1940s and 1950s.

Laurel's 1938 dismissal was an example of the personal and professional friction that had long clouded the Laurel-Roach relationship. Indeed, the comedian had previously been fired by the studio March 15, 1935, over alleged story differences with Roach. And while creative differences had long existed, such as the major conflicts over the *Babes In Toyland* script (1934, later retitled *March of the Wooden Soldiers*), or the team's then-current project (what eventually became *Bonnie Scotland*, 1935), the catalyst for the 1935 firing was "the refusal of Laurel to sign a new term contract with Roach under the terms submitted by the company."[163] (The title of the *Variety* piece from which n. 163 is drawn is consistent with the publication's ongoingly negative critical view of the team— "Stan Laurel Pouts Out, Hardy to Solo.")

As if in a dress rehearsal for the 1938 firing, the 1935 dismissal also found Roach announcing new contingency plans for Hardy almost immediately. Hardy was to be teamed with film comedienne Patsy Kelly and "Our Gang" 's six-year-old Spanky MacFarland. They would appear in a new domestic series to be called "The Hardys." (Some test footage was shot.)

Laurel also had plans; M-G-M was approached about the comedian producing his own features. Actor George Bancroft (the sheriff in John Ford's later classic, *Stagecoach*, 1939) was approached about being Laurel's new film partner. Both M-G-M and Bancroft requested more material before any decision could be made.

In less than a month, however, Laurel and Roach had come to an agreement and the comedian was once again teamed with Hardy. But differences still existed, and when it came time for a new contract in early 1937, Laurel staged an unofficial strike. It was not until October that an agreement with Roach was finally reached. But a change had occurred—the comedian had incorporated and Roach's contract was with Stan Laurel Productions. It was from this two-year 1937 contract that Laurel was dismissed in 1938. But as is apparent from this overview, the Laurel-Roach relationship had become progressively cooler since mid-decade. (It is sometimes suggested that Laurel's incorporating not only provided some of his long-sought-after independence, but was also a way around paying former wife Virginia Ruth the ongoing five percent of his gross salary granted in the divorce. That is, a losing corporation could be most profitable for the comedian.)

Probably the most surprising thing about Laurel's volatile 1938 was that two Stan & Ollie films even appeared: *Swiss Miss* and *Block-Heads*. The latter is particularly popular today, besides being entertaining, it is devoid of romantic and/or operatic subplots. The team does an excellent job of carrying the film itself. Stan & Ollie had been World War I buddies, except Stan did not come back from the front for twenty years—he was not even aware the war was over! When he does return, Ollie decides to take care of him for a while—a position Ollie's wife finds unacceptable. The domestic chaos that follows borrows heavily from the team's previously addressed short subject, *Unaccustomed As We Are* (McCarey story).

Block-Heads, released August 19, just days after the announcement of Laurel's 1938 firing, met with mixed reviews. No doubt Roach's favorite critique of the film came from the *New York Herald Tribune*. Its thumbs-up response credited *Block-Heads'* success to the genius of Harry Langdon, one of the five credited screenwriters.[164] Since Langdon had just been hired to replace Laurel, Roach's move, at least in *Herald Tribune* circles, smacked of brilliance—at least until the opening of the new duo's one-film career, *Zenobia*. The Irene Thirer *New York Post* review of *Block-Heads* (August 30, 1938) was more upfront about the change taking place—"We're sorry they're [Laurel & Hardy] washed up as a team—but welcome back to frozen-faced Harry Langdon . . . ''

Some of *Block-Heads'* initial positive press was probably assisted by way of its swan-song nature. Easily the most significant piece along these lines was done by filmmaker/critic Basil Wright in Britain's *The Spectator* (September 16, 1938), a critique that examined both Laurel & Hardy's career and the appropriateness of this film as a close to that career. Though more modest in scope, *New York Times* critic Frank S. Nugent was equally sympathetic.

Some things, of course, never change. Thus, once again *Variety* panned the effort, again finding it merely a short subject expanded too far. Just as consistently, *New York World-Telegram* critic William Boehnel heralded the film as one of the team's best. As a period side note, both *Variety* and the panning *New York Post* found *Block-Heads'* dark comedy scene, where Ollie mistakenly thinks Stan has lost a leg, one of the film's highlights. And indeed, though the routine is still considered controversial today by some, none of the reviews mentioned herein found fault with it.

Laurel & Hardy's other 1938 film, *Swiss Miss*, is much more uneven than *Block-Heads*, slowed by yet another romantic musical subplot. And besides Laurel's marital woes, he had been physically sick before and during the shooting. Moreover, Roach seemed to interfere more than usual on the production. No doubt this was as a result of Roach's special interest in comedic operettas and the fact that Laurel's personal life was racing towards chaos.

Yet, despite the film's shortcomings, this sometimes zany tale of two traveling mousetrap salesmen visiting Switzerland on business (who would not expect hordes of mice in the land of Swiss cheese?) has its moments. In fact, one of these moments has come to be canonized, appearing as it does in notable film critic James Agee's often anthologized 1949 essay, "Comedy's Greatest Era," which is the starting point for serious study of silent film comedy.[165]

The *Swiss Miss* scene in question finds Stan & Ollie attempting to navigate a narrow, jiggly Swiss Alps suspension bridge while carrying a piano and eventually meeting a gorilla. Though this thrill comedy bit was not actually from the silent film era, it is one of the few examples of visual humor during the sound era that Agee finds worthy of praise. As if a piano were a Laurel & Hardy talisman, especially a piano that needed to be carried, the suspension bridge scene naturally reminds one of the team's award-winning piano escapades in *The Music Box*. But there is a key difference between the two works that goes right to the heart of Laurel & Hardy.

As mentioned previously, the team is at its best when comically mixed in *believable* situations, such as the duo's task in *The Music Box*. But meeting a gorilla on a shaky footbridge in the Alps is not the most typical of encounters, especially when the team is also busy moving a piano. (A gorilla with an organ grinder is fleetingly seen early in the film.) Moreover, while not directly addressing story probability, Laurel & Hardy historian William K. Everson was bothered by the scene's lack of visual realism "due to over-obvious back pro jection and painted backdrops."[166] In contrast, *The Music Box* was shot on location.

Granted this inconsistency with the basic realistic humor precepts of McCarey and Laurel, one still must admit the gorilla-meeting scene does provoke surrealistic laughter. (Agee saw it as a comic "nightmare.") However, surrealism can be better incorporated into a realistic framework. For instance, Laurel & Hardy contemporary W. C. Fields also was often concerned about comic realism.[167] Yet, in a film like *Never Give a Sucker an Even Break* (1941), Fields is able to incorporate several surrealistic scenes. He does this by setting his film at the fictitious studio of Esoteric Pictures, Inc., where Fields is trying to sell a script to the always flighty Franklin Pangborn, who plays a producer. Periodic visualizing of Fields's in-story script, triggered by its being read aloud, creates a film within a film. It gives a qualified legitimacy to any flights of fantasy Fields wants to include in the interior film because it is merely the visualization of a *real* plot element—a script for sale. Thus, when Fields's bottle of alcohol falls from an in-flight airplane, he is able comically to dive out after it without a parachute and suffer no ill effects.

Fields's method here of giving legitimacy to such surrealistic scenes is not unlike the position taken by formalist film theorist Béla Balázs on abstract material. Balázs favored cinema abstractions *if* they were rooted in a story that explained why they were there. Thus, he probably would have accepted this scene of Fields's extreme dedication to the bottle, since this "flight" of fancy was realistically framed—a script being read aloud.

Again, this is not to say the Laurel & Hardy footbridge scene is without humor, but it would be more amusing if the gorilla had been better integrated. As in Fields's film, the comic consumption of alcohol is also a staple in Laurel & Hardy films; witness the delightfully drunken laughing scene in *Fra Diavolo* (see also *The Devil's Brother*) or the bootleg liquor mistaken for mountain well water in *Them Thar Hills*. Therefore, a humorously drunken hallucination or dream might have been a preferable way to include the gorilla scene. Indeed, the second-most written about scene in *Swiss Miss* concerns Laurel's comically ambitious conning of a keg of brandy from a St. Bernard rescue dog.

A hallucination or dream frame to the footbridge material would probably also quiet Everson's concerns about back projection and painted backdrops, since one does not expect precise realism in such a situation. Of course, the ideal incorporation of the surreal into a realistic story occurs when one's fantastic imagery is also real—though no doubt unusual. For example, Laurel & Hardy's surrealistically endless flight of stairs in *The Music Box* really does exist, despite resembling something one would seem more likely to encounter with Dorothy and the gang in Oz.

Coincidentally, at the time of *Swiss Miss's* release, the footbridge sequence generated a real behind-the-scenes controversy. Originally, Laurel had had the film include a bomb being planted in the piano, with detonation to be triggered by hitting a certain note. Consequently, an added bonus of Stan & Ollie's slapstick moving of the piano was to involve the comic tension of their *almost* striking the booby-trapped key.

To Laurel's external chagrin, however, Roach cut the bomb set-up, thus negating the comic motivation for the boys nearly hitting that "explosive" key. But as demonstrated by Agee's praise of the scene, it remains funny—drawing upon the basic comic awkwardness of the duo. More significantly, it underlines anew Laurel's interest in both dark humor and the realistic motivation of the most basic comic business. But as with some of Laurel's black comedy film conclusions, Roach saw fit to cut it. (Ironically, the deleted segment would have also better integrated the scene.)

Laurel & Hardy's next film to be released after *Block-Heads* was *The Flying Deuces* (1939). Done for independent producer Boris Morros, it was an especially memorable production for Hardy, because the film's script girl, Lucille Jones, later became his third wife. Paradoxically, she disliked him at first because she felt the comedian once seemed patronizing when she reminded him about an item of film continuity (making sure different shots of the same scene matched). Their romance started after Lucille fell and suffered a mild concussion on *The Flying Deuces* set. Ironically, this "moving picture" man apparently needed to see a stilled Lucille before he was taken by her beauty. But it took Hardy a while to win her over. She credited his conquest to his eyes: "the kindest, softest, most expressive eyes."[168] Their romance was no doubt assisted by Laurel & Hardy's active production schedule in 1939—productions on which Lucille continued to work. Besides *The Flying Deuces* there were *A Chump at Oxford* and *Saps at Sea*.

Saps at Sea finished shooting in early December 1939. Hardy and Lucille were engaged shortly before Christmas and were married in Las Vegas on March 7, 1940. It had been nearly three years (May 18, 1937) since Hardy had received his divorce from Myrtle. His long-term relationship (since the late 1920s) with sometimes mistress Viola Morse ended with his marriage to Lucille. Consistent with this was a Hardy who dropped the sidelife of playboy to become a gentleman farmer. This also closed a past contradiction in his actions. As once suggested by team author Leo Brooks, Hardy's southern gallantry towards women had him forever forbidding off-color jokes in their presence. Yet, he could still manage to have a mistress. (Morse attempted suicide but eventually learned to accept the action.)

The new couple had a small acreage in the San Fernando Valley. They kept a few animals but concentrated on raising fruit and vegetables—a pastime that World War II soon turned into an act of patriotism when citizens were encouraged to cultivate "Victory Gardens." Hardy had finally found the perfect non-screen marriage partner, and it was a happy union until the comedian's 1957 death.

Unfortunately, Lucille never became close to Hardy's family. The couple's relatively quick romance spelled *golddigger* to many of his relatives. More important, some family members knew and liked Hardy's longtime companion Viola Morse and her young son. Their one-time serious relationship had even involved the purchase of a house for Viola. To both friends and professional colleagues, the comedian and Viola had been a couple for some time. Finally, as the years passed, Hardy's family was less than happy that the comedian was revealing family secrets to Lucille. His background reminiscing often had been creative fiction, and even long after Hardy's death, when Lucille married an ex-newspaperman, the family was concerned that family skeletons might appear.

Hardy's marriage was not the only change taking place in 1940. In April Laurel & Hardy's 1939 concurrent but separate contracts with Roach ended, and the team forever broke with him. They had been planning this for some time. In fact, they had incorporated as "Laurel and Hardy Feature Productions" the previous October, intending to control totally their future comedies. Concurrent contracts and incorporation represented quite a change from the 1930s Hardy whom Roach would later characterize as knowing how to take orders. (Obviously, earlier Laurel-Roach confrontations might have turned out quite differently if Hardy had taken a less "company" line.)

Another change for the period was their involvement in stage work. Teamed for the movies, Laurel & Hardy had done little previous stage work together. While there had been some live entertaining (such as on their 1932 trip to Europe), the 1940s found them much more active on stage. This eventually reflected on first a declining film career and then a non-existent one. But Laurel & Hardy's initial 1940s salvo into stage work—a ten-week, twelve-city tour that began in late September 1940—came at a time when the team was still optimistic about their film future. And the tour gave them no reason to think otherwise. "The Laurel & Hardy Revue," a series of vaudeville sketches also featuring a cast of "Thirty Madcap Merrymakers," was a success. The culmination of this full-length show was the Laurel-written routine, "How to Get a Driver's License," which presented the boys as driving applicants.

Though there had been previous plans for the duo to do some stage work (quite possibly as a way to generate publicity for a now independent production team), the real catalyst for both the tour and the focus sketch was their performance of "How to Get a Driver's License" at an August 22, 1940, Red Cross benefit. The place was the Federal Plaza of San Francisco's Treasure Island. It was Red Cross Day at the fair, with funds going to the War Relief. Nearly 25,000 gathered for an eight o'clock show that also featured Charles Laughton giving Lincoln's "Gettysburg Address." (The actor had presented this previously and so movingly in the 1935 film *Ruggles of Red Gap*.)

As sadly befitted a War Relief program, the *San Francisco Examiner*'s August 23 Red Cross Day coverage appeared in a paper whose front-page headline read, "Nazi Raiders Bomb Heart of London." It must have been an emotional roller-coaster for Laurel—a well-received comedy sketch and a homeland under attack.

Still, the response to "How to Get a Driver's License" was just too good not to take it on the road. And the success of their end-of-the-year tour no doubt helped them secure a contract with 20th Century-Fox the following April (1941).

Hollywood columnist and team fan Louella Parsons also did some strong Fox lobbying on the duo's behalf.

Public homage and the potential attention of movie studios are heady narcotics. But no doubt an additional factor for Laurel & Hardy going on the road was ages old: they needed the money. Searching for a new studio, they were without a regular film income. And even after their 1941 signing with Fox, there were still financial woes. Two of their former wives (Lois and Myrtle) were making noises about back alimony, and both comedians (but especially Hardy) owed the government money for back taxes. In September 1941 the United States sued Hardy for $96,757 in back income taxes.[169] Coincidently, in November 1941 Laurel & Hardy played a tour of American Army bases in the Caribbean. And the duo started another national tour in January 1942. (The Hardy back taxes case would be in the courts for the next decade.)

Interestingly enough, Hardy's old gambling friend Chico Marx soon also found himself on the road (1942, fronting for a band, "Chico Marx and his Ravellies"—Ravelli having been his screen name in both *Animal Crackers*, 1930, and *The Big Store*, 1941). This was a result of the initial breakup of the Marx Brothers in 1941. But neither Laurel nor Hardy was ever in the seemingly ongoing, desperate financial straits in which Chico's gambling placed him. And with his third marriage, Hardy had largely curtailed his gambling.

For Laurel & Hardy there were several memorable events during early 1941. Laurel remarried Virginia Ruth in January, though they separated before the year was half over. In April Laurel & Hardy were guests of Mexico's president at a major film festival in Mexico City. Some Mexican film projects had been under consideration. But on April 23, an agreement was made between Laurel and Hardy Feature Productions and Fox. Exclusively handled by Laurel's friend and attorney but non-agent, Ben Shipman, the team ended up losing creative control instead of gaining it.

The team was now ready to begin the third and most frustrating period of its film career (1941–45, 1951). There were six 20th Century-Fox feature films: *Great Guns* (1941), *A-Haunting We Will Go* (1942), *Jitterbugs* (1943), *The Dancing Masters* (1943), *The Big Noise* (1944), and *The Bullfighters* (1945). In addition, there were two features for M-G-M: *Air Raid Wardens* (1943) and *Nothing But Trouble* (1944), the European production *Atoll K* (1951, released in the United States as *Utopia* in 1954), and a United States government-produced war effort short subject *The Tree in a Test Tube* (1943).

Disregarding the short subject, the general experience Laurel & Hardy had making these films is summed up in one of the titles—*Nothing But Trouble*. While there had at times been friction under Roach, he had given them a great deal of freedom for the most part, from improvising material to shooting stories in chronological order. At the larger and less-personalized 20th Century-Fox and M-G-M, hired hands Laurel & Hardy were not accorded such freedoms, and it shows.

Before addressing some reasons for this loss of control, one should at least note an ongoingly provocative view from Laurel & Hardy revisionist author Leo M. Brooks, Jr. (something which has also surfaced in our correspondence). He suggests 20th Century-Fox has been unduly criticized through the years by both the team and its fans. The studio at least provided cinema work for the team when Laurel & Hardy needed the money, and the duo was hardly being inundated with offers. Of course, the logical answer is the cliché, that "with [studio] friends like this, who needs enemies?" Still, as the following pages suggest, the blame for the poor quality of the final films has probably been overly one-sided.

Regardless of where the blame is placed, there are three key reasons for Laurel's loss of control. First and foremost, the major studios were unwilling to give him, or almost anyone, the nearly total control he wanted. It would have been difficult to negotiate successfully for such freedom, especially in what was still the caste-conscious studio era (1930–45, where everyone had *one* specific job, period). But even if that had not been true, Laurel's very messy personal life had to almost put the kibosh on any serious consideration of such freedom. Moreover, his personal liabilities were hardly ancient history; the most damaging items had recently been in the papers. This was not the way to instill confidence in the money men.

Second, like many creative people, Laurel was less than talented when it came to the business side of his art. This was compounded further when he left his new post-Roach career in the hands of his friend and lawyer Ben Shipman—a nice man but a poor negotiator (at least when he was asked to play agent). For that matter, Laurel was usually less than aggressive when he was in a "nego-tiating" position, whether with wives or with work.

Third, as with Laurel & Hardy's tour activities, these later films helped pay the bills. Indeed, if one did not know what a hopeless romantic Laurel was, one might hypothesize that his 1941 remarriage to Virginia Ruth was a business "proposition." Originally she had received an ongoingly generous divorce set-tlement, but besides alimony and the back taxes, Laurel seems to have been financially inundated with a truly eclectic assortment of bills since the late 1930s, from literally building high walls to his revolving-door court costs. And this says nothing of third wife Illeanna's talent for shopping (when she was not playing at being a real-life screwball heroine), nor does it address the fact that Laurel was always an easy monetary touch for down-on-their luck friends and colleagues.

Sadly, while the team should not be criticized for a studio's shortsightedness, the duo must take the blame both for accepting a restrictive contract and for continuing to make additional 20th Century-Fox films (their five-year 1941 pact called for one film, with merely an option for nine more). A brief 1950 London *Daily Express* interview contains a painfully pertinent revelation from Laurel: "Our last pictures there [Hollywood] were very bad. I knew the scripts were bad before we started. I told the producers. They agreed. But they made us go ahead."[170]

Though all the scripts were hardly done at the onset, the quote dramatically reveals how quickly the team realized their contract was a major mistake. Thus, as Randy Skretvedt suggests in his text on the duo, the fact that Laurel was less than active in the limited input he was given to the initial Fox scripts implies he accepted defeat from the beginning. Ironically, Hardy seems to have been much more involved at this time than his normally dominant behind-the-screen partner. Consequently, as once suggested by Brooks, the team's late films might better be described as Hardy & Laurel films, as the Ollie screen character grows in importance. Still, enough of the duo's old joint material is recycled in these late films to suggest they had more input than is often suggested. Part of the problem, however, probably fell in the time factor. Laurel & Hardy were re-cycling material earlier in their careers, but in the 1930s time was allocated for Laurel to develop creative twists to an old bit. Unfortunately, this 1930s norm became a 1940s luxury.

Possibly there were other mitigating circumstances. In this case, maybe Laurel & Hardy were not unlike their optimistic screen personae—somehow believing things had to improve, despite evidence to the contrary. And just because the studio said one thing, Hollywood was famous for crafty artists who somehow danced around restrictions. As an ironic example, Laurel & Hardy's old mentor McCarey was creating his most critically and commercially successful work at the same time the team was in decline. But even McCarey had to wheel and deal. Bing Crosby and director David Butler observed:

The story he [Leo McCarey] told the studio heads [Paramount] for *Going My Way* [1944] bore no resemblance whatever to the story he finally shot. But he made the tale so absorbing that they had to go for it . . . The production department always demanded 20 or 30 written pages in advance of shooting. So Leo would dictate reams of stuff which he had no intention of using.[171]

Creative subterfuge was not unheard of in Hollywood. Granted, McCarey was in a better position at the time than Laurel & Hardy. Still, in all fairness to the team, one has to assume they had hoped to work around such restrictions. Not surprisingly, it has also been suggested by a then coworker that the team was just too polite about rocking the boat (see n. 173).

The issue of what to do was possibly clouded all the more by the reception of their first Fox film, *Great Guns* (1941). Though decidedly inferior to most of their earlier features, this tale of Stan & Ollie's entry into the army held its own critically and commercially. It did especially well in Great Britain, a nation already involved in World War II.

Billed as the team's "return" to the screen (they had been gone for over a year and a half), this respectably mixed reception for a mediocre film was possibly the result of the traditional glad-to-have-you-back syndrome. Moreover, while *Great Guns* was obviously inspired by Abbott & Costello's first starring film, the immensely popular service comedy *Buck Privates* (1941), America's ongoing preparation for war still made the Laurel & Hardy film timely. And it was not as if *Buck Privates* was the start of a new comedy subgenre. Chaplin had created a classic example of the form in 1917—*Shoulder Arms*. Indeed, Lou Costello's amusing attempts to both march and shoulder a rifle seemed to borrow more than a little from Chaplin's film. Consequently, there is nothing wrong with putting the boys in uniform. Abbott & Costello almost made a minor career of 1940s service comedies, as would Martin & Lewis in the 1950s. And for that matter, Stan & Ollie had frequently appeared in military uniform, such as: *With Love and Hisses* (1927), *Two Tars* (1928), *Men O'War* (1929), *Beau Hunks* (1931), *Pack Up Your Troubles* (1932), *Bonnie Scotland*, (1935), *Block-Heads* (1938), and *The Flying Deuces* (1939).

A service setting is ideal for a comedy team because it provides legitimate reasons for both their close camaraderie and an overly structured setting comically ripe for the traditional misfits. Moreover, there is a natural nemesis in the sergeant (or comparable authority figure), while the men in rank offer a valid pool for any necessary comic oddball additions.

Unfortunately, *Great Guns* was not an ideal setting for Laurel & Hardy. Paradoxically, the film suffered not because it was inspired by Abbott & Costello's *Buck Privates* but rather because it attempted at times to make Laurel & Hardy *into* Abbott & Costello. That is, Abbott & Costello were representative of the new 1940s breed of personality comedians who could fluctuate between incompetent, comic antiheroes and cool, egotistical wise guys with the fast, smart crack. Abbott & Costello, and later Martin & Lewis, operated on this antihero/wiseguy equation. (Interestingly enough, even Lewis's greatest solo work, *The Nutty Professor*, 1963, finds him playing the same antihero/wiseguy duality, a duality often compared to the makeup of the Martin & Lewis team: Lewis plays both an absent-minded professor and a wise-mouthed crooner.)

During the 1940s and 1950s, however, the unquestionable master of combining the antihero/wiseguy formula was Bob Hope, from the Road pictures (opposite Bing Crosby), to such diverse solo outings as his attempt to be a film noir detective in *My Favorite Brunette* (1947), or the Damon Runyon title character in *The Lemon Drop Kid* (1951). Indeed, Hope could sometimes even sandwich the antihero/wiseguy dichotomy into the same verbal pattern. For example, as the baby photographer playing at being a detective in *My Favorite Brunette* he observes in a tough guy voice: ''You see, I wanted to be a detective, too. It only took brains, courage, and a gun. And I had the gun.''

Hope's comic duality compliments modern humor's fascination with the schizophrenic. In fact, Woody Allen, today's greatest film comedian and most self-consciously shrink oriented, often follows the same antihero to wiseguy and back pattern. In *Play It Again, Sam* (1972), Allen bounces frantically between being a Bogart clone and the shlemiel of the week. Allen, an admitted Hope disciple, at times even sounds like Hope. Fittingly, for this examination of an attempted Stan & Ollie change, the Hope service comedy *Caught in the Draft* also appeared in 1941, prior to *Great Guns*, though still not before *Buck Privates*.

While the antihero/wiseguy formula is an interesting and entertaining development in American humor, it does not apply to Laurel & Hardy. They are firmly based in the frustrations of the antihero. Though Oliver tends to be the more dominating, it is not along wiseguy lines. Stan & Ollie's relationship is an ongoing showcase of affection. Moreover, the duo are generally quite polite when they interact with other characters, barring those tit-for-tat escapades when Stan & Ollie have been justifiably provoked. (And even here their shared comic violence also makes them victims, such as the loss of their car and Christmas tree in *Big Business*.) Their more typical politeness is especially true of southern-born Hardy's screen persona, who is very effective at calling up a generously broad helping of this region's courtliness. Thus, it is particularly grating to have the team periodically slip into wiseguy patter during *Great Guns*. For instance, they are accidently responsible for their sergeant's lighting a pipe full of tobacco and gunpowder. It explodes off-screen and he returns to the barracks with a powder-blackened face to confront the boys. Yet, their wiseguy remarks are hardly what one expects of Stan & Ollie:

Stan: "Look, they've assigned us a porter."

Ollie: "You may start over here, my good man. And you may have Thursdays off."

Stan: "Twice a week." (The sergeant is so angry he is literally sputtering.)

Ollie: "Why, it sounds like Sergeant Hippo."

Stan: "It sure does."

Ollie: "In camouflage." (At this point a lieutenant enters and orders the sergeant to clean up. Both exit.)

Stan: "Did you get a load of the big noise [the sergeant]? Old Black Joe." (Laughter by the duo divides Stan's comments and follows them.)

Other than Stan's "Twice a week" comment concerning the number of Thursdays in a week (which is faithful to his less-than-Albert-Einstein image), these wiseguy cracks are far from consistent with the long-established comedy personae of Laurel & Hardy. And what makes the incongruity more problematic is that *Great Guns* also offers scenes of the duo in their traditional antiheroic character. Even the wiseguy material begins with them initially cowering at the return of the sergeant—hardly a fitting foundation for the cracks that follow. While the juggling of the antiheroic/wiseguy persona worked for the 1940s new breed of comedian (like Hope or Abbott & Costello), it so misfires with Laurel & Hardy that one could believe the *Great Guns* screenwriter's only master plan was to be as eclectically funny as possible.

Sadly, comedy values seem to have been compromised. In an earlier (1935) interview with the English publication *Film Weekly*, Laurel had observed: "Laurel and Hardy must never be 'wise guys.' They may only keep on thinking they are and act accordingly. They must never be 'fresh' or resourceful; they must be just plain dumb." Ironically, later in the 1935 interview Laurel added that if a different style of screen comedy became the norm the team would retire: "Laurel and Hardy cannot change, so when the time arrives I shall be ready either to retire or to take up screen writing, directing, or producing."[172] (The interview also finds Laurel reiterating at length on the importance of realism in their comedy.)

Also questionable is the near close of this focus scene from *Great Guns*, where the arrival of the lieutenant accidently rescues the team from the sergeant's wrath. Such an easy victory for the boys, with the sergeant playing the complete fool, is hardly a signature statement for two antiheroic legends. Generally, even the team's rare past victories are comically qualified. For example, despite the conclusion of *Big Business*, in which Laurel & Hardy regular James Finlayson had received an exploding cigar from Stan, the boys have no time to savor the event because they are being hotly pursued by the police.

Unfortunately, the majority of Laurel & Hardy's post-1940 films are fatally flawed along these or similar lines. The exception is the team's 1943 *Jitterbugs*, in which Stan & Ollie help con a huckster who has bilked the heroine's mother out of $10,000. Team biographer Everson is the strongest supporter of *Jitterbugs* as unquestionably the best of their final films. Seeing their other 1940s films as an entertainment desert, he likens *Jitterbugs* to an "oasis." Though many book-length Laurel & Hardy studies (such as Randy Skretvedt's volume) are not entranced with the movie, it is often an undeniably funny film.

At its start *Jitterbugs* does not, however, seem so promising. Ollie is unreasonably gruff with Stan after they run out of gas in the desert. And their early dialogue suggests that the patently asexual Stan is now quite the ladies' man, or at least he tries to be. (This is especially ironic since the film later boasts an attempted seduction of Stan where he is his traditional asexual comic self.) In addition, the duo seem unlikely candidates to be operating a two-man mechanized jitterbug band, their occupation when the film opens. Of course, it allows the team to cash in on the then-current music craze as well as providing a modicum of credibility for the film's title. The qualifying "modicum" appears because the meandering plot soon puts their musical career behind them. However, some period critics were upset with what they took to be a misnomer of a title. (Reviews in *Variety* and *The New York Post* were more bothered than most.) Coincidently, one of the film's few favorable critiques, Bosley Crowther's *New York Times* piece on January 5, 1943, uses the question of the title's appropriateness as a metaphor closing defense of those who find fault with every little thing: "Why do they call it *Jitterbugs*? Say, who let that radical in?" (As a side note, a rare then contemporary appreciation of *Jitterbugs*' unique future status among the late Laurel & Hardy films occurs in Rose Pelswick's *New York Journal-American*, June 5, 1943, review: "Quite an improvement over the previous L & H items [films].")

Regardless, things are much more amusing when the film moves from music to their good deed flim-flam, leaving behind Stan & Ollie's "hep cat" jitterbug ties. And the comic beauty of this finagling is that it necessitates the boys' each playing a different comedy character. Oliver is the ultimate southern-fried colonel, the drippingly gracious and romantic Colonel Bixby. And Stan is comically inspired as the golden-aged eccentric Aunt Emily, whether in a nose-blowing exercise that causes her earrings to fly off in opposite directions or *her* commentary on drinking: "I'm one of those nip and tuck drinkers, one nip and they tuck me away for the night." On occasion Aunt Emily also punctuated her lines with a delightfully comic high-pitched laugh.

Laurel & Hardy purists, however, sometimes bemoan *Jitterbugs'* absence of the more-standard Stan & Ollie comedy shtick. There are three ready defenses for this. First, the team's character departures here are hardly extreme. Stan frequently had played comic antiheroes in drag before, while a romantic and/or southern politeness was forever near the surface in Ollie. Paradoxically, for the time (1940s), one might even prefer Laurel's Aunt Emily to his traditional Stan. Inasmuch as Laurel is showing his age, which hardly goes with the Stan persona (founded on youth, with a baby-like naivete), the added years are perfectly fitting for Laurel's little old Aunt Emily.

A second justification for these acceptably mild departures is that even when Laurel & Hardy's old shtick was repeated during the 1940s (former routines recycled), they did not always play as successfully. A good part of this can be blamed upon a studio that did not fully appreciate the team's classic past material, and thus did not adequately take advantage of it (such as not allowing Laurel to help edit). But other factors tied in—Stan's aging comedy mask could sometimes kill the most promising of humorous situations. (Unfortunately, 20th Century Fox accented the team's age when it changed their make-up from a subdued clown white to a more realistic look. For once, realism was not a Laurel & Hardy plus.) And the men behind the masks were quite possibly slowing down themselves. For instance, their *Great Guns* cameraman Glen MacWilliams, a close friend of Hardy's who owed his position to the comedian, later observed the team would have had more control at Fox if they had simply made some demands.[173]

The third defense for Stan & Ollie's modest character departures in *Jitterbugs* is the most basic in comedy—the new characterizations are very funny. While this is not a justification for anything in the name of humor (especially if it is inconsistent with a comedian's persona), the links between Stan & Ollie and Aunt Emily and Colonel Bixby are sufficient enough for one to appreciate fully the laughter without qualifying it as a guilty pleasure.

Regardless, how did *Jitterbugs* become Laurel & Hardy's desert "oasis"? Like most questions, more than one answer can apply. The most frequently cited is that Fox provided better production values (more-impressive sets and cinematography) because it was grooming the film's heroine (Vivian Blaine) for stardom. Now, while there is no arguing the improved production values, some differences still remain as to why they were forthcoming.

That studio interest in Vivian Blaine was a factor cannot be denied. Indeed, Laurel later referred to Blaine as a classic example of how Fox would drop a

Stan showing his age as early as 1937—a nonretouched publicity still from *Way Out West*

novice on the veteran team and expect them to also act as performance instructors. But a sometimes noted alternative reason for the studio's added attention to *Jitterbugs* is credited to the phenomenal success of the boys' frequent early 1940s touring. This also has to be a component in increasing Fox's interest. But when one closely examines the team's professional activities during this time, the equation "tour success equals studio attention" is not quite so obvious. That is, their second 1940s tour (January and February of 1942) was very successful. For example, *Billboard* magazine observed on February 7, 1942, that in Dayton, Ohio, "Laurel and Hardy, headlining the Colonial's [theatre] stageshow . . . established a new week-end record for the house . . . better than the house has done for weeks."[174] Earlier in the tour the duo had been the top draw in Chicago, appearing at the Oriental theatre in a five-act vaudeville bill supported by a film feature. As if speaking directly to Hollywood, another *Billboard* article on Laurel & Hardy's "live" box office strength observed: "A stronger picture [at Chicago's Oriental], or one featuring the comedy pair, could top this [already high] gross."[175]

Despite this successful tour, their next Fox film (which began shooting in mid-March 1942, was the weak *A-Haunting We Will Go*, not the new and improved *Jitterbugs*. And even *A-Haunting* was followed by something else—the mediocre M-G-M production *Air Raid Wardens*. (Their Fox contract allowed the team to make films for other studios.) But in fairness to the hypothesis that the tour made a difference, *A-Haunting* shooting began so soon after their hit January and February 1942 tour that possibly not that much could be changed on the production. Moreover, while *Air Raid Wardens* was not up to Laurel & Hardy's former standards, M-G-M put forward much more effort to succeed than Fox had thus far. For example, *Air Raid Wardens* boasted such former Roach/Laurel & Hardy alumni as slow-burn comedian Edgar Kennedy, writer Charley Rogers, and cinematographer Walter Lundin. (The mere fact they were being loaned to a major studio has to also be seen as a plus.)

Notwithstanding that possibly these renewals of professional ties were facilitated by M-G-M being Roach's old distributing studio umbrella, another briefer, hit tour (for the war effort) prior to shooting *Air Raid Wardens* might also be credited with increasing M-G-M's attention. Certainly, it was a special topping to Laurel & Hardy's early 1940s stage work.

This mini-tour in length (three weeks, spring 1942) was anything but mini in scope. Called the *Hollywood Victory Caravan*, it was a broad cross section of filmland talent squeezed into a ten-car train canvassing America for Army and Navy relief. Film director Mark Sandrich staged and directed a three-hour show. Bob Hope was emcee, with a regular Noah's Ark of talent, from Gary Grant and James Cagney to Claudette Colbert and Olivia DeHavilland. The goal was to raise $750,000 by entertaining patriotic Americans of thirteen pivotal coast-to-coast cities (Washington, Boston, Philadelphia, Cleveland, Detroit, Chicago, St. Louis, St. Paul, Minneapolis, Des Moines, Dallas, Houston, and San Francisco).

Although it was difficult for anyone to top Bob Hope's energetic talent, especially as the emcee, Laurel & Hardy emerged as the audience favorite. Cagney later said they "stole the show." Their success had a three-part foundation. First, they had established unusually strong film personae (see also Chapter 2). While most in the Caravan talent were known for an assortment of screen characters, Laurel & Hardy forever played Stan & Ollie. Moreover, the identification factor was underlined further by way of the duo's film use of their own names. Interestingly enough, *Newsweek*'s May 11, 1942 coverage of the *Victory Caravan* finds Laurel & Hardy as two of a mere handful of stars pictured.[176]

Second, the very nature of many Laurel & Hardy films—loose plotlines more often peppered with skits than stories—were tailor-made for a show composed of entertainment snippets. Third, although a number of the Caravan troupe had had previous stage experience, few were quite so steeped in the tradition as Laurel, not to mention his still-active involvement in touring. In truth, Laurel & Hardy's recently past concert dates had given them a two-year warm-up for the *Caravan*. Moreover, the duo were just plain good at pressing the flesh— they could easily and pleasantly interact with the public. For example, earlier in 1942 when the team was still on its own tour a *Billboard* author observed: "Generous participation in parties and appearances outside the theatre made them [Laurel & Hardy] a host of friends and helped to up the box office."[177] Of course, during Laurel's later retirement years he became doubly famous for his painstaking attempts to answer all his fan mail and to make himself easily accessible to the public.

Undeniably, when one keeps pace with and outshines some of Hollywood's biggest stars, more than a few film people take notice. Thus, if Laurel & Hardy's early 1940s stage work eventually helped them midway in their last period of sustained filmmaking (as it seems to have done), a special citation should be given to their involvement in the *Caravan*. Thus, any increased efforts by Fox to make *Jitterbugs* work should probably be credited to *both* the studio's desire to promote Vivian Blaine into another Betty Grable and the impressive "live" tour popularity of Laurel & Hardy.

Naturally, one would also like to credit part of *Jitterbugs*' improved entertainment values to an added spark from its comedy team. And if studio awareness increased by way of their successful touring, it would only be logical that the duo would equally feel better about themselves. Regardless, a brief reference in the February 22, 1943 *Newsweek* documented another reason for optimism: "Laurel and Hardy, encouraged by Abbott and Costello's phenomenal success, will attempt a comeback in Twentieth Century-Fox's 'Jitterbug [sic].' "[178] Though brief, the quote reveals much about the situation.

First, since *Jitterbugs* had only been in production a week when this item appeared, it is reasonable to assume there was general optimism going into the project. This is opposed to the confident filmmaker who is upbeat because he both likes the project and already has it in the can (finished). Second, the fact that the film Laurel & Hardy initially saw as a "comeback" did indeed become the greatest of their final vehicles suggests some extra effort on their parts and/ or the studio's. Third, having Laurel & Hardy couch their future aspirations in an Abbott & Costello framework demonstrates nicely just how giant a shadow this new team cast in the early 1940s. Of course, Laurel & Hardy had been indirectly acknowledging this Abbott & Costello connection for the past two years, from *Great Guns* (appearing after *Buck Privates*) to *A-Haunting We Will Go* (following Abbott & Costello's *Hold That Ghost*, 1941). These links between teams, however, did go both ways; Lou Costello seems to have borrowed some of his screen persona's characteristics from Stan & Ollie. Costello's use of Stan's patented cry and blink of the eyes, as well as Ollie's bashful tie-twiddling (which Costello did entirely with his fingers), bothered Laurel more than a little.[179] Still, Abbott & Costello's faster-paced antihero/wiseguy formula had no one confusing the duo with Laurel & Hardy. (Moreover, a younger Laurel had also done some borrowing, such as from Dan Leno.)

Another potential reason behind the unique status of *Jitterbugs* is that Malcolm St. Clair directed and cowrote the original story (with Scott Darling). St. Clair, a former newspaper cartoonist, received his start in films from Mack Sennett early in the silent era. During the 1920s he had demonstrated great comedy range, from co-scripting and co-directing two Buster Keaton short subjects (*The Goat*, 1921, and *The Blacksmith*, 1922) to directing the social comedy *Are Parents People?* (1925) and other Ernst Lubitsch-like films (with whom he was also compared). Inexplicably, his work had gone into great decline during the sound era. Here was a silent comedy kindred spirit for Laurel & Hardy, and someone who had also known artistically better days. Not surprisingly, St. Clair and the team had excellent rapport. Most important, he allowed more of Laurel & Hardy's gift for improvisation to surface.

Unfortunately, their films after *Jitterbugs* do not measure up to this 1943 production. However, there seems to be less of a tendency in them for Laurel & Hardy to do the uncharacteristic thing, such as the previously highlighted wiseguy patter directed at their sergeant in *Great Guns*. This was possibly a result of St. Clair's ongoing presence as a director in their remaining Fox films. Still, limited improvisational freedom was not enough to salvage creatively big studio on-a-deadline productions already encumbered with mediocre scripts.

The entertaining *Jitterbugs* surprise was not repeated in their remaining films, though there were occasional moments of former comedy grace. For example, early in *The Bullfighters*, when it appears that private detectives Stan & Ollie are going to be giving the audience a film noir parody, they corner their suspect in a Mexico City bar. As is appropriate for a genre known for its femmes fatale, their prey is a sexy, hard-as-nails blonde comically known as Larceny Nell but also passing as Hattie Blake (Carol Andrews). She outwits them (the standard film noir game plan) in an inspired bar scene tit-for-tat with eggs.

The comic confrontation works *not* for the reason that the audience is merely feeling nostalgic for *anything* remotely resembling Laurel & Hardy's glory days; an earlier tit-for-tat in the film utilizing their hotel lobby fountain (lots of water!)

falls flat. In contrast, their tit-for-tat run-in with Nell (drawn from *Hollywood Party*, 1934), contains a certain sexually comic tension—perfectly fitting for a film noir parody. Such winning moments make the post-Roach 1940s films all the more frustrating—encouraging the viewer to ponder that age-old question: "What if?"

Making *The Bullfighters* completed their Fox contract, though the studio would have renewed it. To their credit, Laurel & Hardy declined on aesthetic grounds, being far from happy with their late films. But flawed as it was, *The Bullfighters* (with only rare flashes of their former comedy greatness) would have been a much better team swan song than their early 1950s French-Italian co-production *Atoll K*, known in Britain as *Robinson Crusoeland* and as *Utopia* in the United States. This unfortunate film is a very sad conclusion to their joint film career and will be expanded upon shortly.

Professionally, their biggest noise as a team between leaving Fox and the protracted 1950–51 production of *Utopia* was their very successful, nearly year-long (1947) tour of Europe, including a royal command performance on November 3d at the Palladium Theatre. The team headed the list of American performers chosen. The tour had been sparked by a very popular Laurel & Hardy film festival in 1946 London, though their trip had originally included only a few British bookings. Indeed, when the team left the United States in February 1947, *Newsweek* credited their exit to a British musical film production of *Robin Hood*. But while the film never materialized, the tour grew and grew.

Dusting off their "drivers' license" skit, the Laurels and Hardy (Lucille joined the tour later) sailed February 5, 1947, for Europe on the Queen Mary. They docked at Southampton, and the February 10th London *Evening News* coverage opened with a focus on Hardy's weight, including the comedian's own comic observation that he stood in the center of the deck "so that she [the Queen Mary] would not list."[180] Thus, while personally bothered by his weight, Hardy did not avoid the subject professionally when it meant publicity. Indeed, the London *Daily Star* was also taken with his weight (which had increased since the 1932 visit). Their February 12 piece (on the team's London arrival) opened with a look at Hardy's size. They were especially conscious of the wide snake-skin belt and silver buckle that somehow contained his "shop front" stomach. The article was equally fascinated with the laughter-activated movement of his stomach, the red nose, and a second chin much larger than the first. When asked about his eating habits, certainly a question to bother any weight-conscious person, Hardy demonstrated his comedy skills at covering up. Claiming fat was natural for him, he observed, "I've only got to walk past a glass of whiskey and I put on six pounds."[181]

Hardy was being modest about his eating habits. In Chapter 3, the reprinted article "Those Two Goofy Guys" (1930) finds the big comedian treating laryngitis by mixing chocolate ice cream and "rich yellow blobs of cream." And the Chapter 4 critique of Jerry Wilson's "Return of Babe's Night Out" (reminiscences about the mid-1940s Hardy) describes one of the comedian's suppers:

"a 32-ounce New York [steak], medium well, with one dozen new potatoes deep fried in pure ham fat with salad and coffee." (It was an eating habit befitting Hardy's team name among Europe's Germans: "*Dick* & Doof," translating "*Fat* & Stupid"—italics are mine.)

Before opening in London, the duo had warmup dates in Newcastle and Birmingham. The time was also used in gathering possible English background for some of their gags. But as a later affectionate London *Daily Mail* review (March 11) frequently reiterated, the stage team was really more like their films than the films themselves. Fittingly, the critique was entitled "L & H: Just Like a Film."

Team aficionado Laurence Reardon compiled a brief monograph, "Laurel & Hardy in Coventry," which provides a personal slant on the 1947 and 1952 tours by way of the duo's stops in the city of Lady Godiva. Reardon comically informs the reader that ten acts had to be endured before the team appeared. Their 1947 program billing was "Hollywood's Greatest Comedy Couple," with warmup acts like "Australia's Queen of the Air" and "Scotland's Ace accordionists." The booklet is at its best when it chronicles, by way of the numerous witnesses to the tours, what a memorable impact a brief but live Laurel & Hardy contact could have on people. Most amusing were the two teenaged girls who could hardly contain their laughter. Their comedy contortions proved equally amusing to the two women seated behind them . . . two women who turned out to be Laurel & Hardy's wives. Naturally, a meeting with the duo was arranged, at which time the comedy heroes were equally impressive as down-to-earth people.

Earning £1,000 per week, they were royally received throughout England and on the continent. This contrast with the ho-hum attitude of the United States was later more extremely replicated by Stan Laurel disciple Jerry Lewis, who generates such homage in France. In either case, there has often been a tendency in the United States to stamp the duo and Lewis with the label, "For Children Only."

Appropriately, one of the best interviews ever given by the team (primarily Laurel) occurred during their six-week engagement at Paris's Lido nightclub in late 1947. Entitled "têt-à-tête avec deux têtes de pioche," it appeared in the November 25, 1947 issue of *L'Ecran Francais*. This sadly neglected interview is an eye opener, if one can locate a hard-to-find copy. (See Chapter 4's bibliographical essay.) Even before the dialogue begins, there are fascinating background notes on things that were not to be. The team had plans to take their successful tour to South Africa and Australia. Moreover, four Laurel & Hardy films were allegedly to be shot in Europe during the course of the next year—one each in France (for Pathé), England (for producer Alexander Korda), Italy, and Denmark. Of course, the only film to surface from these plans was the regrettable *Atoll K*.

As if to forever play second fiddle to Chaplin, the first question concerned the Karno days of Laurel and his famous former roommate. On their initial visit to the states did Chaplin really tell the New York skyline he would conquer the United States? Laurel couples his "yes" with a reenactment that has an interesting variation from the traditional telling of this famous story. In this French version Laurel has Chaplin's seemingly brash prediction being broadcast with the comedian self-consciously assuming a Napoleonic pose, which entirely changes the mood from youthful boastfulness to tongue-in-cheek kidding.

Laurel, pleased with his acting explanation, unleashes his hysterical, high-pitched laugh so identified with his screen character. It is one some reviewers, including this French one (normally full of superlatives), find disturbing. As if cognizant of the fact, Laurel abruptly shuts the laugh off.

The topic is soon the team's late friend, Harry Langdon (who died in 1944). Laurel observes there were no hard feelings when Langdon had temporarily replaced him. (In fact, Langdon's first biographer, William Schelly, later revealed that the comedian actually asked Laurel's permission.)

Laurel describes Langdon as a very unhappy man the final fifteen years of his life—a period that roughly correlates to the period of time after Langdon's fall from the pantheon of silent comedians. Laurel magnanimously observes that being replaced by Langdon allowed his friend a second chance with the public. (Again, this is consistent with Langdon's hoped-for outcome of the switch.)

Interestingly enough, however, Laurel suggests the team's frequent hiring of Langdon as a scriptwriter was an act of pity. They wanted both to alleviate his misery and to help him earn a living. There is no mention of all the Langdon material that surfaces in *Block-Heads* (examined earlier in this chapter).

Regardless, Laurel becomes impassioned over Langdon's tragically wasted career—ultimately labeling Hollywood the world's cruelest city. As Laurel continues to rail against the film capital and its what-have-you-done-for-me-lately philosophy, an intriguing transition takes place. While presumably still addressing Langdon's sad fate, Laurel's comments apply equally to Hollywood's 1940s misuse and eventual abandonment of Laurel & Hardy. Laurel, known for his rapid mood changes, breaks down—holding his head in his hands. He goes from laughter to despair in short duration.

Later, on a lighter note, Laurel provides a delightful answer to a question concerning the leisure-time moviegoing habits of the duo. Drawing an analogy to a mailman (whom Laurel also imitates), the comedian suggests that just like the person who stays home after delivering mail all week, film comedians like a periodic break from the movies, too. Again, Laurel erupts in a high-pitched laughter which, according to the interviewer, has a false jolliness to it.

Without examining every detail of the interview, two final points merit inclusion. First, Laurel states he was the director on all their team films, regardless of the credits. And though this is sometimes implied by former colleagues in the post-McCarey period, the sudden baldness with which Laurel makes the claim is not typical of the comedian (though his interviews abroad tend to be provocatively informative.) The second item concerns their present French engagement. Evidently, the interview has run right up until their showtime (one of two a day). And though Laurel is pleased with their Parisian reception, he confesses a regret: the comedian wishes he spoke French, because he fears the public does not always understand the gags. And he would like to make them laugh more. (But because of the natural nightclub disruptions, especially the noise, the team declined similar bookings in the future.)

Besides their Paris engagement, and those in England, their first post–World War II tour included stops in Belgium, Sweden, and Denmark (which possibly explains talk of a Danish Laurel & Hardy film). Plus, they returned to both London for the royal command performance and to Copenhagen for a radio performance. The team's American homecoming did not occur until January 1948. What had begun as a six-week tour had stretched to eleven months!

Hardy also demonstrated his versatility by doing some solo work (at Laurel's insistence) in two major films. First, he provided strong comic support for John Wayne in *The Fighting Kentuckian* (1949). (This was an outgrowth of both Hardy and Wayne appearing together in a charity stage production of *What Price Glory?*) And in Frank Capra's *Riding High* (1950), Hardy had a funny cameo as a betting man at the horse track. Given Hardy's real-life fascination with track betting, this amounted to a Hollywood in-joke, especially since *Riding High* starred Bing Crosby, a friend with whom the comedian and others founded southern California's Del Mar Race Track (1937).

On a personal level, the second half of the 1940s were fairly subdued for the duo. Laurel would, however, log one last divorce (1946), again from Virginia Ruth. Laurel watchers were probably even concerned about a pattern that seemed to be reappearing. Laurel married another Russian singer, Ida Kitaeva Raphael, shortly after the divorce, just as he had married the screwball Russian singer Illeanna after his previous Virginia Ruth divorce. And the comedian even married Ida in Yuma, Arizona, where he had gone through two previous ceremonies with Illeanna. But just as the equally eccentric Virginia Ruth did *not* comically haunt this new marriage, the union of Laurel and Ida did not end up in the funny papers. The stable relationship lasted until the comedian's 1965 death. (Team lawyer and friend Ben Shipman, who was much better at handling alimony claims than movie contracts, credited Laurel's revolving door relationship with Ruth giving him a: "permanent case of the triple conniption fits." But Ida did rescue Laurel.)

If a caption were required of this final happy romantic development for an individual who previously had forever worn his heart on his sleeve, one would be tempted to recycle the Peter Bogdanovich title *At Long Last Love* (1975) or possibly Billy Wilder's *Love in the Afternoon* (1957). Paradoxically, while it could not be known at the time, Laurel had again followed the lead of his influential early touring roommate—Charlie Chaplin. The creator of The Tramp had also found a successful permanent relationship with his 1943 marriage to Oona O'Neill. (Interestingly enough, it was the fourth woman each comedian had married, though Chaplin had had no multiple ceremonies with any of his wives.)

Why did this Laurel marriage work, and not the others? Going beyond love and the comedian's standard romantic weaknesses (Ida was a blonde with a European accent), there would seem to have been more of a commitment by both parties. In point of fact, Ida (also an actress who had had minor parts in two Preston Sturges films) told reporters after the ceremony that there would be no more Laurel divorces.

More significantly, Laurel's career was no longer a dominating factor. Granted, there would be numerous projects, such as tours, the unfortunate *Utopia*, and plans that never reached fruition (such as *Robin Hood*). And even after Hardy's death Laurel periodically recorded, by force of habit, potential Stan & Ollie material. But regardless, things had slowed down for Laurel professionally, especially since the team's ethical stand on making quality films (where they had control) had led to no films. Adding to this unwanted slowdown was the late-1940s diagnosis that the comedian was diabetic. The year 1949 would represent one long recovery period for Laurel—appropriately paralleling, in part, the solo work of Hardy. Thus, besides this final Laurel marriage no doubt being a loving one, there was also a need on Laurel's part (more than ever before) for someone to be there.

Hardy remained happily married to the team's former script girl Lucille. Possibly this stability also helped inspire the permanence of the final Laurel marriage. The Hardy union also lasted until that comedian's death in 1957. A January 1946 attempt by Hardy's second wife Myrtle to obtain more alimony (a continuing obsession with her) encouraged, however, at least one major paper to rehash the marital hard times of both Laurel & Hardy.[182] Still, the fact that gossipy material related to the team was now becoming more dependent upon recycled scandal was a moral victory all by itself.

In 1950 Laurel & Hardy began production on a film whose eventual American title now seems a bad joke: *Utopia*. The title is used in reference to the Pacific atoll on which Laurel & Hardy find themselves stranded, and how the now Robinson Crusoe-like duo attempt to establish an ideal country (Crusoeland), even after uranium is discovered and the atoll is inundated by fortune hunters. And just as this failed comedy presented the futility of founding an ideal republic among an international collection of characters (the opportunists), the French-Italian co-production of the film demonstrated the same principle in real life.

Three languages were spoken *and* misunderstood on the set, causing countless production delays and ongoing confusion. Naturally, construction of a script had been even more problematic. Laurel later observed, with only slight exaggeration, "There were two French writers and two Italian writers, and we took along a couple of American writers. [U.S. help was actually brought in later.] Nobody could speak anyone's language, so we got three interpreters, but all they could interpret was 'yes' and 'no.' "[183]

The script continued to be a problem during production. Co-director Leo Joannon (also credited with the story idea for the script) was egotistically difficult. This was even reflected in a stereotypical directing costume of old, which included riding breeches, pith helmet, and various-sized megaphones for different types of scenes. He might have just stepped from a Hollywood time capsule. Laurel found this apprentice Cecil B. DeMille more amusing than the film, though he forever qualified the remark by ironically adding it was hardly a difficult task.[184] Rare were the examples of any production organization. Indeed, the weather also managed to be unbearably hot during the production. A more comic movie might have been made by simply filming the filming.

In addition, as if Thalia, the muse of comedy, were even out to derail the film, both comedians suffered ill health during production—especially Laurel, who underwent prostate surgery before the completion of the movie. He later rued the dedicated persistence that somehow got him through the seemingly endless shooting. What was to have been a three-month production stretched into a year!

The film's ultimate liability, however, is the appalling appearance of both comedians. Stan is the most shocking. His deeply lined face and emaciated body (dysentery contributed to a fifty-pound weight loss during production) would have killed the humor in even more promising material. His childlike persona is nowhere to be seen, having been replaced by a deathly fragile old man inappropriate for laughter. In contrast, Oliver looks as if he has swallowed Stan's lost fifty pounds plus fifty more. While there was a discernible weight gain during the 1940s films, by the time of this last production Ollie had reached less-than-amusing obese proportions. As with Stan, this appearance discouraged laughter and left the viewer almost questioning whether this was an old cinema friend or some mediocre imitator on an off night. Given the film's other problems, appearances such as these have sometimes thrown comparable films into the high-camp category. Laurel himself later observed: "It was so bad it was almost funny."[185]

What had seemed perfectly fitting—making a film where Stan & Ollie were fully appreciated, had turned into an embarrassing mistake. When production was finally completed, one wonders if the April Fool's Day (1951) departure date of Laurel and his wife was self-deprecatingly planned, or just an accident of fate. A further irony for Laurel & Hardy was that 1951 was also the twenty-fifth anniversary of their teaming.

In France and Italy *Atoll K* was released in late 1951. A slightly abridged version entitled *Robinson Crusoeland* appeared in 1952 British theatres. The latter print, again retitled *Utopia*, had a limited late-1954 release in the United States.

Despite both a painful production and finished film, before its U.S. release *Utopia* helped generate a 1951 United States renewal of interest in the team. A July 1951 *Los Angeles Times* article/interview with the duo even underlined this in its punning title: "Hardy Perennials Win Laurels; Rosy Bids Bud from Comics' Europe Work."[186] Consequently, offers were "piling up for this unique and beloved team—offers for TV series, for an Italian stage revue, a Japanese cinema [studio production] and for their [the team's] life story in a Billy Wilder movie.''[187] (Wilder, the celebrated writer/director, seems to have had a penchant for films that could utilize aging comedy teams; roughly ten years later he had equally unrealized plans for a Marx Brothers film.)

The flaw in all this good news was that Laurel's health was still not good. It seems to have cost the team supporting roles in the modest Technicolor musical *Two Tickets to Broadway* (1951; mutual health problems later also kept the team from a cameo appearance in Michael Todd's star-studded *Around the World in 80 Days*, 1956). But early in 1952 Laurel was healthy enough to return to Britain, with Hardy, for another extended tour. As in the British portion of their 1947 tour, they played the maximum length possible under Hardy's alien work permit—nine months. (Like Chaplin, Laurel had not renounced his British citizenship.) Laurel & Hardy had toured with a railroad station skit entitled *A Spot of Trouble*, which Laurel had based on their early short subject *Night Owls* (1930, from a McCarey idea). As usual, they were a major hit.

In the fall of 1953 the team returned to Britain again—touring with the Laurel-authored skit *Birds of a Feather*. As befitted a duo that had gotten so much comic mileage out of drink, *Birds of a Feather* had Stan & Ollie employed as whiskey tasters at a distillery. *But* there was some contemporary comedy updating going on here. Laurel had set the material in a mental institution, because it seems that dear, sweet Ollie (yes, that description is normally reserved for Stan) had decided he could fly and tried just that in a window exit from their spirited workplace. While the comic kicker for the sketch was not all that original— their shrink has, figuratively speaking, mentally jumped the tracks much worse than the boys—it was an interesting departure on what turned out to be their last tour. And because of their previous ties with comic drink and even their occasional moments of dark humor (the script includes a death-like undertaker), it was a comic stretch not unbefitting the duo.

For a comic team who seemed so often to have missed out on poetic justice— such as the terrible last film with the three names (as if people did not know what to call it), two wonderful things happened on this last tour. One was an instantaneous gift that reduced them to stereotypical tears; the other would be years in the making, unfortunately occurring after Hardy's death.

The first was a simple gift from their audience. When their ship reached Cork, Ireland, they were welcomed by the church bells of the city gonging out their ''The Dance of the Cuckoos'' theme song. It was a classic example of populist support of the team. They were definitely more appreciated in Europe.

The second event was a more focused gift from one very devoted fan—the young U.S. student/actor John McCabe, who was then studying in England. Not believing his luck at discovering his comic heroes in the flesh, he pleasantly attached himself to a most willing Laurel. Several years later (1961) there appeared a loving biography entitled *Mr. Laurel & Mr. Hardy*, drawn from a now strong friendship between the comedian and new author. (See also Chapter 4, ''A Laurel & Hardy Bibliographical Essay.'') The book helped generate long-overdue serious attention on the team. It also occurred at a most opportune time, since the frequent reruns of their old films on 1950s television had brought Laurel & Hardy to the attention of a whole new generation of fans. (Appropriately, McCabe would later write the first solo biography of each comedian.)

As a side note, despite the pleasure the team initially felt about a new TV audience, they eventually came to be appalled at the cutting done for commercials as well as disappointed over not receiving any residual-like income. Ironically, while Laurel later (after Hardy's death) sometimes avoided watching their old films because of the editing done for the screen, TV viewing occupied a great deal of time in his final years. In fact, his last move was dependent upon finding an area with a greater availability of TV reception. (For more on Laurel and television, see the interview section of Chapter 4.)

TV recognition also produced a touching comment by weight-conscious Hardy concerning changing attitudes in his neighborhood children. Before the refound fame he had to put up with fat references. The TV broadcast of old Laurel & Hardy films changed these same underage detractors into autograph-seeking fans. TV fan Hardy often avoided screenings of the team's work because he felt uncomfortable watching the large Ollie.

Television was a perennial topic in 1950s team interviews in both the United States and Europe. But Elizabeth Frank's October 14, 1953 *Nottingham Chronicle* (England) tour interview, "Laurel and Hardy Find New Fame: But It Hasn't Brought Them a Cent" (another TV reference), nicely revealed a generally neglected overseas attraction for the team. English music-hall or variety-house entertainment offered a much more humane work schedule for two older comedians in poor health in the 1950s. While they did two shows per day in England, the U.S. circuit demanded six—starting at 11:00 A.M. Thus, Laurel observed, "Variety in America is just murder to the conscientious comic." Later in the interview he added, "What kind of respect can the public feel for an artist who is expected to work six shows six days a week?" Put another way, it is doubtful the team could have handled the sheer physical demands of the U.S. circuit. Moreover, aging perfectionist Laurel spoke all too familiarly about U.S. "kid audiences—who stay for as many as four shows on end—getting rowdier and rowdier as time goes on." As is reflected in England's kinder music hall schedule, Laurel & Hardy praised the country's preservation of the performance as an "event."

British accounts of their tour stops sometimes record a unique audience response to the team's first appearance on stage. Before the applause there was often a collective gasp from the audience, as if to say, "Here are those comic cinema legends in the flesh!"

A high point of the 1953–54 tour was their end-of-the-year month-long stop at the Nottingham Empire Theatre. Laurel's sister Beatrice lived in the nearby village of Bottesford, where she was landlady of the Bull Inn and pub—with its pictorial tribute to the team. Laurel & Hardy visited often and also came for Christmas dinner of turkey and stuffing. Befitting a family holiday, they stayed the night, even logging some serving time behind the bar!

Another London tour exit—October 8, 1952

The downside of the Christmas season included added shows, though nowhere near the normal demands of the stateside variety circuit. During their Nottingham booking there were three shows every Saturday, as well as every day during Christmas week.

Bernard Delfont, who arranged all their post–World War II English tours, had 1953 memories of two wonderful but very different people. Any modest joke made Laurel laugh—with comedy discussion a favored activity. Hardy was both serious and religious and enjoyed reading the Bible in bed mornings.

Given this religious bent, there is comic irony in the fact that Hardy appears to have enjoyed discussing possible retirement to England with local people along the tour, forever changing the specific retreat location to whatever town the team was then playing. Still, he genuinely seemed to like the English countryside and being ingratiating to a host audience hardly originates with him.

What turned out to be their last tour, however, was not without forebodings—it was cut short in May 1954 when Hardy suffered a mild heart attack compounded by other health problems. What had almost become an annual affair—touring in Europe (primarily Britain)—would be no more. And the health problems of both comedians stymied any other joint projects.

The disappointing last project was a 1955 television deal with, appropriately enough, Hal Roach, Jr. The team was to do a series of children's stories (each in color and an hour long) to be called "The Fables of Laurel and Hardy." Laurel was to have that long-desired production control. But shortly before shooting was to begin he suffered a stroke. In time, Laurel almost completely recovered. However, by this time Hardy's health was questionable.

He had been suffering from heart problems since the hot, stressful, and protracted production of *Utopia*. Hardy now weighed over 350 pounds, approximately 100 over his old comedy fighting weight. After another heart attack, it seemed reasonable that some weight be lost. But as if he were back in some 1930s comically surrealist two-reeler (like W. C. Fields's *The Barber Shop*, 1933, where an extended stay in a sauna reduces a giant to a pipsqueak), Hardy dieted off nearly half his body weight—150 pounds. Ironically, in a quest for health Hardy had dieted away his celebrated physical persona. When it became public knowledge in summer 1956 fans were shocked. This depressed Hardy and he became a recluse. On September 15, 1956 Hardy had a massive stroke. Unlike Laurel, there was no recovery.

Suffering two additional strokes nearly a year later, Oliver Hardy died August 7, 1957. He was sixty-five. Laurel observed at the time: "What's there to say. It's shocking, of course. Ollie was like a brother. That's the end of the history of Laurel and Hardy."[188] Actually, with the ongoing popularity of the team, the history of Laurel & Hardy had only just begun. Or, to borrow the title of a 1970s Laurel & Hardy article: "The Legend Grows!"[189]

The touring years and, no doubt, the joint frustration they had experienced at their 1940s mishandling by two major studios helped mold much more of a friendship than had previously existed. And with Hardy's death, Laurel had no inclination to do solo work, though in later interviews he often cited ongoing health problems for keeping him from entertaining (see interview references in Chapter 4).

Stan Laurel died of a heart attack approximately seven and one-half years later, on February 23, 1965. He was seventy-four. For years he and Ida had lived in a small motel-like apartment overlooking the Pacific in Santa Monica, California. Because of his long touring tradition, he enjoyed accommodations that seemed temporary. And watching the ocean was an ongoing fascination. Yet, even the serenity of the sea fueled his wit. Thankfully, visiting fan and friend Jerry Lewis remembered Laurel's comic description of his beloved ocean as they both enjoyed the retired comedian's picture-window view of the Pacific: "It's a nice pool, much bigger than Liberace's." Indeed, on the same occasion, Laurel went on to add the slightest bit of romantic innuendo. Given his past antiheroic record in that department, it provides added poignancy to his amusing whimsey: "I spend hours here [watching the sea] hoping mermaids will surface. But they never do."[190]

As befitted a sea lover and lifelong fisherman, his Oceana Hotel apartment had a maritime appearance, from glass-encased shells to model whaling ships. His Ulverston birthplace by the sea was undoubtedly also a factor in the comfort a nautical world gave him. Moreover, is there not a parallel between the sailor's life and that of the vagabond vaudevillian (which Laurel had loved)—the constant adventure of change through travel. And the metaphor Laurel chooses for a lifetime in entertainment might apply equally to that of a sailor: "I've always played my idiot character as I myself see life—a big dark storm that once in a while is brightened by a rainbow of laughter."[191]

Accounts of his final years sometimes took on a maudlin tone. One such article even resulted in Laurel receiving small-change donations from young English fans who had been led to believe the comedian was living in poverty. Undoubtedly there was some sadness. What life is without it? And this could surface in any account of Laurel's final years, regardless of the article's general tone. For instance, notwithstanding the traditionally upbeat nature of Lewis's reminiscing, Laurel had turned down an invitation to dinner because he did not want fans, especially young fans, to see him so different (aged) from his eternally young screen persona. For the same reason he would tell young neighborhood fans (who did not recognize him) that Stan was away making movies.

One of the extreme accounts of a gloomy Laurel twilight appeared years after his death, and it included Hardy: "Laurel et Hardy: la triste histoire des rois du rive morts dans la misère." Author Joan MacTrevor merely focused on all the negatives of the team's final years, though the article's subtitle says it all: "the sad story of the kings of laughter, dead in misery." But even here MacTrevor cannot suppress Laurel's seeming survival through humor philosophy; she inexplicably includes a Laurel statement that closes with a joke, thus denying the sad story nature of her piece. Moreover, the pivotal observation addresses the one subject that had been the greatest continuous source of Laurel pain:

I have lived well. I loved women intensely and even if they left me, I'll never regret these moments. Six thousand years ago, man had to choose between marrying and going to break stones. That is why this era was called the "Stone Age!"[192]

Another upbeat example of the comedian's final years was always keeping himself accessible (young fans notwithstanding) to the people. And while a number of famous comedians, such as Jerry Lewis, Danny Kaye, Peter Sellers, Dick Van Dyke, and mime artist Marcel Marceau, would also come to pay homage, it was his general availability that remained remarkable.

The extremes to which Laurel allowed this accessibility is best demonstrated by noting that in 1963 he even treated one fan to a five-day visit! Later briefly chronicled as "of mr. laurel and mr. hardy: Huntington [West Virginia] Man Their No. 1 Fan," guest Mike Polacek said of his stay with Laurel and Ida: "They treated me like a king."[193] Polacek also included more about the visit in an article he authored, "my hobby, laurel and hardy."[194] Thus, between the two pieces one discovered that Laurel was both game enough to talk old movies with Mr. Polacek four to eight hours each day, and patient enough to "star" in some of his visitor's home movies. In addition, Polacek's stay was also a fascinating documentation of just how richly varied the drop-in "trade" might have been at Laurel's. For instance, Polacek casually notes that during his visit both silent comedienne Minta Durfee (former wife of Fatty Arbuckle) and Flo St. John (widow of silent comedian Al "Fuzzy" St. John) stopped in to talk and show Laurel old film footage they had of him, Arbuckle, and St. John.

Through the years, then, fans of every age, status and description—even curious tour bus riders—made the comedy pilgrimage to Laurel's door (his address was still listed in the telephone book). Indeed, comedian Jerry Lewis was long after him to become a comedy consultant at a sizable salary. And the fans who did not visit seemed to write letters. The comedian was constantly inundated with fan mail—which he diligently tried to answer, despite failing eyesight. (This was a task he had religiously been pursuing since his filmmaking days.)

Among the celebrity fans, Peter Sellers was strangely unique. Not only was Laurel Peter Sellers's favorite comedian (forever finding wall space in his travels for a large blowup of his comedy idol), the two shared a fascination for Dan Leno, the most prominent English comedian of the late nineteenth century. But whereas Laurel had based part of his screen persona on Leno's comedy character, Sellers passionately believed his own career was being guided by Leno's *spirit*—especially Sellers's comedy timing.[195] This is not unlike Laurel's reincarnation explanation for the skills of young performers. Sadly, neither Laurel nor Sellers seem to have documented their conversations.

Unfortunately, while Hardy lived long enough to see the amazing revival of interest television had brought to the team's old films, he died before the Academy of Motion Picture Arts and Sciences could give the duo a much deserved Oscar for career achievement. However, in 1961 Laurel was honored with an Oscar "for creative pioneering in the field of cinema comedy." Although he was unable to attend the ceremony in person because of a last-minute flare-up of his eye problems, one of Laurel's favorite comedians, Danny Kaye, accepted the statuette for him. (For undisclosed reasons, Laurel's first choice as acceptor, Jerry Lewis, was turned down by the academy.) Laurel was moved by the award, regretting only that Hardy had not lived to see it.

Laurel was also given a special Screen Actors Guild Award for 1963, the same year that pivotal biographer John McCabe began to push seriously for a unique new Laurel & Hardy fan club—what was to become the still-active "Sons of the Desert." In the spirit of the film from which the title is taken, the club is a gentle satire of fraternal orders. Being involved with the organization's inception brought great pleasure to Laurel. Moreover, students of the team owe the club an ongoing debt for their constant search for new insights into the team, which often surface in the many Laurel & Hardy-focused journals.

Sadly but not unfittingly, Laurel's death touched off more controversy from Laurel women. Acting together, the comedian's daughter (by first wife Lois) and his pranksterish former wife Virginia Ruth contested his will twice, because Laurel had left everything (merely a modest inheritance) to final wife Ida.

Evidently, when Virginia Ruth favored a given storyline she was more than a little reluctant to leave it, even when it had become patently ridiculous. Thus, the woman dusted off her old claim that she was still the comedian's legal wife. When this failed, his daughter responded with one of the hoariest claims for contesting wills: that her father was "not of sound mind" when the document was drafted. The court dismissed this claim.

Things were not all cruel in death. Laurel friend and admirer Dick Van Dyke gave the eulogy at the comedian's funeral, underlining Laurel's special gift: "He just wanted to make you laugh, and he did."[196] Laurel even exited this life on a gag line for his attending nurse. Though the exact wording differs according to the source, shortly before Laurel's passing he told the nurse he'd prefer to be skiing now. When she gave the standard rhetorical question, "Do you ski?" he replied, no, but he'd rather be skiing than this . . .

Though his final marker is not quite the "Eighth Wonder of the World," like the miniature tombstone lighthouse he had once coveted as a boy (see nn. 136–38), the man's comedy legacy, in tandem with Hardy's, will give off its own special light as long as there are audiences in search of laughter.

NOTES

1. E. R. Moak, "Tear-Stained Laughter," *Photoplay*, June 1933, p. 40.

2. John McCabe, *Mr. Laurel & Mr. Hardy* (1961; repr. New York: Signet Books, 1966), p. 42.

3. Boyd Verb, "LAUREL WITHOUT HARDY: Gives a Rare Interview and Discusses Their Joint Career," *Films in Review*, March 1959, p. 158.

4. Randy Skretvedt, *Laurel and Hardy: The Magic Behind the Movies* (Beverly Hills, California: Moonstone Press, 1987), p. 18.

5. Harry Brand, [20th Century-Fox Laurel & Hardy Press Release], April 10, 1942, p. 1. (In the Laurel & Hardy files, Margaret Herrick Library, Academy of Motion Picture Arts and Sciences, Beverly Hills, California.)

6. Wes D. Gehring, *W. C. Fields: A Bio-Bibliography* (Westport, Connecticut: Greenwood Press, 1984); Wes D. Gehring, *The Marx Brothers: A Bio-Bibliography* (Westport, Connecticut: Greenwood Press, 1987).

7. John McCabe, *The Comedy World of Stan Laurel* (Garden City, New York: Doubleday & Company, Inc., 1974), p. 11.

8. Fred Lawrence Guiles, *Stan: The Life of Stan Laurel* (New York: Stein and Day, 1980), p. 36.

9. John McCabe, *Charlie Chaplin* (Garden City, New York: Doubleday, 1978), p. 27.

10. "Carl Sandburg Says Chaplin Could Play Serious Drama," in *Authors on Film*, ed. Harry M. Geduld (Bloomington: Indiana University Press, 1972), p. 264. (Originally in *Chicago Daily News*, April 16, 1921, p. 13.)

11. Kalton C. Lahue, *World of Laughter: The Motion Picture Comedy Short, 1910– 1930* (1966; repr. Norman: University of Oklahoma Press, 1972), p. 105.

12. McCabe, *Mr. Laurel & Mr. Hardy*, p. 44. For more possible parallels between these films and the late Laurel & Hardy vehicles, see Jordan R. Young's "Early Ollie: The Plump and Runt Films," *Pratfall* 1 (12), 1975.

13. Theodore Huff, *Charlie Chaplin* (1951; repr. New York: Arno Press and *The New York Times*, 1972), p. 65.

14. McCabe, *Mr. Laurel & Mr. Hardy*, p. 52. This quote, from Hardy's third wife, Lucille, goes on to suggest the comedian went back to New York City in 1918, but other detailed documentation in Lahue's book suggests otherwise (pp. 104–7).

15. Frank "Kin" Hubbard, *Back Country Folks* (Indianapolis: Abe Martin, 1913), p. 45.

16. William Dodgson Bowman, *Charlie Chaplin: His Life and Art* (1931; repr. New York: Haskell House, 1974), p. 70.

17. Gerald D. McDonald, *The Picture History of Charlie Chaplin* (New York: Nostalgia Press, 1965), p. 16.

18. Lahue, *World of Laughter*, p. 90.

19. Guiles, *Stan: The Life of Stan Laurel*, pp. 52–53.

20. Ibid., p. 55.

21. Ibid., p. 58.

22. Skredvedt, *Laurel and Hardy*, p. 25.

23. McCabe, *Mr. Laurel & Mr. Hardy*, p. 42.

24. Jenny Owen-Pawson and Bill Mouland, *Laurel Before Hardy* (Kendal, Westmorland, England: *Westmorland Gazette*, 1984), p. 7.

25. Besides the books mentioned in n.6, see Wes D. Gehring, *Charlie Chaplin: A Bio-Bibliography* (Westport, Connecticut: Greenwood Press, 1983).

26. Maude Cheatham, "The Cinema Caricaturist," *Motion Picture Classic*, April 1922, pp. 38, 73.

27. John McCabe, *Babe: The Life of Oliver Hardy* (London: Robson Books, 1989), p. 52.

28. *The Wizard of Oz* review, *Variety*, April 4, 1925, p. 35.

29. McCabe, *Mr. Laurel & Mr. Hardy*, p. 45.

30. Guiles, *Stan*, p. 72.

31. Ibid., pp. 76–77.

32. For an example of the Marx Brothers M-G-M problems, see Gehring's *The Marx Brothers: A Bio-Bibliography*.

33. Joe Adamson, *Groucho, Harpo, Chico and Sometimes Zeppo* (New York: Simon and Schuster, 1973), p. 209.

34. H. Allen Smith, "A Session with McCarey," *Variety*, January 7, 1970, p. 23.

35. Skretvedt, *Laurel and Hardy*, p. 71.

36. Ibid. p. 46. (Skretvedt reproduces the article but does not note in which Los Angeles newspaper it appeared.)

37. See the author's *Screwball Comedy: A Genre of Madcap Romance* (Westport, Connecticut: Greenwood Press, 1986).

38. McCabe, *The Comedy World of Stan Laurel*, p. 61.

39. John McCabe, compiled by Al Kilgore, filmography by Richard W. Bann, *Laurel & Hardy* (New York: Ballantine Books, 1975), p. 13; McCabe, *Mr. Laurel & Mr. Hardy*, p. 99.

40. Guiles, *Stan*, p. 110.

41. Gehring's *Leo McCarey and the Comic Anti-Hero in American Film* (New York: Arno Press, 1980).

42. Peter Bogdanovich, "Leo McCarey Oral History" (Los Angeles: American Film Institute, 1972), p. 20.

43. Most Laurel & Hardy studies accept the McCarey position on pacing expounded in both his American Film Institute Oral History and in Serge Daney and Jean-Louis Noames's "Taking Chances: Interview with Leo McCarey," *Cahiers du Cinema* (in English), January 1967, pp. 43–54 (*Cahiers* original, February 1965). McCabe's *Mr. Laurel & Mr. Hardy* has the credit going to Laurel. But this work tends to grant the comedian a greater creative hand than McCabe's subsequent works in both the team and Laurel.

44. Bogdanovich, "Leo McCarey Oral History," p. 23.

45. Ibid., p. 24.

46. Walter Kerr, *The Silent Clowns* (New York: Alfred A. Knopf, Inc., 1975), p. 318.

47. Peter Bogdanovich, "Hollywood," *Esquire*, February 1972, p. 8.

48. Skretvedt, *Laurel and Hardy*, p. 97.

49. Bogdanovich, "Leo McCarey Oral History," p. 20.

50. Frank Capra, *The Name Above the Title* (New York: Macmillan, 1971), p. 40.

51. Ibid.

52. Bogdanovich, "Leo McCarey Oral History," pp. 29–30.

53. Charles Barr, *Laurel & Hardy* (1967; repr. Los Angeles: University of California Press, 1974), p. 79.

54. Gerald Mast, "More Fun Shops," in *The Comic Mind: Comedy and the Movies*, Chapter 12, 2d edition (1973; repr. Chicago: University of Chicago Press, 1979), p. 191.

55. Skretvedt, *Laurel and Hardy*, p. 119.

56. Bogdanovich, "Leo McCarey Oral History," p. 21.

57. Daney and Noames, "Taking Chances: Interview with Leo McCarey," p. 43.

58. McCabe, *The Comedy World of Stan Laurel*, p. 212.

59. "Ruth Laurel Remembers," *Pratfall*, vol. 1, no. 5 (1971), p. 6.

60. Skretvedt, *Laurel and Hardy*, p. 121.

61. Ritchie Calder, "Laurel in Shirt Sleeves Holds Family Party," *Daily Herald* (London), July 25, 1932, p. 9.

62. Andy Anderson, *Battle of the Century* review, *Motion Picture Exhibitors Herald-World*, February 11, 1928, p. 64.

63. S. B. Kennedy, *Liberty* review, *Motion Picture Exhibitors Herald-World*, April 27, 1929, p. 65.

64. *Soup to Nuts* review, *Motion Picture Exhibitors Herald-World*, May 4, 1929, p. 76.

65. *Big Business* review, *Motion Picture Exhibitors Herald-World*, June 15, 1929, p. 161.

66. "There is no substitute for laughter" (Hal Roach/M-G-M ad), *Motion Picture Exhibitors Herald-World*, March 9, 1929, n.p.

67. Guiles, *Stan*, p. 113.

68. Ibid., p. 114.

69. Ibid., p. 121.

70. "Funny Mr. Hardy's UNFUNNY Alimony Troubles," *The American Weekly*, January 27, 1946, p. 4.

71. "Oliver Hardy File," Billy Rose Theatre Collection, New York Public Library at Lincoln Center. There are numerous brief clippings (without complete citations) on the relationship of Hardy and Myrtle.

72. "Hardy and Wife Reconciled," *New York Times*, October 4, 1933, p. 27.

73. "Oliver Hardy File," Billy Rose Theatre Collection.

74. Verb, "LAUREL WITHOUT HARDY," p. 156.

75. McCabe, *Mr. Laurel & Mr. Hardy*, pp. 104–5.

76. Dennis Pope, "Dennis Pope on Stanley LAUREL [&] Oliver Norvell HARDY," *Film*, Autumn 1967, p. 33.

77. Verb, "LAUREL WITHOUT HARDY," p. 156. See also Skretvedt, *Laurel and Hardy*, p. 186.

78. Skretvedt, *Laurel and Hardy*, p. 184.

79. Daney and Noames, "Taking Chances: Interview with Leo McCarey," p. 43.

80. McCabe, *The Comedy World of Stan Laurel*, pp. 62–63.

81. Pete Martin, "Going His Way," *Saturday Evening Post*, November 30, 1946, p. 66.

82. Walter Blair, *Native American Humor* (1937; repr. San Francisco: Chandler Publishing Company, 1960), p. 169. See also Gehring's detailed look at the roots of the antihero in *Screwball Comedy: A Genre of Madcap Romance*, pp. 13–35.

83. See also Gehring's "W. C. Fields: The Copyrighted Sketches," *Journal of Popular Film & Television*, Summer 1986, pp. 65–75.

84. Albert F. McLean, Jr., *American Vaudeville as Ritual* (Lexington: University of Kentucky Press, 1965), p. 106.

85. McCabe, *Mr. Laurel & Mr. Hardy*, p. 46.

86. See both n. 80 and the McCarey-authored "Comedy and a Touch of Cuckoo," *Extension*, November 1944, p. 5. (The *Extension* piece, however, does not directly address Laurel & Hardy.)

87. Martin, "Going His Way," p. 65.

88. Sidney Carroll, "Everything Happens to McCarey: During those sparse times

when he isn't breaking his valuable neck, Leo McCarey does direct some extraordinary pictures," *Esquire*, May 1943, pp. 43, 57.

89. Carroll, "Everything Happens to McCarey," p. 57.

90. Ibid.

91. Bogdanovich, "Hollywood," p. 8.

92. James Thurber, "The Man Who Hated Moonbaum," in his *My World—And Welcome to It* (1937; repr. New York: Harcourt, Brace and Company, 1942), pp. 59–71; Burton Bernstein, *Thurber: A Biography* (New York: Ballantine Books, 1976), p. 238.

93. Bogdanovich, "Leo McCarey Oral History," p. 9.

94. Ibid., p. 83.

95. Ibid., p. 53.

96. Bernstein, *Thurber: A Biography*, pp. 438–39.

97. "Oliver Hardy File," Billy Rose Theatre Collection.

98. Guiles, *Stan*, p. 128; Richie Calder, "Laurel in Shirt Sleeves Holds Family Party," *Daily Herald* (London), July 25, 1932, p. 9.

99. Skretvedt, *Laurel and Hardy*, p. 245 (drawn from a source, *Today's Cinema*, without further citation).

100. Calder, "Laurel in Shirt Sleeves Holds Family Party," p. 9.

101. Owen-Pawson, *Laurel Before Hardy*, p. 12.

102. Calder, "Laurel in Shirt Sleeves Holds Family Party," p. 9.

103. "Laurel & Hardy to Broadcast To-night: Their Talk May be on Tombstones," *Daily Herald* (London), July 26, 1932, p. 3.

104. "20 Hurt In Laurel and Hardy Stampede: Women Crushed At Midnight Welcome," *Daily Herald* (London), July 30, 1932, p. 1.

105. "Fight To Greet Actors: Thousands at Glasgow Welcome Laurel and Hardy," *New York Times*, July 30, 1932, p. 16.

106. "Theatrical Folk Back From Europe: Laurel and Hardy Return on the Paris After Stenuous Tour of Britain," *New York Times*, August 31, 1932, p. 12.

107. Guiles, *Stan*, pp. 131–32.

108. Ibid., p. 132.

109. Skretvedt, *Laurel and Hardy*, p. 260.

110. Ann Glaze, "No Laughs In Laurel Home-Life, So Comedian And Wife Separate," *Movie Classic*, February 1933, p. 28.

111. Ibid.

112. Herman Hesse, *Steppenwolf*, trans. Basil Creighton, rev. Walter Sorell (1927; repr. New York: The Modern Library, 1963), p. 29.

113. Ibid.

114. "Obituary: Mr. Stan Laurel," *The Times* (London), February 24, 1965, p. 15a.

115. Skretvedt, *Laurel & Hardy*, p. 248.

116. "Oliver Hardy File," Billy Rose Theatre Collection.

117. Guiles, *Stan*, p. 128.

118. Ibid.

119. Will Rogers, "Some Vivas for Mexico" (November 15, 1931, syndicated weekly newspaper article), in *Will Rogers' Weekly articles*, vol. 5, *The Hoover Years: 1931–1933*, ed. Steven K. Gragert (Stillwater: Oklahoma State University Press, 1982), p. 87.

120. Bruce Crowther, *Laurel and Hardy: Clown Princes of Comedy* (London: Columbus Books, 1987), p. 77.

121. Leonard Maltin (editor and chief contributor), *The Laurel & Hardy Book* (New York: Curtis Books, 1973), p. 74.

122. Philip K. Scheuer, "Comics Famous 'By Accident'," *Los Angeles Times*, December 29, 1929, Part III, p. 18.

123. Dorothy Spensley, "Those Two Goofy Guys," *Photoplay*, July 1930, p. 136; Skretvedt, *Laurel & Hardy*, pp. 201–202.

124. Donald W. McCaffrey, Chapter 5, "Duet of Incompetence," in *The Golden Age of Sound Comedy: Comic Films and Comedians of the Thirties* (New York: A. S. Barnes, 1973), p. 92.

125. Groucho Marx and Richard Anobile, *The Marx Bros. Scrapbook* (New York: Grosset & Dunlap, 1974), p. 80.

126. Skretvedt, *Laurel & Hardy*, p. 201.

127. McCabe, *The Comedy World of Stan Laurel*, p. 74.

128. McCabe, *Mr. Laurel & Mr. Hardy*, p. 55.

129. Skretvedt, *Laurel & Hardy*, p. 277.

130. Guiles, *Stan*, p. 141.

131. Jack Scagnetti, *The Laurel & Hardy Scrapbook* (Middle Village, New York: Jonathan David Publishers, 1976), p. 61.

132. Guiles, *Stan*, p. 144.

133. Frank S. Nugent, *Way Out West* review, *New York Times*, May 4, 1937, p. 29.

134. Skretvedt, *Laurel and Hardy*, p. 324.

135. "Funny Mr. Laurel Who Keeps on Getting Married," *New York Journal-American*, February 23, 1941, p. 5.

136. "Laurel & Hardy to Broadcast To-Night: Their Talk May be on Tombstones," p. 3.

137. Ibid.

138. Owen-Pawson and Mouland, *Laurel Before Hardy*, pp. 33–35.

139. Skretvedt, *Laurel and Hardy*, p. 345.

140. "Newest Upheaval in the Not-So-Private Life of Sad-Faced Mr. Laurel," *New York Journal-American*, December 10, 1939, n.p., in the "Laurel & Hardy Files," Billy Rose Theatre Collection, New York Public Library at Lincoln Center.

141. *New York Journal-American* article from January 29, 1939, in the "Laurel & Hardy Files," Billy Rose Theatre Collection.

142. "Laurel Weds No. 3 as No. 2 Gives Chase," *New York Daily News*, January 2, 1938, n.p., in the "Laurel & Hardy Files," Billy Rose Theatre Collection.

143. "Stan Laurel Asks Court to Restrain First [sic] Wife," January 12, 1938, n.p., in the "Laurel & Hardy Files," Billy Rose Theatre Collection.

144. "Funny Mr. Laurel Who Keeps on Getting Married," p. 5.

145. Ibid.

146. Ibid.

147. "Sad Pan, Frying Pan Met, Says Stan Laurel," *New York Daily News*, October 26, 1938, n.p., in the "Laurel & Hardy Files," Billy Rose Theatre Collection.

148. Ibid.

149. "Laurel Held as Drunken Driver," *New York Herald-Tribune*, September 30, 1938, n.p., in the "Laurel & Hardy Files," Billy Rose Theatre Collection.

150. Guiles, *Stan*, p. 180; McCabe, *BABE: The Life of Oliver Hardy*, p. 140.

151. *New York Journal-American* article from January 29, 1939, in the "Laurel & Hardy Files," Billy Rose Theatre Collection.

152. Ibid.

153. "Funny Mr. Laurel Who Keeps on Getting Married," p. 5.

154. *New York Journal-American* article from January 29, 1939, in the "Laurel & Hardy Files," Billy Rose Theatre Collection.

155. "Funny Mr. Laurel Who Keeps on Getting Married," p. 5.

156. James Thurber, "A Box to Hide In," in *The Middle-Aged Man on the Flying Trapeze* (1935; repr. New York: Harper & Row, 1976), pp. 224–27.

157. H. Allen Smith, "A Session with McCarey," *Variety*, January 7, 1970, p. 23.

158. "Funny Mr. Laurel Who Keeps on Getting Married," p. 5.

159. Ibid.

160. *New York Daily Mirror* article from October 31, 1939, in the "Laurel & Hardy Files," Billy Rose Theatre Collection.

161. "Langdon Replaces Stan Laurel; Teams With Hardy in Comedy," *New York World Telegraph*, August 18, 1938, n.p., in the "Laurel & Hardy Files," Billy Rose Theatre Collection.

162. Skretvedt, *Laurel and Hardy*, pp. 352, 354.

163. "Stan Laurel Pouts, Out, Hardy to Solo," *Variety*, March 20, 1935, p. 2.

164. Skretvedt, *Laurel and Hardy*, p. 349.

165. James Agee, "Comedy's Greatest Era," in *Agee on Film*, vol. 1 (New York: Grosset and Dunlap, 1969), pp. 2–19 (originally appeared in *Life*, September 3, 1949).

166. William K. Everson, *The Films of Laurel and Hardy* (1967; repr. Secaucus, New Jersey: Citadel Press, 1972), p. 183.

167. See Gehring, *W. C. Fields: A Bio-Bibliography*.

168. Scagnetti, *The Laurel & Hardy Scrapbook*, pp. 72–73.

169. "Hollywood Dollar-Dolors," *Time*, September 22, 1941, p. 55.

170. "Together Again," *Sunday Express* (London), May 7, 1950 (n.p. cited). In the "Laurel & Hardy Files," British Film Institute (London); contract references are drawn from Skretvedt, *Laurel and Hardy*, pp. 373, 374.

171. Bing Crosby and David Butler, "Remembering Leo McCarey," *Action*, September-October 1967, p. 12.

172. W. H. Mooring, "With MacLaurel & MacHardy in Bonnie Scotland," *Film Weekly*, June 28, 1935, pp. 8, 9.

173. Skretvedt, *Laurel and Hardy*, p. 381.

174. "Laurel and Hardy: $10,700 in Dayton," *Billboard*, February 7, 1942, p. 17.

175. "Laurel and Hardy Top Chi With 18G; Ork Holdover 32G," *Billboard*, January 24, 1942, p. 24.

176. "Victory Caravan," *Newsweek*, May 11, 1942, p. 33.

177. "Laurel and Hardy: $10,700 in Dayton," p. 17.

178. "Entertainment Lines," *Newsweek*, February 22, 1943, p. 12.

179. Guiles, *Stan*, pp. 202–3.

180. "Laurel & Hardy: The Above Have Arrived," *Evening News* (London), February 10, 1947 (n.p. cited). In the "Laurel & Hardy Files," British Film Institute (London).

181. [Laurel & Hardy in 1947 London], *Daily Star* (London), February 12, 1947 (n.p. cited). In the "Laurel & Hardy Files," British Film Institute (London).

182. "Funny Mr. Hardy's UNFUNNY Alimony Troubles," *The American Weekly*, January 27, 1946, p. 4.

183. "Stan Laurel Dies; Movie Comedian," *New York Times*, February 24, 1965, p. 41.

184. Guiles, *Stan*, p. 213.

185. "Stan Laurel Dies; Movie Comedian," p. 41.

186. Philip K. Scheuer, "Hardy Perennials Win Laurels; Rosy Bids Bud from Comics' Europe Work," *Los Angeles Times*, July 8, 1951, pp. 1, 3.

187. Ibid., p. 3.

188. "Oliver Hardy of Film Team Dies; Co-Star of 200 Slapstick Movies," *New York Times*, August 8, 1957, p. 23.

189. Ray Atherton, "The Legend Grows!" *Classic Film Collector*, Winter 1970, p. 35.

190. Jerry Lewis (with Herb Gluck), "Book Six," in *Jerry Lewis In Person* (New York: Atheneum, 1982), p. 228.

191. Ibid., p. 226.

192. Joan MacTrevor, "Laurel et Hardy: la triste histoire des rois du rive morts dans la misère . . . ," *Cine Revue*, June 6, 1987, p. 43.

193. Homer Alley, "of mr. laurel and mr. hardy: Huntington [West Virginia] Man Their No. 1 Fan," *8mm Collector* [now known as *Classic Images*], February 1964, p. 9.

194. Mike Polacek, "my hobby, laurel and hardy," *8mm Collector* (February 1964), p. 9.

195. Peter Evans, *The Mask Behind the Mask* (1968; repr. New York: Signet, 1980), p. 193. See also award-winning film critic Alexander Walker's authorized biography, *Peter Sellers* (New York: Macmillan, 1981), p. 206.

196. "Van Dyke Delivers Stan Laurel Eulogy," *New York Times*, February 27, 1965, p. 25.

2

stan & ollie:
the comic antiheroes

Opening title for *Big Business*: "The story of a man who turned the other cheek—and got punched in the nose."

Laurel & Hardy exerted a significant influence upon American humor and upon popular American culture in general. Though critics have not always accorded them the same lofty status as some of their 1930s contemporaries, such as W. C. Fields or the Marx Brothers, their impact is undeniable in four ways: as important cultural icons; as developers of a change in film comedy pacing (which also eased their transition from silent to sound film); as movie pioneers in the innovative early use of comic sound; and, most important, as valuable participants in the evolution of the comic antihero into mainstream American humor.

As with the film personae of most clowns, from Charlie Chaplin's "Tramp" with the "east-and-west feet" to the comically eclectic Marx Brothers, any examination of Laurel & Hardy's influence must begin with their status as icons.

The images of skinny Stan and chubby Ollie have been reproduced on nearly every conceivable product, from playing cards and coloring books to dolls and "The Dance of the Cuckoos" (their theme tune) music boxes. Late in life a mildly upset Laurel even mentioned buying an ashtray decorated with the duo's likeness. The comedian's irritation came from the irony of having to pay for something the team had inspired. Not surprisingly, there was some Laurel bitterness that the duo shared so little in the merchandising income of the Laurel & Hardy names and personae, not to mention the continued showing of their old films on television for which they did not receive residuals.

The same thing had happened to the Three Stooges team. Contemporaries of Laurel & Hardy, their careers had also been "born again" when their old

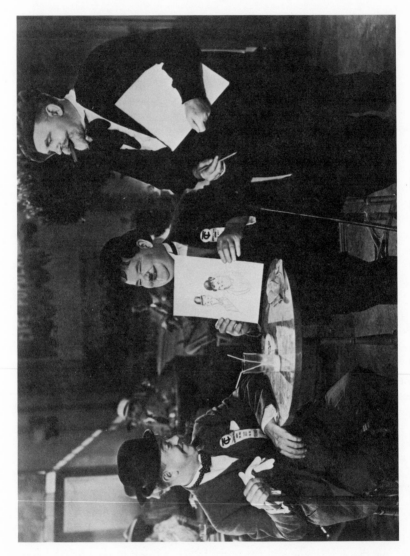

Stan & Ollie seem to be footnoting their status as comedy icons in *The Flying Deuces*

films reappeared on 1950s television. But while the Stooges also were deprived of income from past films, they came out of retirement (two of the original three still being alive), added a replacement, and profitably returned to film production. However, between the poor health of both Laurel and Hardy and the latter's relatively early death, there was never a chance for them to follow the Stooges's example for cashing in on a late-career revival.

In 1960, when Laurel was actually approached about the rights to both the team name and likeness, a financial arrangement was made with actor/producer Larry Harmon (who created and first played the character of Bozo the Clown). Harmon's plan, which he later implemented, was to make Laurel & Hardy film cartoons and sell team-related merchandise. The proposed cartoon series generated most of the initial attention, but the marketing aspect of the agreement was no doubt close to Laurel's heart, since he was well aware of unauthorized sales of team-related products.

Interestingly enough, through the later efforts of Harmon, the sale of Laurel & Hardy items were eventually part of a landmark ruling on the marketing rights of celebrity heirs. In August 1975 New York Judge Charles Stewart ruled that publicity generated by celebrated but deceased individuals represented a form of property rights still controlled by the heirs.[1] As a period *Los Angeles Times* article on the ruling so nicely headlined: ''Laurel, Hardy Legacy: A Victory for Widows' Rights'' (see n. 1).

Shortly before his 1965 death Laurel had asked Harmon to ''see that Ida [Laurel] and Lucille [Hardy] would always be protected in the sale of Laurel and Hardy products.''[2] Late in the decade Harmon became aware of a major new line of competing Laurel & Hardy memorabilia, especially a wristwatch manufactured by the Richard Feiner company. Upon investigation Harmon discovered that Hal Roach had been selling Laurel & Hardy rights to a number of companies, presumably for different products!

In an irony of ironies, therefore, Laurel & Hardy's old boss, as well as others, were taken to court. Even in death, it seemed there was no cessation to the volatile Laurel-Roach relationship. Still, after five years of expensive and frustrating legal action, Harmon's promise to Laurel concerning the widows was honored with a favorable court decision.

Enough, however, on the marketing of Laurel & Hardy. What is there about their personae that even makes their mere caricatures so popular? There are two answers. First, and most basic beyond their obvious ties to comedy, the team quite literally looks funny. Theirs is the most fundamental of comic contrasts— the ongoing interaction between a fat person and a skinny person. And they further accent the difference in various comic ways. For instance, Stan's scarecrow dry hair is forever combed straight up, as if he had just had an electrical shock, while Ollie's hair is invariably slicked down close to his head. More subtly, when Stan is confused or frightened, he goes into his patented elongated vacuous facial expression (tears being optional), vertically culminated by his reaching up and scratching the top of his head (like a comic El Greco, if the master of lengthened figures had done clowns). In equally subtle contrast, Ollie's most memorable comic "mask" (expression) occurs when he broadens his face in disgruntlement over another boner by Stan, tilting his head slightly downward and allowing his many chins to pile up onto his chest. And unlike Stan's elongating hand motion to the top of the head, Ollie's corresponding trademark gesture happens during times of shyness, when he plays with his tie, thus breaking its perpendicular lines.

Of course, instead of inferring humor, one might also translate the meaning of these fat-skinny contrasts into some metaphysical mindset, such as unconventional symbols for feast and famine. Granted this is rather a deep-dish suggestion. But in the spirit of "Ripley's Believe It or Not," just such a Stan & Ollie correlation once occurred at a remote shrine in China, where their picture was being used on an altar for just that reason. This is not an invitation to dust off one's knees and begin worshipping the duo. It does, however, underline anew both the worldwide pervasiveness of the team as well as the almost primal contrast in their body shapes.

The second factor behind the universality of their personae as icons (after simply looking funny) is that they represent the ultimate symbol of comic frustration. Of course, rare is the humor figure that does not know some degree of comic frustration. But Laurel & Hardy established new highs for comic incompetence as they participated in the evolution of America's comic antihero (to be expanded upon later in the chapter). In contrast, such pivotal Depression-era Laurel & Hardy contemporaries as the Marx Brothers, W. C. Fields, and Mae West created screen icons more closely related to comic anti-establishment dissent. The Marxes at their best comically dismantle everything from countries (*Duck Soup*'s Freedonia, 1933) to high art (*A Night at the Opera*, 1935). Mae West's aggressively sexy double-entendred humor focuses on leveling men and mores. Even W. C. Fields, whose screen roles vacillated between hucksters and antiheroes, is most often iconically seen today in the former guise—as the high hatted, gloved con man making a comic pitch out the side of his mouth. For example, the fraudulent Fields is the model for the crooked lawyer Larsen E. Pettifogger in Johnny Hart and Brant Parker's current newspaper comic strip, "The Wizard of Id" (since 1964). And advertisers invariably latch onto the huckster image of Fields, such as the very successful potato chip ad campaign with cartoon "spokesperson" "W. C. Frito."

The fundamental attractiveness, therefore, of icons like the Marx Brothers, Fields, and West (also after their equally funny appearances) is that they represent comic outrageousness—saying and doing things most people feel but seldom act upon because of societal pressures concerning acceptable behavior. Thus, Fields feels no inhibitions about booting a brattin' kid in the keister, the Marxes enjoy throwing fruit at their designated pompous matron Margaret Dumont, and West is an ongoing advertisement for sexuality. In contrast, Stan & Ollie as icons symbolize comic frustration—the forefathers of today's Charlie Brown. Instead of representing envied actions, one either equates Stan & Ollie's problems with exaggerations of personal problems or feels comically superior to two such lamebrained characters. But even when the duo is at their chuckleheaded best, such as their opening title description from *The Hoose-Gow* (1929)—"Neither Mr. Laurel nor Mr. Hardy had any thoughts of doing wrong. As a matter of fact they had no thoughts of any kind"—one still feels an empathy for two such warm and decent characters. *The Times* of London probably said it best when it praised the team as "an expression of well-intentioned muddle-headedness in a harsh and practical world."[3]

A second major influence of Laurel & Hardy, after their two-pronged significance as icons, was their contribution (with McCarey) to a change in silent comedy pacing (see Chapter 1). As opposed to silent comedy's more typical fast motion, Laurel & Hardy came to represent an innovatively slowed pace. This inspired slower comedy rhythm (such as their very methodical take-your-turn tit-for-tat violence) had four supporting factors. First and foremost, it was fresh and funny—the requirement that makes the other points possible. The duo's only significant slower-paced silent competitor was Harry Langdon, and his career self-destructed just as Laurel & Hardy's was taking off (1927). Second, the slower pacing anticipated the more realistic needs of sound film production, allowing Laurel & Hardy to make the smoothest transition to "talkies" of all silent comedians. Third, this reduced speed enabled the team to display a comic tendency best defined as anticipation. As critic/historian Walter Kerr has suggested, while the typical silent comedian hid the gag in the setup, the team "*showed* everyone the joke, explained it most carefully, anatomized it."[4] For instance, the insert of a misplaced roller skate just before the oblivious Oliver steps on it comically telegraphs the impending pratfall. Thus, while their material might seem hoary with age (even for the late 1920s), this was perfectly consistent with a methodical comedy style that embraced viewer *anticipation* instead of the more traditional *comic surprise*. (Unfortunately, it is this ritualistic nature that sometimes turns off the contemporary viewer, who finds the duo's films too drawn out.) The fourth supporting factor concerning their slower pacing was its appropriateness for screen personae who were equally "slow" in the brain department.

Their silent comedy gift of slower pacing and its accompanying aid in their transition to sound film also had another important dimension—the team's continued use of visual comedy. Despite the duo's early grasp of the comic potential of the new sound technology, Laurel & Hardy were still an ongoing demonstration that one need not jettison a silent comedy shtick to succeed in sound films. After Chaplin, who made even less of a concession to sound (the Tramp spoke only once, and then not until 1936), visual comedy remained alive and well in the sound world of Stan & Ollie. I am particularly reminded of the simple but comically deliberate hand gestures Ollie frequently uses in the award-winning *The Music Box*. Like a silent comedy conductor, he frequently makes words seem superfluous.

For a period contrast, one might counter Laurel & Hardy's visual slapstick with the verbal slapstick of the Marx Brothers. That is, despite the often canned theatre nature of the Marxes' first two movies (*Coconuts*, 1929, and *Animal Crackers*, 1930—screen adaptations of two earlier Marx Brothers plays), they were first and foremost pioneers of *comic sound potential* during the early "talkie" years. While this is most obviously linked to the machine-gun delivery of Groucho or ethnic Chico, even the comic silence of Harpo was closely tied to sound, from his ever-present bicycle horn to the fractured English translations of his mime by dialect comedian Chico. Moreover, Harpo's best sight gags were invariably set up by a verbal comment, such as the *Duck Soup* call for a cigarette lighter that results in Harpo pulling a blowtorch from underneath his magic coat.

No such necessary link between sound and comedy existed for Laurel & Hardy, though paradoxically their voices (which nicely matched their physical personae) came to be famous, too.

Despite Laurel & Hardy's emphasis on visual comedy, their third important influence—joining their significance as icons and comedy pacing innovators—was their creative use of early sound (such as comic off-screen noise and the addition of cartoon-like sound effects). The patentedly more sound dependent Marx Brothers notwithstanding, Laurel & Hardy did have two central traits that lent themselves nicely to sound film—bumbling incompetency and comic tit-for-tat violence. A critic and documentary pioneer John Grierson observed in 1935: "They are clumsy, they are destructive . . . the world of sound is theirs to crash and tumble over [making this] a first creative use of [film] sound."[5]

In the 1930s celebrated realist filmmaker Alberto Cavalcanti also graded the team highly in this category: "They were the pioneers of sound comedy."[6] But whereas Grierson felt Laurel & Hardy's sound innovations were most assisted by the duo's lack of dependence upon (and thus distraction by) verbal comedy, Cavalcanti more generally credited the team's wisdom in minimizing any change during the coming of sound. Indeed, between the slower pacing and modest need of dialogue, the punning critic would have been tempted to label Laurel & Hardy "soundproof."

A fourth and final significant Laurel & Hardy influence is their Leo McCarey-orchestrated participation in the evolution of the comic antihero in mainstream American humor. Such humor was typified by the *New Yorker* writing of authors Benchley, Thurber, Day, and Perelman (see also the author's book on McCarey and the comic antihero[7]). Thus, credit for this antiheroic blossoming of the 1920s, as *the* American humor historian Walter Blair observes in his watershed *Native American Humor* is usually given to "the magazine [*The New Yorker*] which was more responsible than any other medium for the rise of a new type of humor."[8]

While McCarey's Laurel & Hardy did not invent the comic antihero, their phenomenal late-1920s rise to prominence in that comic guise paralleled the center-stage emergence of the character on the national scene. Five distinctive characteristics of the comic antihero emerge from extensive study of the subject: his constant frustration, his childlike naivete, his abundant leisure time, his apolitical nature, and his life in the city.[9] Each characteristic also constitutes a break with what had formerly been the dominant character type in American humor—the capable crackerbarrel Yankee (see n. 7.)

The core characteristic here, of course, is frustration. Stan & Ollie succeed at very little. As with their fictional counterparts, any attempts to deal with an irrational world in a rational matter are generally doomed from the beginning. The duo's only parallel with the capable Yankee is that they do manage, as the Benchley comic antihero does, to be persistent (which they complement with slow thinking). A famous illustration is their piano-moving exploits in *The Music Box* (1932). Thus, the following brief Laurel & Hardy overview demonstrates the comic richness of their antiheroic appeal. The examples are drawn from their early films in order to parallel the time when the comic misfit was moving to the center stage of American humor.

First, Stan & Ollie's frustration is centered around conflict with both wives and machines. Their wives dominate them, though Ollie generally finds himself to be the most comically misused, (as was the case with Thurber's "battle of the sexes"). Still, even when the story seems to overlook the woman, there exists a foreboding tension just beyond screen space. For example, the opening title of *Should Married Men Go Home?* (1928) asks the question: "What is the surest way to keep a husband home? Answer: Break both his legs."

The domestic "front" provides the team with one of their most popular settings for a pivotal Laurel & Hardy theme—escape. That is, they are often trying to sneak away from the restrictions of marriage, if only for an evening. These matrimonial "jail breaks" also give one a more logical understanding of what might first seem an illogical other Stan & Ollie setting—their propensity also to turn up in prison, with the accompanying expectation that an attempted comic escape will be forthcoming. Yet for this team, marriage and prison are just two comic extremes of what the boys symbolically are always trying to escape—the debilitating restrictiveness of modern life itself.

This subjugation, real or imagined, also includes an irony befitting an anti-heroic world view. An extended escape by Stan & Ollie is not only rare, it is probably not in their best interests. Domination by prison guards and wives might also be viewed as supervision for truly *childlike* antiheroes. Regardless, the price of their security is suppression, especially when one sees their increased incompetency on their own. Indeed, one might make a comic analogy between Stan & Ollie's suppression for security tendencies (at the risk of comic chaos on their own) and the still-provocative hypothesis of film theorist Siegfried Kracauer towards the German Expressionism film movement of the 1920s (paralleling the early Laurel & Hardy career).[10] Kracauer felt the limited narrative choices provided by fatalist German Expressionism—tyrants or chaos—aided the rise of Hitler, the tyrant who rose from the chaos of Germany's post–World War I Weimar Republic. While no comparably sweeping sociological generalizations seem to relate to Laurel & Hardy, the growth of antiheroic humor was not hindered by the 1930s Depression which made most people feel antiheroic.

The other primary source of frustration for the antihero is his dealings with the mechanical. For Stan & Ollie (especially Ollie), mastering a mechanical device is another way to assert manhood. But unlike the escape attempts, this attempt at technological dexterity represents not so much proving manhood (necessitating secrecy from one's wife) but rather playing it out before her and for her benefit.

In *Hog Wild* (1930) Stan & Ollie are systematically destroying a house in order to get a radio antenna on the roof. Granted, Ollie's wife has set him to the task, but it is a matter of male pride for him to accomplish it. Thus, when he comes crashing down the chimney, like some out-of-season Santa in civvies (after several other unplanned exits off the roof), his wife tells him maybe he ought to call it off. Ollie refuses, however, with a resounding, "I'll put it on the roof if it's the last thing I do!" (Had the film been produced in today's black comedy-conscious world, Ollie just might have received his wish.)

The second commonality between the antihero and Stan & Ollie is their childlike nature. Several of their films begin with Stan just dropping in at Ollie's home, as if to say, "Can you come out and play?" Comedy film historian Gerald Mast goes so far as to say, "The starting point of every Laurel and Hardy film is that they are overgrown children."[11] Certainly the relationships with their wives are more that of parent and child than of husband and wife. There is seemingly no sexual bond and the mothers/wives make the decisions. Moreover, the periodic escape attempts by the "boys" might best be equated with that nearly universal childhood dream (invariably pondered if not always acted upon) of running away from home, even for only a short adventure. And such pivotal comedy components as Stan's crying routine and Ollie bashfully playing with his tie are direct links to childhood.

In *Brats* (1930) they literally double as both fathers and sons. Thus dual-focus narrative convincingly illustrates that the Stan & Ollie adult is no different from the child. While the twosomes play at separate games (checkers and pool vs. blocks and boxing), both sets tend also to fight and be comically destructive. Appropriately, whereas the earlier activities of the fathers and sons were usually reciprocal, the finale is something of a shared experience. The children have left water running in the bathtub since early in the film, and when little Ollie asks for a bedtime drink his father unleashes a tidal wave by merely opening the door.

Playing upon the title of this film, Mast observes that the world of Stan & Ollie "is populated solely with brats. The childish spite of the central pair runs up against the equally childish spite of their opponents [the celebrated "tit-for tat" encounters]."[12] Though one might question whether Stan & Ollie's realm is "solely" composed of brats (see this chapter's later examination of Tiny Sandford's cop role in *Big Business*, 1929), it does point up the centrality of the childlike characteristic to the team's comedy.

A third shared trait between the team and the comic antihero is the frequent leisure-time focus of their activities. While there are Stan & Ollie exceptions to this, they still seem to have a preponderance of free or play time, which also reinforces one's image of them as children. Historically, this also reflects a period (1920s) when increased leisure time for the masses was first becoming a reality. And it also demonstrates, as noted by author Hamlin Hill, a retreat from the ever-more complex and dangerous modern world. That is, the antihero deals with this frightening outside realm by not dealing with it at all. Instead, he focuses "microscopically upon the individual unit . . . that interior reality—or hysteria . . . In consequence, modern humor deals significantly with frustrating trivia."[13]

An excellent example of Stan & Ollie leisure time activities occurs in *A Perfect Day* (1929), a film that also nicely complements some of the antiheroic points examined thus far. As the title indicates, it was just the right sort of a day for a picnic. Stan & Ollie, their wives, Uncle Edgar (Edgar Kennedy, with a bandaged gouty foot), and the family dog prepare for a carefree day.

Stan & Ollie make the sandwiches while their wives attend to other details. Just when the sandwiches have been nicely arranged on a tray being held by Ollie, the kitchen's swinging door shoots Stan into Ollie and the sandwiches are broadcast all over the room. The two fight, make up, and eventually rearrange the sandwiches. But all the mayhem has encouraged the dog to attack Uncle Edgar's bad foot. When Hardy tries to tear the family pet off Edgar's foot, he rebroadcasts the sandwiches.

Eventually all is ready and the car is packed. Neighbors yell goodbye and the trip begins, almost. A tire hits a nail in the driveway and now there is a flat to fix. As Ollie fixes the tire, Stan accidently assumes the dog's role of attacking poor Edgar Kennedy's foot. He manages to sit on the foot, step on it, slam it in the car door, and, in the grand finale, drops a tire jack on it. Eventually the tire is fixed, but numerous other comic frustrations deny the bunch their picnic. So much for the fate of antiheroes, even on a "perfect day."

There is more to Stan & Ollie's free time, however, than just the domestic scene. They play golf in *Should Married Men Go Home?* (1928), while their original plan in *We Faw Down* (1928) was a night of poker with the boys. But their non-domestic leisure time more often found them in a nightclub, such as with unplanned dates in *Their Purple Moment* (1928), their adventure at the Pink Pup Club in *That's My Wife* (1929, with Stan in drag as Ollie's wife), and *Blotto* (1930), where they manage to get drunk on a non-alcoholic beverage.

The fourth common characteristic linking Stan & Ollie to the comic antihero is a non-political nature. The closest they come is probably one of their prison or police films. Still, there are no real issues at stake. The comic interactions are more a game of hide-and-go-seek between overgrown kids. Gerald Mast, while comparing law enforcement characterizations in the films of Charlie Chaplin and Mack Sennett, makes a comment pertinent to the world of Stan & Ollie— "The prison cops in [Chaplin's] *The Adventurer* [1917] . . . shoot rifles at the escaping Charlie, and their bullets, unlike the bullets in Sennett comedies, look as though they could kill."[14] Like Sennett's cops, Laurel & Hardy's men in uniform are harmless. Indeed, the Laurel & Hardy cop is often given enough personality (something generally lacking in Sennett films) to even make him likeable. For instance, Laurel & Hardy stock player Tiny Sandford has a small but endearingly memorable cop role at the close of *Big Business*. He runs through a roller coaster of comic emotions as he first incredulously observes a classic tit-for-tat confrontation, and later tearfully commiserates with the boys as they momentarily feel remorse for their amusingly violent actions.

The utter incompetency of the comic antihero encourages the non-political stance. He is constantly buffeted about by the day-to-day frustrations of a seemingly irrational world. This figure is hardly capable of planning his leisure time, let alone becoming political. *Crucial* issues for Laurel & Hardy included things like keeping their derbies on or safely lighting a gas stove.

Just to play a comic devil's advocate, one might still wonder: if a political event were thrust upon an antihero, would he respond? No. Even then he would probably miss it because of a vacuity reminiscent of Laurel & Hardy, which fittingly might be called the "derby disease." That is, pioneer antiheroic writer Robert Benchley, in a well-documented study of news photographs taken of "cataclysmic events," found that:

If you want to get a good perspective on history in the making, just skim through a collection of news-photographs which have been snapped at those very moments when cataclysmic events were taking place throughout the world. In almost every picture you can discover one [antihero] guy in a derby hat who is looking in exactly the opposite direction from the excitement, totally oblivious to the fact that the world is shaking beneath his feet. That would be me, or at any rate, my agent [such as Stan & Ollie] in that particular part of the world in which the event is taking place.[15]

Not surprisingly, non-controversial comedy has long been a major selling point with Stan & Ollie audiences, just as it has no doubt contributed to the fact that many critics have not taken the duo seriously. Appropriately, one period critic who *did* recognize the team's significance, novelist Graham Greene, also praised the importance of their non-political stance. His 1940 review of the team's *A Chump at Oxford* ranked it:

with their best pictures—which to one heretic [Greene] are more agreeable than [the often political] Chaplin's; their clowning is purer; they aren't out to better an unbetterable world [later that year Chaplin released his black comedy on Hitler, *The Great Dictator*]; they've never wanted to play Hamlet [an unrealized Chaplin project, as well as a frequently cited *serious* role when a comedian starts to go deep-dish—somberly self-reflective].[16]

The fifth and final connection between Stan & Ollie and the comic antihero is that they are citizens (read: victims) of the city. Born of a period that for the first time found America's urban population outnumbering rural residents, Laurel & Hardy's classic films often presented the masses comically running amuck, be it the epic pie fight of *The Battle of the Century* (1927) or the cartoon-like traffic jam/demolition derby called *Two Tars* (1928). Even when one finds them in the seemingly more subdued California suburbs, those rows upon rows of identical white bungalows represent a bottled humanity just waiting for an excuse to explode comically—such as the team's greatest tit-for-tat encounter with their stock company regular James Finlayson in *Big Business*.

Ironically, Laurel & Hardy soon experienced in real life (1932) the violent chaos of massed humanity—their first joint visit to Europe (see Chapter 1), where huge admiring crowds became dangerously out of control. For a darker period send-up of the people one is also reminded of novelist and scriptwriter Nathanael West, especially his *The Day of the Locust* (1939), in which an uncontrollable movie crowd kills the central character.

The city is synonymous with all the frustrations of the antiheroic modern world, from America's fundamental Jeffersonian democracy fear of the cities (the unnatural mixing of too many people) to the anti-individualism of an ever-escalating mechanization of society. Of course, the Laurel & Hardy film turns such frustrations into fun. The large urban pool of people becomes a reservoir of comedy types, and the machines forever give the boys comic fits. Indeed, the antiheroic car of cars—the Model-T Ford—is often associated with them. And it need not be a focus of a film, such as the problematic automobile of *A Perfect Day*. For instance, the streetcar demolition of Stan's Model T at the close of *Hog Wild* was a most fitting close to the team's (but especially Ollie's) urban nightmare. This includes the antenna excursions that kept Ollie falling off the roof, and later being nearly flattened in traffic after falling off a ladder . . . from the back of the Model-T.

Thanks also to the tit-for-tat encounters, one sees just how thin modern urban man's veneer of civilization is. Interestingly enough, despite the cleansing total comedy violence, Stan & Ollie and their comic combatants still take turns while wreaking havoc. This telling residue of politeness—even in violence—nicely demonstrates the artificial facade of graciousness with which modern urban society frequently covers its stress points.

Naturally, this does not say Stan & Ollie are any more capable in the country, as their comic problems in *Them Thar Hills* (1934) witnessed. But it does suggest the obvious—there are more potential conflicts in the city, as well as temptations, which often means the same thing, since antiheroes like Stan & Ollie are constantly frustrated. Thus, a boy's night out might be ever so more inviting if there are nightclubs nearby, especially as in the classic early Laurel & Hardy films made prior to the repeal of Prohibition in 1933.

For the antihero, the often-harried urban setting can also be emasculating, which is hardly something this comedy victim needs, since his dominating wife already wears the pants in the family. But whereas this last reference to pants was metaphorical, there is something just off-center enough about the antiheroic city that its comic male victims sometimes literally appear in drag.

For Stan & Ollie, this most often means the former plays the girl. Without getting too Freudian in interpretation, this is perfectly in keeping with a modern (antiheroic) comedy movement where gender roles were often topsy-turvy to begin with. Such sexual inversions are even more obvious in screwball comedy, which, beginning in the mid-1930s, builds upon antiheroic comedy. This new genre dressed up the urban surroundings and added beautiful people, but this was more of a reflection of the need to mass market feature films than a substantive difference. The outcome was essentially the same: an eccentrically comic battle of the sexes, with the male generally losing.

Besides the emasculating appropriateness of periodically seeing one of the team in drag (in *Twice Two*, 1933, they both don women's clothing to play each other's wives), it is altogether fitting that Stan & Ollie's special friendship is occasionally portrayed as that of an actual couple, comic as that may be. Their friendship is clearly more important than anything else, including their screen marriages.

For instance, in *That's My Wife* (1929), where Stan convincingly plays Ollie's wife (an ongoing gag has a drunk flirting with Stan), the thin one has definitely supplanted his stout friend's spouse. Stan had dropped in on Ollie and his wife for two years! She had demanded a choice of her husband: Stan or her. When Ollie proved indecisive, she left. One should hasten to add, of course, that Stan's new identity as Mrs. Ollie was only a *temporary* ploy to suggest the fat one was happily married and therefore qualified to meet an eccentric inheritance requirement.

Consistent with their antiheroic world, a comic couple dichotomy of Ollie as male and Stan as female (whether in drag or not) still finds the "woman" as the ultimate winner (or, more precisely, Ollie as the primary sufferer). This occurs despite the fact that Stan is hardly the physically or verbally abusive wife with which Ollie usually has to cope.

These are the five core characteristics of the comic antihero—the twentieth-century humor evolution in which Laurel & Hardy played such an important part. This chapter also examined three other significant influences of Laurel & Hardy: as comedy icons, developers of a pivotal change in American film comedy pacing, and as movie pioneers in the innovative early use of comic sound.

While these have been the key thrusts of Laurel & Hardy's impact on American humor and popular culture, other items could no doubt be mentioned, for instance, their ongoing influence on comedians. This is best exemplified by the parallels between the team and early television's classic *Honeymooners* duo of Jackie Gleason and Art Carney as Ralph Kramden and Ed Norton.

As with Stan & Ollie, Ralph & Ed are in the age-old comedy contrast tradition of fat man/skinny man. Like Ollie, Ralph thinks he has all the answers, only to suffer constantly comic frustrations. His companion on these misadventures is the dumb but amazingly loyal Stan-like Ed. While Ralph & Ed bring a more blue-collar backdrop to the *Honeymooners*, it is still a program fundamentally wrapped around their leisure time, especially their bungled attempts to obtain permanent leisure time—via their ever-changing get-rich-quick schemes. And though Ralph is much more verbally combative with wife Alice (Audrey Meadows) than Ollie ever was with a spouse, the wife also controls things in the *Honeymooners*. Finally, with Ralph & Ed, as with Stan & Ollie, there is no designated straight man. Both team members share the laughter.

The ties are so many that one is tempted to read more into Gleason's popular 1950s catchline using a Laurel & Hardy stock company figure—"The ever popular Mae Busch.'' Regardless, Gleason was an acknowledged fan of early film comedy, and on at least one *Honeymooners* episode Ralph & Ed consciously played at being Stan & Ollie. These roots to an earlier team seemed to come out in truly diverse ways.

There are countless other examples of Laurel & Hardy influence. These would include their international fan club, the "Sons of the Desert,'' or Lou Costello's appropriation of the famous Stan cry and blink of the eyes when problems became a bit too much for his childlike screen character. Costello also did a variation with his fingers of Ollie's tie twiddling. Laurel bitterly resented these liberties, no doubt in part because Abbott & Costello usurped Laurel & Hardy as the film public's favorite comedy team in the early 1940s. In contrast, Dick Van Dyke's persona draws more broadly from the inspired physical comedy presence of Stan. They appropriately became close friends (see Chapter 1), and Van Dyke has been active in past celebrations of Laurel's career. Laurel & Hardy had a strong influence also on the British comedy team of Morecambe & Wise (see Chapter 4) and on Johnny Carson—such as his Ollie-like direct address to the camera in moments of comic frustration or his occasional fond aping of both Stan's and Ollie's mannerisms and their celebrated comic anthem, "Here's another fine mess . . .''

Countless artists in other media (and with radically different target audiences) have been influenced by the team. Two of the most diverse examples are Nobel Prize-winning playwright Samuel Beckett's existential *Waiting for Godot* (1957), and award-winning children's author/illustrator Maurice Sendak's *In the Night Kitchen* (1970).

Beckett, sometimes considered the most important of the post–World War II playwrights, draws strongly on Stan & Ollie for the derby-wearing characters Vladimir and Estragon in *Godot*. (For a thorough breakdown of their ties, see Jordan Young's fascinating essay "Popularity Grows on Borrowed Roots.''[17]) But critic/historian Kenneth McLeish provides a more manageable capsulization of his own: "The shifting, double-act, busy-doing-nothing relationship of Vladimir and Estragon . . . is based on that of Laurel and Hardy.''[18] In contrast, the three cooks of Sendak's *In the Night Kitchen* are identical clones of Ollie.

While it is hardly recommended procedure to compare existential plays and children's literature, if a general connection (besides Laurel & Hardy) were made between the two works, it would be in their dark comedy natures. Granted, there is a world of difference between examples, especially with a play sometimes unofficially referred to as *Waiting for God*. Still, a key point here is how the ongoing comedy relevance of Laurel & Hardy is maintained, at least in part, by the team's anticipation of today's ever-popular dark humor. In fact, pivotal black comedy novelist Kurt Vonnegut dedicated his book *Slapstick* (1976) "to the memory of Arthur Stanley Jefferson and Norvell Hardy, two angels of my time."[19]

For Vonnegut, this very loosely autobiographical novel has Stan & Ollie ties because their *slapstick* films are "what life *feels* like to me. There are all these tests of my limited agility and intelligence. They go on and on." And for Vonnegut, Stan & Ollie's "fundamental joke" is that they try their hardest at every test, always in "good faith" that this time will be different. Even though this is why Vonnegut, or the viewer in general, finds Laurel & Hardy funny, there is also a certain "common decency" about their patient methodical persistence in the face of life's constant frustrations.

If anything, the continuing entertainment impact of Laurel & Hardy has begun to escalate in recent years. For instance, film writer/director John Hughes's inspired 1987 *Planes, Trains and Automobiles* has Steve Martin and John Candy in a classic Stan & Ollie love-hate relationship of continuous comic disaster, including the mandatory destruction of a car. (And in the true spirit of a wrecked Stan & Ollie Model-T, Martin & Candy's totaled automobile produces one final laugh when it manages to work even after its comic Armageddon.) For the discerning viewer, it was hard to miss the comic inspiration for Hughes's film, or as *Variety* observed: "Steve Martin and John Candy repeatedly recall a contemporary Laurel & Hardy."[20]

In late 1987 the most direct and moving recent homage to the duo appeared in Ray Bradbury's affectionately poignant short story, "The Laurel and Hardy Love Affair."[21] This bittersweet tale chronicles a romance built upon a special fondness for Stan & Ollie. As sentimentally one-dimensional as that may sound, Bradbury is very effective in his intermingling of a real-life relationship with a host of Stan & Ollie basics (including tie twiddling and frequent picnicking by the celebrated 131 steps which the team endlessly take the piano up in *The Music Box*, 1932). Indeed, the ultimate severing of the couple's relationship is made all the more moving because just as they defined their love in Laurel & Hardy terms (right down to calling themselves "Stan" and "Ollie"), their breakup makes one feel as if Laurel & Hardy—the ultimate bonded couple—had broken up as well. Moreover, Bradbury's application of Stan & Ollie traits to a basic romance reminds the reader that one of the greatest yet often most-forgotten influences of any phenomenon is how it resurfaces in the little things of day-to-day existence, little things that slowly mold one over a lifetime. Such has been the case with Laurel & Hardy.

These Laurel & Hardy influences have surfaced often just in 1988, for instance. Film director/producer Martin Brest's critical and commercial hit *Midnight Run* has direct links to Laurel & Hardy. The film stars Robert De Niro and Charles Grodin as a bantering male couple in another love-hate relationship of nonstop fighting and making up, with soft-spoken Grodin a delightful contrast to loud, domineering De Niro (one plays Stan to the other's Ollie). And, like *Planes,*

Trains and Automobiles, Midnight Run also comically features a constant change in types of transportation.

Brest-directed films often feature such male teamings (see the comic coupling of Judge Reinhold with John Ashton in *Beverly Hills Cop*, 1984). And Brest has observed:

I think it all has to do with the fact that when I was growing up, the things I used to watch on TV that I enjoyed were Laurel and Hardy movies and "The Honeymooners." Those are the things that entertain me more than anything. Having them as sort of role models.[22]

On the hit television show "Newhart" there is more than a little of Stan & Ollie in the comic interaction of Newhart's Dick Loudon character (Vermont country inn owner) and Tom Poston's George Utley (inn handyman). Most obviously, Newhart's persona plays off the simpleton nature of Poston's character. In a 1988 article, Newhart observed:

There's a lot of Laurel & Hardy in the relationship, with me being Hardy and him being Stan Laurel. I do everything but look at the camera and say, "Did you see what he just did? Can you believe it?"[23]

Newhart might also have added that, as in the antiheroic interaction of Stan & Ollie, the dominant Loudon is more likely to play the final fool, because unlike Utley, he tries to make rational sense (after all, this *is* crackerbarrel Yankee Vermont) of an irrational world.

Other 1988 Laurel & Hardy surfacings start with the limited-run critical and commercial success of *Waiting for Godot* at Lincoln Center's Mitzi E. Newhouse Theatre. Steve Martin and Robin Williams starred, with at least one reviewing critic remembering Laurel & Hardy.

Casting Martin and Williams, whose first fame came from their respective standup comic work, would certainly have met with Laurel & Hardy approval. But one cannot help thinking what if the veteran team had been able to appear in the play they helped inspire, especially since Beckett's fascination with silent film comedians would seem to be further heightened by the ambiguity of their old age. Witness his use of Keaton in the movie *Film* (1964) two years before the comedian's death. Though the part was originally offered to Chaplin, Keaton (like Laurel & Hardy) seems much more appropriate for Beckett's tragicomic world. While Chaplin's Charlie is generally in control, *if* he so desires, Keaton's screen persona could beautifully suggest fatalist defeat even in victory, such as the close of his *Cops* (1922) or *College* (1927).

Additional 1988 links to Laurel & Hardy are as eclectic as a rambling storyline for Stan & Ollie. They range from notable actor Jack Gilford's funny/sad imitation of both comedians in *Cocoon II* (with old age, naturally, being *the* factor for both the scene and the movie), to renowned black-comedy cartoonist Gary Larson "starring" Stan & Ollie in one of his "The Far Side" cartoon strips. The boys are seen running down a long highway (towards the viewer), with an atomic bomb mushroom cloud rising in the background. The Ollie caption simply reads: "Now you've done it!" Larson has merely served up an amusingly pessimistic modern version of "Here's another fine mess . . . " One safe bet is that Laurel & Hardy will remain "contemporary" for some time to come.

NOTES

1. Vernon Scott, "Laurel, Hardy Legacy: A Victory for Widows' Rights," *Los Angeles Times*, August 29, 1975, Part IV, p. 22.

2. Ibid.

3. "Mr. Stan Laurel: A Great Comedy Partnership" (obituary), *The Times* London, February 24, 1965, p. 15a.

4. Walter Kerr, "Laurel and Hardy: The Saving Turnaround," in *The Silent Clowns*, Chapter 34, (New York: Alfred A. Knopf, 1975), p. 330.

5. John Grierson, "Summary and Survey: 1935," in *Grierson on Documentary*, ed. Forsyth Hardy (New York: Harcourt, Brace, 1947), p. 134.

6. Leonard Maltin (editor and chief contributor), *The Laurel & Hardy Book* (New York: Curtis Books, 1973), p. 74.

7. See especially Gehring, *Leo McCarey and the Comic Anti-Hero in American Film* (New York: Arno Press, 1980).

8. Walter Blair, *Native American Humor* (1937); repr. San Francisco: Chandler Publishing Company, 1960), p. 168. For more background on the comic antihero, especially foreshadowing of the character in various media prior to the 1920s, see Chapter 1.

9. See especially Wes D. Gehring, "The Comic Anti-Hero in American Fiction: Its First Full Articulation," *Thalia: Studies in Literary Humor*, Winter 1979–1980, pp. 11–14; Wes D. Gehring, "Film's First Comic Anti-Heroes: Leo McCarey's Laurel & Hardy," *Ball State University Forum*, Autumn 1979, pp. 46–56; Wes D. Gehring, "Background of the Comic Antihero," in *Screwball Comedy: A Genre of Madcap Romance* Chapter 2, (Westport, Connecticut: Greenwood Press, 1986), pp. 13–35.

The antihero is the opposite of the once dominant capable crackerbarrel Yankee figure. See especially: Wes D. Gehring, "The Yankee Figure in American Comedy Fiction," *Thalia: Studies in Literary Humor*, Winter 1978–1979, pp. 43–49; Wes D. Gehring, "Frank Capra: In the Tradition of Will Rogers and Other Yankees," *Indiana Social Studies Quarterly*, Fall 1981, pp. 49–56; Wes D. Gehring, "The Neglected Career of Kin Hubbard's Abe Martin: Crackerbarrel Figure in Transition," *Indiana Magazine of History*, March 1982, pp. 26–37.

10. See Siegfried Kracauer's *Theory of Film: The Redemption of Physical Reality* (New York: Oxford University Press, 1950).

11. Gerald Mast, "More Fun Shops," in *The Comic Mind: Comedy and the Movies*, Chapter 12, 2d edition (1973; repr. Chicago: University of Chicago Press, 1979), p. 191.

12. Ibid., p. 192.

13. Hamlin Hill, "Modern American Humor: The Janus Laugh," *College English* (December 1963), p. 174.

14. Gerald Mast, *A Short History of the Movies*, "The Comics: Mack Sennett and the

Chaplin Shorts,'' in *A Short History of the Movies*, Chapter 5, 3d ed. (1971; repr. Indianapolis: Bobbs-Merrill, 1981), pp. 76–92.

15. Robert Benchley, "Johnny-on-the-Spot," in *From Bed to Worse: Or Comforting Thoughts About the Bison* (New York: Harper & Brothers, 1934), p. 255.

16. Graham Greene, *A Chump at Oxford* review, *Spectator*, February 23, 1940, p. 248.

17. Jordan Young, "Popularity Grows on Borrowed Roots," *Pratfall*, vol. 1, no. 5, pp. 7–9.

18. Kenneth McLeish, "Samuel Beckett," in *Arts in the Twentieth Century* (New York: Viking Penguin, 1985; Markham, Ontario: Penguin Books Canada Limited, 1986), p. 463.

19. Kurt Vonnegut, see "Dedication" and "Prologue" in *Slapstick* (New York: Delacorte Press/Seymour Lawrence, 1976), pp. 1–19.

20. "Planes, Trains, and Automobiles" review, *Variety*, November 25, 1987, p. 14.

21. Ray Bradbury, "The Laurel and Hardy Love Affair," *Playboy*, December 1987, pp. 76–78, 210–11. See also the Bradbury book *The Toynbee Convector* (New York: Alfred A. Knopf, 1988). A condensed version appeared in the September 1988 *Reader's Digest*, pp. 149–52.

22. Hellel Italie, "Director Martin Brest is considered a bit of a smart aleck," (wire service story), *Waterloo Courier* (Iowa), August 10, 1988, p. C–3.

23. Elaine Warren, "He Forgot His Own Name—And Was Hired on the Spot," *TV Guide*, November 5, 1988, p. 11.

3

Laurel & Hardy:
PERIOD REFLECTIONS

Opening Title for *The Finishing Touch* (1928): "The story of two boys who went to school for nine years—and finished in the first reader."

In order to broaden the book's Laurel & Hardy perspective, this chapter includes the reprinting of the Helen Louise Walker interview "Ka-Plop and Ka-Bloop: Laurel and Hardy Reveal What Makes You Hear Such Funny Things" (*Motion Picture Classic*, June 1930), the Dorothy Spensley article/interview "Those Two Goofy Guys" (*Photoplay*, July 1930), and my own "Encore: An Interview/ Article Collage" of pivotal and/or provocative Laurel (team spokesman) observations drawn from often early sources.

The Walker piece recommends itself for four reasons. First, it is one of the more ambitious early Laurel & Hardy interviews. Second, Hardy assumes a more active part than is often the case in team interviews. Indeed, if one knew nothing about the duo beyond this interview, it might be wrongly assumed that Hardy was the off-screen team leader, just as his was the dominant film character. Thus, when the Walker-interviewed Hardy even contests a Laurel position with a joke (though at his own expense), it is an entertaining surprise that rarely occurred outside their movies. In fact, Hardy's comic comeback as to who was hit by the most pies in *The Battle of the Century*—"I guess more of them landed on me! In the first place, there's more *of* me!"—is reminiscent of Hardy's screen character. It is as if a bit of Oliver momentarily surfaced in Hardy's everyday conversation.

A third plus for the Walker interview is that the comedians seem genuinely very enthusiastic about exploring and sharing the comedic possibilities of sound during this period of technological transition. There is even a reference to how a sound-effect problem was solved in the previous year's Douglas Fairbanks, Sr./Mary Pickford feature film *The Taming of the Shrew* (1929). Moreover, the often reticent Hardy goes on to add pertinent observations about the "old days" with Larry Semon. The interview suggests that at times or with given subjects (such as cinema's comic use of sound), Hardy's commitment to the production process was greater than often suggested. (For another more visible Hardy interview see Chapter 4's examination of Alice L. Tildesley's 1930 piece "Funny Film Faces: How They Got That Way.")

Of course, as a tongue-in-cheek aside, one might simply credit Hardy's special interest herein to his healthy appetite. Certainly, the interview's most entertainingly protracted comic commentary occurs when Hardy discusses (with great pleasure) the tasty items the film industry has substituted for such things as mud (whipped cream and cocoa) and snowballs (pineapple sherbet, egg whites, corn flakes). One might comically ponder if whipped cream and cocoa had any influence on the frequency with which mud puddles appeared in the adventures of Stan & Ollie.

Fourth, the Walker interview briefly reiterates the team position against impromptu comedy in public (see the 1929 Eleanor Parker piece examined in Chapter 4). Consummate professionals, Laurel & Hardy did not wish to compromise their high comedy film reputation with unplanned, potentially mediocre public performances as Stan & Ollie. However, as suggested earlier, this principle did not preclude the occasionally very brief, reflexive public assumption by the team of their screen personae. In fact, after they politely decline Walker's request for them to improvise a Stan & Ollie comic quarrel, the interviewer's description of their joint solidarity on the issue is right out of their movies: "They looked at one another, their mouths curved upward [into smiles], and nodded in unison."

Part of the attraction of Spensley's "Those Two Goofy Guys" is as a companion piece to Walker's interview. Appearing nearly concurrently, Spensley has written a big picture overview of the team, while Walker lets the subjects themselves address a more narrow focus (the comic use of film sound).

Spensley, however, has also based his piece on an interview with the team. But for whatever reasons he has chosen to transcribe most of it into his own words—possibly just a note-taking convenience, since Spensley interviewed the team over dinner (while Walker and the duo discussed comic sounds in the working atmosphere of a studio publicity office). Or, it might have been that Hardy's laryngitis kept it from being an adequately balanced interview to Spensley. (The cynic might also claim developing laryngitis is more in fitting with Hardy's reputation for disinterest in this sort of thing.) Or finally, the fact that the team was not as comfortable with interviews conducted in public (which this seems to have been) might have resulted in Spensley's deciding the material was best put in his own words.

Regardless, what emerges is a broad-based look at two new comedy celebrities. Both their amazing fame and diverse backgrounds are examined briefly. The realistic foundation of their comedy is underlined, as is their scientific "clocking" (counting): each Laurel & Hardy short subject must have at least seventy-five identifiable laughs.

Spensley also provides a period insight into the popularity of Laurel's crying shtick. The routine is so often requested, publicly and privately (thanks to his four-year-old daughter), that Laurel confesses: "I don't like to cry." Spensley finds the comment enough of a comedy bombshell to twice quote the comedian on the subject in an article otherwise largely devoid of Laurel or Hardy original comments. Indeed, Spensley seems to be trying to reduce Laurel (via the repeated line) to some sort of comic Greek chorus of one. While the revelation now carries little impact (both the crying shtick and the admission are, after all, old news), the subject still represents another way to gauge the team's fame. When Laurel's dislike of the bit comes up in much-later interviews, one assumes it is a natural outgrowth of his responding to the request over the course of a career . . . not by 1930! Moreover, later comments generally limit the topic to simply his displeasure, without elaborating on the nonstop requesting that triggered it.

"Those Two Goofy Guys" is also not without small bonus points of interest, such as the duo's culinary tastes at the press date. Fittingly, Laurel the sailor, who loves to fish in his own boat, dines on baked barracuda. Even more appropriately, chef Hardy of the rich eating habits and mighty girth is treating his laryngitis with a chocolate ice cream concoction.

These, then, are some of the highlights found in the contrasting period perspectives by Walker and Spensley. But for the student of Laurel & Hardy, the reprints will undoubtedly offer additional insights, if no more than instructing one by what is *not* included. Finally, the "Encore" sampling ties this chapter together by offering a closing showcase for some insightful comments from an often relatively young Laurel.

For a critical examination of additional interviews pertinent to the study of Laurel & Hardy, see Chapter 4.

THOSE TWO GOOFY GUYS

By Dorothy Spensley

Three and a half years ago Stan Laurel and Oliver "Babe" Hardy were just a couple of bright boys knocking about Mr. Hal Roach's studio.* Today the world is laughing at them. They are billed over feature pictures with sex appeal heroines in theater electrics. They are inserted in initial talkies of grand opera baritones [*The Rogue Song*, 1930]. This, to their regret.

They are the comedy sensations of the season.

And all because they have learned, by a lucky stroke, that the public likes to see itself caricatured on the screen; that the public can laugh at the maunderings

*Reprinted from *Photoplay*, July 1930, pp. 72, 136.

of a fat man who shakes a warning pudgy forefinger at a sensitive simpleton who is prone to weep.

They must be a success because they are waylaid for autographs. They are asked to talk over the radio. Festive nights are given for them at leading hotels. Fans, loitering in preview theater lobbies, sidle up and ask Stan to cry. Cry like he does in pictures.

"And I don't like to cry," said Stan, wrinkling his nose over the baked barracuda.

"There, there! You won't have to cry."

Babe looked relieved, because he was in on this, too. He had laryngitis, and was eating chocolate ice cream for it.

"I don't like to cry," said Stan, smiling bravely as he forked the barracuda.

And you won't have to, or we'll know the reason why, won't we Oliver? But Oliver was folding the rich yellow blobs of a pitcher of cream into the dark loam of the ice cream. He weighs well over two hundred and fifty, and his middle name is Norvell. He was reared to be an attorney, in Atlanta, Georgia. And he's married.

Oliver is the punctilious gentleman of the comedies; the dainty, particular dear who is social mentor for Stan. You've noticed it in their thirty-two comedies. He is the one who gently chides Stan when Stan does the wrong thing. He is the exasperated darling who puffs his cheeks and looks long and hard at Stan when, say, he drops the eclair down the hostess' back.

But Stan is the one who whimpers. He is the one who crescents his brows, blinks his eyes, gulps, draws his lips into a quivering wounded slit, and weeps. He is the underdog with the lacrymose pan.

To us, he will always be Whimpering Stan. Everywhere he goes they ask him to weep. That's why he doesn't like to cry. Even when he goes home at night, Lois, his four-year-old, meets him at the gate with a request for daddy to weep. His wife has laughed at his whining pan for six years.

Oliver drives a sportive coupe, and Stan a Ford. But when Stan takes the family out on a Sunday, it's in a Pierce-Arrow.

Who thinks of the gags?

"We both do," says Whimpering Stan, grinning.

"We both do," says Punctilious Oliver, soberly.

It takes three men to make Laurel and Hardy comedies. Stan writes the skeleton story and takes it to the set where Jim Parrot, director, brother of Charlie [sic] Chase, another Roach comedian, and Oliver, go into a huddle.

The laugh-getting gags are worked out as they shoot. It takes seven days to make a comedy that must elicit seventy-five laughs. They count the laughs at previews. That's what they call "clocking" a comedy. If it "clocks" less than that something is wrong. One comedy brought one hundred and twenty laughs. A record. The comedies are usually two-reels. If they sustain the laugh interest, they are allowed to run two and a half or three.

What does the public laugh at? Homely situations, mostly. Everyday occurrences. Consider "A Perfect Day." It's built on the simple situation of a family preparing for a picnic, packing the basket, assisting gouty uncle to the balky Ford. "Night Owls" is not built so much on the antics of thieves, but rather the utter idiocy of two humans trying to enter a house without a key. Ordinary stuff. Everyday situations, but etched by comedy hands; seen through the merry squint of comedy eyes.

Whimpering Stan has more to do with the comedies than he reticently admits, it is said. It is he who plants the seed of the story and watches it bloom into something funny. A man of about forty, with blond hair and live blue eyes, he has seen plenty of stage experience.

He is a Lancashire lad, born in Ulverston, England, of professional parents. His childhood was spent in the music halls. In 1910 he came to America with Fred Karno's London Comedians. Charles Chaplin was in the troupe. Stan understudied him, and when Charlie left to go into pictures, Stan stepped into his oversized shoes. Like Chaplin, he realizes that a laugh is close to a tear, and he sprinkles his stories with the faintest suggestion of pathos.

That bristling pompadour of Whimpering Stan was arrived at by accident. He had played in a convict picture and so had Babe [*The Second Hundred Years*, 1927]. Both had shaved their heads. At the end of the picture Stan sailed for England and Oliver went vacationing. When Stan returned his hair covered his head like a porcupine's thatch. Roach saw it and that was the beginning of Stan's stylish bob.

They roister about the lot, Babe and Stan sometimes clowning for favored visitors. Babe sings, and Stan plays the piano. They have no desire to make feature length pictures unless they find a sure-fire story. They have seen too many comedy teams hit the rocks in seven-reel specials.

KA-PLOP AND KA-BLOOP: Laurel and Hardy Reveal What Makes You Hear Such Funny Things

By Helen Louise Walker

SCREEN TEST:*

Do you know what noise a fat man makes when he falls into a mud puddle? A thin man? Can you spell the sound?

Do you know what a "ka-Bloop!" is? How is it made?

A "gullup"? A "crattle"?

Have you a little sound library in your home?

Do you know the difference between a "zowie" and a "swizsh"? Do you care? You do?

*Reprinted from *Motion Picture Classic*, June 1930, pp. 70, 103, 105.

Then read this article and you will learn all this and much more which the up-to-date movie-goer should know.

Comedians do not fall down and go "boom" any more. Dear me, no. This is very passe. When the up-to-date comedian falls down, he goes "blump." I have the words of Laurel and Hardy for it and, after all, they should know exactly how comedians fall.

You see, with the addition of sound to comedies, funny noises have become important and the old-fashioned "whams" and "zowies" of the comic strips, which were imitated in the early sound comedies, simply will not do any more at all.

For instance, in a recent picture, Mr. Hardy (he is the round one) was required to sock Mr. Laurel (the sad one) on the head. In the old days, they tell me, the sound would have been recorded as a mere garden variety of "thud." But not now. In this scene, the sound of the sock on Mr. Laurel's head was recorded as a resounding and unexpected "clank" and the effect was obtained by a prop man somewhere smiting the brake drum of an automobile with a mallet.

"It was a great improvement," the pair informed me with satisfaction, "because it was both unexpected and incongruous. Those are the qualities which make people laugh at noises in pictures."

BARRELS OF FUN

"Well—just what is a 'blump'?" I wanted to know. "The noise you make when you fall down?"

"When *I* fall down," Hardy informed me, seriously, "they drop a big empty barrel on a stone floor. When Stan (Laurel) falls down, they drop a *little* barrel. That makes the right sized 'blump' for each of us."

"I see. There's a lot more to this funny-sound business than I had imagined." Yes, *Watson*, a good deal more.

"Oh, my yes! Why, we have a whole library of sounds on file. You know— whenever we get a particularly good effect, we file a strip of the sound track away so we can use it again in another picture. We get them from other studios, too. Whenever we hear of a good noise being 'shot' on some other lot, we send over and ask them for a bit of the record of it. A sound like—oh, a good siren, or a donkey braying, a particularly good crash or squeak or an odd effect with voices. We have hundreds of 'em."

PIE PERFECTION

"We have to keep studying sounds all the time. There are, for instance, what we call 'gooey sounds.' Those include the noise a pie makes, hitting you in the face. That is a sort of 'ka-slush,' which is much better than the sound we used to use, which was more of a 'ka-plop.' A pie makes its own noise pretty well. But if it seems to us that it isn't emphatic enough, we can always add to it by dropping wet towels on the pavement."

"We made a picture not long ago in which we used more than five thousand big, gloopy custard pies [*The Battle of the Century*, 1927]."

"And most of those pies landed on me," sighed Laurel.

"I guess more of them landed on me!" retorted Hardy. "In the first place, there's more *of* me!"

"We didn't mind the pies so much, though. You get used to pies, in this business. But this was an outdoor set and there were a lot of bee-hives not far away. The pies attracted the bees and we were simply covered with the things. They couldn't sting us because the stuff—the custard—was too thick all over us. But they certainly gave us a lot of trouble."

'SOFT' SOUNDS

"Other 'gooey' sounds, of course, have to do with soft food being thrown—and snowballs. A snowball makes a 'plosh.' And mud. When you fall into a small mud puddle, you record a little 'plop,' but when it is a big mud puddle, then it is a big 'blop.' The small sound is easy, but we get the big one—the 'blop'—by running a big truck through thick mud.

"Just lately we have been doing some research in the laboratory on gurgles. We use those when one of us swallows something, or when we are under water, or something like that. We used to use just a plain 'glub.' But we want something better—more of a 'ka-bloop-ka-bloop-ka-bloop.'

"The best effect we have been able to get so far was by putting one end of a hose in a barrel of water and then blowing through the other end. The air going through the water in the barrel makes a fair 'ka-bloop.' But I think we'll get something better. We're working on something which will make a good 'gul-luping' sound, too. That's really good for swallowing.

"We got a good effect the other day when Stan had to swallow a nickel. We dropped an automobile crank into a metal washboiler and it made a good 'plink.' "

CRASH CACOPHONY

"You're getting into crashes!" interrupted Laurel. "They're pretty difficult, too. A rattley crash—a sort of—of—'crattle,' we call it—we do with broken glass in a wash-boiler. A splintery sound we make with thin boards—smashing them.

"You know, you never can tell how a noise is going to record. Remember when Mary Pickford hit Doug on the head with a stool in 'The Taming of the Shrew'? It didn't sound at all like a man being hit on the head with a stool when she really did it. It sounded like someone thumping a watermelon to see whether it was ripe.

"I think what they finally did was to hit a small keg with a padded mallet.

"A kiss can get you into more trouble—I mean, of course, the *sound* of a kiss—in pictures, than almost anything else. You can't imagine what they sound like, sometimes! Who was it—Ian Keith and Dorothy Mackail?—who broke all the microphones with one kiss? *What* a kiss!

"We had to do some snores the other day. Babe and I made the snoring noise and then a prop man blew a little tin whistle after each snore—for the little 'whee' sound, you know."

IMPROVING ON NATURE

"We make the sound of a slap by whacking the floor with a big wet mop—and a 'kurrunch' we do with broken glass.

"But we've improved a good deal on the old-fashioned 'zowie' A 'zowie' is the sound you make when you swing at somebody and miss. You know, the blow just whizzes past his ear. Well, we call that a 'swizsh!' now and we do it by running a wind-machine—one of those things like a big fan—against canvas. That's a good sound.

"One of the strangest things is the sound a gun makes over the microphone. A real gun makes a feeble little 'crack,' which is no good at all. It's a funny thing, but we have had much better effects for gun shots by merely bursting a paper bag close to the microphone.

"Another good way, if you want a very loud sound, is to slap a leather cushion with a paddle.

"We do horses' hooves with cocoanuts. 'Bop-kok! Bop-kok!' You know the sound."

"Comedy-making has changed a lot since the old days," Hardy remarked, becoming reminiscent suddenly. "I can remember when I used to make pictures with Larry Semon in the old days. If we wanted mud to throw at each other, we whipped up some thick soap suds and mixed the stuff with lamp black. Ugh! Often, if we were in a hurry, we just went out and got some real mud."

TASTY MUD

"But comedies are getting effete. Now, if you please, when we want mud, we take whipped cream and mix it with cocoa! It isn't so bad when you get it in your mouth.

"We're making a picture now with snowballs [*Below Zero*, 1930]. And we make them out of pineapple sherbet, beaten whites of eggs and corn flakes. Not bad at all, if you swallow some!

"Stan ate a good deal of rice pudding mixed with fire-extinguisher not long ago. Remember the picture where the rice boiled out of the radiator of the car [*Hoosegow*, 1929]? We put the fire-extinguisher in the rice pudding to make it boil out that way."

"It wasn't bad at all," Stan reassured me. "The fire-extinguisher didn't have much taste—and it was quite good pudding!"

These two look disconcertingly like their screen selves, when you meet them. Sitting there in the publicity office, I fully expected them to begin tearing each other's coats at any moment.

"Couldn't you do just a *little* quarrel—or a small argument—for me?" I pleaded.

"No, indeed!" They were very firm. "We aren't that clever at acting!"

They looked at one another, their mouths curved upward, and nodded in unison. Perfect agreement. And a happy thing to see in this town where most comedy teams do most of their fighting off the screen.

They're having a good time, putting comedy on a sound basis—making up noises, as well as faces.

"ENCORE: AN INTERVIEW/ARTICLE COLLAGE"

Compiled by Wes D. Gehring

In 1929 Laurel called the team's revolutionary reduction in comedy pacing, which was both a Stan & Ollie trademark and the perfect transition into sound films, "slow-slapstick." To him, the key example was the duo's epic pie fight— *The Battle of the Century* (1927):

We went at it, strange as it may sound, psychologically. We made every one of the pies count.

A well-dressed man strolling casually down the avenue, struck squarely in the face by a large pastry, would not proceed at once to gnash his teeth, wave his arms in the air and leap up and down [as in a speeded-up Mack Sennett film]. His first reaction, it is reasonable to suppose, would be one of numb disbelief. Then embarrassment, and a quick survey of the damage done to the person. Then indignation and a desire for revenge would possess him; if he saw another pie close at hand, still unspoiled, he would grab it up and let fly.[1]

In another 1929 interview, with tongue firmly in cheek, Laurel had these thoughts on the coming of sound: "Well, I guess I'll be looking for a good job as a janitor or something." Addressing Hardy, he further kidded, "This is our end, Oliver."[2]

If the antiheroic Stan & Ollie were pigeonholed under any one comedy theory, it would be that of superiority, for as a 1929 Laurel observed, "People like to laugh at the misfortune of others. It's human nature. So we merely exaggerate those misfortunes. We multiply everything, making humour in the very fact of repetition."[3]

Consistent with the nonpolitical nature of an antiheroic persona, Laurel did not believe in comedic message movies. Thus, in another 1929 article he stated, "Too many people believe that the world rests on their shoulders. A comedian should remember just one thing. That is, 'Laugh and the box office is always busy.' "[4]

Despite the nonmessage use of exaggerated repetition, the team's comedy is based in realism. In 1935 Laurel said, "You never yet saw us in a picture that had no dramatic logic. Almost anything we do could happen between friends, if there happened to be two friends like Laurel and Hardy . . . Coincidence can be exaggerated but must still loiter somewhere within the realm of possibility."[5]

Even with such articulation, filmmaking Laurel could not be sure of the comedic success of his current project. On the set of *Bonnie Scotland* (1935) he opined:

But when it comes to making a film, I'm so near to the darned thing I can neither see nor feel it. Everybody tells me it is going to be the best we've made. All I know, by this time, is that I want to get it finished as quickly as possible.

By the time we're nearly through with a film . . . I never seem able to make up my mind whether it is a howling success or a crying shame.[6]

Bonnie Scotland was followed by another Laurel & Hardy operatic parody, *The Bohemian Girl* (1936). Laurel, ever the silent comedian despite being well into the sound era, said:

Music is to comedy what seasoning is to any palatable dish . . .

We have found that good music is an ideal background for comedy. The contrast of fine singing voices and classical instrumental numbers with carefully chosen humorous situations is ideal "theatre." It is just startling enough to be entertaining when the various elements are properly blended.[7]

The year after the release of *The Bohemian Girl* a team classic appeared, *Way Out West* (1937). While the extent to which Laurel & Hardy improvised has been exaggerated, during the production of this western spoof Laurel revealed:

We needed a scene giving a reason for us to be ordered out of town. In the script, Hardy had a gun which he accidently fired at the sheriff, as a result of which we were ordered on our way. But when we began to shoot the scene, we saw it was neither plausible nor funny.

In talking things over, it occurred to us that it might be amusing if we caught a ride on the stagecoach, got into a flirtation with a girl in it, who would turn out to be the sheriff's wife, and complain about us when we drove into town, thus getting us into conflict with her husband. So far it has developed into several comedy situations which make us believe we've hit the right thing.[8]

Despite, however, their connections with improvisation, it would be more logical to celebrate the well-honed nature of the team's comedy—the numerous comedy variations on a single theme that reappear throughout their work. The most famous example of their preference for polished perfection was their anguish over a surprise debut on live television's 1954 *This Is Your Life*. Laurel called it "a staggering experience . . . we certainly never intended to start out on an unrehearsed network show!"[9] Still, as early as 1929 Laurel stated, "The reason we avoid all public appearances [is because] people expect us to be funny all the time. We are like everyone else with a regular business. Comedy is our business.''[10] As Hardy further articulated in this piece, improvisation did *not* allow for quality control. They could not always live up to their high studied comedy standards.

Naturally, a *real* quality control problem for Laurel was his marriages. But despite messy career-damaging relationships, his wit surfaced here, too à la his legendary observation: ''You know my hobby—and I married them all.'' Less familiar are his funny but still hopeful 1943 comments after his final break with frequent wife Virginia Laurel: ''I guess you can't warm love over. After the first time the flavor's gone . . . [But] I wouldn't say I'll never marry again. That's a hard thing to say. You never know what the future will bring.''[11]

As if life's happiness were based upon some celestial balancing act, while his film career was all but over by the mid-1940s, Stan Laurel's next marriage was a *lasting* success.

NOTES

1. ''Comics Famous By Accident,'' *The Los Angeles Times*, December 29, 1929, Part III, p. 18.

2. Eleanor Parker, ''Two Prize Idiots,'' *The Picturegoer*, October 1929, p. 43.

3. Ibid.

4. Loretta K. Dean, ''THOSE FUNNY BOYS: A Few Inside Facts about the Screen's Funniest Pair of Comedians and the Man Who Has Photographed Most of Their Pictures,'' *American Cinematographer*, October 1929, p. 39.

5. W. H. Mooring, ''With MacLaurel & MacHardy in Bonnie Scotland,'' *Film Weekly* (England), June 28, 1935, p. 8.

6. Ibid.

7. ''Music Laurel's Seasoning,'' *New York Daily Mirror*, February 28, 1936, n.p. cited. In the ''Laurel & Hardy Files,'' Billy Rose Theatre Collection, New York Public Library at Lincoln Center.

8. Eldon K. Everett, ''[A Lost Article from] 1937—An Interview with L & H,'' reprinted in *Classic Film Collector*, Winter 1976, p. 38.

9. ''No Laughing Matter,'' *TV Guide*, April 23, 1955, p. 14.

10. Parker, ''Two Prize Idiots,'' p. 43.

11. ''One More Crash in Love Can Not Sour Stan Laurel,'' *Milwaukee Journal*, July 6, 1943, n.p. cited. In the ''Laurel & Hardy Files,'' Billy Rose Theatre Collection, New York Public Library at Lincoln Center.

4

A Laurel & Hardy
Bibliographical Essay

"Nobody loved them but the public." This popular early refrain about the team addressed their frequent lack of critical success, or even serious attention.

This bibliographical essay furnishes, in a logical manner, those key reference materials that are most helpful in studying the lives and careers of Laurel & Hardy. All works are divided first by length and then by subject. The pivotal works discussed are also found in the bibliographical checklist in Chapter 5. Numerous foreign language items are examined but the primary focus of this bibliographical essay is Laurel & Hardy print material available in English.

The first section is devoted to book-length sources written about the comedians. These materials are subdivided into four categories: Laurel & Hardy viewed by an insider (an author who knew the subject firsthand), general biographies, critical studies, and references. While these books sometimes focus on one of them, they do not entirely divorce themselves from the team (though the Jenny Owen-Pawson and Bill Mouland *Laurel Before Hardy* comes close). Thus, even these are treated as team biographies.

The second section comprises shorter works and includes articles, interviews, book chapters, and monographs. Its two subdivisions are Laurel & Hardy critical essays and print interviews/reminiscences with Laurel & Hardy and colleagues or families. There is also a brief account of existing Laurel & Hardy archives and film sources.

BOOKS

Laurel & Hardy Viewed by an Insider

For Laurel & Hardy this category very nearly does not exist. Unlike my experience in doing biographies on Charlie Chaplin, W. C. Fields, and the Marx Brothers—where book sources included the comedians themselves, their children, a grandchild, a wife, and a mistress—a Laurel & Hardy volume has yet to have such an origin (though Laurel's exwife Virginia Ruth had a major impact upon Fred Guiles's *Stan: The Life of Stan Laurel*). Considering the significant importance and length of the duo's career, not to mention the sometimes stormy marriages and personal lives of the two (especially Laurel), this is rather surprising. It is particularly startling when one considers the number of tell-all insider books that have appeared in recent years. And though it is easy to sometimes denigrate such works as, at best, opportunistic, there can often be pleasant surprises. For instance, the book *W. C. Fields & Me* (1971), by the comedian's longtime mistress Carlotta Monti (coauthor Cy Rice), is a very insightful look at one of Laurel & Hardy's major comedy contemporaries. Along similar lines is the book by Chaplin's second wife Lita Grey (with Morton Cooper)—*My Life with Chaplin* (1966). Though these relationships produced a number of messy scandals (the marketing of both volumes played upon sensationalism), Grey's book is surprisingly even tempered in its informative telling.

The Laurel & Hardy insider work is, however, miles away from any such prior cases of controversy. It is the result of a fan who became a friend, a student who became a professor—John McCabe. His pioneering *Mr. Laurel & Mr. Hardy* (1961, a timely work on the team following the 1950s revival of interest in the duo via television) is an affectionate examination of the men and their movies. This fondness is even reflected in a title that recycles the comically dignified manner in which Stan & Ollie were often introduced in their films. It was born of McCabe's close friendship with an older Laurel, whom the author first met in 1953 England, where the team was touring and McCabe was an American graduate student at the Shakespeare Institute in Stratford.

Working with the close assistance of Laurel, this book (and McCabe's later *The Comedy World of Stan Laurel*, 1974), is the closest the comedian came to an autobiography. *Mr. Laurel & Mr. Hardy* is also enriched by a rare and insightful interview with the very private Hardy, the subsequent assistance of the rotund comedian's widow Lucille, and periodic commentaries on humor and/or Laurel & Hardy by numerous prominent comedians, from Groucho Marx to Marcel Marceau.

Later editions of this perpetually in print volume added a Dick Van Dyke foreword drawn from his 1965 funeral eulogy for Laurel, and an eclectic "The Rest of the Story" final chapter that included everything from Laurel's measured response to being honored with a special Oscar (pride humorously kept in balance—the statuette was nicknamed "Mr. Clean"), to McCabe's cofounding (with Laurel's blessing) of an organization celebrating the team—The Sons of the Desert. (See Chapter 1 for more on the great Laurel & Hardy film from which it draws its name.) Subsequent club chapters—"tents"—would, in accordance with the organization's tongue-in-cheek constitution (also included in *Mr. Laurel & Mr. Hardy*) derive their names from other Laurel & Hardy film titles. The book is also indexed, and includes a filmography of the team's movies and their solo film work.

The danger with any *insider* volume is that of built-in bias, given the unique personal relationship between subject and author. Subjectivity can be a weakness and a strength. Prominent film historian David Robinson's positive *Sight and Sound* review (Winter 1961/1962) of the book correctly labels McCabe's position as that of an "idolator." Yet, McCabe's loving enthusiasm generally pushes any barometric reading of the work more towards strength than weakness. Moreover, as a pioneering book on the team, a certain degree of fanaticism is to be expected, or maybe even needed (as with any such work), to break old traditions of neglect.

All this is not to say the book is without problems. *Mr. Laurel & Mr. Hardy* is mildly flawed both by not giving the team's mentor Leo McCarey more credit and by not at least touching on the darker side of Laurel (see Chapter 1 for more on these items). While there was a time I was unduly harsh on McCabe for these very reasons (*Films in Review*, November 1979), the book's positive aspects (including its historical timeliness) outweigh these complaints. In addition, with McCabe's later (by thirteen years, 1974) *The Comedy World of Stan Laurel* he went a long ways toward rectifying these two omissions.

The original goal of *Mr. Laurel & Mr. Hardy* had been merely a closer look at the team's construction of movies. However, McCabe had included enough rich material from the other side of the screen to make an interested public and critics hungry for more.

The considerable detail McCabe then brought to the private Laurel (as well as an ongoing look at the public team) in *The Comedy World of Stan Laurel* is also peppered with an eclectic but fascinating assortment of reproduced documents. These include the Laurel-authored stage script "The Drivers' License Sketch" (variations of which were used between 1939 and 1947), an excerpt from a rambling unpublished Laurel biography written by his father in 1939, and the Laurel-authored stage sketch "Birds of a Feather" from the team's last British tour, October 1953–May 1954.

Indeed, because there is so much rich historical material, one is almost tempted to include the indexed *The Comedy World of Stan Laurel* in the reference section of this essay. But the affectionate McCabe biographical framework that holds the work together more logically places it in the insider category. Interestingly enough, McCabe's consciously eclectic approach to the book (he refers to it as "miscellany") is a further reflection of the insider categorization. McCabe correctly realizes that Laurel's approach to comedy was also often a mixed, anything-goes pluralism, though generally with a realistic foundation. (This pluralism also might help explain the origin of Stan's occasional lapses into "white magic"—see Chapter 1.)

Fittingly, McCabe has most recently (1989) added still another watershed work to his ongoing Laurel & Hardy scholarship. His *BABE: The Life of Oliver Hardy* is the first biography of the rotund one. Such a work has been long overdue, and McCabe entertainingly fills in many blank spots in the life and often troubled times of Hardy. In addition, McCabe further fleshes out the biography of Laurel. Indeed, the book often reads as a joint biography of the team.

While Laurel continues to be given a certain affectionate deference, it is pleasant to have the pivotal team historian acknowledging the comedian's foibles more readily than before. And the same can be said of his chronicling of the often volatile private life of Hardy, though on occasion McCabe can work too hard defending questionable Hardy actions, such as the comedian's sexual dalliances during an admittedly difficult second marriage.

Despite his mammoth size, the comedian had been a biographical invisible man. Between Hardy's no information or misinformation ways, McCabe's greatest accomplishment was just getting a story down on paper. And he has effectively accomplished this in a stylistically tight biography devoid of the eclectic detours (however interesting) of his earlier team-related writing.

Credit it to an insatiable appetite for Hardy information or McCabe's writing skills, but I finished the book still wanting more. Normally, this is the ultimate compliment one can pay an author. Unfortunately, without trying to negate any of McCabe's very real accomplishment, part of my disappointment was the realization that much of Hardy's life story has simply been lost to the ages. This is further underlined by the fact that McCabe wrote the text—the author with the best possible pipeline to the subject.

Undoubtedly, additional Hardy biographies will periodically surface, with some no doubt focusing on indiscretions McCabe chose not to explore. But the irony remains, how can such an honored and loved shadow of the screen (about whom one knows every comic characteristic) have left so little relating to the man behind the screen?

Just as *Mr. Laurel & Mr. Hardy* was a pioneering work on the duo, *The Comedy World of Stan Laurel* and *BABE: The Life of Oliver Hardy* were equally precedent-setting books on the team components. Moreover, McCabe has had a direct impact upon other Laurel & Hardy texts. For instance, he is the author of the text for the reference work *Laurel & Hardy* (1975, to be addressed shortly), which was compiled by Al Kilgore, with a filmography by Richard Bann. And McCabe provided much-credited assistance to Fred Guiles's *Stan: The Life of Stan Laurel* (1980, also soon to be examined). Thus, one might be tempted to call McCabe the poet "laure[l]ate" of the team. Certainly he has had a major impact upon shaping and even preserving (via his biography friendship with Laurel) the behind-the-screen heritage of this team.

General Biographies

One might best make the transition from "insider" works to "general biographies" by beginning with Guiles's *Stan: The Life of Stan Laurel*. Besides having a pivotal McCabe connection, Guiles also interviewed a number of Laurel & Hardy friends and contemporaries, ranging from Hardy's widow Lucille to Roach composer Marvin Hatley (the author of the team's signature "The Dance of the Cuckoos"). But the primary source was Laurel's off-center wife Virginia Ruth. Indeed, she first contacted Guiles about doing such a biography. Thus, while not quite an "insider" biography, period reference people make it the next best thing. Moreover, juxtaposing two such diverse key source persons as Virginia Ruth and McCabe (an exwife vs. an academic fan, an intimate during Laurel's professional heyday vs. a friend at the close of the comedian's career . . .) makes for a very provocative book.

As one might expect, while Laurel & Hardy "warts" are kept to a minimum in the McCabe books, especially in the earlier *Mr. Laurel & Mr. Hardy*, Guiles's biography provides a more complete private picture of both comedians—scandals and all. And most pointedly, it plays up a very talented though still underrated comedian (Laurel) whose personal life was often as erratically unstable as his classic films were funny. Consequently, the ultimate irony was that while Laurel sacrificed so much of his personal life for his workaholic comedy needs, what private time survived (and it seldom remained "private" long) soon scandalously lessened the chances of Laurel ever being fully in charge of the career he loved—making movies.

The book also includes a sizable amount of personal background on Hardy, though the comedian's extremely reclusive nature will unfortunately, no doubt, forever keep his biographical profile much slimmer than his comedy partner's. Also, recognition of McCarey's significance to the team is liberally sprinkled throughout the work.

The candor with which Guiles addresses the often messy personal life of Laurel (and to a lesser extent Hardy) is refreshing if for no other reason than that such information had previously been downplayed and/or found to have been seemingly incongruous to the man and his asexual persona, especially when contrasted with the subdued gentlemanly politeness of Laurel in his senior years. However, the Guiles biography seems slightly too enamored of the negative. Just as the McCabe material, despite its importance, can be at times saccharin, Guiles occasionally errs in going too far the other way. It is not that his revelations are wrong (as shocking as they may be), or that Guiles includes no Laurel positives (he does). But the biography just seems couched in a subtle negativism—perhaps the legacy of an ex-wife (Virginia Ruth) as a key source, despite an attempted balancing from McCabe.

Unfortunately, because the book is without footnotes (as are all the volumes examined thus far), one cannot keep a running tabulation on how close the balance of the two sides (Virginia Ruth and McCabe) was in the final input. But suffice it to say, a more complete picture necessitates a reading of both Guiles and McCabe.

Stan: The Life of Stan Laurel is also mildly flawed by Guiles's occasional tendency to contradict himself. For instance, a few pages after documenting a less-than-loyal action of Laurel towards some friends, Guiles notes Laurel's extreme faithfulness to old cronies. In point of fact, both statements are true, though the latter tendency is more the norm. Such dual capabilities are at the heart of the comedy sphinx that was Laurel. Guiles obviously understands this, but his transitional writing does not always bridge such contradictions.

Guiles shows a good sense of period performers and entertainment cycles as a historic backdrop for the world of Laurel & Hardy, but he sometimes is too terse or pat in his treatment of that material. For example, he blames Buster Keaton's fall from the pantheon of comedy greats simply upon the coming of sound movies. In truth, it was much more complex than that, also involving an alcohol problem, marital difficulties, and a fascination with comedy so complex that it made him less than sophisticated or interested in the private sector. It was a problem list surprisingly like Laurel's (see Chapter 1 for more on this). Such missed opportunities would have enriched the Guiles text. Indeed, if he had acted upon the shared problems of Laurel and Keaton, Guiles might have started with a still from *The Comedy World of Stan Laurel*, which pictures a seemingly drunk, after-hours Keaton partying with Laurel & Hardy and Jimmy Durante.

A warmer, slice-of-life volume is Jenny Owen-Pawson and Bill Mouland's *Laurel Before Hardy*. Despite its 1984 publication date, this is a relatively rare book in the United States, having been printed in England. The page-one goal of the text was to offer something entirely new—Laurel's "first few years in Ulverston, England [his birthplace]; the places he loved; the people he knew from his childhood, and those who probably helped to shape him into a great comedian."

The catalyst for the book was the early 1980s convening of an "International Convention of the Sons of the Desert" in Ulverston. Besides revealing much about the early years of Laurel, it is also a guide to how Ulverston was intertwined with his life. For instance, during Laurel & Hardy's triumphant 1932 visit to Europe, Laurel reminisced briefly with a London *Daily Herald* reporter about a grave marker shaped like a miniature lighthouse (complete with light) that had fascinated him since childhood. However, this *Daily Herald* article (see both Chapter 1 and the "Shorter Works" section of this chapter) is predictably lacking in fleshing out any background on this unconventional tombstone that had so impressed a young boy. *Laurel Before Hardy* fills in such gaps, chronicling that the marker was erected in 1897 (when Laurel was seven) in memory of "Thomas Watkins Wilson M. D.," who frequently vacationed in Ulverston. But apparently the attention getter for local children was what one would now call its eternal flame—a gas light that for years shone from atop the monument, twenty-four hours a day.

Laurel Before Hardy also provides more detail about the comedian's family and Ulverston neighbors than any other Laurel texts, and offers a wealth of rare period photographs that document his family and the town itself—with most of the Laurel-related historical sites still standing.

Two additional items guaranteed that the book would not become one of those bloodless genealogy books some families publish. First, it has early and late samplings of cheery Laurel correspondence, from a 1910s card to his beloved Ulverston grandmother to an extensive collection of 1950s letters to a British Laurel & Hardy fan. Second, *Laurel Before Hardy* boasts a number of charming anecdotes about the very young Laurel. Such as his boyishly mischievous ways resulting in his being the family child most frequently locked in the windowless woodshed as punishment. But adult suspicions were aroused when these "sentences" were accepted so willingly by the boy. Upon investigation it was found that the perennial little "prisoner" had hidden candle, matches, and comic reading material in the shed! What an interesting foreshadowing of a man who would one day become famous for comedy. Regardless, young Laurel's inspired "escape" from punishment is also an excellent example of Laurel making the best of a bad situation (what psychologists now call "reframing"), a talent he would put to frequent use as an adult.

Two years after the publication of *Laurel Before Hardy* the Dutch volume *De wereld ven Laurel en Hardy* (1986) appeared. Written by Thomas Leeflang, it was translated into English by Phil Goddard in 1988—*The World of Laurel and Hardy*.

The text is primarily biographical, though critical commentary surfaces frequently, including an opening that addresses the "why" behind the team's ongoing popularity. Unfortunately, Leeflang's book is flawed by numerous errors, from wrongly dated stills to stating Jerry Lewis and Dick Van Dyke paid the rent on Laurel's final apartment! Some mistakes might be attributed to a hasty translation production, as was suggested in an unsigned review in the Spring 1989 issue of *Bowler Dessert* (a British journal devoted to Laurel & Hardy). But there are enough other basic errors, such as calling Groucho the oldest Marx brother (it was Chico), stating McCarey won two Oscars (actually, three), and the apartment comment, to note that a good part of the problem rests with the original text.

This is unfortunate. The book contains insightful critical comments and obscure biographical facts, such as a list of books Laurel ordered from England in the 1930s. Fittingly, they were about English variety artists, especially his beloved Dan Leno. Thus, the mistakes distract from these positives, and leaves one wondering about the volume's unevenness.

The book also addresses the film fan collector, such as including a section on the monetary value of original Laurel & Hardy publicity stills. Appropriately, still reproduction quality in the text is quite good.

A final volume in the biography category, Jack Scagnetti's *The Laurel & Hardy Scrapbook* (1976) includes (as its title suggests) a rather eclectic assortment of items. Like several of the team reference works, the *Scrapbook* is an oversized, profusely illustrated volume and offers the reader a wide assortment of pictures, including film still publicity material, private snapshots, and team memorabilia.

With the book's one-paragraph synopsis of each Laurel & Hardy film and a reproduction of the "Sons of the Desert" constitution, an argument might be made for placing the volume in the reference section. But there is still enough of a life and career prose overview—six short chapters plus an introduction— that the book is best placed in the biography section. Indeed, Scagnetti's work is one of the first Laurel & Hardy book-length studies to address directly Laurel's one-time messy personal life.

Critical Studies

While the first McCabe book on the team (*Mr. Laurel & Mr. Hardy*, 1961) includes some comedy theorizing, *the* pioneering work is British author Charles Barr's *Laurel & Hardy* (1967). It is insightful and beautifully written, with a comically provocative opening (inspired by the Arthur C. Clarke short story "Expedition to Earth"). Barr asks what if some future alien society could only know the history of man on earth by way of one ancient surviving relic—a Laurel & Hardy film. Laughable . . . or is it?

Barr's work comprises eighteen short but detailed chapters, an index, bibliography, and a ranked filmography (with Laurel & Hardy movies graded against a five-level system, ranging from "Dud" to "Great"). Barr early on recognized both the significance of McCarey to the team and the superiority of Laurel & Hardy's silent films over their sound vehicles, especially the vast majority of their features.

Though close analysis of comedy puts off some people (a group that included Laurel), such scrutiny merely represents an attempt to understand better something one holds dear. And Barr ranks very high in his ability to perform this task without provoking that equally age-old complaint: "You've killed the comedy" (by analyzing it). Like Laurel & Hardy slapstick, Barr's insights are direct and easy to enjoy. For instance, his passing observation on the duo's screen characters could not be more perceptively succinct: "Stan is dumb, Ollie impatient: all the subtle variations of their relationship, and there are many, are based on this distinction, which doesn't change."

Barr's entertaining and intelligent examination of the team also works on another level—Laurel & Hardy credibility. Many fans of and authors on the team are almost apologetic when anything smacking of comedy analysis occurs. Yet, every student of the duo knows they have never received the critical attention they deserved. Thus, readable serious attention, like Barr's *Laurel & Hardy*, encourages others to look beyond the pratfalls.

Besides, if any further justification is needed for analysis, such as a response to the hoary adage that the author/entertainer never had such-and-such interpretation in mind (one to which Laurel also adhered), one need only provide the now classic reply, "Trust the tale, not the teller." That is, if a given work moves one in some way, that is reason enough to examine it along those lines.

Eleven years after Barr's work, Italian writer Marco Giusti's *Laurel & Hardy* was published (1978). Volume 57 of the "Castora Cinema" auteur series, it justified the team's inclusion by crediting them with being directors of their directors. The slim volume is often poetically revealing. In fact, the introduction alone provides more thought-provoking observations than the contents of several whole books examined in this chapter. For example, Giusti uses Hardy's childhood "lobby watching" habit (studying characters) as a metaphor for why viewers forever enjoy the team—Stan & Ollie are so realistic it is like interacting with cherished friends and family. Moreover, this addresses the occasional complaint that their films have minimal (if any) storylines. Giusti suggests sharing cinema time with Stan & Ollie is an end in itself, not unlike the simple shared time spent with loved ones. Overall, Giusti credits the team with a believable realness to the public greater than that of more celebrated period contemporaries like Chaplin and Keaton. This thought-provoking suggestion has generated critical attention since its original introduction by Laurel & Hardy authors Raymond Borde and Charles Perrin (examined later in the chapter). For example, a variation of it occurs in the next text under study.

British author Bruce Crowther's *Laurel & Hardy: Clown Princes of Comedy* appeared in 1987. Besides its main text commentary (including numerous stills and biographical background), this indexed volume includes a filmography, selected radio and television activity, British tour bookings for 1952 and 1953–54, a select discography, bibliography, and a foreword by Ernie Wise of the Laurel & Hardy-influenced British comedy team of Morecambe & Wise. Because of these additions one might justify placing the volume in the reference section, but there is sufficient critical commentary to maintain its present categorization.

Crowther is another team author apologetic about analysis. But thankfully, since his criticism is often perceptive—or at least interestingly provocative—he does not avoid the task. My main complaint with his approach is that his justifiable critical elevation of Laurel & Hardy seems to be matched often with a lowering in significance of Charlie Chaplin, as if there were only a finite amount of comedy praise to be distributed. However, one important exception in his comparisons of Chaplin's Tramp and Stan & Ollie finds Crowther positing that however much one relishes the comic adventures of Charlie, most viewers *today* would have an easier time relating to the frustrations of the duo. Crowther might have drawn an analogy by comparing Fred Astaire and Gene Kelly. The masterly Astaire, the dancer who forever plays the professional top-hat-and-tails dancer in movie after movie, is someone the viewer idolizes for his sophisticated style. In contrast, one is much more likely to identify with the seemingly more casual dance of Kelly, who accents this by usually *not* playing a professional dancer but rather a more "everyman" figure who appears to dance spontaneously just for the joy of a given moment. Thus, while one finds comic poignancy throughout

Charlie's fund-raising adventures for the blind girl of *City Lights* (1931), it is easier to identify with Stan & Ollie's attempts to put an antenna on the roof in *Hog Wild* (1930). Though the analogy is not without flaws, it is interestingly provocative.

Besides both critical commentary and background information on Laurel & Hardy's films, Crowther's book interweaves a considerable amount of biographical material, including their sometimes checkered pasts. Clearly influenced by the revelations of Guiles's volume (which is occasionally cited), Crowther still manages to write a more upbeat book on the team—possibly because their endearing films generate so much attention.

Scott Allen Nollen's *The Boys: The Cinematic World of Laurel & Hardy* (1989) is disappointing. With an introduction by John McCabe and twelve critiquing chapters, beginning with "Why Take Laurel & Hardy Seriously?" one's hopes are high. Unfortunately, Nollen too often mistakes compendiums of examples for analysis. He does this so often a more cynically ironic reviewer might have created a special *Lists* of Laurel & Hardy subsection. But then there is the problem of misinformation, such as Nollen's conflicting thoughts on screwball comedy (at one point he suggests it was a product of the 1940s) or that "the Boys" were the only likeable people in their films.

In making his case for Laurel & Hardy criticism, Nollen displays little awareness of what significant analysis has been done (both during the team's heyday and after), though he does on occasion thankfully draw from the work of McCabe and Barr.

There is no denying Nollen reveres the team and knows their films (such as the section of Chapter 6 when he discusses all the movies in which Stan ate nuts!), but these are not the sole requirements for playing critic. And even when he embraces the provocative, such as the duo's homosexual overtones (a subject their childlike nature immediately renders ludicrous), he provides no new insights. It is not that Nollen merely wants to titilate the reader, though his later comment on Stan's enjoyment of bananas might suggest this: "an aspect of esoterica that psychoanalytic theorists would probably enjoy discussing." It is just that this genuine film fan seems unwilling or unable to move beyond the most surface "reading" of these film texts.

Reference Texts

The largest number of Laurel & Hardy books falls into this category. Though one might cite several explanations for this, the most logical reason is the grassroots popularity of the duo. Rarely darlings of the critics, the ongoing success of Stan & Ollie rests, like a Frank Capra film, in the hands of the people. And the majority of the team's authors have given the public Laurel & Hardy facts rather than thematic or critical analysis.

Appropriately, one of the most central reference books, editor Leonard Maltin's *The Laurel & Hardy Book* (1973), has the following citation on the title page: "Official book of Sons of the Desert, the international Laurel and Hardy organization." The volume, largely written by the prolific but ever insightful Maltin, has a grab-bag assortment of chapters certain to please the team fan. For instance, one of the more important chapters, "The Laurel and Hardy Stock Co.," devotes several pages to each of the following performers: James Finlayson, Mae Busch, Charlie Hall, Walter Long, Anita Garvin, Rychard Cramer, Arthur Housman, and Tiny Sandford.

These supporting characters, so important to the Laurel & Hardy films, seldom receive adequate attention elsewhere. Unfortunately, the thinness of some biographical sketches, through no fault of the detail-conscious Maltin, points up just how little is known about several performers. While full enjoyment of the book (especially the "Stock Co." chapter) is dependent upon having seen several Laurel & Hardy films, one need not be a team aficionado to enjoy the volume.

The book is not, however, devoid of critical perspectives on the duo. Maltin has penned an especially fresh chapter on the critics, revealing Laurel & Hardy's longtime lofty position among British reviewers. Other chapters vary from gag appearances by the clowns to their working methods and style (which draws from the American Film Institute's Oral History with Leo McCarey).

Finally, there are two brief chapters by John McCabe, indexes to the solo films of both Laurel & Hardy (compiled by R. E. Braff), and a Laurel & Hardy filmography (compiled by Richard Bann). Interestingly, McCabe and Bann (plus Al Kilgore) later joined forces to compile their own team reference book—*Laurel & Hardy* (1975, to be examined later in this section).

Sharing center stage with the Maltin book in the reference section is Randy Skretvedt's phenomenally detailed (462 pages) *Laurel and Hardy: The Magic Behind the Movies* (1987). Skretvedt, a longtime devotee of the duo (including first involvement with the Sons of the Desert as a teenager), has written a book that, at its most fundamental, closely examines their films from both sides of the screen. But it hardly stops there. Skretvedt also pleasantly inundates the reader with a wealth of Laurel & Hardy biographical material. This naturally dovetails into his goal of keeping one abreast of the team's behind-the-screen activities. There are occasional references to period commentaries on the team, especially as reviewed in *Variety* and the *New York Times*. This book might have also qualified for several other categories in this biographical chapter, but a reference placement seems most fitting.

The inclusion of the criticism is surprising in light of Skretvedt's preface, which finds him generally disappointed in the voluminous amount of writing on the team—another example of a Laurel & Hardy author negating the more analytical approach. Naturally, Laurel's aversion to the dissection of comedy is also noted early in the text—the opening page of the prologue. Unfortunately, Skretvedt's lesser view of print sources is honored when it comes to full citations. Despite the book's many pluses, there is neither a standard bibliography nor footnotes, a characteristic it shares with the Maltin book. (The Skretvedt volume does include a one-page "Sources" section, but it contains largely interview references and incomplete print citations, such as "back issues of" such-and-such a journal.)

Since a text citation by nature is rarely complete, this is frustrating. The interested reader (of Maltin and Skretvedt) who wants to pursue further information from an article and/or personally evaluate it is forced to first play secretary (recording the partial reference) and then detective finding it. One might liken it to the hoary treasure hunt tale, where only half a map is available. As most Laurel & Hardy books provide little or no references, one should be happy for those random references that do occur, partial citation though they may be.

Skretvedt's goal was to base the text largely on the reminiscences of Laurel & Hardy co-workers. This approach had been inspired by his earlier encounters with some of these same people at Sons of the Desert meetings to which they were frequently invited. If for no other reason, the interweaving of these Laurel & Hardy-focused oral histories make for an interesting and provocative book—especially since Skretvedt does not whitewash his subjects, as has often been the case with other team authors; he addresses, for instance, Laurel's sometimes dark sense of humor (see Chapter 1).

Though in no way a mere coffee table book, the volume is richly illustrated, often with rare stills and photographs and even rarer period publicity posters. An amusing corollary to this, and acknowledged by Skretvedt, is that the comic caricatures of the duo are often rather mediocre likenesses. This is doubly surprising, since the posters are otherwise imaginatively and amusingly drawn.

Skretvedt is generous with his crediting of McCarey's influence, even drawing from a Peter Bogdanovich interview of the director (uncited source—the American Film Institute—sponsored McCarey oral history), where McCarey discusses the duo's style and pacing. Fittingly, Skretvedt focuses on McCarey's often overlooked greatest impact on the team (besides teaming them): his molding of Laurel & Hardy stories. Ironically, as one pages through Skretvedt's credits for the duo's films, McCarey's story credits (as well as the category itself) are sometimes missing, such as on the pivotal *Hog Wild* (1930) and the delightful *Brats* (1930, McCarey story credit shared with Hal Roach). Is this an omission or a suggestion that sufficient ad-libbing occurred on the set to eliminate the category? The ad-libbing hypothesis is sometimes implied between the lines. Regardless, this needs to be clarified.

Despite these modest qualifiers, Skretvedt's work remains one of *the* Laurel & Hardy books (reference or otherwise) for both students of the team, or comedy in general.

After the center stage reference placement of the Skretvedt and Maltin books, one should best move on to two "films of" texts: William Everson's *The Films of Laurel and Hardy* (1967) and the previously noted collaboration of McCabe, Kilgore, and Bann on *Laurel & Hardy* (1975).

The latter volume is the most ambitious of the two (400 pages to 223), with a more detailed rehashing of the storylines, complete credits, and more photographs. Each *Laurel & Hardy* film entry also has a quality rating that amusingly plays upon the traditional four-star system. That is, "Excellent" is designated by four little black derbies, "Above average" by three, "Average" by two, and "Below average" by one. Fittingly, the "Preview" (Preface) of *Laurel & Hardy* states "no single volume can serve as encyclopedic survey of Laurel and Hardy . . . What this book offers is a pictorial overview . . . together with all pertinent statistics and supplemental information necessary for an understanding of their career."

Both books offer supplements to their primary "films of" focus, with the Everson text being the more elaborate. His volume offers brief biographical sketches of each comedian; an introduction that examines the ironies and dangers of their 1960s cult status; a section on "The Years Before the Teaming"; a look at "The Modus Operandi of Laurel & Hardy," including their frequent alienation of women viewers and their propensity for dark humor; and sections on "The [film] Compilations" in which their work appeared and "Deleted Scenes" (stills from sequences which did not make final prints).

The supplements to the collaborative *Laurel & Hardy* are a "For Stan and Ollie" section that gives comments on the duo from a truly eclectic collection of famous Laurel & Hardy fans, from Marcel Marceau to Lenny Bruce; a "Preview" that includes everything from biographical material to an examination of each comedian's basic "mannerisms" (such as Stan's cry or Ollie's tie twiddling); a largely pictorial "The Roach Years"; and brief late text entries on their "Career Turnabout" (their 1940s cinema decline), "Final Footage" (career pluses *after* the films, despite the reference to "Footage"), and "The Sons of the Desert" (a brief history and the constitution of the club that is an ongoing celebration of the duo). Unlike Everson's one closing section of "Deleted Scenes," the collaborative *Laurel & Hardy* includes deleted material individually from each film in question—look for the subheading "Production Sidelights."

As a pure source for each film storyline (as well as everything from reproductions of their comic opening titles to quotations of comically pertinent dialogue) the McCabe, Kilgore, and Bann *Laurel & Hardy* is to be preferred over Everson's volume. It is not only more thorough but also more accurate. For a kind yet straightforward look at storyline errors in *The Films of Laurel and Hardy*, see Dick Bann's "Cutting Room Floor" column in *Pratfall* magazine (volume 1, number 6).

Despite these problems, the Everson text still represents an excellent complement to the collaborative volume in the area of critical commentary. He liberally peppers each film entry with background material of often insightful proportions, something for which the storyline detail of *Laurel & Hardy* does not allow time.

Another natural pairing of Laurel and Hardy reference books occurs with Raymond Borde and Charles Perrin's *Laurel et Hardy* and Jeane Pierre Coursodon's identically titled volume.

The longer (133 page) Borde and Perrin volume might best be called the French version of *The Films of Laurel & Hardy*. Drawing upon John McCabe's initial Laurel & Hardy book, Borde and Perrin first list the solo filmographies of the comedians before moving on to a slightly more ambitious look at the team's films (including a short synopsis of each movie but not full credits). Borde and Perrin also include a film rating system of a four-star variety, which possibly influenced the derby demarcations of the later McCabe, Kilgore, and Bann book. The most interesting aspect of the Borde and Perrin volume and its one filmography departure, is its eighteen-page '' Dictionnaire De Gags.'' Using a one-word title for various comedy sketch material, such as those involving ''alcohol,'' or ''torture,'' the authors alphabetically examine, in brief, variations of each category while noting the films in which they occur.

Other text highlights include references to important but obscure writings on the duo, especially Louis Chavance's 1930 essay ''Laurel et Hardy'' (see this chapter's shorter works section), which Borde and Perrin refer to frequently. Indeed, the authors are rightfully bothered by how much continues to be unknown about Laurel & Hardy, including a wish for more insight into McCarey's collaboration.

In Borde and Perrin's general team overview they have high praise for the Laurel & Hardy silents, though the smooth transition to sound is examined in an insightful manner. The authors also reveal that Laurel & Hardy's 1930s short subjects were often shown in France as compilation, feature-length Stan & Ollie adventures; they provide a refreshing new slant on the team's dubbing of foreign language versions of their films.

Frequent references to an obscure Laurel & Hardy interview in L' Ecran Francais (November 25, 1947; see this chapter's shorter works section) provides additional ''new'' material to an interesting reference.

Jean Pierre Coursodon's monograph-length Laurel et Hardy (54 pages) devotes not quite half its length to a team filmography, again with a brief story synopsis for each movie but without full credits. The rest of Coursodon's work is a combined biographical/critical look at Laurel & Hardy, from pre-team days to their 1940s decline and the final Atoll K derailment. Of special interest is Coursodon's division and examination of the team's film career, his analysis of their screen personae, and theoretical comments on their work and Henri Bergson's comedy of superiority.

While each French text includes stills, neither is as profusely illustrated as the Everson or McCabe, Kilgore, and Bann texts. Indeed, this accounts for part of their relative shortness compared to these two American volumes, though the scope of the French references was never that ambitious.

One French text, however, with more ambitious goals is Roland Lacourbe's splendid Laurel et Hardy: Ou l'enfance de l'art (1975). It is an extensive compendium of Laurel & Hardy material, ranging from a detailed filmography and time line to several chapters of critical commentary on their work. The volume also includes reprints of John McCabe's 1954 interview with Hardy (from Mr. Laurel and Mr. Hardy), the 1959 Films in Review session with Laurel, and a chapter overview of their career. The book is further enriched with numerous stills and reproductions of obscure drawings—from a comic strip and a water color to even *Pratfall* magazine covers. And whereas many Laurel & Hardy texts lack and/or minimize the bibliography, Lacourbe's section is both ambitious and annotated.

Finally, two unusual Laurel & Hardy reference books should be noted, including an asterisk for super fan designation by the name of their author—Leon Smith. These privately published volumes are *A Guide to Laurel and Hardy Movie Locations* (1982) and the sequel *Following the Comedy Trail* (1984, which also includes some Our Gang movie locations). In each case, the Smith book provides photographs, maps, and directions for fans wishing to visit original Laurel & Hardy film locations. Though sometimes little has changed about the sites, the norm finds them drastically altered, underlining the work that went into Smith's "verification" of each location.

While the Smith books might not turn up on your standard Laurel & Hardy bibliography, they seem an apt way to conclude this book section as well as to document the unusual grassroots popularity of an old team whose fans still want to visit yesterday's production sites. But, as the blurb on the *Following the Comedy Trail* cover observes, "Smith's decision to delve into another book on Laurel and Hardy was prompted by fan mail from readers in this country and overseas who urged him to find 'more and more' movie locations." Thus, one might fittingly add that in 1985 *Pratfall* magazine brought out its own special edition, monograph-length team location guide entitled *Laurel and Hardywood.*

SHORTER WORKS

Laurel & Hardy Critical Essays

Any number of essay-length critical pieces might have been chosen. This section, proceeding chronologically, examines some of the most important. When an author is responsible for more than one pivotal essay, all his work is grouped together. The same principle is applied to journals that have been unusually rich and/or influential in their examination of Laurel & Hardy material.

It is most fitting that a section devoted to shorter critical pieces on Laurel & Hardy should begin with the late 1920s pocket-sized reviews of the *Motion Picture Herald Tribune* (see also Chapter 1). Drawing from their "What the Picture Did for Me" section—verdicts on the films by the exhibitors themselves—there is a triple justification involved. First, while the team was never better than in these early short subjects briefly though persistently chronicled upon by the *Motion Picture Herald Tribune*, shorts by their very nature seldom generated the critical attention of a feature. Thus, these rave reviews document a pivotal Laurel & Hardy period that often has been given critical short shrift. Second, because the team had seldom been embraced by intellectual critics from various Valhallo schools of thought (who might genuflect only to a Chaplin), it seems especially appropriate that the *Motion Picture Herald Tribune* "critics" are an eclectic collection of John and Jane Q. Publics whose critiquing is based upon a democratic reading of the people (their theatre audiences). And third, just as the best Laurel & Hardy films are short and to the comedy point, these highlighted *Motion Picture Herald Tribune* pieces are abbreviated hosannas that get the job done quickly. For instance: "Laughed myself sick at this one. Metro has word comedy in a class of its own. We featured this comedy."

Robert Herring's *Close Up* article on the team (May 1930) is surprisingly contemporary in its early recognition of Laurel & Hardy universals. He is especially perceptive when discussing the theme of destruction, both as slapstick and as a general metaphor for their screen lifestyles. He calls the duo a "marriage of extreme inconvenience" and nicely fleshes out their characterizations. For example, when analyzing Stan's propensity to frustrate Ollie, Herring effectively also shows how the thin one's comically dumb actions can still be an expression of love for his partner. Thus, when Ollie plays conjuror and Stan gives away the tricks, this merely demonstrates he is "proud of Hardy, of being with him, and wants to show you how wonderful the tricks are."

Another perceptive 1930s work is Louis Chavance's *La Revue du cinema* (no. 7) essay "Stan Laurel et Oliver Hardy." It combines the analytical approach of the Herring piece with the *Motion Picture Herald Tribune*'s more-grassroots appreciation of the team; like the *Tribune*'s "Laughed myself sick" quote, Chavance is fond of describing the team's comic skills along "laugh until [it] hurts" lines.

"Stan Laurel et Oliver Hardy" is anchored in a general comparison of French and U.S. film comedies. While noting France's pioneer status in this area (such as the films of Max Linder), Chavance is very complimentary towards America's comedy capabilities. For example, he feels the tit-for-tat frenzy of a Laurel & Hardy film could only be conceived in America.

While comparing national cinemas can be controversial, Chavance is on surer, more critically helpful ground when he zeroes in on the team. Consequently, he describes Laurel & Hardy as the only comic actors with no sentimentality. Their comic violence is a spiteful poetry. Sentimentality would distract from this comic purity—which is also displayed in their simple contrasting shapes.

Chavance is bothered by the negative portrayal of women in their films. He even has a wish that a new male-female variation could be introduced. But he also knows this would not fit the team's comedy. Consequently, he is willing to leave their comedic misogyny alone, observing that the big laugh is not possible without some comic distortion.

Chavance talks at length, and in poetic terms, about the team's tit-for-tat comic violence, with a special focus on *Two Tars* (1929). In general, he finds a joy of destruction in their work. He also likens their comic conflicts to the musical discord Stan & Ollie would produce if they were members of a symphony orchestra.

Chavance is an early example of a critic who prefers Ollie over Stan, though he notes the 1930 norm is just the opposite. (Much later Ollie's increased recognition was bolstered by Laurel's greater 1950s appreciation of Hardy's talent.) Here as elsewhere in the essay, Chavance anticipates future and/or ongoing pertinent Laurel & Hardy issues of interest.

Of the significant more-mainstream publications reviewing the heyday of the team's feature work (1930s), the *New York Times* merits special kudos. While not granting the duo carte blanche praise in the nature of James Agee on Chaplin or Alexander Woollcott on Harpo Marx, the paper was routinely insightful in its Laurel & Hardy excursions, frequently displaying complementary comic embellishments of its own. (For a darker interpretation of the *New York Times* on Laurel & Hardy, see Wes Heath's "A Critique of the Critics," addressed later in this chapter when *Pratfall* magazine is examined.)

The most gifted of the several Laurel & Hardy *New York Times* reviewers was Andrè Sennwald, who died tragically at the age of twenty-eight from gas poisoning in early 1936. His January 12, 1934 hosanna to *Sons of the Desert*, the team's greatest feature (though many period reviews hardly supported this view) demonstrates just what a loss his premature death was: "At the Rialto [theatre] spectators are checking their dignity with the doorman; an audience yesterday spluttered, howled and signed in sweet surrender." Or, Laurel & Hardy are "A Quixote and Panza in a nightmare world, where even the act of opening a door is filled with hideous perils, they fumble and stumble in their heartiest manner." (See also his *Babes in Toyland* review.)

After Sennwald, the *New York Times* period critic most perceptively appreciative of Laurel & Hardy was Frank Nugent. As demonstrated earlier in his May 4, 1937 celebration of *Way Out West* (see Chapter 1 for his firmly tongue-in-cheek preference for "the humor of anatomy" over "the anatomy of humor"), he was very capable of recognizing comic talent and writing about it with a knowledgeable wit.

Nugent's August 30, 1938 review of the initially underrated *Block-Heads* wisely recognizes the traditional priority most personality comedians (whether Red Skelton or the Marx Brothers) give to characterization over plot, as well as demonstrates a comedy connoisseur's awareness of Laurel & Hardy: "Masters of the delayed and double takes, the slow burn, the dead pan, the withering (or vacuous) looks, the tailspin and asthmatic wheeze, Laurel and Hardy seem equally at ease with or without plot material."

Even the *New York Times* more socially oriented Bosley Crowther (so instrumental later in the Supreme Court's decision granting motion pictures First Amendment rights) recognized the importance of personality over plotline for the duo. Crowther's February 20, 1940 review of *A Chump at Oxford* closed with "Laurel and Hardy have been managing for so long to get by without one of those [stories] that its absence is imperceptible. The idea is to laugh, not to think. You'll get the idea, all right."

Indeed, possibly because Crowther was a late convert to Stan & Ollie's comedy, his January 4, 1938 review of *Swiss Miss* (which Agee would later salute in his famous "Comedy's Greatest Era" essay) had about it the appreciation known only to the *new* disciple. Thus, Crowther compared the team to both Chaplin and Disney (still high praise, but very lofty stuff in the 1930s). And his comment on the operetta in which the duo find themselves immersed is positively contemporary in its preference (both for *Swiss Miss* and any of their other operetta films): "There is too much operetta on the whole, but the Laurel-Hardy episodes are so delightful that the film even takes [the romantic, operetta lead] Walter Woolf King in its stride."

Though these highlights hardly exhaust the interesting *New York Times* Laurel & Hardy reviews or reviewers (see, for instance, Mordaunt Hall's June 10, 1933 critique of *The Devil's Brother*), it nicely demonstrates an open-minded appreciation of "lowly" slapstick by a most prestigious publication. Unfortunately, this was not always the case when it came time to assess the merits of Laurel & Hardy. The perfect example of this involves the team's treatment during the same period from *Variety*, the bible of the entertainment industry. The following brief examination of *Variety* is this chapter's only exercise in negative critiquing, but it is justified because of *Variety*'s great influence, especially since their Laurel & Hardy complaints were (and sometimes still are) echoed by others.

Variety panned just about everything Laurel & Hardy did, including the duo's most celebrated features; its *Way Out West* critique (May 5, 1937) described the film as "tough sledding," *Block-Heads* (August 3, 1938) was "an awful letdown," and *Swiss Miss* (May 11, 1938) was "Just a filler-in and not a very good one." Even the great *Sons of the Desert* (a top-ten grossing feature), gets very little *Variety* praise (January 9, 1934), and that most reluctantly: "It will get laughs but no new business and will have to be satisfied with sub-normal receipts in a majority of the important spots."

Indeed, besides the last review's surprising coolness, its "sub-normal receipts" projection misses by a country mile. Such miscalculations, critically or commercially, are unlike *Variety*, at least for the period under examination. This is normally the most astute of entertainment publications. For example, its period film critiques of Laurel & Hardy contemporaries like the Marx Brothers are insightful. In fact, *Variety*'s review of *Duck Soup* is unique because of its farsightedness. At a time when many critics were panning what is now considered the team's greatest work, *Variety* gives it a contemporary-sounding review (see my 1987 book on *The Marx Brothers: A Bio-Bibliography*). What was there about Laurel & Hardy that proved alienating to various *Variety* critics? A comparison of their Laurel & Hardy pannings provides some clues, as well as an early source for similar complaints by others. Three factors stand out.

First, for *Variety* and some other period critics, Laurel & Hardy were strictly kid stuff. Though *Variety* is seldom quite so direct about this, one finds it baldly stated in the first paragraph of its *Swiss Miss* review: "Of little box-office value, except for the children." A more interesting demonstration of this period prejudice surfaces when one looks for a positive Laurel & Hardy film review in *Variety*. Though this is a rare commodity, a perfectly glowing critique of *Babes in Toyland* occurs on December 18, 1934. Not surprisingly, this was also a film especially earmarked for the youth market—reminders of which are sprinkled throughout the piece, from "a film par excellence for children" to "the best juvenile product to date."

Second, though slapstick has never been entirely divorced from American film, the "Golden Age of Sound Comedy" (1930s) was obviously competitive with physical comedy. Appropriately, *Variety* was constantly pooh-poohing Laurel & Hardy visual material, the essence of their work. For example, *Block-Heads* was a "hodge-podge of old-fashioned slapstick and hoke." When rare *Variety* praise did come Laurel & Hardy's way, it was often linked to dialogue. For example, see the publication's reviews of *Our Relations* and *A Chump at Oxford*. Alternately, panning *Variety* critiques often bemoan the team's lack of witty dialogue, such as their reviews of *Block-Heads* and *Way Out West*.

A third *Variety* complaint (and the most common to surface in dissenting Laurel & Hardy reviews by other publications) pertains to a lack of storyline— what was addressed in Chapter 1 as the attempt to stretch Laurel & Hardy short subjects to a sometimes meandering feature length. This is a more fundamental criticism than the subjective complaints on Laurel & Hardy's slapstick comedy and childishness. Still, *Variety*'s period Laurel & Hardy critics (and others) missed the point that the *New York Times* reviewers knew so well: one's primary concern with personality comedians like Laurel & Hardy is the significance of characterization over storyline. Indeed, when one discusses his or her favorite movie personality comedian with friends, it is enough simply to say, "I saw so-and-so's latest film." Invariably, the conversation then focuses on that personality comedian's celebrated characterization and specific shticks (such as the special dumbness of Stan).

At the same time that *Variety* was showing little appreciation for Laurel & Hardy, the team was receiving its most insightful period praise from England. No doubt this was assisted by that country being Laurel's birthplace. But if explanations were that simple, Hardy's U.S. ties should have improved the team's stateside reviews.

Regardless, a survey of this sympathetic British analysis of Laurel & Hardy must begin with the great documentary producer, theorist, and critic John Grierson. Though best known now for his pioneer work in documentary, his 1920s and 1930s criticism is an invaluable source of farsighted critiquing. For the student of film comedy, his most pivotal essay is "The Logic of Comedy," a 1947 interweaving of earlier film critiques, including a Laurel & Hardy piece from the October 29, 1931 *Everyman*. Anthologized in *Grierson on Documentary*, this seemingly unlikely source produces a most compelling analysis of Laurel & Hardy as well as their comedy contemporaries (especially the Marx Brothers).

Grierson's "The Logic of Comedy" is insightful in three ways—all of which anticipate future developments in Laurel & Hardy criticism. First, without undercutting Laurel, Grierson feels that Hardy has so developed his screen persona (by 1931) that Ollie has gone from being the team's "minor partner [to] the major one.'' While many duo followers might disagree with that assessment, there is no denying the still positive reevaluation of Hardy's screen character. Ironically, Laurel, the dominant partner behind the camera, was eventually a major factor in the new appreciation of Ollie. (See McCabe's 1961 *Mr. Laurel & Mr. Hardy*, where Laurel talks of being bowled over by his old teammate whenever one of their films is on TV.)

Second, Grierson recognized early the black-comedy aspects of Laurel & Hardy's comedy, especially their all-important ties with violent destruction and a legacy of ''chaos''—an apt Stan & Ollie description Grierson often uses.

Third, Grierson indirectly anticipates the comic antihero's non-political status—his fate to be forever frustrated by the little things of life. Grierson achieves this by limiting his Laurel & Hardy film references to the film originally being reviewed, *Laughing Gravy* (1931), in which Stan's middle-of-the-night hiccups (of nearly bed-shaking proportions) begin another of the team's domino effect descents into a comedy hell. That is, Stan's hiccups awaken their dog, Laughing Gravy, causing him to bark; this awakens their ''no pets allowed'' landlord . . . and ''another nice mess'' has begun.

As a *Laughing Gravy* aside, what could be more antiheroic than having your dog play the title character? And while this is hardly one of the duo's great films (the McCabe-Kilgore-Bann book rates it two-and-one-half derbies—slightly above average), it makes an interesting selection. Grierson nicely demonstrates the team's *standard* frustration (and accompanying comic chain reaction) in a *standard* or basic Laurel & Hardy film. In effect, a trait or characteristic is sometimes most apparent in a modest or even mediocre work, where one is not distracted from a given pattern by a special artistry.

Interestingly enough, Grierson's view of comedy at its best usually has dark overtones and/or elements of antiheroic problems. For example, in this same ''The Logic of Comedy'' essay, Grierson offers a macabre interpretation of the Marx Brothers' *Animal Crackers* (1930) close, with Harpo's spray-gun knockout of the whole case, including the comedian, being interpreted by the critic as comically insane murder by the Marxes' resident madman. (A more traditional ''reading'' of the scene would be to assume Harpo's spray is something less than lethal, such as ether.) Consequently, given Grierson's comedy perspective, it is easy to see why he rated Laurel & Hardy so highly.

A second pertinent Grierson essay is his ''Summary and Survey: 1935'' (originally appearing in ''The Arts Today,'' 1935), also anthologized in *Grierson on Documentary*. As the title suggests, this is a much broader piece that touches only briefly on comedy, let alone Laurel & Hardy. Yet Grierson's strong praise of the duo's very creative use of sound nicely compliments his earlier celebration of the team (see Chapter 2). Moreover, Grierson was singling out Laurel & Hardy as the silent comedians who made the most ''effective use of sound.''

Regardless, the student of comedy is lucky to even have Grierson commentary on Laurel & Hardy. In ''The Logic of Comedy,'' he ponders the wisdom of analyzing the world of Stan & Ollie—not because their films do not merit such attention but due to concern that public critiquing would self-consciously hinder their future work. Grierson feared Laurel & Hardy would be burdened with an added artistic responsibility and thus lose their "gift of honest slapstick," something he had seen happen to other comedians. For Grierson, this comic loss of what might be called the clown's artistic naivete is best exemplified by what he considers the critical analysis spoiling Charlie Chaplin's persona. But Grierson feels so strongly about the team's comedy significance that he still opts (thankfully) for critique.

Another pivotal Laurel & Hardy critic from 1930s Britain is filmmaker Basil Wright. This chapter covers four of his essays: the *World Film News* cover article "Blest Pair of Sirens" (June 1937); *The Spectator* review of *Block-Heads* (September 16, 1938), which quickly turns into a Laurel & Hardy career celebration; the *World Film News* "The Last of Laurel" (October 1938), a *Block-Heads* review that stays closer to its subject; and a brief section in Chapter 3 of his later book *The Long View* (1974).

Initially, the most striking thing about "Blest Pair of Sirens" is the lofty praise with which Wright showers the two. It is not empty homage, since important elements of their comedic art are highlighted items soon to be addressed. But it is important to pause briefly on this adoration because it is so outside the Laurel & Hardy criticism norm in the United States. It reads more like the ongoing celebration one expects of an essay on Chaplin.

Not surprisingly, Wright places the team "with Chaplin, among the few great mimes." (He is particularly fond of their dance number in *Way Out West*.) On the other hand, Wright credits Laurel & Hardy with being the only "serious rivals" to sound comedy's Marx Brothers, implying that these two teams are the measuring stick for all personality comedians of the sound era. While Wright acknowledges Laurel & Hardy's discovery of song, he should have accented its importance to the *Way Out West* dance number. Not only is their dancing mime funny, they verbally complement the scene (on the same high level) with their delightful singing. (See Chapter 1.)

Wright also affectionately excels at dissecting the team's comedy technique: from their "Mutual destruction" (uncredited example from the tit-for-tat violence of *Big Business*); to "variations on a simple theme" (such as different ways to fall off the roof in *Hog Wild*). He also examines the team phenomenon of "Delayed Reaction" (with Wright's example being the mistaken sacking—literally—of their boss instead of title character Fra Diavolo, a film also known as *The Devil's Brother*.

Despite these Laurel & Hardy accolades and Wright's methodical understanding of their comedy tools, he still indirectly demonstrates a self-consciousness about the team's often less-than-lofty critical stance; he both opens and closes the piece on a defensively personal level, not without a dark comedy element: "Maybe you don't find them funny? . . . I hope you will many times be forced to sit through a Laurel and Hardy feature film, tortured by the unceasing laughter of an audience of ordinary people."

Wright's second piece, done the following year (1938), was a homage to a Laurel & Hardy career that was then thought to be over. In fact, early in the essay Wright refers to it as "in the nature of an obituary." But very soon it becomes more in the nature of a rejoicing wake—thankful for the comic gifts the team would be leaving behind.

Though technically appearing in Wright's film review column (from *The Spectator*—"The Cinema"), he quickly moves from the team's "last" film to especially memorable earlier efforts, including *Way Out West, Aerial Antics* (British title of *Hog Wild*), and an indirect piano-moving reference to *The Music Box* (1932) and *Swiss Miss* (1938). Wright thought so highly of *Way Out West* he wishes it had been the team's "last" film. Yet, he has positive things to say about *Block-Heads*—especially a comic lunacy that could find poor muddle-minded Laurel guarding his World War I trench twenty years after the war was over. Indeed, he seems to enjoy every major comedy scene in *Block-Heads*, from the subdued dark humor of Ollie thinking Stan has lost a leg (see Chapter 1) to the slapstick with the automatic garage door involving another expendable Stan & Ollie automobile. Wright eventually makes an advantage of both *Block-Heads'* lunacy and eclectic nature—crediting its broadness as fitting for a "final" film.

No doubt due to the apparent close of the team's career, Wright almost entirely avoids his sometimes apologetic nature (for such high Laurel & Hardy praise) found in his *World Film News* article, though *The Spectator* piece does conclude with the self-conscious defense: "Should haughty persons resent so long a eulogy on two film actors, let them remember that a good laugh is as hard to come by as a good cry."

The third Wright piece, "The Last of Laurel," complements the previous broadbased *Block-Heads* review, because it actually centers on the film itself. However, as the title suggests, Wright manages to comment on the apparent demise of the team, too. But a lighter tone demonstrates he has weathered the personal shock that such a duo could be derailed: "May the curse of the Ritz Brothers light on all who are not [Laurel & Hardy fans]." The final item, the extended aside from *The Long View*, makes a fitting close to the Laurel & Hardy–Wright connection, both because historical perspective only bolsters his continued praise of the team and he now had a warm memory of having met Laurel.

One might easily extend this survey of period English critical appreciation of Laurel & Hardy much further, especially with attention to novelist Graham Greene and filmmaker Alberto Cavalcanti. (For more on them, see Chapter 2, especially in reference to Greene's *A Chump at Oxford* review in the February 23, 1940 *Spectator*.) In fact, the breadth of this regard might best be demonstrated by the lauding of Laurel & Hardy from so unlikely a source as novelist Henry Miller. In his essay on cinema, "The Golden Age" (see the 1939 Miller anthology *The Cosmological Eye*), he calls the team's *Battle of the Century* (1927) "the greatest comic film ever made," though he ironically cannot remember the film's title. Miller's reasoning for bestowing this honor on the film famous for

Posed antiheroic violence for *Block-Heads'* garage door scene

its epic pie fight at first seems simplistic—"it brought pie-throwing to apotheosis." But when he expands upon this generally—"In every art the ultimate is achieved only when the artist passes beyond the bounds of the art he employs"—Miller indirectly echoes Grierson's comments on Laurel & Hardy's comic ties to "chaos," my own view of them as *the* comic antiheroes, and what Wright's "Blest Pair of Sirens" best defines as the team's ultimate connection to the "woes of Sisyphus." Unfortunately, Miller soon steams off in a different direction, but his fleeting Laurel & Hardy insight again underlines a key point of this section—the team was much more likely to be accorded the status of comic artists in England (or Europe in general) than in the United States.

Returning to U.S. criticism, Laurel & Hardy were not only underrated in many circles, they were often without a rating at all. For example, the team went routinely unreviewed in such influential journals as the *New Republic* and *The Nation*. It was not as if Laurel & Hardy films were outside the criticism norm for these publications. For instance, the *New Republic*'s Otis Ferguson, probably the premier American film critic of the 1930s, was W. C. Fields's greatest and most poetically insightful period champion, with his ongoing critiquing seminar on Fields as a comedic "national treasure" and an American Falstaff. Moreover, Fields did not represent analytical slumming for Ferguson, what is popularly referred to in recent years as a critic's "guilty pleasures." This always provocatively perceptive writer, who died in World War II, excelled as a reviewer of any number of *popular culture* disciplines, long before that phrase entered the language. Thus, he was as comfortable exploring the blues of Bessie Smith as he was the films of Fields. For such a critic (the influential precursor of such important 1940s mainstream reviewers as James Agee and Robert Warshow) generally to avoid Laurel & Hardy speaks volumes about the team's general lack of artistic credibility in the states.

As an insightful critic of Fields, Ferguson's neglect of Laurel & Hardy was also unfortunate due to the comic antiheroic parallels he might have drawn between these comedians (excepting, of course, those times when Fields assumes his con-man persona).

While period critiques of Laurel & Hardy were often not as plentiful as one might expect, there were still reviews to be found, and an interesting source of such criticism was the many New York City newspapers. Though not every one reviewed Laurel & Hardy films, this was still a time when there were well over a dozen major newspapers published in Manhattan alone. The most striking message that comes from a survey of period New York papers is that while *Variety* is in no danger of losing its status as the most vitriolic reviewer of Laurel & Hardy, some of the New York papers had complaints along similar lines. That is, they had problems with what they called the team's weak feature-length storylines and comedy more geared to a juvenile audience. But unlike *Variety*, the majority of these New York papers also worked at finding something positive in the Laurel & Hardy films. (Too often *Variety*'s negative position actually seemed reminiscent of those old punning attacks on an elitist publication—one that is usually *sneersighted*, or goes along for *deride*.)

In contrast, there were certain New York papers with a special soft spot for Laurel & Hardy. *New York World-Telegram* film critic William Boehnel was a strong supporter. In his May 4, 1937 review of *Way Out West*, he called the team the "last frontier" of slapstick, maybe not "as slick and smart as its more refined counterpart, but it is usually eminently more enjoyable and certainly more eternal." (See also his August 30, 1938 review of *Block-Heads*.)

Another "Gotham City" newspaper champion of Laurel & Hardy was the *New York American*. Its backing transcended changes in critics and even the newspaper itself, as it became the *New York Journal-American* in 1937. Thus, its unsigned *Sons of the Desert* review (January 8, 1934) correctly did cartwheels over Laurel & Hardy's greatest film—something that was not quite so obvious to all period critics. Moreover, its praise for the "Laurel-Hardy formula . . . as the martyr husbands" was especially perceptive because what seems obvious now (the comic superiority of this particular portrayal of antiheroic husbands) was just as likely then to be lost among other domestic battles royal—both Stan & Ollie's as well as those of other period screen clowns. (For example, the January 1, 1934 *New York Sun* review of *Sons of the Desert* had trouble, in part, with the film for that reason—their old material reading of husbands trying to slip out on their wives.)

Another *New York American* piece of note was Robert Garland's May 4, 1937 review of *Way Out West*, which again demonstrated knowledgeable recognition of what might be the only rival to *Sons of the Desert* as Laurel & Hardy's greatest feature film. Garland was also cognizant of (though he touches upon it only briefly) a key to the team's ongoing success—an item pursued more fully in recent years. Their humor is based in studied obviousness. (One is reminded of Hardy's childhood habit of people watching in hotel lobbies—see Chapter 1.) Theirs is the comedy of anticipation—one sees the bit coming and savors its execution. Their telegraphing of a gag even goes to the point of adding inserts (close-ups of a given object that will soon be the catalyst for the comedy), such as a shot of a wayward rollerskate shortly before Hardy will step on it.

Garland also reminds the viewer that the team's comedy bread and butter is still a throwback to silent film, a fact easily lost sight of in sound film's golden era (1930s). This, no doubt, is a foundation for some of the negative reviews; critics found their slapstick old-fashioned. Interestingly, Garland provides this physical comedy reminder in a film in which Laurel & Hardy also best demonstrate their sound comedy capabilities.

Rose Pelswick's June 5, 1943 critique of *Jitterbugs* in what had become the *New York Journal-American* continued the paper's knowing support of the team. Though the film was not in a class with Laurel & Hardy's best 1930s films, *Jitterbugs* was above average—which made it a big improvement over their other 1940s work (after *Saps at Sea*, 1940).

While Pelswick noted *Jitterbugs'* diamond-in-the-rough quality, a goodly number of her reviewing colleagues merely saw it as more 1940s mediocrity from the team. Moreover, several critics even felt manipulated by the title *Jitterbugs*. For example, Archer Winston's *New York Post* critique (June 5, 1943) stated: "the title promises something the picture does not deliver. With the exception of a single jitterbug sequence, and that of mediocre quality, there is nothing to excite a hepcat or depress one who is not hep."

No doubt use of the title was an attempt to capitalize on the then-current dance craze. And though the picture was good compared to their other work during this period, the fact that the team was being marketed in this way (a trendy title only loosely attached to the brief screen time of Stan & Ollie as a two-man jitterbug band) demonstrates just how far their fortunes had fallen in just a few years. Plus, it is more evidence of how the larger Hollywood studios with which they worked in the 1940s (after their final split with Roach) did not understand their basic comedy story needs. (See Chapter 1.)

Regardless, Archer Winston's complaint about a misleading title seems an overreaction. Comedy in general, and Stan & Ollie in particular, are very good at meandering away from whatever thin plotline *might* have existed in the beginning. Besides, were there really that many "hepcats" who came to the movie strictly because of that title? Whenever one is dealing with such classic clown genre personalities as Laurel & Hardy, the storyline is traditionally just another peek at whatever comedy shtick—specific routines and/or variations of them—animates their all-important screen comedy personae.

That is why one often hears things like: "I saw a Laurel & Hardy film last night" (or the comedian(s) of your choice), without bothering (or often needing) to provide a title. It would be much more logical if comedy titles returned to a tendency often seen in early silent comedy—placing the character's name in the title because he/she is the one thing that holds the eclectic comic grab bag together. For example, the films of Max Linder, John Bunny, Mabel Normand, Fatty Arbuckle frequently played up their names in this manner: *Max in a Dilemma* (1910), *Bunny at the Derby* (1912), *Fatty Joins the Force* (1913), *Mabel's Married Life* (1914), *Fatty and Mabel Adrift* (1916), etc. Though not without later precedents, such as the series of Abbott & Costello films which began with *Abbott and Costello in Hollywood* (1945) or the more recent Pee Wee Herman films—*Pee Wee's Big Adventure* (1985) and *Big Top Pee Wee* (1988)—names in the title are relatively rare, though still often appropriate. Of course, a semblance of this name-game approach does connect to Laurel & Hardy. They used their own names within their films throughout their careers, which reminds the viewer that their unique ongoing comedy characters generally take precedence over everything else—the same message of the name in the title. (In the 1930s Laurel & Hardy's short subjects were sometimes edited together in Europe and released at feature length with their names in the title.)

Of course, to come full circle on *Jitterbugs'* title question one might merely quote *New York Sun* film critic Eileen Creelman's simple answer in her June 5, 1943 review:

Laurel and Hardy, of all people, don zoot suits and appear in a film called *Jitterbugs* . . . Neither Stan Laurel nor Oliver Hardy are the age, build or type for zoot suits. This is probably the [comedy] point of it all.

Though Creelman observes, "The jitterbug sequences do not last long," it is merely a point of information, not a condemnation. And her closing underlines this "anything goes" titling, at least if it is amusing. Moreover, she could also have recommended a name in the title approach, since her final remarks key upon the dominance of clown characters like Laurel & Hardy—"By now [1943] moviegoers should know just how they feel about this slapstick pair. *Jitterbugs* is centered about them."

There are any number of New York City newspaper reviews with which one might close this segment. I limit mine to two short critiques of *Way Out West*: Blaud Johaueson's *New York Daily Mirror* piece and Dorothy Masters's *New York Daily News* review (both from May 4, 1937).

One is first attracted to the essays because of the joyful exuberance both authors bring to their subjects. But beyond mere enthusiasm, these critics demonstrate a knowledge of Laurel & Hardy's earlier work and a fundamental acceptance of the team as significant artists. They offer no apologies for the duo's slapstick or low-comedy tastes, something to which even the pro–Laurel & Hardy English critics succumb.

Another against-type attraction is that two such euphoric reviews should come from women—the gender often alienated by Laurel & Hardy because of Stan & Ollie's frequent run ins with domineering, frying-pan-toting wives. This is not to say Laurel & Hardy are limited to a male audience, but males are decidedly in the majority.

Interestingly enough, Laurel & Hardy's key 1930s personality comedian contemporaries, W. C. Fields and the Marx Brothers, also enjoy a largely male audience. Like Laurel & Hardy, the antiheroic Fields often suffers through screen marriages to heavy-handed wives (especially Kathleen Howard). In contrast, the Marxes, or more precisely, Groucho, is best known for his comic verbal attacks on stuffy society matron Margaret Dumont.

Regardless, if women critics were to rave about any of Laurel & Hardy's features, it is fitting that Johaueson and Masters should rate *Way Out West* so highly. There is not a frying pan in sight and comic saloon temptress Lola Marcel (Sharon Lynne) is an inspired bad girl. As Johaueson observes, Lynne is "still a first rate siren." As if Johaueson and Masters were balancing their praise of *Way Out West*'s two central female roles, Masters singles out Rosina Lawrence— the unknowing heiress Mary Roberts, who slaves for Lois and Mickey Finn

(James Finlayson) in Cinderella-like drudgery. Stan & Ollie are her most unlikely rescuers.

More than most *Way Out West* reviewers, Johaueson is especially taken with the film's parody nature—"a hilarious burlesque of the heroic westerns," with Stan & Ollie nicely described as "two knights . . . sadly addicted to blunders." Johaueson's unofficial symbol for this parody is the boys' partner in slapstick, Dinah the burro, who has a pivotal role in Stan & Ollie's comically misguided attempt to break into Finlayson's saloon (see Chapter 1). With tongue firmly in cheek, one might even count the role as another (though highly unconventional) woman's role. Certainly, it would not be inconsistent with Johaueson's attention to Dinah.

While Johaueson begins her review with a parody slant, Masters's piece opens with a fascinating sociological description of the riotous joy with which New York's Rialto Theatre audience responded to *Way Out West*. This is one of those invaluable pieces of time seldom recorded but which bring the period to life. Even if Masters had had nothing else to say, her opening would have been worth preserving. Her observations are also nicely complemented by *New York Post* critic Archer Winston's review. He was so moved by the *Way Out West* response of young Rialto patrons that he opened his review with a focus on a specific boy and his father as they succumbed to a laughter of "hysterical abandon." (Winston is so thorough as to record one of the comedy bits that was so convulsing audiences: Stan overhears a saloon patron complain about a piece of meat being "tougher than shoe leather." This triggers a light to go on in Stan's muddle-headed mind—he places the meat in his shoe, nicely covering a hole in his sole.)

Pivotal Laurel & Hardy literature in the 1940s is not nearly so plentiful as in the decade just examined for three reasons. First, their film career essentially ended with the 1945 feature *The Bullfighters*, though there would later be the regrettable *Atoll K* in 1952. Consequently, there is no large store of film reviews and articles that a new product is forever generating (as was the case in the productive 1930s). Second, although there continued to be a strong Laurel & Hardy following, their 1940s film work as a whole showed a definite decline—not the best catalyst for an ongoing public analysis of their work. Third, there was a new team on the block—Abbott & Costello—and they represented not only more comedy competition but a new type of competition: faster-paced, more tough-spirited, emphasizing the verbal, and with a constant flip-flop between being antiheroic and wiseguy (see Chapter 1). Consequently, Laurel & Hardy's once innovative antiheroic humor was no longer on the cutting edge. This was made worse in the 1940s, starting with *Great Guns* (1941), when their material seemed determined to remake them into a second-class Abbott & Costello (see Chapter 1).

Once-great careers in decline can, of course, inspire insightful revisionist writing on what is going wrong. One excellent Laurel & Hardy example of this, which also recognized early the unfortunate attempt by a new studio to make over the team, occurs in the *New York Times*'s October 3, 1941 review of *Great*

Guns. For example, "Not that the boys are slipping [the forever Laurel & Hardy supportive *New York Times*]; but alas! how desperately do they need a script-writer with an understanding and appreciation for their particular style of fun-making." However, sensitive critical explorations of their decline, such as this *New York Times* piece, were in the minority.

As so often is the case, it was not until after the close of Laurel & Hardy's film career (using 1945 as the more appropriate date) that a modicum of serious literature on the team began to appear—the trickle-down theory applied to film aesthetics. Two such late 1940s essays were Simon Watson Taylor's " 'HERE'S ANOTHER FINE MESS!': A dissertation on Laurel and Hardy—the ambassadors of the unprivileged" (*Film Survey*, Spring 1947) and James Agee's "Comedy's Greatest Era" (*Life*, September 3, 1949).

It seems most fitting, because of England's past critical hosannas for the team, that one of these new era essays should be penned by an Englishman—actor, poet, and surrealist writer Taylor. Quite possibly, his " 'HERE'S ANOTHER FINE MESS!' " was the result of another English connection. Shortly prior to the publication of Taylor's essay, Laurel & Hardy were having a critically and commercially successful tour of English music halls. Even *Variety* (March 1947), normally less than kind to the team, was moved to report very favorably on their London Palladium show.

Regardless as to whether the catalyst for the essay was a touring Laurel & Hardy (as a later English tour was for the writing of John McCabe), Taylor's piece is a good post-1945 starting point as it both addresses some earlier unresolved Laurel & Hardy issues and explores some new ones.

Taylor's essay begins with an ambitious examination of why one laughs. Though comedy theory is hardly an easy way in which to draw readers, he quickly moves to his hypothesis: laughter is "to reassure ourselves; to laugh is to break out for a short time from the restricting barriers of the hard realities of existence."

More specifically, to "reassure ourselves" is to be made aware of the total incompetency of others as they attempt to meet life's ridiculous demands. And to briefly "break out" from reality is to have a "sense of fantasy." In the reassurance department, Laurel & Hardy (the ambassadors of incompetency) are a perfect example for Taylor. Even the most frustrated viewer should be pleased that his problems are not those of Stan & Ollie. Put another way, this portion of Taylor's theory merely embraces the most hoary of comedy hypotheses: superiority.

Ironically, surrealist Taylor implies that Laurel & Hardy are a special example of his theory because of their *realistic* foundation in modern times. Realism has often surfaced in examining Laurel & Hardy, and in this case, Taylor suggests the viewer's modern problems are more likely to be addressed (and at least temporarily purged) in the films of Laurel & Hardy as opposed to those of Chaplin or the Marx Brothers.

How does Taylor embrace a "sense of fantasy" in Laurel & Hardy if the duo has such a realistic base? He feels that the team has a special ability to draw the viewer into their screen world, beyond the general voyeurism associated with watching movies. For Taylor, Stan represents the hopeless individual victimized by modern society, while Ollie symbolizes humanity's vain attempt to fight back. Taylor's prose on these characterizations falls somewhere between insightful elegance and overwriting. For example, listen to his description of Ollie:

oozing dignified courtesy, pompous rectitude and native cunning from every pore—only to have his elaborate facade knocked tumbling to the ground at the first contact with the cold, heartless world controlled by prototypes: the muscular toughs, astute business men, shrewish wives and inhuman policemen.

But despite Taylor's pretty prose, his argument for the team's sense of fantasy (via its mesmerizing realism and the unique voyeurism that accompanies it) seems weak until he implies that this is the same reason Laurel & Hardy do not receive the comic respect of a Chaplin or the Marx Brothers. Taylor feels one is more uneasy laughing at Stan & Ollie because they are so close to the viewer's own frustrating real world. Whether one accepts this or not, it is a refreshing switch from the standard excuse for the Laurel & Hardy put-down—primitive and repetitive slapstick.

If this Taylor approach to a "sense of fantasy" in Laurel & Hardy is too deep-dish, he does provide another more straightforward example: when Stan & Ollie become involved in their classic tit-for-tat acts of shared comic violence. Focusing on Hardy, who most often takes the comic physical abuse of these confrontations, Taylor labels the team's tit-for-tat scenes "unsurpassed *reductio ad absurdum* of the concept of violence." He strongly feels their *subversive* comedy goes well beyond comparable material by Chaplin and the Marx Brothers. And with his own brand of comedy elitism, he roundly dismisses viewers who define subversive humor by way of the Three Stooges and Abbott & Costello.

If Taylor's way with words and provocative thinking has not won the reader over to the Laurel & Hardy mutual admiration society, his comic conclusion just might tip the scales. It is as poignantly effective as criticism gets. Referring to humanity's metaphorical individual as victim, Taylor inspiredly recycles basic Stan & Ollie material as passwords of humanity: " 'Oh, Olly [sic]! I'm frightened' . . . and 'Here's *another* nice mess you've got us into.' "

An early companion piece to Taylor's essay is James Agee's celebrated "Comedy's Greatest Era" (see also Chapter 1). Though Laurel & Hardy aficionados might feel they have just cause to take Agee's name in vain—for not including the team in his silent comedy pantheon four of Chaplin, Keaton, Langdon, and Lloyd—kind though fleeting things are said about the duo. Titleless references are made to *The Battle of the Century* (1927) and *Swiss Miss* (1938). And Agee compliments earlier English critics when he credits Laurel & Hardy with being "the only comedians who managed to preserve much of the large, low style of silence and who began to explore the comedy of sound." Indeed, Agee's important but abbreviated commentary even boasts references to the pivotal Leo McCarey. Consequently, while the Agee piece does not boast the elegant poetry-like Laurel & Hardy focus of Taylor's essay, the former work has since become such a watershed work (often considered the starting point for the serious study of silent comedy), that even its brief positive Stan & Ollie strokes are significant.

The majority of the team's best work during the 1940s occurred not in the movies but rather on stage, from bond rallies to tours (see also Chapter 1). Thus, much as with the solo activities of the Marx Brothers during this period (their film career as a team also being on the wane), an appreciable amount of Laurel & Hardy criticism is all but lost in less-than-mainstream hinterland publications. For example, the November 3, 1940 *St. Louis Post Dispatch* featured a very informative piece on Laurel & Hardy and their Hollywood revue, from various acts on the bill to a brief discussion of the duo's "Drivers' License Sketch." More important, author Calvin McPherson entertainingly implies that their routine was liberally laced with the team's physical shtick:

Just to see Stan Laurel scratching the top of his head with all five fingers, as if he were mixing a batch of biscuits, or watch him tune up for a whimper, has always been genuine pleasure. Hardy's flick of the necktie, his greasy daintiness and impatience with Laurel make the fun complete.

McPherson's review also includes a surprising aside on the team, coming as it does from a heartland fan who also happens to be a critic. He confesses to being a "sucker" for Laurel & Hardy material—"in some of the world's worst motion pictures and several of its best." With the negatives no doubt reflecting the glut of poor pictures Laurel & Hardy did in the 1940s, it is still interesting that the sympathetic McPherson should so breezily acknowledge such a dichotomy in their work.

Naturally, major entertainment trade papers like *Variety* and *Billboard* often kept one modestly abreast of hinterland activities. For example, the February 7, 1942 *Billboard* carried a brief account on the team's box office clout in Dayton, Ohio, where they established new stage show records. Besides reminding one of Laurel & Hardy's perennial popularity in small-town America, the short piece goes on to note the team's "generous participation" in local activities—which indirectly feeds the standard critical image of Stan & Ollie as nice (though rather vacuous) guys. (See also *Billboard*'s brief comment on their stage success in Chicago, January 1942.) Moreover, the team's stage work was not limited to heartland appearances. Thus, more-visible print media commentary on their tour periodically surfaced, from the *Variety* review (March 1, 1947) of their London Palladium appearance to the *New York Times* piece (October 22, 1947) on their November 3 command performance before the British royal family.

Ever perceptive British film comedy historian David Robinson eclipsed all pre-1954 essays on Laurel & Hardy with his *Sight and Sound* (July-September 1954) piece, "The Lighter People." Though hardly lengthy (four and one-half pages), it managed to cover a broad spectrum of Laurel & Hardy material as well as making references to three important and previously herein examined essays: Grierson's "The Logic of Comedy," Wright's "Blest Pair of Sirens," and Agee's "Comedy's Greatest Era."

Robinson's article begins with the now almost obligatory reference to the team's lack of recognition—"Among the larger talents, Laurel and Hardy still remain outside the pale of the intelligentsia's recognition." But without trying to elevate them to Chaplin level (Robinson readily acknowledges their "bad films"), he pushes for their general recognition as "very, very good clowns."

Before the critical analysis meat of the essay, Robinson briefly provides some background material on the comedians both before and after their teaming. With the revelations of recent years, this proves to be the essay's only weak section. For example, Roach is mistakenly given credit for teaming Laurel & Hardy, the implementation of the comedy duo did not occur as quickly and effortlessly as is suggested, and no mention is made of Leo McCarey. Robinson might also have been more expansive on the team's innovative early use of sound for comedy. (Interestingly enough, he picks *The Big Noise*, 1944, as the best of the duo's final five 1940s films, which clashes with today's popular pick—*Jitterbugs*, 1943; see Chapter 1.)

Robinson is at his best when his focus becomes analysis, such as his definition of the basic Laurel & Hardy story structure—"the proposition of an enterprise; the progressive frustration of its execution; and its final catastrophic abortion, which leaves them where they were at the beginning, or even one unhappy step backwards."

His delineation of the team's screen personae is excellent, especially on Ollie's "elephantine elegance." For instance, "His walk is assured, head in the air (with the consequences one might expect)." Taking a more traditional critical stance of Stan as comedy character, Robinson keys upon the parallels between Laurel's character and those of the celebrated earlier clown, Dan Leno (this remained a popular subject among future Laurel & Hardy authors). Robinson also examines the "pure simpleton" nature of Stan, reminding one that any rare bit of comic wisdom that might appear is purely accidental.

Laurel & Hardy detractors sometimes criticize the team for having a relative dearth of material. Others imply this when they suggest the duo is monotonous. If and when the student of Laurel & Hardy addresses this issue, a ready alibi is the ever-popular difference of taste—one either likes or dislikes them. Robinson refreshingly goes beyond this in two ways. First, while admitting their material is not extensive, he argues that it avoids monotony by dispensing "pleasures of *recognition*" to the viewer. Robinson likens the phenomenon to the music-hall use of catchphrases. But one could draw examples from diverse entertainment periods and mediums, from Jack Benny's patented "Well," to Steve Martin's "One wild and crazy guy." (Both were used in numerous settings, from stand-up stage work to television.)

Robinson's "pleasures of *recognition*," or Laurel & Hardy shtick, include familiar dialogue, such as "Another fine mess," and physical bits, for example, Ollie's comic expression of speechless disgust at Stan's latest demonstration of inspired stupidity. One is reminded of the auteur theory as it was originally applied to film directors. That is, a fundamental part of this critical stance was defining the artist through certain scenes and/or situations that routinely surfaced in his/her work, such as John Ford's propensity to include a graveyard scene in his films more effectively to underscore his favored populist theme. Thus, Robinson's position might be likened to a minimanifesto on the comedian as auteur. Of course, recognizing a comic pattern does not necessarily make something funny for everyone, just as repeated scenes do not by themselves make an auteur director great. But the main point here is that Robinson has addressed an often-avoided subject with an interesting, provocative answer.

The second way Robinson defends the team from raps about limited material is to recognize Laurel & Hardy's "seemingly infinite capacity for variation on a single theme." He finds this best demonstrated in the team's *The Music Box* (1932) and *Aerial Antics*, which he bolstered by an extended quote from Wright's "Blest Pair of Sirens."

Finally, Robinson's essay is arresting when it briefly cites a previously published but unfootnoted dialogue between the duo on their theory of comedy. This segment is especially intriguing in light of the team's normal reticence about attempts to explain comedy. Indeed, as noted earlier, Laurel eventually became almost hostile in his refusal to play comedy theorist. Consequently due to both the dialogue's comic insightfulness and its inherent rarity, here is the extent of what Robinson included:

O.H.: The fun is in the story situations which make an audience sorry for the comedian. A funny man has to make himself inferior . . .

S.L.: Let a fellow try to outsmart his audience and he misses. It's human nature to laugh at a bird who gets a bucket of paint smeared on his face—even though it makes him miserable.

O.H.: A comedian has to knock dignity off the pedestal. He has to look small—even I do—by a mental comparison. Lean or fat, short or tall, he has to be pitied to be laughed at.

S.L.: Sometimes we even feel sorry for each other. That always gets a laugh out of me. When I can feel sorry for "Babe."

Fittingly, this approach to comedy, traditionally defined as the theory of superiority, matches that of the pivotal Leo McCarey.

Comments on Laurel & Hardy in Robinson's later book *The Great Funnies: A History of Film Comedy* (1969) are noteworthy. Though interesting, the scope of the volume, including its equal attention to stills, severely limits what can be said about any one comedian. The team does, however, headline the brief chapter, "Laurel and Hardy, W. C. Fields." Robinson's comments are largely abbreviations of some subjects addressed in "The Lighter People," from the team's inspired stupidity to their "best" films being "variations on limited gag material." Always cognizant of perceptive Laurel & Hardy literature, such as his earlier references to Grierson, Wright, and Agee, on this occasion he draws from Charles Barr's *Laurel & Hardy* (1967)—Stan & Ollie are "supreme liberators from bourgeois inhibition, yet essentially they are, or aspire to be, respectable bourgeois citizens."

Robinson does pare down his original list of favored Laurel & Hardy feature films. The earlier piece saluted (in order of notation) *Way Out West* (1937), *Our Relations* (1936), *Fra Diavolo* (1933), *Swiss Miss* (1938), and *Block-Heads* (1938). The later Robinson chapter on the team limits the list to a trilogy of (in order) *Our Relations, Way Out West,* and *Block-Heads*. (For more on Robinson, see his *Sight and Sound* review of McCabe's *Mr. Laurel & Mr. Hardy,* both of which are dealt with in the book section of this chapter.)

Besides Robinson's 1954 essay, "The Lighter People," the year also saw the publication of English author John Montgomery's pioneering book on film clowns, *Comedy Films: 1894–1954*. Unfortunately, the book's treatment of Laurel & Hardy is disappointing (as is its examination of several other comic personalities). The duo receives neither the major focus of a chapter nor even an extended commentary in some subsection. At "best," Laurel & Hardy rate a mere page at the close of Montgomery's Chapter 16, "The Eccentrics," which is otherwise devoted to W. C. Fields and the Marx Brothers. Uncharacteristically, here is an English author not so enamored of the duo. Ironically, in light of the comedy theory dialogue just cited in Robinson's same-year essay, Montgomery closes "The Eccentrics" chapter with a Laurel quote belittling attempts to define comedy.

Montgomery's grouping of Laurel & Hardy with W. C. Fields and the Marx Brothers, though actually minimizing the amount of print space the duo receives, seems to be the 1950s norm. In writing books on Fields, the Marx Brothers, and other comedians, I have established a network of comedy source references that are generally egalitarian in their treatment of clown characters. However, one readily finds, at least during the 1950s, that while Laurel & Hardy are often packaged with Fields and the Marxes, they receive nowhere near the attention of these comedy colleagues. For instance, Arthur Knight's *The Liveliest Art: A Panoramic History of the Movies* (1957), a perceptive overview of world film history, focuses on the Marxes and W. C. Fields as "an almost perfect [comic] balance of sight and sound." There is little more than an aside on Laurel & Hardy.

Unfortunately, the 1957 catalyst for more-meaningful consideration of the team was the August 7 death of Hardy. Though countless career-rehashing obituaries surfaced, two of the better ones appeared in the *New York Times* and the *London Times* (both August 8, 1957). The normally staid *London Times* was so sensitive as to close with a reference to his passion for golf, even noting his handicap. And as thorough as the *New York Times* piece was, the newspaper topped itself the next day with a short but moving editorial page tribute to both

Laurel & Hardy entitled "The Fiddle and the Bow," drawn from the paper's observation, "You recall only skinny Laurel playing against fat Hardy as a bow plays against a fiddle, and you think of the gay, ingenious music." (Agee had once said of the team: "They fit as a fiddle to the bow.") Regardless, the *New York Times* found a qualified way to grant them the highest praise: "We expect that sequences from their films will become as classic as the fun of Chaplin, the Marx Brothers, W. C. Fields, and Buster Keaton." (See also, the *New York Herald Tribune*'s Hardy obituary, August 8, 1957.)

The best article to next consider is critic Peter Barnes's "Cuckoo," from the August 1960 *Films and Filming*. Thought provoking and sensitive, the essay is yet another example of English appreciation of the duo at prestigious criticism levels and is especially timely. It heralds the cult rediscovery of Laurel & Hardy; the intellectuals finally following the lead of the public. And while it notes the lofty recognition of Stan & Ollie in the 60s now being a "part of the archive Series '50 Famous Films' at the [British] National Film Theatre," it more pointedly notes the impact of two very influential silent comedy compilation films— Robert Youngson's *The Golden Age of Comedy* (1958) and *When Comedy Was King* (1960), both of which include Laurel & Hardy material.

The shared 1960 date of the article and the latter compilation film is also important, because it is with the second Youngson work that critical attention starts to refocus on underappreciated silent comedians, such as Laurel & Hardy. Fittingly, after 1960 Youngson's compilation tempo increases, as does his eventual interest in Laurel & Hardy: *Days of Thrills and Laughter* (1961, includes duo material), *M-G-M's Big Parade of Fun* (1964, more Laurel & Hardy included), *Laurel and Hardy's Laughing Twenties* (1965), *The Further Perils of Laurel and Hardy* (1967), and *Four Clowns* (1970, Laurel & Hardy are joined by Buster Keaton and Charley Chase). (For other compilations during this active period see the "Filmography.")

Barnes's article also notes such significant Laurel & Hardy comedy contributions as slowed pacing and gags based in anticipation (though no mention is made of Leo McCarey). He also reminds one of what might be called the cartoon principle: while the world of Stan & Ollie is constantly buffeted by comic destruction, "no one is really hurt. The characters are indestructible." Barnes makes the provocative further point that though the boys are "endlessly discomforted," they are "never humiliated." Like everything else comic, the answer to this lies in the eyes of the beholders. But one certainly has to admit that Stan & Ollie (especially Ollie) always attempt to remain dignified regardless of their ongoing comic catastrophes.

Revisionist Laurel & Hardy criticism often uses Chaplin as a whipping boy, and the Barnes piece is no different. One comment is that Chaplin pathos is a dangerous precedent (demanding laughter *and* tears) to establish. However, Barnes comically tempers this with his tongue-in-cheek analysis of a Laurel & Hardy scene as if it were Chaplin-authored. Drawing from *Bonnie Scotland* (1935), Barnes picks the routine where the out-of-step marching of army recruit

Stan gradually becomes the regiment norm, as one soldier after another assumes Stan's cockeyed gait. Barnes feels that if Chaplin had done it, the following serious critical commentary would have surfaced: " 'a devastating satire on the herd instinct and the military machine,' 'a subtle attack on the idea of togetherness,' 'a superb illustration of the power of suggestion,' and so on." Ironically, as comically argumentative as this was (1960), it remains true today for too many people.

Like Robinson's 1954 essay, "The Lighter People," Barnes defends Laurel & Hardy repetition by comparing it to the polished routines of the music hall (also applicable to vaudeville), where performers toured for years with the same material. However, Barnes holds his justification to this point, where (as previously noted) Robinson more fully addresses it.

Three closing items of interest in Barnes's "Cuckoo" are a strong essay opening (celebrating the nature of comedy), a maudlin close where he ceases being a critic and becomes a sentimental fan, and another rare kernel of comedy theory from Laurel: "Never try to outsmart the audience." Calling this comment "Laurel's comic credo," Barnes correctly applies it to the team's comedy of anticipation, where the viewer knows what is coming. (Interestingly, this position, like Laurel's comments on comic realism, contradicts the comedian's sometimes use of fantasy—see "white magic" in Chapter 1.)

The *London Times* article, "Fun with Laurel and Hardy: Seeking the Foolproof Job" (March 16, 1961) compares the masterful ways in which both Chaplin and Laurel & Hardy could sustain a story based on the simplest of situations. Though the unacknowledged author still gives Chaplin the edge in this ability, he places Laurel & Hardy ahead of Buster Keaton, Harold Lloyd, and Harry Langdon (the comedians, with Chaplin, generally considered silent comedy's pantheon four—See Agee's "Comedy's Greatest Era"). Besides being on target with Laurel & Hardy's "Chaplin touch," it is appropriate they should be receiving pantheon-level attention. Later in the year (August 18, 1961), John Hogbin's *Eltham and Kentish Times* (England) article, "Laurel and Hardy Retain Their Appeal," credited the team's ongoing popularity to the "simplicity of their gags."

During winter 1962–63 film critic Manny Farber's essay "White Elephant Art Versus Termite Art" appeared in *Film Culture*. Though only briefly touching on Laurel & Hardy, the references that occur are significant and provide a comically basic demarcation of art. The article is an attack on overly formalistic works (white elephants) where an "artistic" signature is self-consciously present—"a yawning production of over-ripe technique shrieking with presciosity, fame, ambition . . . now turned into a mannerism."

The majority of Farber's piece is spent delineating examples of this white-elephant art (what is more self-conscious than a white elephant?), with such provocative examples as Truffaut's *Jules and Jim* (1961) and *Shoot the Piano Player* (1962), films still generally held in high critical regard. However, when

Farber contrasts the white elephant with the preferred termite art, his opening example is Laurel & Hardy. "Good work usually arises when the creators . . . seem to have no ambitions towards gilt [flashy self-consciousness] culture, but are involved in a kind of squandering-beaverish endeavor that isn't [specifically directed] anywhere or for anything." This termite-like art is metaphorically below the surface, with no distracting style coming through to derail viewer attention. Consequently, Farber represents one more critic celebrating the team's foundation in realism, the comic ambiguity of day-to-day living. One is reminded again of documentary pioneer John Grierson on two counts. First, besides his general appreciation of Laurel & Hardy and their comic transformation of the everyday world, Grierson observed in "The Logic of Comedy" that clowns "are, in essence, super realists: that is to say, they are tragedians in disguise. Their endings are happy for everybody but themselves." Second, and even more pertinent to the Farber essay, is the comically famous Grierson undercutting of an overall formalistic film by director Joseph Von Sternberg—"When a director dies, he becomes a photographer."

Since the 1960s—but especially during the early part of that decade, a pivotal source of Laurel & Hardy essays was the publication *8mm Collector*, which later became *Classic Film Collector*, and then *Classic Images*. The pieces are best grouped into three general categories: analytical articles, reprints of earlier essays on the duo, and personal thoughts on the team by film collecting fans and occasionally Laurel himself. Without attempting to touch on all the pieces, some of the most pivotal will be addressed briefly.

The analytical essays are best delineated by Allan Hoffman's ongoing examination (Summer 1969–Spring 1971) of "The Twilight Years" of the team. Writing in his "dick und doof" ("fat and stupid," as Stan & Ollie are known in Germany) column, he provides a sensitively balanced look at Laurel & Hardy's less-than-happy 1940s screen career. For instance, he notes early in the first issue: "popular 'legend' has it that the studio executives were a 'tyrannical' group, delighting in every opportunity to 'sabotage' the team's career. A dramatically appealing and satisfying story, but one that seems highly unlikely."

Instead of the proverbial "end with a bang," Laurel & Hardy exited with a whimper, thanks to large studios that were not vindictive, but rather preoccupied with (to the studios' thinking) higher priorities. And this was worsened by their great misconception of the Stan & Ollie world—the most ironic of errors since it occurred in an alleged *film* town. Still, as previously noted, the team itself must shoulder some of the blame for their 1940s decline.

Hoffman performs a balancing act near the close of the final installment of "The Twilight Years." After his detailed look at these generally very disappointing films ("At their best" in *Jitterbugs* and *The Dancing Masters*—both 1943), Hoffman adds, "In spite of all we may say against these films they somehow still manage to amuse." He then notes some positive viewer responses towards these same films that have left him so sober faced. Thus, his message is that regardless of purists, "those unfamiliar with the body of their work are frequently very satisfied with the Fox films." (The vast majority of their last films, starting with *Great Guns*, 1941, were released by 20th Century-Fox.)

More Hoffman balancing occurs when he plays the proverbial armchair quarterback (make that critic) by asking what if the 1940s Laurel & Hardy had kept clear of 20th Century-Fox. His hypothesis suggests that the team would probably not have found things any more to their liking at Universal, Paramount, and Columbia (M-G-M had already failed them in *Air Raid Wardens*, 1943, and *Nothing But Trouble*, 1945). He does, however, wonder aloud about the Columbia short-subject department. Though representing a "step down" for the team, Laurel & Hardy could have worked with silent comedy colleagues like Buster Keaton and Harry Langdon and comedy directors Clyde Bruckman and Del Lord.

Hoffman might be underestimating Universal, since for a time the studio specialized in resurrecting former stars in modest *A* pictures, such as Mae West and W. C. Fields in the western parody *My Little Chickadee* (1940). Moreover, Universal gave Fields a great deal of freedom in his last two starring features—*The Bank Dick* (1940) and *Never Give a Sucker an Even Break* (1941)—a time ironically paralleling a Laurel & Hardy loss of control at Fox. Regardless, Hoffman has written an insightful and provocative serial piece on that always hard-to-examine subject—the decline of the artist. A *Classic Film Collector* companion piece to the Hoffman series can be found in Dennis Gifford's "The Latter Days of Laurel and Hardy" (Fall/Winter 1968). Gifford examines the late films, discussing as well their availability on 8mm.

Gifford's *Classic Film Collector* "Laurel & Hardy" (Summer 1968) is a rambling article ranging from his film fan encounter with the duo to an examination of missing segments from team films available for purchase in 8mm. An expanded examination of Gifford's meeting with the duo is found in his later regular *Films and Filming* column, the "Flavor of the Month" (for October 1984). Another thoughtful *Classic Images* commentary on the duo appeared as "The Universal Appeal of Laurel and Hardy" (July 1981). Also informative was the brief examination of the team's greater 1930s box office ranking in Great Britain.

The second category of articles (reprints) from this publication with the musical-chair titles is probably its richest, drawing an eclectic assortment of materials from any and all periods. Consequently, subject matter and date can be as diverse as the October 1929 *American Cinematographer* article "THOSE FUNNY BOYS: A Few Inside Facts About the Screen's Funniest Pair of Comedians and the Man Who Has Photographed Most of Their Pictures," to the 1961 Associated Press wire service piece, "Stan Laurel at 70: I'm All Washed Up." The former article was reprinted as "The Screen's Funniest Comics" in the February 1964 *8mm Collector*, while the second piece resurfaced in the Spring 1965 *8mm Collector*. Both will be examined further in this chapter's shorter works section, "Interviews/Reminiscences." There is also a rare look at a Laurel & Hardy script provided by the reprint in the March 1986 *Classic Image* of *The Fixer-Upper*'s (1935) shooting script.

Other reprints of special interest include numerous commentaries on Laurel's death, especially the often cited "Laurel and Hardy: Au Revoir" in the Spring 1965 *8mm Collector* (originally appearing in the February 28, 1965 *Philadelphia Sunday Bulletin*). An interesting session with Laurel & Hardy film editor Bert Jordan appeared as "A Life of Comedy" in the Spring 1968 *Classic Film Collector* (credited to the Summer 1967 *Cinemeditor*). This piece will also be examined chronologically later in this chapter's shorter works "Interviews/Reminiscences" section. And finally, see also the "Comic Couple Now a Cult" in the Fall 1971 *Classic Film Collector* (originally in the July 8, 1971 *Hollywood Citizen News*).

The third type of article from this publication, personal thoughts of film collectors and occasionally Laurel himself, is probably best demonstrated by Mike Polacek's "my hobby, laurel & hardy," from the February 1964 *8mm Collector*, with the same issue also carrying a reprint of an article on Polacek, "of mr. laurel and mr. hardy: huntington man their no. 1 fan" (both will be examined later in the chapter).

The death of Laurel in 1965 naturally generated a number of first-person accounts of the team, sometimes mixed with critical evaluations of their comic artistry. Thus, 1965 became the year of Stan & Ollie in review. For first-person accounts at this time, see this chapter's "Interview/Reminiscences" section.

French journal *Cinema* ran a perceptive (though brief) critical overview on Laurel & Hardy after the former's death. Titled simply "Stan Laurel est Mort" (no. 95, 1967), it credited the team's calculated slowness as the key to their originality. Moreover, the essay was generously sprinkled with bits and pieces only a real student of Laurel would appreciate. For example, a throwaway comparison with Langdon's screen persona, which found Stan less vacant than Harry, less "holy virgin." This unsigned critical commentary is an impressive and focused homage to the passing of a master clown.

Between July 1965 and January 1966 *Films and Filming* serialized a lengthy philosophy-of-comedy thesis by critic Raymond Durgnat that would later surface in expanded form as *The Crazy Mirror: Hollywood Comedy and the American Image* (1969).

Durgnat's chapter on Laurel & Hardy, "Beau Chumps and Church Bells," is in the eclectic tradition of the text itself. While the book is stimulating, the material is presented in a scatter-gun, short chapter approach, as Durgnat attempts to touch bases with a large number of comedians. Thus, the brief Stan & Ollie chapter ranges all over their antiheroic landscape, from tit-for-tat comedy to a European welcoming via church-bell renditions of their theme song. But Durgnat is at his best and most focused when discussing the duo's ties with the theatre of the absurd. For instance, he credits the piano-carrying comedy of *The Music Box* as being "a perfect little epic of monotonous futility, ornamented with odd little lyrical moments (as when the manhandled music box seems to mutter to itself, melodiously . . .)." He also addresses what, for him, are really minor differences between the "ultra-high-brow" theatre of the absurd and the "ultra-low-brow" comedies of Laurel & Hardy. Durgnat finds that while they complement each other, the more significant nod goes to Stan & Ollie, because regardless of life's absurdities, they realistically retain sparks of emotion not to be found in a Beckett tramp.

Coincidence also played a part in the increased 1965 visibility of the team. From July 20 to September 18, the Gallery of Modern Art put on "A Tribute to Hal Roach"—a retrospective film series primarily featuring Laurel & Hardy works in celebration of Roach's 50th anniversary in motion pictures. A special twelve-page program was published by the gallery to commemorate the event.

In September 1965 Robert Youngson's *Laurel & Hardy's Laughing 20s* was released. *Variety*'s early review (August 11) noted the influence of McCarey and Stevens. But the most detailed look at this chronological examination of the duo is film critic Judith Crist's excellent *New York Herald Tribune* critique (November 18), "Playing at the Beekman Theatre," this tells a story all by itself. That is, during the 1930s the team seemed to be forever opening in New York City by way of working-class Brooklyn. In contrast, 1965 cult figures Stan & Ollie were at one of Manhattan's prestigious East Side film theatres—Frances Herridge's *New York Post* review (November 18) liked the anthology so much that even the narration received praise, a characteristic of this and other comedy compilations that often prove irritating. For example, *Variety* had said of this narration, "It all but includes instructions telling us when to laugh. There are plenty of places . . . when laughter is likely to be provoked . . . but let us spot them ourselves. Don't push." Regardless, one saccharine line from Kathleen Carroll's *New York Daily News* review (November 18) nicely sets a period tone of the team's ever-more reverential status—"Their faces alone warm the heart."

Fittingly, for a year so sprinkled with Laurel & Hardy events, 1965 also saw the film opening of director Blake Edwards's *The Great Race*, a homage to film comedy's slapstick past, especially that of Laurel & Hardy. Appropriately, this film (starring Tony Curtis, Natalie Wood, and Jack Lemmon) had the following dedication: "for Mr. Laurel and Mr. Hardy."

Kalton Lahue's book, the *World of Laughter: The Motion Picture Comedy Short, 1910–1930* was published in 1966. While there is not a Laurel & Hardy section per se, there is a sprinkling of relevant material, especially on their solo days (see especially Chapters 6, 7, and 9).

On July 14, 1967 *Time* magazine did a special film piece on "The L & H Cult," and the ever-escalating Laurel & Hardy interest beginning with watershed 1965. Thus, it touched on everything, from the Sons of the Desert's rapid fan club growth to the ongoing proliferation of Laurel & Hardy items, such as the then-forthcoming publication of film historian William Everson's *The Films of Laurel and Hardy*.

Later in 1967 the fall issue of the British journal *Film* featured the article "Dennis Pope on Stanley LAUREL & Oliver Norvell HARDY." (Because of unusual title lettering this article sometimes mistakenly appears in bibliography as co-authored by an O. Norvell!) Initially, the piece chronicles the growing interest in the team, from prestigious public screenings of their comedies to the 8mm home consumption of these same, ever-popular works. But Pope examines reasons for the team's decline after they left Roach as well as crediting their "continuing universal appeal . . . largely . . . to . . . visual comedy."

The most interesting aspect of the article is the inclusion of the 1962 Laurel & Hardy film season for the Canton Film Appreciation Group of Cardiff. This was not just any film fan schedule, because Laurel worked with author Pope on choosing the films. The season was composed of six programs, the first three being roughly chronological in their order; the last three were a selection of "the best of Laurel & Hardy":

1. *Golf* (Hardy alone), *Roughest Africa* (Laurel alone), *Sailor Beware* (an all star comedy), *Putting Pants on Phillip* (first L & H short), *The Battle of the Century, Leave 'em Laughing, Double Whoopee.*

2. *Unaccustomed As We Are, Brats, Helpmates, Pardon Us.*

3. *Thicker than Water* (last short), *Block-Heads, Saps at Sea* (last film for Hal Roach).

4. *Fra Diavolo, Busy Bodies.*

5. *Bonnie Scotland, County Hospital.*

6. *Way Out West, The Music Box.*

No information is provided about how film availability or the sponsoring club's financial position affected the choices. Moreover, to limit "the best of Laurel and Hardy" to three short programs asks the impossible. Still, knowing that Laurel was part of the selection process makes this an interesting addition. For example, while highly regarded *Way Out West* receives deservedly preferential treatment (sharing closing program honors with the Oscar-winning *The Music Box*), where is *Sons of the Desert*?

The following year (1968) Everson wrote "The Crazy World of Laurel," an insightful essay that appeared in the Canadian film journal *Take One.* Everson covers a wide range of topics, and while not everything is new, he often manages to give certain items a perceptive twist. For instance, there is the obligatory look at Laurel & Hardy's gift for "milking" material and the viewer's comic joy at *anticipating* the gag. But Everson is also quick to concede that "when their material was below par, or the directional pacing was off, this same kind of construction would produce exasperating slowness and heavyhandedness."

As in other works on the team, Everson places great importance on their measured comic violence and the direct address of Ollie. But he surprises the reader by finding the latter motif "probably even more effective" than tit-for-tat violence. Moreover, he differentiates between Ollie's visual-only direct address and the verbal/visual variety of later comedians like Bob Hope. Everson believes that because Ollie never speaks during direct address, "He thus never comes *out* of the picture, but rather invites the audience to join him *in* it.'' This is an interesting hypothesis; in Woody Allen's *Purple Rose of Cairo* (1985) Jeff Daniels's screen character first initiates verbal and visual direct address with audience member Mia Farrow, then literally steps *out* of the movie. Still, any time a film character acknowledges his audience, even with Ollie's direct address type, it gives him an outsider's presence, simply by his special comic awareness that there is an outside.

More of a subtle comic intimacy is established when the direct address follows the Ollie pattern and limits itself to the visual, since the spoken word is by its nature more self-consciously disruptive to a storyline. Yet, the great verbal/visual direct address of Bob Hope or Groucho Marx generally occurs as a brief aside (a comic soliloquy) and, naturally, the other screen characters are oblivious to the event. Thus, a special comic tie seems to be created between the audience and the focus screen character regardless of the type of direct address. But whatever one's position on this point, this Everson piece is often thought-provoking. In truth, there are silent direct-address examples prior to Hardy's Ollie, such as Charlie Chaplin's film-closing wink at the camera in *Behind the Screen* (1916) or Fatty Arbuckle's comically inspired motioning of the camera to tilt upward as he changed to a swimsuit in *Fatty at Coney Island* (1917). However, this also is pertinent, since Everson's lack of earlier examples seems to imply Hardy's screen character pioneered the technique.

Other interesting points examined in this essay include the superiority of the team's early silent films, their use of black comedy, the apparent importance of director William Seiter on *Sons of the Desert*, and their special comic use of sound. Most refreshing is the Everson close that gently takes the team to task for not artistically challenging themselves more. It is a brave question rarely asked, let alone allowed to close an article on Laurel & Hardy, where the sugary is much more the norm, but it is asked in the nature of an interested friend, whose fondness for the subject is forever front and center.

The Laurel & Hardy journal *Pratfall* first appeared in 1969, though the initial issue is not dated. In correspondence with the journal's current editor/business manager, Lori S. Jones, she kiddingly observed, ''We did that on purpose [omitted the date] so they'd be 'timeless.' '' The importance of this publication to Laurel & Hardy study is best stated by merely quoting the subheading that originally appeared on the *Pratfall* cover—''The 'Way Out West' [tent of 'The Sons of the Desert'] Periodical Tribute to Stan and Ollie.'' The founder and editor (through 1983) was Larry Byrd.

Early *Pratfall* issues remind one of the later *Freedonia Gazette*, which also featured an explanatory cover subheading: ''*The* Magazine Devoted to the Marx Brothers.'' That is, both journals are brief, inexpensively published devotions of love that maintain a fierce loyalty to their respective teams. While *Pratfall* in the 1980s has not been able to maintain as regular a publication schedule as the *Gazette*, issue after issue has produced worthwhile articles. The pieces can be placed in four primary categories: reprints of early, often obscure, articles and reviews on Laurel & Hardy; interviews with people from the team's personal and/or professional past; critical pieces on Laurel & Hardy's artistry written specifically for *Pratfall*; and biographical essays on regular members of the cast and crew.

Though there is neither time nor space to comment on all articles in each category, some essays merit attention. In the reprint category are Eleanor Parker's October 1929 *Playgoer* magazine piece, "Two Prize Idiots," in a 1969 *Pratfall* (vol. 1, no. 3); Joseph Jefferson's (Laurel's father) January 1932 *Picturegoer Weekly* article, "My Lad Laurel," in a 1970 *Pratfall* (vol. 1, no. 4); a collection of Laurel & Hardy–related comments of Grierson from *Grierson on Documentary*, which resurfaced as "GRIERSON on Laurel & Hardy" in a 1978 *Pratfall* (vol. 2, no. 3); and Jordan Young's 1978 "Laurel & Hardy Meet The Pink Panther," in which Blake Edwards discusses the influence of Laurel & Hardy and Leo McCarey on the Pink Panther series, in a 1982 *Pratfall* (vol. 2, no. 5). The first two pieces are examined later (chronologically) in this chapter's "Interviews/Reminiscences" section. And assorted Grierson critical pronouncements on the team, drawn from *Grierson on Documentary*, have already appeared in this and the first two chapters.

Interviews with people from the team's personal and professional past might best be represented by noting "The Way It Was"—an interview with film producer Joe Rock in a 1970 *Pratfall* (vol. 1, no. 4) and "Ruth Laurel Remembers"—the most possessive former wife of Laurel reminisces in a 1971 *Pratfall* (vol. 1, no. 5). Both will be examined later in the chapter.

New Laurel & Hardy criticism was a regular part of *Pratfall*, at least during the early years. Essays meriting recognition include Jordan Young's "Popularity Grows on Borrowed Roots," an insightful look at how the team seems to have influenced Samuel Beckett's *Waiting for Godot* in a 1971 *Pratfall* (vol. 1, no. 5); Henry Presbys and James Limbacher's "L & H & Henry Ford," an informative look at the added laughs to be drawn from the Model T Ford, affectionately referred to as the Tin Lizzie, in a 1974 *Pratfall* (vol. 1, no. 11); Simon Watson Taylor's "Here's Another Fine Mess," a reappreciation of the team that also addresses comedy theory, and Wes Heath's "A Critique of the Critics," both from a 1977 *Pratfall* (vol. 2, no. 2). The Heath essay attacks what he finds to be less-than-kind *New York Times* reviews of Laurel & Hardy films. I referred to his article earlier in this chapter when my survey of *New York Times* Laurel & Hardy reviews offered a *positive* rather than a negative verdict. Such differences are what make criticism both educational and entertaining. But Heath has somehow missed a number of very positive comments on the team by assorted *New York Times* critics. Moreover, he sometimes accents the negative by focusing on a mere line or two from a review. Still, the piece is good at reminding one of the condescending manner in which some critics (and the *New York Times* had no corner on the market) treated Laurel & Hardy movies as well as slapstick films in general. (Of related interest, see the short period essay "Babe Hardy, The Fat Boy with Vim," in the February 20, 1916 *Florida Metropolis*, a Jacksonville newspaper.)

Also of special interest is Jordan Young's "Early Ollie: The Plump and Runt Films," in a 1975 *Pratfall* (vol. 1, no. 12). Ten years before the days of Stan & Ollie, Hardy was the heavy half of the Vim Comedies team of Plump & Runt (with Billy Ruge as Runt). In 1916 they did thirty-five Plump & Runt films, the same number of shorts Charlie Chaplin did in his film baptismal year (1914) with Sennett. And while no one is trying to place these shorts on a plane with Chaplin's, they are fascinating for the student of Laurel & Hardy. Author Young provides a complete list of the films (arranged by production date), with a paragraph-length story description and an even briefer "review" from a period trade paper. This fleshed-out list constitutes the brunt of the article, with Young often finding the films "sounding like typical L & H situations," including character interaction.

Any pre–Laurel & Hardy information is valuable, but mere conjecture from an author who has not viewed all the films is very qualified evidence, especially since a reading of the actual plot synopses finds numerous exceptions to the later celebrated duo, as in those early Laurel & Hardy movies where they both appeared but had yet to be teamed effectively. As noted in Chapter 1 (n. 11), Hardy himself does not credit any pre–Stan & Ollie–like developments occurring before the 1925 *The Paperhanger's Helper* (1 reel version of *Stick Around*), in which he is teamed with Bobby Ray.

This new criticism category can close with a reference to "Stan on Stage," a *Billboard* listing of Stan and Mae Laurel's vaudeville appearances compiled by Jim Kerkhoff in a 1972 *Pratfall* (vol. 1, no. 8). While obviously not criticism per se, the article provides tour dates and locations throughout the nation, and a wealth of largely neglected period criticism suddenly becomes readily accessible.

Representative pieces for the final *Pratfall* category, biographical essays on regular members of the cast or crew, best include Hank Jones's "Here's to Finn!" (a tribute to James Finlayson) in the 1969 inaugural issue of *Pratfall*; "Edgar Kennedy: The Slow Burn" in a second 1969 issue (vol. 1, no. 2); Vivien Burgeon's "THE BIG SNEEZE: A Visit with Billy Gilbert" in a third 1969 *Pratfall* (vol. 1, no. 3); and Jim Shadduck's 1972 "The Ku-Ku Song Man!", a biography of T. Marvin Hatley, author of the team's theme song and other memorable Laurel & Hardy music (vol. 1, no. 7).

Obviously, *Pratfall* represents an invaluable source for the student of Laurel & Hardy. Unfortunately, it is little known in academic circles. Although the scholar is hardly its target audience, it still has something to offer, as the previous pages demonstrate. It is not alone, however, in its anonymity. Though best known in the United States, *many* other Laurel & Hardy journals are published around the world. Often modest in scope—more newsletter than magazine— these labors of love are frequently printed by different Sons of the Desert tents. Fittingly, the majority of these publications are based in Great Britain—home to both Laurel and forever greater critical team attention. Two of the slicker examples are *The Laurel & Hardy Magazine* (the *Helpmates* tent of Gillingham, Kent, England) and *Bowler Dessert* (Editor William A. McIntyre of Largs, Ayrshire, Scotland).

Not surprisingly (outside Sons of the Desert circles), neither publication is well known in the United States (they are not listed on interlibrary loan computer bank holdings). Both journals were referred to in British author Bruce Crowther's *Laurel and Hardy: Clown Princes of Comedy*. But when I requested Philip Sheard's *Bowler Dessert* article "Laurel and Hardy Visit Any Old Port" (no. 23) at London's British Film Institute, they had not heard of the journal. (This is the only specific article citation Crowther drew from these two publications.) One must deal directly with the editors of the journals.

Among similar other Laurel & Hardy works I am very impressed with the Leo M. Brooks, Jr./*Them Thar Hills* American Tent newsletter *Shifting Sands* (now defunct). Brooks's essays tend to be provocative. For example, "Worth a Thousand Words" and "Virginia Lucille Jones Hardy Price" (both in the October 1988 *Shifting Sands*). The former addressed the controversial 1938 *Look* photograph of a weeping Laurel, the latter the hostility of Hardy's family to his last wife. (The new, since 1989, Brooks newsletter is entitled *Front Row*.)

As these and other Brooks essays show, he is a revisionist Laurel & Hardy historian—addressing subjects not all students of the team wish to hear. This is never more apparent than in the final issue of *Shifting Sands* (December 1988). Three of his brief articles, "Mae Charlotte Dahlberg," "Felix Knight and the Boys," and "Hardy and Rogers: (*What Might Have Been*)," were probably blasphemous to some team fans. The first somewhat softens the image of Mae, while placing more blame for Laurel's then-dormant career on the comedian himself. The second suggests Hardy was an "unhappy man" in the 1930s and volatile on the set. The third piece reminds the reader that Hardy loyalty during much of the period tended to go with Roach rather than his partner during those famous Laurel-Roach conflicts.

One should hasten to add Brooks is not playing *Mommie Dearest*. He genuinely likes the team but stands clear of any kind of rose-colored glasses approach. In fact, his editorial-like close to the final *Shifting Sands* issue, entitled "Teamwork," states: "A number of members of the Sons [of the Desert] have almost turned the worship of Stan Laurel into a cult. If Stan were alive today, he would be the first to speak out against this." All in all, the ongoing grassroots publications generated by the interest in Stan & Ollie are amazing.

In 1969 *New York Times* film critic Vincent Canby wrote the Laurel & Hardy piece, "Slapstick that Sticks." Appearing in the midst of the team's cult craze, Canby briefly discusses the "patronizing" dangers of such fads while referring to earlier similar concerns by team author Everson. Outside the anthology film features of Robert Youngson, Canby has little time for the Laurel & Hardy compilations because they "destroy the very conscious, internal rhythms of their gags."

Fittingly, Canby recommends Hal Roach Studio's 1969 reissue of the following complete and unedited Laurel & Hardy package: the feature *Way Out West* (1937) and five short subjects, *The Hoose-Gow* (1929), *Brats* (1930), *Hog Wild* (1930), *Helpmates* (1931), and *Busy Bodies* (1933). And just as appropriately, Canby plugs Charles Barr's *Laurel and Hardy* (1967; see the earlier book section of this chapter), which offers a solid study of the team's comic pyramiding of a gag.

The majority of Canby's essay is devoted to these six films. He credits *Way Out West* with having at least two classic scenes—the tickling routine with Stan and the team's block-and-tackle sketch that accidently launches a donkey. Canby also has praise for the film's musical numbers.

His continued accolades for the short subjects include the provocative observation: "Neither Hardy [Ollie] nor Laurel [Stan] ever makes any real bid for our sympathy [despite the direct address of Ollie]. They get it but they never ask for it—which, I think, is one of the reasons they wear so well." However, many critics, myself included, read Ollie's direct address as a bid for sympathy, as if to say, "Would you look at what I have to put up with?" But in the general pursuit of their comedy shtick, Canby seems on more secure ground making such Laurel & Hardy claims.

In the close of his article, Canby again reiterates the importance of *not* taking Laurel & Hardy comedy routines from the original films. Out of context, they often lose their appeal, though film anthologist Youngson at least recognizes the cruciality of longer excerpts . . . if one must rely on this approach.

A Canby side note, as if borrowing a page from Laurel & Hardy film buffs, is his added fascination with the backdrops in those Laurel & Hardy films—Los Angeles circa 1930. (See the book section of this chapter for references to Leon Smith's *A Guide to Laurel and Hardy Locations* and the *Following the Comedy Trail* sequel.)

Canby's article was later reprinted in Stuart Byron and Elisabeth Weis's anthology, *The National Society of Film Critics on Movie Comedy* (1977). The collection contains what were then contemporary essays, often in film revival format, of a wide spectrum of comedy subjects, from Mack Sennett to Luis Buñuel.

The Canby piece, reprinted as simply "Laurel and Hardy," was the only essay on the team in *Movie Comedy*. A thumbnail comparison of how their 1930s personality comedian contemporaries rate in the text finds both the Marx Brothers and W. C. Fields with two essays each, while Will Rogers and Mae West are omitted.

In January 1970 the *Village Voice* published a superb Laurel & Hardy critique by critic William Paul. Though entitled "Film: *Way Out West*," it is better described as an insightful overview of Stan & Ollie's antiheroic relationship, with a focus on comic violence, or, as Paul so nicely describes it, "anarchy by accident."

The filtering of the piece through *Way Out West* is an outgrowth of Paul's

Stan's "white magic"—about to light his thumb

examination of an attempt in West Germany to repackage Laurel & Hardy's arthouse image via this film. Consequently, Paul does some hypothesizing on why *Way Out West* was chosen. He differentiates between this movie and other more-typical (and presumably less popular among upper-class West Germans) Laurel & Hardy vehicles. Paul concentrates especially on its minimal use of comic violence (one of their ''gentlest comedies'') and the fact that Stan & Ollie eventually succeed (rare indeed) at their main task (delivering the deed to the heroine), though there are naturally a number of comic frustrations along the way.

More-perceptive points along these and additional lines are made, though Paul seems to have overstated the reasons for the team's initial lack of success with the cultural and social upper classes in general: ''No intellectual establishment could afford to embrace films which delight in the triumph of man's irrational side over his intellect.'' There has always been at least an appreciative segment of the cultural/intellectual audience that savors this very thing, whether in the Marx Brothers 1930s or the Monty Python 1970s. Indeed, during the 1950s poet Dylan Thomas, speaking to experimental filmmakers, defined film poetry as a scene where Stan shoved Ollie down some stairs!

Another provocative position by Paul returns one to the appropriateness of ''white magic'' in the world of Stan & Ollie. Paul finds its addition palatable because the unthinking Stan is simply unaware of the laws of nature, thus making surrealistic gags like lighting his thumb (as if it were a cigarette lighter) acceptable.

Regardless, the piece also provides additional observations of a less controversial nature, such as Paul's excellent handling of Stan & Ollie's warm comic camaraderie via their musical duets. With the *Way Out West* number in front of the saloon as the focus, Paul notes ''they are dancing as if this were the way they always behaved whenever they heard music . . . L & H demonstrate a sense of grace that rivals Chaplin, but more importantly they create the sense of a purely physical communication.''

Also in 1970, prolific film author and critic Leonard Maltin published *Movie Comedy Teams* (updated in 1985), with the opening chapter devoted to Laurel & Hardy. Though sometimes uneven in content, it is the best book on film comedy teams. Maltin's Laurel & Hardy chapter is excellent—fitting for a duo he ranks as the screen's greatest team. Their front and center placement in the book is accented further by the introduction by comedian Billy Gilbert, a familiar face in several Laurel & Hardy films (including *The Music Box*) and an active participant behind the scenes. (But, as Gilbert goes on to note, he also worked with a number of other outstanding comedy teams.)

Maltin opens his chapter by commenting on screen comedy's history of less-than-adequate attention from film students and scholars, not to mention the neglect suffered by Laurel & Hardy. He then credits their later cult status to three things: constant showing of their films on television, Robert Youngson compilation movies, and John McCabe's affectionate biography *Mr. Laurel and Mr. Hardy*.

Maltin includes a fifty-plus page survey of their joint film career and briefly examines their solo work. As usual, Maltin is extremely informative in a limited space. His more-significant observations include high praise for the team's early silent short subjects, crediting *Sons of the Desert* as their greatest work, finding major fault (among the Roach films) with *Swiss Miss* (1938), and noting the acceptability for both *Jitterbugs* (1943) and *The Bullfighters* (1945), two late career films sometimes lost among the numerous poor films in which the team then found themselves. The chapter also includes a Laurel & Hardy filmography.

In addition, Maltin did shorter Laurel & Hardy chapters for two of his later books, *The Great Movie Shorts: Those Wonderful One- and Two-Reelers of the Thirties and Forties* (1972) and *The Great Movie Comedians: From Charlie Chaplin to Woody Allen* (1978). In the former work Maltin begins by addressing the "why" behind Laurel & Hardy's success. He credits both the relaxed production atmosphere at the Roach studio and the team's ability to create likeable "real people," which also helps explain the public's still-unique affection for the duo.

Maltin also quoted George Stevens on the central importance of Leo McCarey to the team, praised the short subject as the team's "purest form," revealed that Laurel (like Chaplin) referred to his screen persona as the "little fellow," and reminded the reader that while the team forever remained loyal to physical comedy, slapstick had become a "dirty word" by the 1930s. (The chapter concludes with a filmography of their *sound* short subjects.)

The third Maltin reference cited, *The Great Movie Comedians*, was prepared while he was serving as guest director of the "Museum of Modern Art's Bicentennial Salute to American Film Comedy." The Laurel & Hardy chapter from this excellent work avoids becoming a mere rehash of Maltin's previous chapters on the team. Among many points, Maltin beautifully describes a pivotal example of Laurel's mime in *Wrong Again* (1929), where the comedian demonstrates a wide range of comic responses to a broken statue he has reassembled incorrectly. Maltin then ties this in with McCarey, who had directed the film and considered it a "special favorite." Fittingly, Maltin underlines McCarey's significance to the team, and quotes the director on his development of Laurel & Hardy's slower pacing.

Maltin also nicely articulates a point Roach was seemingly attempting to make in the earlier cited essay by the producer. That is, even when Stan & Ollie find themselves entwined in the most comically "outrageous exaggeration," the scene's success is dependent upon "the team's fundamental basis in reality . . . [in] credible situations and characters."

Maltin adds that "because their comedies were basically down-to-earth," Laurel occasionally enjoyed devising comic bits based in camera trickery—self-consciously funny filmmaking at the expense of realism. Maltin draws his ex ample from a Grierson favorite—the *Way Out West* scene where a partially-clad Ollie exits the scene only momentarily yet returns fully dressed. When curious Stan wonders how this was possible, Ollie simply but comically admonishes him, "Never you mind."

One might also have used the *Way Out West* scene where Ollie's head goes through the trap door and Stan's attempt to pull him out briefly results in a stretched neck of junior giraffe proportions. Yet, it can be argued that these examples are such an extreme break with the team's normal brand of comic reality that the humor seems flawed by the inconsistency (regardless of how funny they may be as an isolated scene). But Maltin's comment on why Laurel was fond of occasional camera trickery no doubt also applied (or was an indirect reference) to the comedian's now and again use of his special effect's "white magic," such as the recently mentioned lighter-like nature of Stan's thumb in *Way Out West* or the *shadow* of a window shade he could pull down in *Block-Heads* (1938).

The "white magic" is more of a comic inconsistency problem. For example, while Ollie's ability to get dressed occurs in a comically unbelievably short time, character authenticity is still maintained—Stan's mystification on how Ollie did it reinforces the inspired stupidity at the very heart of Laurel's screen persona. And as noted in Chapter 1, to give Stan "white magic" powers regardless of the comic surprise this produces, detracts from the wonderful muddleheadedness of the character and lessens the humor dependent on it.

On less-controversial ground, Maltin states the team's occasional musical sketch works "not because Stan and Babe [Ollie; see Chapter 1] are immensely talented singers and dancers but because they are wholly engaging personalities and present these little interludes with such pleasure and lack of pretension."

Maltin then nicely ties the team's performing joy into an essay-concluding observation on the "key word" for Stan & Ollie: love. It is central to both their comically resilient relationship and their cockeyed encounters with the rest of the world, tit-for-tats notwithstanding. The chapter closes with a filmography of their movies together, including several sometimes forgotten guest appearances in short subjects.

In 1971 Gerald Mast's *A Short History of the Movies* (now in its fourth edition) appeared. While not lengthy in its critiquing of personality comedians like Laurel & Hardy, Mast provides a generally informative survey of the team, from a provocative definition of their childlike nature to an analysis of their comedy in terms of theorist Henri Bergson.

In 1973 Mast wrote the best historical overview of film comedy yet available: *The Comic Mind: Comedy and the Movies* (now in its second edition). And though one would have hoped for more Laurel & Hardy material (they receive three pages to Chaplin's three chapters!), Mast is again thought provoking in his team analysis. At the center of his writing is a further embellishment of the team's childlike behavior, though he continues to define them in comically harsher terms than the norm, calling them "nasty children." But Mast is right on the comedy target when he credits Stan & Ollie with the knack to "convert a group of normal people into a mass of pie slingers, shin kickers, and pants pullers. They bring out the worst in everybody. And to bring out the worst in folks is to belittle human pretensions to anything better." And as cited in Chapter 1, Mast notes both the superiority of the team's silent work and the importance of McCarey.

In the Fall 1971 issue of *The Saturday Evening Post* Ron Cooper did a tribute to the ongoing popularity of the team—"Ollie and Stan: Two Minds Without a Single Thought." Richly illustrated with film stills, it largely rehashed the cult status they had already achieved by then, including the formation of the "Sons of the Desert" fan club and the subsequent birth of the periodical *Pratfall*.

In 1973 comedy film historian Donald McCaffrey's book *The Golden Age of Sound Comedy: Comic Films and Comedians of the Thirties* appeared, with Chapter 5, "Duet of Incompetence," devoted to Laurel & Hardy. This excellent chapter and the book as a whole is the best of McCaffrey's film comedy texts.

As with the rest of the book, the strength of the Laurel & Hardy chapter is in the refreshing straightforwardness with which McCaffrey reexamines the world of Stan & Ollie. For example, he perceptively says of *Block-Heads*, "In no other feature does Ollie's comedy of frustration seem more artfully handled. All his warm, gentlemanly efforts to assist a friend backfire."

McCaffrey is neither afraid to take on the sacred cow (he suggests *Way Out West*, 1937, is "overrated") nor to champion a much less acclaimed work, *Our Relations* (1936). However, he rates *Sons of the Desert* (1933) as their "masterpiece," noting both an impressive trio of critics seconding that verdict and providing his own strong case. His proof revolves around the tight consistency of the comic storyline—where every action seems to dovetail back into the plight of antiheroic husbands. McCaffrey also draws a fleeting but effective parallel here with the best and equally antiheroic husband films of the team's comedy contemporary W. C. Fields: *It's a Gift* (1934), *The Man on the Flying Trapeze* (1935), and *The Bank Dick* (1940).

Fittingly, McCaffrey is also good at relating Laurel & Hardy themes and characteristics to other period comedians, including Abbott & Costello, who eventually usurped the duo in the 40s (going beyond the book's 1930s focus). Such comparisons are especially diverting when he focuses on the period's numerous other comedy teams—certainly the heyday of this phenomenon. Moreover, his general praise of Laurel & Hardy is not merely the knee-jerk stroking of a comedy favorite. In the opening to his examination of the unique warmth inherent in the Stan & Ollie relationship, he matter-of-factly credits the Marx Brothers as being better comedy artists. But his point is that even they could not touch the comic love generated between Stan & Ollie or between the team and their audience—"the bond of two struggling, inferior men whose everyday life is plagued by [comic] obstacles."

Consequently, from an essay opening that requests more credit for the long underrated talent of Hardy to a close that asks for a comedy pantheon placement of Laurel & Hardy next to Chaplin and Keaton, McCaffrey seldom deviates from serving as a thought-provoking guide to the world of Stan & Ollie. Numerous stills are also included in the work.

In September 1973 author/archivist Charles Silver's sensitive and insightful essay "Leo McCarey: From Marx to McCarthy" appeared in *Film Comment*. While Laurel & Hardy are not the focus of the piece, Silver nicely demonstrates how a later classic McCarey film like *Duck Soup* (the Marx Brothers, 1933) "features innumerable bits of [comic] business that can be traced to the Roach films McCarey inspired, supervised, or directed."

Indeed, the best tit-for-tat sequence outside of McCarey's Laurel & Hardy work is *Duck Soup*'s inspired confrontation between Roach regular Edgar "slow burn" Kennedy and Harpo Marx. Silver observes, "The progressive destruction in the peanut-and-lemonade-stand sequences are variations on two McCarey-supervised mini-masterpieces, *Big Business* and *Two Tars*."

Similar ties are drawn between McCarey's Laurel & Hardy work and his pivotal screwball comedy *The Awful Truth* (1937). McCarey's gifted 1930s re-implementation of antiheroic basics he originally devised for Laurel & Hardy excellently demonstrates the period significance of his comedy gift.

In 1974 the obscure but helpful essay "Ollie and Stan: They Bore Life's Burdens with Courage" appeared in *Southland Sunday* magazine (*Long Beach Independent Press-Telegraph*). Written by free-lancer Richard Trubo, it is another piece on Laurel & Hardy as cult figures. However, Trubo manages to add new twists to such overviews, including the team's cult status in China and a short interview with then *Pratfall* editor Larry Byrd.

Author/critic Walter Kerr makes a first-rate Laurel & Hardy contribution in *The Silent Clowns* (1975). Conveniently, Kerr does for the silent era what McCaffrey did for the 1930s. The team receives a Kerr focus in both Chapter 33, "Laurel and Hardy: The First Turnaround" and Chapter 34, "Laurel and Hardy: The Saving Turnaround."

As these headings suggest, both chapters are tightly interrelated. "The First Turnaround" zeroes in on the solo careers of Laurel & Hardy, with Kerr stating "each of the two clowns had been working in what proved to be a 'wrong' direction." Consequently, their Stan & Ollie screen personae represented a real change: "the first turnaround." Though this slightly simplifies things (see Chapter 1 and the piece to be examined following Kerr), it is still entertainingly insightful on detailing the many differences between the pre-team screen characters of Laurel & Hardy.

In the second and more crucial of the two Laurel & Hardy chapters, "The Saving Turnaround," Kerr examines the team's watershed reduction of comedy pacing just prior to the coming of sound. Because of this "turnaround," their film careers not only survive (the "saving" of the title) but prosper in the sound era, something none of their silent comedy contemporaries were able to do. Kerr reminds one in a refreshing manner of the uniqueness of the team's slowdown— "the *comedy* of Laurel and Hardy came to consist of the pauses between the effronteries . . . [comic violence itself was not new]. What is distinctively funny about these two men is the time-lag . . . with which the unthinkable [tit-for-tat] is . . . allowed to play itself out.'' For more on the team's inadvert anticipation of the naturalistic pacing that is sound film, see Chapter 1.

Kerr also makes an interesting claim for the new pace surfacing in other Roach films soon after its full articulation in the world of Stan & Ollie. However, Kerr misses a good opportunity for a hypothetical explanation when he merely credits it as an ''infectious'' style. He might have noted the *Cahiers* interview of McCarey where the director takes credit for both the slower pace and the tit-for-tat violence. McCarey was in a power position as a Roach supervisor whose influence went beyond the team (though they remained his ongoing pet project). Thus, one might have expected rapid assimilation. Conversely, the McCarey nightclub party anecdote concerning the public birth of tit-for-tat comedy violence included Hal Roach (see Chapter 1). Consequently, any new comedy developments that McCarey might have realized and grafted to it (like slower pacing) that night would be of special applicable interest to Roach and his studio.

Unfortunately, while Kerr acknowledges the importance of Leo McCarey to the team later in Chapter 34, there is a chance he is not familiar with the *Cahiers* interview. Kerr suggests the team's unique pacing was a Roach lot ''collaborative achievement'' with a great deal of inadvertent assistance from Hardy. There is no reference to the prior published McCarey claim.

A bonus of Chapter 34 is Kerr's discussion of post–silent era Laurel & Hardy, just as McCaffrey followed the team beyond his 1930s focus. Not surprisingly, given the silent comedy base from which Kerr is coming, he finds the sound films (which for him mean the features) inferior. (Earlier Kerr had revealed the team's classic silent short *Big Business* to be his favorite.) To Kerr, Laurel & Hardy's ''absence of passion, for women or for other goals, would deny them the extended narrative base on which feature films generally depend.'' Though this seems to sell the duo short on the methodical persistence (passion?) they bring to escaping their wives (*Sons of the Desert*) or delivering a deed (*Way Out West*), it does provide another explanation for what Kerr reluctantly calls their ''limited'' nature.

One might, however, reframe the negative connotation of Kerr's ''limited'' by connecting it to critic Hamlin Hill's poignant commentary on modern American humor in *College English* (December 1963), where the put-upon individual, the antihero, eventually deals with this frightening outside world by not dealing with it at all; instead the antihero focuses ''microscopically upon the individual unit . . . that interior reality—or hysteria . . . In consequence, modern humor deals significantly with frustrating trivia.'' Along these lines, the Stan & Ollie as Sisyphus analogy is hardly a limitation if their ''frustrating trivia'' can be connected to a central theme as is successfully done in *Sons of the Desert* and *Way Out West*. Moreover, if an example of an unquestioned film comedy star whose pantheon status has not been hindered by minimal passion is needed, one has only to mention Buster Keaton or Jacques Tati's screen character Mr. Hulot. In

Keaton's case, far from being a liability, his blank visage (the celebrated "Great Stone Face") was integral to both his screen persona and comedy success in general.

Keaton's methodical screen persona is also sometimes compared to Sisyphus. If Laurel & Hardy's most noted example of this is *The Music Box* (1932), Keaton's is in *Daydreams* (1922), where he finds himself endlessly walking on a riverboat paddlewheel, or trying to walk in the face of the *Steamboat Bill, Jr.* (1928) cyclone. (Even the otherwise mediocre Keaton sound feature *Speak Easily* (1932) includes the comedian on both a treadmill and a revolving backdrop.)

Tati does not so much represent the treadmill tendencies of Laurel & Hardy as an independent obliviousness to the treadmill nature of the world around him. Thus, instead of Stan & Ollie's comic involvement in "frustrating trivia" (a subtle, antiheroic escape from the traumatizing modern world), the "frustrating trivia" surrounds Mr. Hulot. Indeed, late in Tati's career he so decentralizes the comic "trivia" away from Mr. Hulot in *Playtime* (1967) that the "trivia" itself becomes the star. (Obliviousness is also to be found in Keaton, whom Tati credits as being central to his comic art.)

Regardless, Kerr's application of "limited" to the world of Stan & Ollie is more appropriate when he links it to the cavalier filmmaking techniques behind the duo's thrill comedy. That is, camera angles and/or the absence of establishing long shots in their periodic use of thrill comedy (*Liberty* focused on it entirely, 1929) immediately telegraph the message that no real danger is involved. (This is just the opposite of the true comic chills provided by the thrill comedy of their contemporary Harold Lloyd.) Consequently, whatever one's views on Kerr's Laurel & Hardy pronouncements, he is intellectually stimulating.

The cover story for *Liberty* magazine's Summer 1975 issue was Alvin Nizer's "Laurel and Hardy." Nizer suggests the team's "universality" is becoming ever more apparent to the public, and what is more important—to the critics. Drawing from the team's own observations on comedy, Nizer credits their appeal to the duo's attempts to be real. He also provides a basic career overview, with periodic critical commentary, such as, "Laurel and Hardy did their best work before the advent of sound."

At the very end of 1975 a Laurel & Hardy record single of their "Trail of the Lonesome Pine" (from *Way Out West*) made it to number two on Britain's Top 10 best-selling record charts. Stan & Ollie's mid-1970s record chart breakout (amid all those rock stars) bears special attention. The hit song seems to have been in no little way assisted by a November 1975 revival of *Way Out West* on British television, while the tune's success hardly discouraged United Artists's (which produced the single) late 1975 marketing of their long-playing record salute to the team, *Laurel and Hardy: The Golden Age of Hollywood*. The album is critically noteworthy since it alternates musical numbers with comic verbal tracks from their films—twenty-two extracts from sixteen Laurel & Hardy movies. Add to this excellent packaging, extensive notes by John McCabe, and numerous photos, and one has a product for both scholar and fan. For good accounts of the hit single, see Ed Blanche's *Los Angeles Times* piece, "Laurel and Hardy Make the Top Ten" (February 18, 1976) and a 1977 Chris Fellner *Pratfall* essay, "L & H Hit the Charts" (vol. 2, no. 2).

Some final late 1970s Laurel & Hardy criticism entries include Philippe le Guay's "laurel et hardy: una allégorie de la catastrophe" (*Positif*, July-August 1978), my two revisionist articles, "Film's First Comic Anti-Heroes: Leo McCarey's Laurel and Hardy" (*Ball State University Forum*, Autumn 1979) and "Leo McCarey: The Man Behind Laurel & Hardy" (*Films in Review*, November 1979), and James Robert Parish and William Leonard's detailed guide *The Funsters* (1979), with a survey chapter on Laurel & Hardy.

Le Guay's article merits special attention because it is one of the most ambitiously analytical essays examined in this text. The article is broken into four categories, plus a short introduction and conclusion. The first section, "Une dialectique de l'humiliation," links Stan & Ollie destruction to humiliation and the ties between force and superiority. Comparisons are made between Laurel & Hardy and the comedies of Chaplin and Keaton, especially as they pertain to comic contrasts in size. Le Guay suggests the duo do not follow the normal pattern, since skinny Stan frequently takes the initiative, with fat Ollie paying the comic penalty.

Stan & Ollie comedy is about humiliation, because their tit-for-tat encounters with others never avoid destruction. Indeed, as the team patiently awaits its next comically violent turn they are clinically attentive (curious instead of self-protective) about their adversary's next move. Thus, Le Guay finds the duo's comic fights more tragic than comparable conflicts in Chaplin and Keaton films, because Stan & Ollie battles aim for total humiliation . . . total loss of dignity . . . total metaphorical destruction of the individual.

The second section of Le Guay's article, "La reduction à l'object," posits that since *all* manner of comic violence is permitted in Stan & Ollie's world, their antagonists might be defined as puppets . . . so many objects—a state sometimes also applicable to Stan & Ollie themselves. Though not without merit, this line of argument neglects the strong sense of preestablished comic personality they bring to each film, which is often also true of their comic adversaries, such as Jimmy Finlayson. Le Guay's argument better applies to Sennett's machine-like Keystone Cops. Indeed, it is because one *knows* Stan & Ollie that one is moved by their constant frustration, or that Le Guay can so easily link their names with tragedy.

In its favor, however, this section of the essay does effectively define the hopelessness of the human condition through Stan & Ollie. Again, the myth of Sisyphus is applied as the central theme of their art. Not surprisingly, *The Music Box* (1932) is noted as the ultimate example, but with the well-taken reminder that the owner (Billy Gilbert) of the battered but finally delivered piano destroys it himself at story's end. Laurel & Hardy's efforts have suffered the ultimate negation.

Part three is "L'inaccessible harmonie." The Stan & Ollie object is a comic menace waiting to happen, which is often underlined with the insert shot. Thus, just as critic Jean-Pierre Coursodon defines Laurel & Hardy audience interaction as comic certainty versus comic surprise, one might liken it to a humor version of what Hitchcock does to the suspense thriller.

Fittingly, Le Guay uses this section to underline the team's base in reality. That is, since their movement knows neither the ballet of Chaplin nor the gymnastic gift of Keaton, one quickly tags their comic clumsiness as in the "mere mortal" category. While the author might be underestimating the occasional display of physical grace on Ollie's part, Chaplin and Keaton are in an uncontested class all their own.

Le Guay draws a parallel between the unattainable physical harmony (slapstick frustration as symbolic of their ongoing comic antiheroic nature) and the team's often less-than-harmonious interaction with music, be it playing instruments (*You're Darn Tootin'*, 1928) or moving one (*The Music Box*). Again, one might quibble, since the team is also capable of harmonious musical actions, including some brief but pleasant dancing in *The Music Box*! Still, Le Guay makes an interesting point, as well as once again drawing a parallel to Hitchcock—this time with reference to *The Man Who Knew Too Much* and the failed gunshot disrupting a musical orchestration.

Because of Stan & Ollie's persistent disharmony with the world, Le Guay provocatively suggests the team be labeled not victims but rather agents of destruction. Again, he defends his position with the methodical manner in which the duo embrace the comic violence of tit-for-tat.

The fourth category, "Feu sur le spectateur," finds the spectator within a Laurel & Hardy film seldom in a neutral zone. The team's tit-for-tats forever draw in the distant spectator—possibly the only type of comic *surprise* to surface in a Laurel & Hardy film. And while the viewer outside the film is in no danger of getting a misthrown pie in the face, the occasional direct address visual asides by Ollie implicate one in the spreading comic violence. (For Le Guay, the Hitchcock connection here is *Rear Window*, where spectator Jimmy Stewart finds there is no neutral zone.)

These four points lead Le Guay to suggest that in the realm of Stan & Ollie laughter represents both a pleasantly total negation of all values and an opportunity for the viewer metaphorically to join in the subversive liberties of their comedy.

In 1980 the first series of reference books appeared in *Magill's Survey of Cinema: English Language Films*. Edited by Frank Magill, each volume is composed of contemporary critiques of significant English language films. The essays, written specifically for the project, are approximately three pages long, contain principal cast and credits, and are arranged alphabetically.

The Laurel & Hardy film reviewed in the first series is *Way Out West* (1937). In 1981 a second collection of volumes was published in *Magill's Survey of Cinema*. This selection reviewed the team's *Babes in Toyland* (1934, see also

March of the Wooden Soldiers). In 1982 Magill introduced a series on silent films, reviewing Laurel & Hardy's classic short subject *Big Business* (1929).

Besides listing cast and credits, the volumes include story synopses, comments on the central players' careers at the time of the film's release, and critical analysis often drawing upon both the film's initial response and its reputation today. Thus, for a generally capsulated look at these specific Laurel & Hardy films or that of another favorite, the Magill series is a good starting point. (Of the three Laurel & Hardy film surveys mentioned here, the best is critic Robert Mitchell's examination of *Way Out West*.)

In the early 1980s two book-length studies of film comedy teams appeared: Garson Kanin's *Together Again! Stories of the Great Hollywood Teams* (1981) and Jeffrey Robinson's *Teamwork: The Cinema's Greatest Comedy Teams* (1982). Though neither book is in a league with Maltin's previously discussed volume, each work devotes a chapter to Laurel & Hardy.

The one by the multitalented Kanin is of the oversized, coffee table variety, with the traditional accent on stills. The accompanying text in the Laurel & Hardy chapter is very uneven. While it offers sometimes lengthy quotes from the two comedians and supports reality as a foundation for team effectiveness, it also has some glaring flaws. There are numerous mistakes, such as crediting early solo Laurel parodies (such as *Mud and Sand*—see Chapter 1) to the team and stating the duo "never acted without each other" once they were teamed. Kanin can also be rather saccharine in his statements: "Speaking for myself, I cannot like anyone who does not like Laurel and Hardy, nor love anyone who does not love them." He claims, "In 104 films they never ran out of comic ideas, insane invention, charming conceits." Kanin correctly contradicts this in his closing remarks, stating their "later pictures failed." And this was not the only such inconsistency. Consequently, the chapter is a major disappointment, especially considering Kanin's name is on it.

Jeffrey Robinson's *Teamwork* chapter on Laurel & Hardy is a major improvement on the Kanin counterpart. Robinson provides more of a historical/biographical background on which to affix his analysis. At his best, he can be very perceptive. For instance, Robinson compares the different manners in which Laurel & Hardy and Abbott & Costello play the same soda-fountain sketch. The routine has each team with limited funds but not wishing to show it. In each case the dumber team member (Stan and Lou Costello) is to turn down an order request simply as a whim and not because of financial woes. The comedy comes from Stan and Lou each being moved still to make an order whenever he is asked.

When the two teams perform the skit one sees "how slowly paced Laurel and Hardy were. It's extraordinarily slow. But that pace loaned itself extremely well to the balance of dialogue and mime that Laurel and Hardy worked with in their short films." Robinson might also have added that despite the general comic differences that arise between Stan & Ollie, a sense of frustrated affection still exists. This is absent from the screen personae interactions of Bud Abbott & Costello, and Bud's comically violent retaliations against Lou (and Moe Howard's against the other Stooges) forever alienate the viewer from Abbott. In contrast, comic sympathy for Ollie's Stan-orchestrated frustrations sometimes even has one rooting for the larger teammate—an unthinkable development in the Bud & Lou relationship. (As a side note, the focus sketch previously discussed has a vaudeville history that can be traced back to the celebrated turn-of-the-century team of Weber & Fields, if not earlier.)

Robinson provides close analysis of several Laurel & Hardy films while also addressing comedy basics, such as a "formula for comedy" dependent upon a film being clocked. Thus, a Laurel & Hardy two-reeler was supposed to evoke a certain, definite number of laughs. If not (after a sneak preview), material was added and/or reworked.

Like most critics, including Laurel & Hardy themselves, Robinson feels going to features was a mistake, with the team's short subject attributes working most effectively in the feature *Sons of the Desert*. As with any survey chapter, one can neither include everything nor be forever fresh in analysis. But Robinson does a commendable job of assimilation—made to look all the better following Kanin. The essay also includes numerous stills and a brief filmography (title, year, and studio) of all films in which Laurel & Hardy both appeared.

A 1982 companion work to Robinson's *Teamwork* chapter is Albert Bermel's ambitious study *Farce*. Laurel & Hardy receive special attention in Bermel's chapter on "The Talking Thirties." Though somewhat brief, Bermel still manages to be stimulating. For instance, he compares the team's slowly methodical comic violence to the technique Buster Keaton the boy used in vaudeville to draw a bigger laugh—he waited several seconds after slapstick victimization before saying "Ouch!"

Another observation is reminiscent of Robinson's comparison of the team to Abbott & Costello. Although Bermel does not become so specific as to focus on a shared routine, his general overview parallels Robinson's: Laurel & Hardy's physical comedy provides an effective comic balance when combined with the auditory. That is, Laurel & Hardy's "superiority as a farce team over, say, Abbott and Costello consists largely in the matched [slapstick] rhythms, which give their performing a planned, visually fascinating coherence."

Because Bermel's book is a broad historical overview of farce, examining work as early as that of Aristophanes, it also provides an opportunity for readers to do their own comparing through the ages.

William Schelly's 1982 study, *Harry Langdon* (the first book on the comedian), devotes a full chapter to "Stan, Ollie and Harry." Besides providing one of the more thorough examinations of *Zenobia* (1939, the one film to costar Hardy and Langdon), Schelly looks closely at the friendship of the three comedians (especially the mutual-admiration society of Laurel and Langdon). Naturally, the chapter's special drama involves Roach's quasi-teaming of Hardy and Langdon after the 1938 firing of Laurel. Appropriately, for a man (Laurel) seemingly better at male friendships, Langdon only accepted the role after getting Laurel's blessing. (For more on this see Chapter 1.)

Janice Anderson's *History of Movie Comedy* (1985) is an excellent film comedy overview in a competitive field. The "Laurel and Hardy" segment is included in the chapter "Monkey Business: The Movie Teams." The duo is dealt with intelligently, with the author correctly zeroing in on the humanity of the two, be it the warmth of their screen relationship or the good spiritedness with which they forever meet their frustrations. An added plus for readers is that the book boasts both a wide spectrum of comedians outside the United States as well as quality reproductions of stills and color posters: an unusual combination of insightful commentary and good pictures.

In 1986 Volume 2 of *Current Research in Film* appeared. Edited by Bruce Austin, it included a Richard Alan Nelson essay with the arresting title, "Before Laurel: Oliver Hardy and the Vim Company, A Studio Biography." Though the piece is well worth reading (especially in its ongoing message for film historians to better utilize local period news sources in their research), the essay does not deliver on the title's co-billing of Hardy. The piece is much more taken with its methodological approach and the studio itself. And when it specifically focuses on Hardy, part of its content is merely recycled Jordan Young on the "Plump and Runt" series, examined earlier in this chapter.

Once these qualifiers are noted, however, it is only fair to credit the article with providing a thorough background on a studio central to the early Hardy, and as one might expect, the lengthy bibliography includes numerous entries from local period sources (Vim Studio was based in Jacksonville, Florida). There is also a list of company personnel and a studio filmography.

In 1987 numerous articles appeared marking the 60th anniversary of the 1927 teaming. London *Daily Mail* film critic Shaun Usher's essay on the subject (with that most fitting of titles, "The People's Clowns") is a good yesterday-and-today sort of Laurel & Hardy overview, though Roach is mistakenly credited with teaming them. Thus, subjects covered range from the Marx Brothers initially receiving greater critical attention to the more recent, ongoing, interest generated by the Sons of the Desert following. Usher also quotes influential British film historian Leslie Halliwell's observation that Laurel & Hardy were "the greatest comedy team of all."

Halliwell's verdict comes from another 1987 work, *Double Take and Fade Away*, a book sometimes referred to as *Halliwell on Comedians*. This prolific author opens his seventh chapter on American film comedy from 1930–45, with a six-page focus on Laurel & Hardy. Despite the limited space potential of such a broad-based book, Halliwell does a masterful capsulization of team highlights that is both very readable and genuinely affectionate without becoming maudlin. Not surprisingly, he also calls them "the supreme example of thirties laughter."

An earlier work by this author, *Halliwell's Hundred: A Nostalgic Choice of Films From the Golden Age* (1982), had dedicated two brief chapters to the team. The focus films were *Sons of the Desert* and *Way Out West*, though

Halliwell used both works as platforms with which to launch into eclectically interesting generalities about the team. As a culminating tribute, the book is "Dedicated to the memory of Mr. Laurel and Mr. Hardy."

Another British author penning Laurel & Hardy material in 1987 was Jerry Palmer, whose book *The Logic of the Absurd: On Film and Television Comedy* has a chapter largely devoted to the duo, "The Semiotics of Humour: The Logic of the Absurd." It is a belabored semiotic examination of surrealism and comedy surprisingly drawn from the world of Laurel & Hardy. Though his examples are legitimate (such as the descending elevator in *Liberty* that squashes a policeman to midget size), the team is a curious choice given both the generally realistic foundation of their work and the fact that most of their comedy is based on anticipation. An example is the insert shot that shows the nail or skate Ollie is about to step on. Still, on a general comedy level, Palmer provides new twists on an old phenomenon—comic surprise.

As if in celebration of the teaming, a moving Ray Bradbury short story entitled "The Laurel and Hardy Love Affair" appeared in the December 1987 issue of *Playboy*. Though hardly a traditional example of criticism, the piece is so immersed in Stan & Ollie basics it manages to serve a critiquing purpose. Like the educational side of effective parody (being thoroughly versed in the subject under comic attack), a true appreciation of this Bradbury story is dependent on a working knowledge of Laurel & Hardy. Indeed, one might credit stories like this as the most palatable of *critical approaches*.

Fittingly, the endless flight of steps in *The Music Box* plays a pivotal role in the story, as well as both patented Stan & Ollie gestures—tie twiddling and top-of-the-head scratching—and such team tag lines as "Another fine [sic—nice] mess you've gotten me into" and "Why don't you do something to help me!" But most important to the story's success, just as it is to the team itself, is the great love and affection Stan & Ollie share for each other. The romantic couple of Bradbury's story represent a surrogate Stan & Ollie, from appropriating their names and the same contrasting shapes to those gestures and taglines. Thus, when the Bradbury couple mirror their love through a joint appreciation of Stan & Ollie, it is a relationship more readily understood by the reader, with a built-in carryover of affection from the real team.

Bradbury, however, closes with a real emotional tumble—the Stan & Ollie-like couple break up—providing the added poignancy that would have accompanied a permanent split of the real team. Again, one's carryover of affection for Stan & Ollie has enhanced the Bradbury story. Moreover, the shock one feels at the break up underlines the uniqueness of the real duo—who can imagine Stan without Ollie?

Author Lawrence Christon would no doubt have difficulty imagining such a split. His *Los Angeles Times* piece on the duo, with a title borrowed in part from Luis Buñuel—"The Discreet Charm of Laurel & Hardy" (January 10, 1988)—is a warmly informative overview of their lives and comic times, which generally avoids merely cloying praise. Indeed, Christon is just as apt to temper sweetness with comedy, such as his George Burns quote describing Laurel as so nice, "You wanted to take him home."

Christon demonstrates a thorough understanding of his subject matter and chronicles it in a manner entertaining even to the Stan & Ollie aficionado. Plus, in rehashing the standard background, he is capable of adding the refreshing aside. For instance, when discussing the well-known popularity of the team with period leaders like Franklin Roosevelt and Benito Mussolini, Christon suggests the team was enjoyed "perhaps not only for their merits as comedy diversion, but because their quality of self-contained naivete had to be a small source of nostalgia for anyone dealing in *Realpolitik*."

Happily, Leo McCarey is recognized for the significant role he played in the teaming and molding of the duo, and it is not merely a fleeting credit. McCarey is well served by the article, though Christon primarily focuses on his pivotal slowing of Laurel & Hardy pacing.

While the article does not provide a credit for the mind behind the inspired stupidity of Stan & Ollie (it was Laurel—see Chapter 1), Christon does praise McCarey for recognizing "that slowing the tempo not only put people's reaction times more in sync with what was going on in front of them, but it was more in keeping with two characters who were a mental half-step behind."

Christon also closes with an effective "The Boys as Heroes" section, where he addresses the continued popularity of the team. The answer for Christon is that Stan & Ollie "were indefatigably committed to the old idea of virtue, however quaint, and would go to any length to see it redeemed." This is reminiscent of Vonnegut's prologue to *Slapstick* (see Chapter 2), where the novelist pays homage to the inherent decency of Stan & Ollie, despite all the frustrations they experience in a less-than-rational world.

As almost an aside, Christon touches on sociological criticism when he draws a parallel between the team's general frustrations and the 1930s Depression, a backdrop for so much of their career. Though probably a factor, such a connection neither explains Stan & Ollie's popularity today with younger audiences (years after the 1930s), nor does it address the fact that Depression-like poverty was not a basic theme for the duo (though exceptions existed, such as *One Good Turn*, 1931). If anything, part of the team's popularity was, like the period screwball comedy couple, based in the comic irony that *despite* having much in their favor, these comic antiheroes still could not succeed. For instance, even before *Hog Wild* arrives at Stan & Ollie's celebrated attempt to erect a radio antenna, one is introduced to a pompous, well-off Ollie who is having a major snit in front of his wife and the maid merely about a lost hat . . . a hat which, unbeknownst to him, is right on his head!

Regardless, Christon is correct in accenting the Vonnegut-like "virtue" factor over the sociological approach when trying to decipher Stan & Ollie's timelessness. Amusingly, this and the other valuable contributions of "The Discreet Charm of Laurel & Hardy" occur after an early Christon remark on the impossibility of critiquing the team: "They had a quality that can't be intellectually decanted.'' The piece thus rebuts the unfortunate cliche that deciphering comedy destroys it.

Another 1988 article (September 16–23), from a seemingly unlikely place (the British publication *Radio Times*) produced an excellent put-it-in-perspective article on why the team did not receive the 1930s critical reception they deserved. Written by Philip Jenkinson, for the ''In the Picture'' column, it recounts the team's often less-than-auspicious period film standings. Besides recycling the standard little respect from critics position, Jenkinson reminds one that even the forever loyal 1930s public ''twice voted RKO's Wheeler and Woolsey as their favorite funny men.'' Consequently, it becomes most ironic that a Laurel & Hardy film from this period, *Way Out West*, is considered ''one of the most inventive . . . comedies ever made.'' (Jenkinson might have added the further irony that most of today's film audience has not even heard of Wheeler and Woolsey!)

There were a number of events in the 1980s that generated news stories about the duo—stories sometimes of an analytical nature. Of course, the mere fact the team was still generating such attention decades after its heyday is a critical commentary all its own.

Seven topics come to mind: the ever-increasing visibility of the Sons of the Desert fan club; the push by a new Hal Roach Studios (a Canadian-based firm that bought the original film rights from Roach Sr.) to find lost Laurel & Hardy films and to strike new copies from the best 35mm prints available; Larry Harmon's push to put the team's image on a United States postage stamp; the production of a musical play based on their lives; Hal Roach's honorary Oscar; Ulverston's Laurel & Hardy Museum; and the colorization of their films.

First, of the many Sons of the Desert pieces, two of the more novel are Katherine Ainsworth's *Los Angeles Times* article, ''A Captive of a Comic Cult Confesses'' (July 20, 1980), and the *Los Angeles Examiner* journalist Rip Rense's ''They Haven't Deserted Stan and Ollie'' (October 19, 1981). Also, see Rense's 1983 piece on a then-new package of Laurel & Hardy films (below).

Ainsworth's piece is as entertaining as its title. She is a ''Sons of the Desert'' member who is confessing. It is largely an affectionately witty background on both the club's history and its monthly activities, but it also manages to include a brief celebration/critique of Laurel & Hardy from President Jimmy Carter. In a letter sent to the ''Sons of the Desert's'' first international convention (Chicago, August 1978), Carter observed,

I certainly welcome this opportunity to join you in furthering public awareness of the great contribution of these films to American humor. Oliver Hardy was Georgia's gift to the world of film comedy. As a Georgian, I am extremely proud of this. And I also share your gratitude and that of millions of Americans to England for lending us the immortal Stan Laurel. Together, they taught us that comedy can be humane as well as raucous, sweet as well as slapstick.

The Rense essay provides a view of the sillier side of a ''Sons of the Desert'' meeting, focusing on the ''Way Out West'' tent. Of course this fits nicely in with Laurel's egalitarian request that the club have only "half-assed dignity." As if in the spirit of Stan & Ollie, the night's reported events even took on the qualities of a two-reeler, from honored guests unable to attend to difficulties putting up a screen.

A pocket-sized Laurel & Hardy critique (featured prominently in the article) by the evening's emcee misses the essence of the duo but probably tells more about loyal fans: the team "appealed to extremely intelligent people because of the subtlety of their gags—and they have always appealed to folks who aren't particularly genius caliber because of the slapstick. But they have always appealed to everyone." That is, while many intelligent people enjoy Stan & Ollie, there is nothing subtle about their telegraphing approaching gags. Indeed, removing the element of surprise is a Laurel & Hardy cornerstone. Ironically, the quote's self-deprecating reference to slapstick is probably an apologetic habit born of often less-than-kind critics. Finally, as loving and loved as Stan & Ollie are, they have detractors who often find them excruciatingly methodical, seeing the team's celebrated slowdown in pacing as a liability. Regardless, the devotion of Stan & Ollie fans everywhere, both inside and outside the "Sons of the Desert," has allowed the team's comic legacy to be immeasurably enriched.

Second, criticism that might be subheaded "Laurel & Hardy Lost and Found" is nicely represented by both Rip Rense's *Los Angeles Herald Examiner* piece, "Pies Will Be Flying at Premier of Laurel and Hardy Treasures" (July 11, 1983), and Mervyn Rothstein's *New York Times* essay, "A Filmic Bouquet of Laurel and Hardy Rarities" (December 15, 1984).

In both cases, the catalyst behind the reviews was the rerelease of six earlier Laurel & Hardy films: *Duck Soup* (1927), *You're Darn Tootin'* (1928), *Double Whoopee* (1929), *Liberty* (1929), *Habeas Corpus* (1928), and *Big Business* (1929).

Duck Soup (not to be confused with the later Marx Brothers film of the same title) was the special event of this Laurel & Hardy package. The film had long been thought lost, but a print had surfaced in Belgium. All the other films had been struck from original camera negatives. Rothstein's piece takes a special look at *Duck Soup* and how much that was soon to become patented Stan & Ollie was surfacing.

Rothstein's essay also provides general recognition for McCarey, who had a credited hand in each of these highlighted six films (see this volume's "Filmography"). In fact, Rothstein provides short career backgrounds for McCarey as well as Laurel & Hardy. He also includes a brief thumbnail storyline of each film.

Rense's article is more casual about this special Laurel & Hardy film program; instead of zeroing in on the films themselves, as Rothstein does, Rense focuses more on the unique phenomenon of the team's staging of a 1980s "comeback." Moreover, as is befitting a relaxed piece, Rense has Hardy's widow as his authority figure, as opposed to Rothstein's use of scholarly film figures such as William Everson and James Agee.

Among the observations Rense draws from Hardy's widow Lucille is one that bases the team's success upon the comedy theory of superiority: "Their type of comedy was something everyone could understand. Even the smallest child could watch and say, 'See? I'm smarter than *he* is.' " Not surprisingly, this observation on comedy is quite close to that of Hardy's (see Chapter 1).

Lucille, who was then married to newspaper publisher Ben Price, also inadvertently noted the antiheroic nature of Stan & Ollie, who "never tried to put anyone down. They put themselves down first." Of course, one might quibble about their tit-for-tat comic violence being a putdown. But even then they always seemed to have a justifiably comic reason for such retaliation. Lucille's position on the team reminds one of the inherent "common decency" Vonnegut had found so attractive.

All in all, the Rense and Rothstein essays act as a Laurel & Hardy composite, complementing each other both in relationship to these specific rereleased short subjects and to their comic charisma in general.

The search alone for these comedy treasures was sometimes entertaining enough to squeeze out the criticism entirely. For instance, in yet another Rip Rense *Los Angeles Herald Examiner* piece, "Stumbling Upon the Lost Films of Laurel and Hardy" (December 9, 1982), he reports upon several finds, including a Nome, Alaska, basement discovery—beneath an old ice skating rink (where the cold had preserved the films). One might also examine Darren Leon's *Los Angeles Times* "A Search for a Cinematic Bag of Gold" (January 11, 1983), though the opening quotes concerning the theft of Stan & Ollie's money should be attributed to *The Devil's Brother* (*Fra Diavolo*, 1933), not *The Bohemian Girl* (1936).

In either case a special hosanna should be cited for the archival detective work of Roach chairman of the board Earl Glick, studio vice president Herb Gelbspan, studio library curator Mark Lipson, and numerous archivists for implementing a special five-year plan to find lost Laurel & Hardy films, as well as ones no longer available in 35mm (meaning the best available prints). And what better project for another "Hal Roach Studio" than to search out the work of what had been the original company's bread-and-butter comedy team?

Indeed, while much of this cinema sleuthing was no doubt done out of love for the duo, it was good business. As Glick observed in the Rense essay, "We think that there might be a tremendous audience out there." (Interestingly enough, the early 1980s also produced a sizable find of "lost" "Honeymooners" episodes, with the Laurel & Hardy-influenced "team" of Gleason and Carney (see Chapter 2).

Third, Larry Harmon, the original Bozo the Clown, generated a great deal of news copy with his successful lobbying of the United States Postal Service for a commemorative stamp marking the 60th anniversary of Laurel & Hardy's teaming. (For example, see the *Los Angeles Daily News* article "Bozo Stuck on Paying Tribute to Laurel & Hardy," October 30, 1985). Ironically, after all

Harmon's work to obtain government approval, he has delayed (or possibly killed) the project over a question of design (see Chapter 1). As a historical side note, Laurel & Hardy's comedy contemporary W. C. Fields had previously been honored with a commemorative stamp marking the 100th anniversary (1880–1980) of his birth. And it was announced in April 1989 that the centennial of Laurel's birth (1890–1990) would also be marked with a special stamp.

Fourth, on September 12, 1984, London's West End (English theatre's equivalent of Broadway) saw the opening of the Laurel & Hardy musical *Block-Heads*. Recycling the name of their 1938 feature, the flawed production (which mixes their private lives with their public career) is best examined in Irving Wardle's *London Times* review (October 18, 1984), with an abbreviated critique also appearing on October 21. Wardle found Stan & Ollie wonderfully realized by Mark Hadfield and Kenneth Waller, but the private-life portion of the storyline did not always portray the duo sympathetically. Fittingly, Wardle entitled his review "A Fine Mess . . . ".

The musical was to have opened on Broadway the following season (1985). However, its mixed reception in London no doubt doomed any such plan, especially with Broadway production costs being three times that of the West End. For more on the planned United States opening, see Enid Nemy's *New York Times*'s "Broadway: A Musical About Laurel and Hardy Due Next Season" (June 8, 1984) and the *Times*'s "West End Opening for Laurel and Hardy Play" (June 14, 1984).

Fifth, earlier in 1984 (April 9) the Academy of Motion Picture Arts and Sciences gave Hal Roach an honorary Oscar "in recognition of his unparalleled record of distinguished contributions to the motion picture art form." The filmmaker, then 92 years old, still healthy and active, had long outlived Laurel & Hardy as well as such duo-related principals as McCarey and Stevens. (See Aljean Harmetz's *New York Times* piece, "Hal Roach to Receive Special Oscar," March 12, 1984.)

Sixth, the 1980s saw increased attention being paid the Laurel & Hardy Museum established (in 1976) in Laurel's hometown of Ulverston. One of the best essays on the subject is the 1983 British *TV Times* article (August 6–12) titled "Stan is Home." Author Alan Kennaugh has drawn together an interesting assortment of Laurel-Ulverston connections and how they influenced the comedian's professional and private life. Fittingly, museum founder and curator Bill Cubin is a major source of information.

Seventh, from the very beginning of the 1980s the colorization of old Laurel & Hardy films has been a topic of interest. For instance, see the April 22, 1980 London *Daily Star* Trevor Walls article, "Stan Gets a Tan by Computer." Critical raves for the duo from pieces like this are normally only seen between the lines—Laurel & Hardy continue to have such popularity their films are chosen as pioneering subjects for colorization.

Of course, the artistic ethics of colorization remain a debated subject. But there is no debating the persistent popular success of Laurel & Hardy through the years. And as long as humanity honors laughter, works like this will forever explore the comic gifts of Stan & Ollie.

Interviews/Reminiscences with Laurel, Laurel & Hardy, Colleagues, and Families

Any number of interviews and reminiscences with Laurel, Laurel & Hardy, colleagues, and families might have been chosen. This section, proceeding chronologically, examines some of the most important. The interviews or reminiscences label is applied liberally, embracing pieces that have a significant amount of dialogue, even though the article might not traditionally be labeled an interview.

Loretta Dean's October 1929 *American Cinematographer* article, with its essay-length title, "THOSE FUNNY BOYS: A Few Inside Facts About the Screen's Funniest Pair of Comedians and the Man Who Has Photographed Most of Their Pictures," is a good starting point for this section both because of its early date and the fact that questions are asked of the team *and* photographer Len Powers.

It begins with biographical material on all three individuals and then slides into an exchange of complimentary comments culminating with a trio chorus of "So that makes us a mutual admiration society." But the piece does move beyond this apparent camaraderie fluff to a more pointed commentary.

Powers relates the difficulty of filming when the team starts to ad lib. He credits their "funniest gags" to such moments. (For more on the team's improvisation, see Chapter 1.) Ironically, his solo example is drawn from *Birthmarks*, which does not compare with their best films from this period. Powers praises the duo further when he reveals his leisure-time entertainment includes Laurel & Hardy theatrical screenings—this from their cinematographer!

Powers mentions that the two are great practical jokers and reveals a like spirit himself. He relates how he met an anticipated gag with one of his own. Discovering a Laurel & Hardy plan to dunk him on location, he responded by wearing old clothes over a swimming suit. But the screen comedians still won the day. Despite Powers's prepared open invitation for a dunking (by leaving himself in an assortment of vulnerable by-a-pond positions), Laurel & Hardy did not bite. And who knows, perhaps this was Laurel & Hardy's intended gag all along—something leagues beyond the minds of Stan & Ollie.

The article also reveals the casual world view to which each comedian adheres: " 'Life is serious enough, anyway,' says Hardy, 'so why do a lot of worrying? Just take things as they come.' " Laurel agrees *but* adds the successful comedy qualifier, " 'He's right; too many people believe that the world rests on their shoulders. A comedian should remember just one thing. That is, laugh, and the box office is always busy.' " As was sketched in Chapter 1, Laurel's personal life was the archetypal rudderless ship, but comedy was never taken so lightly.

However, because of his inherent shyness, even comedy assertiveness must have been challenging, at least in the early years. Thus, Dean describes Laurel as "So shy that he slips into previews after the lights have been lowered, and ducks out before they come on again."

As a closing note, it is unusual among Laurel & Hardy authors to describe Hardy as Dean does—"really of the intelligentsia." The article includes no Hardy quotes bolstering this, and other Dean descriptions match the now-standard norm (i.e., Hardy is the "essence of geniality and modesty"). This is not meant to question the comedian's intellectual skills but merely to draw attention to an irregularity in this article.

Also appearing in October 1929 was Eleanor Parker's *Playgoer* magazine visit with the duo, "Two Prize Idiots." The piece is at its best examining the subject of personal appearances. Beginning with a stereotypical Hollywood opening (a mob of waiting fans outside a theater, the arrival of the stars, the radio announcer with a microphone in the lobby . . .), Laurel & Hardy find they have very little to say (funny or otherwise) when called to an impromptu mike. According to Laurel, "That's the reason we avoid all public appearances. People expect us to be funny all the time. We are like everyone else, with a regular business. Comedy is our business. We can't [forever] go around . . . doing comedy." The more reticent Hardy added, "if we try to be funny, and didn't succeed, people would say, 'Oh, they're not half so good as we thought they were.' So we refuse all [public appearance] requests [keeping] what funniness we have for the screen." Of course, this policy would do a complete flip-flop in the 1940s, as their screen career faded and the stage became their focus assisted by personal appearances.

The Parker piece is peppered with other points of interest, from the team's initial fear of sound film to Laurel's basic superiority approach to comedy: "People like to laugh at the misfortune of others. It's human nature." Parker reveals, "When Laurel and Hardy are making a picture, the scene of their activities is the Mecca of the entire studio." At another point, even the editor of *Playgoer* adds an aside—M-G-M studio heads "haven't boomed the brilliant pair half enough." The article eventually comes full circle as the team's complete lack of self-consciousness when performing is contrasted with their preference to avoid playing the clowns in public. Of course, every role has exceptions. For Laurel & Hardy, it was the time an on-location shoot precipitated a Los Angeles neighborhood school to dismiss class and allow the youngsters to watch the duo at work. This time, when the "Be funny" public request came, Laurel & Hardy responded with a special half hour of fun just for the children.

Another late-1929 article is Philip K. Scheuer's "Comics Famous 'By Accident,' " from the December 29 *Los Angeles Times*. Unlike the previous two pieces, the interview portion of this essay involves only Laurel, with a brief and cutting Scheuer aside suggesting Hardy's views are not necessary. Despite the title, the focus is on the team's early response to sound film and their innovative slowdown in comic pacing. According to Laurel, the latter, herein referred to as " 'slow-slapstick,' " evolved from *The Battle of the Century* (1927). This film predates the one McCarey pinpoints as most crucial to the pacing change—*From Soup to Nuts* (1927, see Chapter 1). But it should be added that McCarey closely supervised *The Battle of the Century* and he saw it as one of his more personal Laurel & Hardy films (see Chapter 1).

Laurel's comment on the latter film and "slow-slapstick" turns upon the entertaining hypothesis that a sudden and unexpected pie to the face would not immediately result in visual and physical anger so much as "numb disbelief," followed by "embarrassment and a quick survey of the [pie] damage done to his person." Only after this progression would any comic retaliation take place. While this example does not seem long enough to mirror some prolonged Laurel & Hardy "slow-slapstick" scenes, it does evolve from the realistic base that was important comically to both Laurel and McCarey. An additional attraction to this Laurel story is that it fittingly moves from "slow-slapstick" to comic revenge. Though it does not address the next humor move (the tit-for-tat comic violence), it is a good example of what Laurel saw as a psychological approach to humor.

Lastly, the Scheuer essay finds Laurel expressing reservations about making features and touches briefly upon "clocking" laughs, something expanded upon thoroughly in the July 1930 *Photoplay* articles, "Those Two Goofy Guys," reprinted in this text. The latter article is paired in Chapter 3 with the reproduction of another 1930 piece, though with a more explanatory title: "Ka-Plop and Ka-Bloop: Laurel and Hardy Reveal What Makes You Hear Such Funny Things" (*Motion Picture Classic* magazine, June).

Alice L. Tildesley's "Funny Film Faces: How They Got That Way" (an article examining Laurel & Hardy and other period comedians) was published in 1930. But the 1972 *Pratfall* (vol. 1, no. 8) reprinting of the Laurel & Hardy segment of the piece is without a citation. (Reference sources for articles reprinted in *Pratfall* are often incomplete, though seldom omitted.) The Laurel & Hardy interview is at the M-G-M lot where the two are on loan to provide comic relief in the feature film *The Rogue Song* (1930), with Metropolitan Opera star Lawrence Tibbett topping the bill.

Interviewed on M-G-M's cafe sun porch, the team was stopping traffic with their rose-pink and purple satin outfits (it was to be an "all-color" film). Self-conscious about the attention, Laurel observed, "Over on the Hal Roach lot, where we belong, they take us more for granted."

The realistic comedy base implied in the Scheuer piece is directly addressed in this piece. For Laurel, their comedy is the "human sort of stuff that could happen to anybody." Hardy seconds this, adding, "The minute you wisecrack you're fresh; people resent it. Comedy must be believable."

Ironically, wisecracks, which Laurel also negates as inappropriate for their comedy arsenal, will be unfortunately written for them during their 1940s film decline (see especially *Great Guns*, 1941, in Chapter 1).

Of additional special interest is Laurel's comment, "We write our own stories and our own dialogue. Sometimes the picture just grows from what happens. Sometimes it develops from an incident in our own homes.'' He credits the basic premise to be washing machine salesmen in *Hats Off* (1927) to a real-life pest he had recently encountered. Unfortunately, no more is said about the evolution of a film for which McCarey is given a great deal of credit.

This interview also expands upon the team superiority approach to comedy touched on in the Parker piece. Laurel calls Stan & Ollie ''Just a couple of dumb fellows,'' while Hardy says, ''We're two chaps without too much sense; I'm the one that thinks I have more than Stan has. But really, I haven't as much. That's all there is to it.''

The interview comes full circle when Hardy's serious face, as he discusses his tough early entertainment years, provokes laughter from cafe onlookers. (Tildesley describes it as ''The grave face of a preposterous baby.'') Hardy, given a rare interview close over his partner (as well as having been more personally open than usual throughout), poignantly observes, ''Expect we'd better be glad they think we're funny. Stan and I have had a lot of hard knocks. So long as people like us, we're willing to let 'em laugh!''

On January 9, 1932, *Picturegoer Weekly* ran the interview/article ''My Lad Laurel by Stan's Father.'' It is a moody piece fluctuating between fatherly pride and sadness that movies have killed theater as he once knew it. Moreover, Mr. Jefferson confesses that his love of stage drama made him ''not entirely pleased'' with his son's childhood interest in comedy. This is ironic, since the multitalented A. J. at one time considered himself a comedian, listing it as his occupation at the time of Laurel's birth. Moreover, Laurel later credited much of his comedy skill to A. J. (see Jerry Lewis's memories of this later in the chapter). Regardless, the piece finds A. J. challenging Laurel to stretch himself cinematically—''Although he is soaring in salary and popularity, I would tell you there is much more in him than the films have brought out of him as yet.'' He places Laurel on a level with Chaplin, and wishes for more comedy pathos from his son. Coupled with this is Jefferson's unhappiness over the Americanization of Laurel's comedy—the implication being any artistic potential is lost. The article is best described as a crisp portrait of father rather than son.

Laurel's father also kept a fascinating diary during his lengthy mid-1930s visit with his film star son. See Chapter 1 for more on this unpublished family-owned document. (A private collector who wished to remain anonymous gave me access to his copy.)

As if acknowledging a call from the past, 1932 is the year of Laurel's celebrated English homecoming (with Hardy). The visit generated a great deal of press in his native land. Especially enlightening is the London *Daily Herald*'s July 25 coverage, ''Laurel in Shirt Sleeves Holds Family Party,'' which includes a large front-page picture of the comedian with his father and stepmother. The Ritchie Calder piece, examined thoroughly in Chapter 1, reports on the comically self-styled ''Prodigal Son'' opening a small family reunion at London's Savoy Hotel to the press.

The following day, July 26, the *Herald* ran a shorter piece about the duo on radio—"Laurel & Hardy to Broadcast To-night." In a brief dialogue with an unnamed reporter, Laurel surprisingly turned the subject to a graveyard light-house in his native Ulverston. (For more on this, including a photograph, see Chapter 1.)

England's *Film Weekly* ran a July 29 tongue-in-cheek article entitled "Laurel High-hats Hardy." Switching their comedy roles, Stan is now frustrated by a dumb partner—first-time British tourist Ollie. The piece reads like a comedy sketch, with Stan forever repeating the refrain (after more Ollie stupidity), "Oh, Ollie!" They are allegedly sharing their troubles with humorist Ian Fox.

The most widely reported incident of their trip was an out-of-control crowd that welcomed the team to Glasgow at midnight on July 29. Here was a comic celebration gone macabre, or, as the front page London *Daily Herald* (July 30) article titled it, "20 HURT IN Laurel and Hardy Stampede." Most initial reports of the incident did not include direct quotes from the team, opting instead for paraphrasing. Thus, in the *Herald*, "Laurel and Hardy confessed that in no part of the world had they received such a tumultuous reception." The *New York Time*'s brief report, "Fight to Greet Actors" (July 30) included a variation upon the previous quote and another, mentioned already, "Laurel wept with emotion." For more on this and their northern tour, see the August 4, 1932 *Kinematograph* article, "Laurel and Hardy: Enthusiastic Admirers in the North."

The team received continuous coverage from *Kinematograph* during their visit. Another recommended piece from this publication is the August 18 "At Laurel's Father's Home Suburb," which includes a brief paraphrasing of a Hardy speech praising his friendship with Laurel.

Back in the United States the team was briefly profiled in a *New York Times* article, "Who's Who This Week in Pictures" (October 2, 1932). Laurel's portion is largely devoted to references to Chaplin, from early Karno troupe understudy days with film's soon-to-be most celebrated comedian, to Laurel crediting Chaplin for his initial foray into movies. Given both Laurel's own eventual great film success and the medium's ongoing rise in credibility, his comments at the time of Chaplin's motion picture-bound departure from Karno are comically innocent: "We [the troupe] all thought Charlie was a fool for leaving the superiority of the stage for the doubtful medium of moving pictures." Possibly closer to the point, however, was Laurel's next comment: "Charlie was getting $60 a week of which he was sure, and he was a great hit." In the volatile world of vaudeville, financial security plus success was not to be taken lightly. Of course, this was something Chaplin felt himself (see both Chapter 1 and my *Charlie Chaplin: A Bio-Bibliography, 1983).

A failing marriage received public scrutiny in Ann Glaze's *Movie Classic* magazine interview with Laurel, "No Laughs in Laurel Home-Life, So Comedian and Wife Separate" (February 1933). Laurel presents a moving but rather sanitized look at his problem marriage. The piece is at its best when discussing the frequently dark private side of comedians in general (though it no doubt would apply to many performers) once the show is over (see Chapter 1).

In June 1933, E. R. Moak's "Tear-Stained Laughter" appeared in *Photoplay* magazine. As the title indicates, the essay, like "No Laughs . . . ", examines the dark side of being a clown. In this case, however, it is a biographical chronicling of all the hard knocks Laurel and Hardy went through before their successful teaming. It is a maudlin article only redeemed by the occasional elaborating quote from Laurel or Hardy (though not the conventional interview). For example, when Hardy was five years old, his widowed mother was in severe economic straits and unable to provide for the children's Christmas. Thus, she revealed to them the myth of Santa. Hardy observed in 1933, "Mother did what she thought the square thing, but we were so young to be disillusioned—and there were so many blows awaiting us later on."

Both the article's tone and its time-line proximity to Laurel's marital problems of "No Laughs . . . " might suggest it was a hedge against any potential bad publicity, especially since sad side biographical material is hardly standard fare for Laurel & Hardy, as opposed to the well-chronicled Dickensian childhood of a Chaplin. Ironically, a passing remark near the close implies there are no domestic problems in Laurel's household.

W. H. Mooring's "With MacLaurel & MacHardy in Bonnie Scotland," from the June 28, 1935 *Film Weekly*, is an outstanding interview with Laurel. Though billed as a team session, it is more correctly described as a lengthy Laurel monologue on filmmaking, Laurel & Hardy–style. Though their production *Bonnie Scotland* is the backdrop for this entertaining minilecture, Laurel focuses more on their team comedy in general.

Besides being such a delightfully longwinded session with Laurel, it is an important interview for three reasons. First, it is another excellent example of the importance of a realistic base in their work. Coupled with this is the diverting fun of Laurel totally lost in personal comedy theory, complete with third-person commentary on their film personae. Second, Laurel's comments to *Film Weekly*'s "Hollywood Representative" Mooring, as the filmmaker differentiates between American and English screen comedy suggests he has fully embraced his adopted country. Third, there are two rare references to the potential demise of the team. One states they would retire before trying to change their comedy characters. The second reveals Laurel's initial concern with the original *Bonnie Scotland* story and the comedian's implied near-break with Roach. For more on this rewarding interview, see Chapter 1.

Laurel & Hardy are credited with coauthoring the September 1935 *Hollywood Reporter* newspaper article—"You, Too, Can Be a Comedian!" In an era when a great deal of celebrity ghostwriting was being done (even the active pen of Groucho Marx is alleged to have been so assisted on occasion), it is more than likely that Laurel & Hardy worked with an uncredited author, especially since they were not normally essayists. (Indeed, Hardy even disliked writing letters!)

Regardless, it is an entertaining piece that includes material of both a direct and indirect duo nature. For instance, the article recommends that when a prospective comedian is ready for the studio audition, he/she should first ''hire an old Model T break-away Ford [a pivotal prop in the world of Stan & Ollie] so that you can drive up in front of a producer's sanctum and do your stuff in front of his office window prior to making personal contact.''

Indirectly, one is reminded of Hardy and his fellow gambling buddy Chico Marx when the article reveals that playing bridge is a good social contact in the movie colony, that many ''aspiring comics have made the grade by filling in as a fourth at this game.'' The Marx Brothers' film that same year (1935) was the M-G-M critical and commercial hit, *A Night at the Opera*, largely made possible by Chico's bridge-playing friendship with M-G-M production head Irving Thalberg. While the Marx Brothers were hardly ''aspiring comics,'' the surprising 1933 flop of their previous film—*Duck Soup* (ironically now often considered their best movie) had ended their association with Paramount and put their film career in the doldrums. (See my *The Marx Brothers: A Bio-Bibliography*, 1987.)

From the second half of the 1930s to the early 1940s, news items featuring quoted material from Laurel or Hardy often focused on the marital battles royal of the skinny one. The most full-blown examples seem to have appeared in the *New York Journal-American* newspaper. Examined more thoroughly in Chapter 1, representative articles include: ''Sad-Pan Stan's Comic Wife Troubles'' (January 29, 1938), ''Newest Upheaval in the Not-So-Private Life of Sad-Faced Mr. Laurel'' (December 10, 1939), and ''Funny Mr. Laurel Who Keeps on Getting Married'' (February 23, 1941). The three articles can also be found in the Laurel & Hardy files of the Billy Rose Theatre Collection of the New York Public Library at Lincoln Center. (A fourth *New York Journal-American* file piece of a similar nature appeared on January 29, 1939, but the title was unnoted.) Though this newspaper seemed to specialize in lengthy overviews of Laurel's domestic problems, it hardly had a corner on the phenomenon as a news item. For instance, see the *New York Daily News*'s ''Sad Pan, [Wife's] Frying Pan Met, Says Stan Laurel'' (October 26, 1938), or the philosophically amusing *Milwaukee Journal*'s ''One More Crash in Love Can Not Sour Stan Laurel'' (July 6, 1943), which finally found Laurel (of all people) observing ''I guess you can't warm love over.''

There is no denying the *New York Journal-American* articles misuse Laurel's marrying ways for copy/comedy space. But there is usually a comic slant to the pieces, often with amusing quotes from Laurel (especially in the hilarious 1941 essay—extensively quoted in Chapter 1). This seems to make these unfortunate situations more palatable (as opposed to scandalous) to the general fan. If anything, such domestic shambles (eventually marrying four women a total of eight times), might have further reinforced Laurel's screen status as an incompetent. Indeed, the frying pan headline might have been retrieved from a Stan & Ollie film. Moreover, no matter how fond one is of Laurel, his domestic adventures did reach darkly comic extremes—which he himself eventually was big enough to poke fun at—such as walling in his grounds (''Ft. Laurel'') allegedly to keep out blondes.

Even *Look* magazine's controversial 1938 Laurel photo essay, "The Saddest Man in Hollywood Is a Comedian: Stan Laurel," featured a comic line about his much-married life. And this from an article famous for its picture of a real-life weeping Laurel, distraught over his marital woes.

Of course, one must admit, Laurel's romantic marrying ways differ from the generally asexual Stan. Still, the articles are all obviously subject-grounded in frustration, a fundamental theme for antiheroic Stan & Ollie.

The often tongue-in-cheek acceptability of these articles is best demonstrated by contrasting them with a later, *not* recommended essay on Hardy—the *American Weekly*'s "Funny Mr. Hardy's UNFUNNY Alimony Troubles" (January 27, 1946). Though a cursory comparison between this piece and the recently examined Laurel articles reveals some basic parallels (such as messy domestic lives), the Hardy article includes no softening of the subject via a comic touch. There is neither an entertaining commentary from the comedian himself (the introverted Hardy was difficult to quote on any subject) nor a past domestic record that would rival Laurel's.

Naturally, however, Laurel & Hardy quoted print material from the late 1930s to the early 1940s was not limited to Laurel's marital musical chairs. Unfortunately, much of it seems to be lost or forgotten in less-than-mainstream publications. This is nicely represented with the discovery by the American magazine that has done the most (after *Pratfall*) to celebrate the life and times of Laurel & Hardy—*8mm Collector* (later known as *Classic Film Collector* and *Classic Images*—title changes that can slow down research).

In 1976 *Classic Film Collector* published ''1937—An Interview with L & H.'' It had been discovered and prefaced by Eldon K. Everett (no original source given, beyond it being a 1937 newspaper clipping). It provides both a fascinating window on the genesis of a particular *Way Out West* (1937) scene and further thoughts on the realistic foundation of the team's theory of comedy.

The scene in question must produce a humorous reason for the sheriff to later throw the duo out of town. The script had Ollie accidently firing a gun at the sheriff, but on the set the provocation became the innocent stagecoach flirtation of Ollie with the sheriff's wife.

This additional affirmation of a realistic comedy theory is arresting for two reasons—it is one of the strongest Laurel & Hardy declarations on realistic comedy theory yet available, and it is the often absent or quiet Hardy who makes the statement. He observes, in part, ''Nothing is funny unless people can believe it could have happened. That's why impossible things like a comedian coming along and eating doorknobs isn't funny. Nobody eats doorknobs.''

After the 1945 completion of their feature film *The Bullfighters*, Laurel & Hardy's American performing days as a duo were largely over. But there were very successful British music hall tours in 1947, 1952, and 1953–54, and the unfortunate European production of their last film, *Atoll K* (1950–51). Obviously, a good source of interview material during this period is found in European archives. One such example was found at the French Cinémathèque (Paris)—entitled "têt-à-tête avec duex têtes de pioche," it appeared in the November 25, 1947 issue of *L'Ecran Francais* (no. 126). It was done during a French extension of their 1947 tour. This is an extremely rich interview, with a sometimes emotional Laurel discussing numerous subjects. They range from the tragedy of Harry Langdon (coupled with the business harshness of Hollywood), to Laurel claims for his auteur status as a filmmaker. The only disappointment in the piece is that while Laurel acts as the team spokesman (as is usually the case) and thus dominates the dialogue (with Hardy's blessing), the interviewer also matter-of-factly notes *but does not record* several early solo career stories Hardy had related!

The Laurel & Hardy files at the British Film Institute (BFI) house several much shorter 1947 articles clustered around the team's February arrival in England. The best of the group, with regard to commentary from the duo, appeared in the February 12 London *Daily Star* (article title not cited). Though the comedian's remarks are often paraphrased, several familiar subjects are covered, from Hardy's size and fascination with golf to Laurel's interest in fishing and his Ulverston birthplace. (A briefer 1947 piece along similar lines had surfaced in the February 10 London *Evening News*: "Laurel & Hardy: The Above Have Arrived."

Two other BFI-held articles/interviews of interest, but dating from the 1950s, are "Together Again" (May 7, 1950, London *Daily Express*) and Elizabeth Frank's "Laurel and Hardy Find New Fame: But It Hasn't Brought Them a Cent" (October 14, 1953, *Nottingham Chronicle*). The former piece addresses two Stan Laurel sore spots, the poor scripts of the team's final American films and the fortune Laurel had lost in alimony payments. The latter interview, as the "But It Hasn't Brought Them a Cent" subheading suggests, examines the 1950s TV fame that does not pay. Of more interest in the latter piece (since TV frequently comes in for attack during their 1950s interviews) is the team's preference for British music-hall touring as opposed to the American vaudeville variety. (For another brief interview related to their old films being on TV and the medium in general, see the London *Daily Express* for October 14, 1953, citation incomplete.)

In July 1951 the team (back in the United States) did a *Los Angeles Times* interview with Philip Scheuer: "Hardy Perennials Win Laurels; Rosy Bids Bud from Comics' Europe Work." Despite the upbeat punning title and the good-spirited dialogue that follows, today the article is sadly ironic. For instance, it still manages to be optimistic about the team's then yet-to-be-released film—the regrettable *Atoll K*, and the offers for many professional projects that would never see fruition.

Despite the piece's cheery, projected comeback style, it manages to survey the team's past ten years of woe, from the unfortunate 1940s films to the problems encountered during the European production of *Atoll K*. Laurel & Hardy's thoughts on their 1940s films could be bitter. Hardy observed (''wrathfully,'' according to Scheuer) that by 1945 the team had done ''four or five [films] for the studio [20th Century-Fox], and we asked for our release. The first one, *Great Guns*, was funny and it made money. After that they never gave us stories—or casts.''

In contrast, while Laurel & Hardy had been less than happy about the *Atoll K* production, they were able to interject some comedy into this portion of the interview. Though not on a comic par with some of the *New York Journal-American* articles, the team's comments on their pompous French director are often amusing, from his riding breeches and pith helmet costume (as Cecil B. DeMille wore,) to indulgently arty shooting habits. The latter had prompted Laurel to observe dryly, ''He was doing a travelogue.'' Consequently, as with Laurel's eventual kidding of his marrying ways, this 1951 interview further demonstrates an ability to deflect pain with humor.

The Scheuer interview also finds Laurel & Hardy marking this time (1951) as an approximation of the 25th anniversary of the Stan & Ollie partnership (technically, the anniversary date was 1952), and they briefly reminisce about their early career years as a team. In addition, briefer segments touch on an assortment of items, from the team's then-current vogue in Europe to their ''modest'' private homes. Fittingly, at least for the optimistic tone of the interview, it closes with a listing of future Laurel & Hardy projects, projects on which time would, unfortunately, run out.

Later in 1951 the team was featured in *TV Time Magazine*—''Popularity Rains on Laurel & Hardy: An Exclusive Interview.'' As with the Scheuer piece, this interview by Natalie Best begins with the phenomenal popularity of their films on early television. But not surprisingly, given the nature of the publication, the focus does not leave the world of television (the Scheuer interview informatively rambles along on several topics). Also, most fittingly, the *TV Time Magazine* Laurel & Hardy interview presents the team's most positive look at the medium. The justifiable Laurel anger and sadness that greets the subject of television in later interviews concerning television's re-editing of their films is not present here. Especially pleasant was the return to an increased visibility. Hardy observed:

It does our hearts good . . . A year ago nobody knew us. When I went up to the corner grocery some kid would say, ''Get out of the way, fat.'' Now they stop and say ''You're Oliver Hardy aren't you! Can I have your autograph?''

Hardy later added that television's revival of their old films made for a pleasant review of their career—''We'd forgotten a lot of the good old gags. Remember the one where Stan played a tune on the bedsprings? [I] thought we'd die we laughed so hard.''

Conversely, the new medium of television was providing them with new material, which they hoped to use on their own future small-screen program.

Laurel, forever the parodist, asked, "How about kidding the commercials? You know the commercials are getting just exactly like the old time pitch men who used to sell gadgets and neckties from little card tables in doorways along the streets."

The interview ended on a comic note, with Laurel expanding upon a Hardy joke. When asked how much he weighed, a favored period response by Hardy was to plead ignorance, since his scales did not go over 300 pounds. On this occasion Laurel quipped, "Oliver, why don't you get two scales and put one foot on each one and add them up?"

On December 1, 1954, Laurel & Hardy appeared on Ralph Edwards's live NBC television program, "This Is Your Life." Years later Jim Britain transcribed the show for *Pratfall* magazine, where it appeared as a two-part piece in vol. 1, nos. 8 & 9 (1972). Special program guests included Leo McCarey, who related a real-life example of Laurel indirectly getting Hardy in trouble just as Stan always does to Ollie. During the skyscraper production of *Liberty* (1929), Hardy attempted to relieve the high-rise anxiety of Laurel by demonstrating the effectiveness of the safety platform some fifteen-twenty feet below their scaffold set. He jumped down to the platform—which he crashed through, falling an additional twenty feet to the ground. Somehow he escaped serious injury. Though the film was eventually finished, Hardy's good deed could not have been much comfort to Laurel.

Though polite, Laurel & Hardy had been less than pleased at their surprise appearance on "This Is Your Life." An early in-print articulation of this appeared in a *TV Guide* interview the following year (April 23, 1955). "No Laughing Matter: Laurel & Hardy Find Themselves on TV . . . for Free." While the title is a reference to old Laurel & Hardy films shown on television from which the team received no income, the article begins with their displeasure over the Edwards broadcast. According to Laurel, "Babe and I are both great television fans, and we've been planning to do something on TV. But we certainly never intended to start out on an unrehearsed network show!"

One is reminded of the 1929 Eleanor Parker piece, "Two Prize Idiots," where even then these two consummate professionals preferred avoiding live public appearances that might damage their big-screen image as very funny men. Moreover, in the 1950s, with Laurel's ill health having delayed their television plans, the team was all the more sensitive to orchestrating the correct public image. Consequently, their thoughts on the Edwards show were understandable.

The *TV Guide* interview also has them briefly discussing their enormous popularity outside the United States and some purposefully vague thoughts on the type of television show they would like eventually to have—and it would not be live.

Associated Press writer Bob Thomas (best known now as a celebrity biographer/interviewer) did a July 26, 1956 piece on them (later reprinted without full citation in *Pratfall*) entitled "Comedy Veterans Plan Comeback." Interviewed separately because of Laurel's poor health (he was still recovering from a stroke), both comedians were optimistic about eventually doing their own television show.

An eclectic assortment of topics surfaced, many of them familiar to followers of the team, such as the hoped-for program and their lack of income from the constant screening of their old films on television. Amazingly, on doctor's orders, Hardy had lost 150 pounds, bringing his weight down to 210. (Laurel later felt this huge weight loss was the precipitating reason for Hardy's death the following year, 1957.)

In the Thomas interview, however, Hardy is naturally upbeat about this physical change, ironically crediting his wife for being a "good taskmaster" in limiting calories. Another irony, which the team would have had to face had Hardy lived, is briefly suggested by Thomas. "His [Hardy's] fans might have difficulty recognizing him these days. His hair is thin and gray, and his multitude of chins has diminished."

Laurel does not want to rush his convalescence for fear of a relapse during the anticipated production of their small-screen program. Laurel also has an added incentive for obtaining a show: "I'm anxious to get some new films [programs] on TV so we can get those darned old [Laurel & Hardy] ones off. It makes me so mad to see them because they're cut [edited] so poorly." This was an issue he became much more vocal about with the passage of time. The increased bitterness was, quite possibly, also fed by the realization that with Hardy's death there never would be a new Laurel & Hardy television show to substitute for their poorly presented old films on the small screen.

After Hardy's stroke robbed him of both speech and movement in September 1956, there were periodic visits from his partner. Coverage of one such meeting appeared in the November 11, 1956 *London Dispatch*. The title of reporter Gerald McKnight's article/interview said it all: "Sad Reunion of Two Men Made World Laugh." The piece includes quoted material from Laurel, his wife, Ida, and Hardy's wife, Lucille.

Naturally, Hardy's death was well covered by the press. Indeed, as demonstrated earlier in this chapter, articles like the *New York Times*'s "The Fiddle and the Bow" could rise to heights of poetic criticism. But unlike later coverage of Laurel's death (which generated even more attention), there seemed less tendency for the commentaries on Hardy to include interview material—whether recycled from the comedian or new items from others. Of course, since Laurel had often acted as team spokesperson, there was less Hardy material from which to draw. Moreover, because Laurel lived longer (with cult status growing yearly) and since he had always made himself more accessible to the public (from general fans to celebrities like Dick Van Dyke), it is only logical there were more personal accolades surrounding Laurel's passing.

Still, Hardy's death obviously generated published personal commentaries, especially Laurel's widely quoted "I'll Never Work Again." (For example, see the brief London *Evening News* piece with that quote as its title, August 8, 1957.) A more ambitiously maudlin article is found in the *News Chronicle*'s

"Hardy of Laurel and Hardy Dies with Last Message to Wife Unspoken" (August 8, 1957). It includes an extended statement from Hardy's wife, Lucille. More typically, however, if anyone was cited, it was team survivor Laurel. For instance, Rene MacCall's telephone interview with Laurel in the London *Daily Express*'s confusingly titled: "Hardy (The Fat Half of Laurel & Hardy) Dies— To Stay Fat" (August 8, 1957). The interview is much easier to follow than the title, which merely meant Hardy had long stayed overweight against doctor's orders and this is what had killed him.

A few months after Hardy's death Bob Thomas did another interview with the skinny one—"Stan Laurel, Ill at 67, Can't Bear Old Films" (see the December 5, 1957 *New York World-Telegram and Sun*). According to Laurel, two things kept him from watching their films on TV. First and most important, "they're so cut up" by time slot–conscious TV distributors. Second, "They seem too slow nowadays. That was because we had to leave time between the gags for the audience to laugh. You don't need that spread in TV."

It had been two years since Laurel's stroke and he stated, "I'll never be able to go back to work. I just don't have the strength for it." He played down the doctor's "slight stroke" diagnosis, realizing "Even if you get back to normal physically, you're mentally demoralized. I'm afraid even to go down on the beach, for fear I'll fall."

Without doubting these health comments for an instant, Laurel was undoubtedly still mourning the loss of a longtime partner, and his mood was naturally all the more somber. Possibly, however, Hardy's death allowed Laurel to be much more frank about his own frail health, suggesting that the skinny one had never really been that confident about a comeback. But as long as Hardy had been alive, a team return to glory was not an impossibility.

Regardless, this second Thomas interview is an absorbing session, managing to squeeze in a number of topics, including his hobby-like letter writing to friends and fans and an ironic fascination (given the plight of his old films) with the small screen—"I've got to be where I can get TV. [He was planning to move to an area where more television stations were available.] These nights of nothing to do can drive you crazy."

Several months after Laurel's death Bob Thomas interviewed Dick Van Dyke on his hosting duties for a forthcoming Laurel & Hardy television special. The article is examined later in this chapter.

A brief *Theatre Arts* piece, "Deepest Cut" (September 1957), sandwiched between the Thomas interviews, is a useful companion work to the first Thomas session with Laurel. For example, an especially noteworthy link provides a further insight into Laurel's desire to have the team's old films taken off television: "Some of them [Laurel & Hardy films] are so butchered [edited by TV] that they don't make sense, so I'm at a loss to explain why they're still popular." Laurel also expresses the wish he could be allowed to edit the old team films, if they really must be cut for television—a request that surfaced through the years in several Laurel interviews.

The "Laurel & Hardy Files" in the Billy Rose Theatre Collection of the New York Public Library at Lincoln Center contains the November 16, 1958 print interview, "Laurel Smiling Again But Not for the Films." The interview, in part, was a response to a rumor that the comedian was living in poverty. "One little girl sent me a dollar. She probably thought I was starving. I sent her back $2. She made a good investment."

Though he had "had many requests to appear on TV shows," he repeated his response of the previous year: "It would be too much of a physical strain." The interview closed on the topic of Laurel's finances. While implying TV appearance money would be nice, he observed, "I'm not rich by any means, but I can get by with the little annuity I provided for myself."

The following year (March 1959) *Films in Review* printed one of the most thorough Laurel interviews. Conducted by Boyd Verb and entitled "Laurel Without Hardy," it examines their joint career and provides Laurel's views on several related subjects. Career topics addressed include the coming of sound ("We said as little as possible"), working scripts (basic starting point to be comically peppered during production), and the team's international success (even greater abroad than in America).

More generally, Laurel feels that young comedians are burning themselves out on television—which demands new material on a weekly basis. He also reveals that the original plan for a Laurel & Hardy television program had them doing 39 episodes (then the length of a season). But "I refused and told them the only way I'd make pictures was once every three months."

Among other general topics, Laurel rated Chaplin as easily the greatest comedian, education as the key to any career (regretting he had neglected his own as a child), and his fondness for the comedy of Jackie Gleason and Art Carney. (Laurel also thought they would be the perfect team to impersonate himself and Hardy in any future biography film.)

One final observation begs to be made, though it begins on a well-worn Laurel subject—television's shabby reediting of their films. But this rendition rekindles interest because Laurel also adds a lengthy example of a specific case. The comedian had watched one of his favorite films, *The Devil's Brother* (1933; see also *Fra Diavolo*) and found its length cut in half, with even that full of commercials. And while Laurel & Hardy were only supporting characters in the film, the team's pivotal and very funny first scene, where the two are robbed of their life savings, was completely eliminated. Consequently, the "new" introductory scene became their comic robbery of the central character. However, without that introductory set-up scene of their own comic victimization, Laurel felt "all sympathy for us was gone." Though this may be an overstatement on Laurel's part, loss of that segment does eliminate a comic symmetry (from victim to victimizer) and another funny example of Stanlio & Ollio (as they are referred to in the film, playing off Diavolo) failing miserably at a task they have just observed. Indeed, Ollio nearly hangs for his deed. Weeping Stanlio is pardoned . . . if he does a good job hanging his partner! More dark comedy is added when

Stanlio even offers to have his friend stuffed so they can always be together. (As a side note, this is also the film that features both Stanlio's classic "earsie-kneesie-nosie" body parts slapping routine, and probably the best of their out-of-control laughing sketch.)

Late in 1959 reporter Jeffrey Blyth sought Laurel out for the London *Daily Mail* interview "The Twilight of Clowns." In contrast to the often career focus of the *Films in Review* article, Blyth concentrates on Laurel's retirement years. Unfortunately, he turns the story into a melodrama, suggesting Laurel is nearly destitute and "almost a forgotten man." This added to Laurel's embarrassment—because this was during the period in which the comedian had already been receiving cards from concerned fans, sometimes containing money. Laurel went to great pains to return it and explain the real situation. The irony here, however, is that while Laurel's retirement was financially adequate, his modest apartment was hardly Fort Laurel.

The next year (August 1, 1960) an interview of Laurel by journalist Rick Du Brow appeared in the *New York Morning Telegraph*—"Stan Laurel, Now 70, Rips Modern Hollywood Practices." In the article the comedian found "Modern Hollywood" abysmal—"a shrinking island surrounded by money-grabbing, back-stabbing, and too much politics."

He sees politics as a two-part problem. First, with fewer films being made there is naturally more competition for positions and thus more game-playing—politics—among the participants. Second, Laurel is even more bothered by the kind of politics that finds the performer offering his views on national issues: "What right have they [Hollywood stars] to impose their thoughts on the public, which certainly knows as much as they do . . . Some of our stars are . . . taking themselves too seriously."

As with many Hollywood veterans, Laurel is also bothered by both the expense and lack of need for such 1950s technological developments as the wide screen. He points to the importance of the story over technology, and supports his position with period references to critically acclaimed exceptions to this trend, movies like *Marty* (1955) and *Room at the Top* (1959), "both simple black and white films on small screens, and both made fortunes." The interview also ends along Hollywood veteran lines, with the comedian reminiscing about the happy, less-harried days of Laurel & Hardy's film heyday.

In 1961 Larry Goldstein did an extensive Laurel interview, and after the comedian's death four years later Goldstein further embellished this Laurel piece. (See *Pratfall*'s 1977 reprint, vol. 2, no. 2, "An Interview with Stan Laurel.")

At the interview's beginning Laurel differentiates between types of low comedy—the Laurel & Hardy variety "contains an element of sympathy and simple truth that is absent in common slapstick, especially as practiced by the Keystone Kops and the Three Stooges." It is a well-taken point, though the elitist posturing is rare for Laurel; it does not surface again in the interview. Quite simply, the viewer is concerned with the comically violent plight of Laurel & Hardy, while the Keystone Kops and the Three Stooges seldom produce comic empathy, despite the occasional laugh. This is especially true of the Kops, whose machine-like comic rigidity removes any human concern about them and makes them the perfect poster boys for Henri Bergson's classic theory of comic "inelasticity" (when human beings become machine-like).

Laurel also offers further thoughts on the team's revolutionary slowdown in pacing: "This violent-pause effect . . . gave the audience a chance to relax and gave them a breather until the next brick fell on Ollie's head." There is an implied tie-in here with the previously mentioned "simplicity and simple truth," because Laurel sees this drawn-out comic pain as a "what's the use" sort of pathos.

The interview showcases a certain irony when Laurel compares the team's work with current trends in comedy: "We never dealt with satire or suggestive material. Although some of our films were broad parodies or burlesques of popular dramatic themes, there was no conscious attempt at being either sarcastic or offensive." While Laurel's nonpolitical defining of the comically antiheroic Stan & Ollie is well taken, the trends in 1950s American film comedy were often apt to be running from satire, too. Indeed, late-1950s interviews with Laurel & Hardy comedy contemporary Groucho Marx have him bemoaning the period absence of the satirical world in which the Marx Brothers thrived during the 1930s. (See my *The Marx Brothers: A Bio-Bibliography*, 1977.) After all, was not a less-satirical period a pivotal reason, after television, for why Laurel & Hardy enjoyed such a 1950s revival of interest?

Sometimes the later in life an interview takes place the simpler the explanations become. This piece is not without such oversimplifications. For example, Laurel has the duo's film career ending because "the public just got tired of low comedy. They began to demand more art in filming and less corn."

What hurt Laurel & Hardy in the 1940s was not the decline of low comedy but rather a lack of comedy understanding and support from 20th Century-Fox and M-G-M. If appreciation of low comedy had disappeared, there would not have been the phenomenal revival of interest for the team during the 1950s. Thus, it was not the times but rather the loss of quality control that hurt Laurel & Hardy, something acknowledged by Laurel in other interviews.

While low comedy has known varying degrees of popularity during the ages, it has never been completely banished from entertainment. Even while Laurel & Hardy were struggling during the 1940s, writer/director Preston Sturges had very successfully married sophisticated wit to low-comedy slapstick in films like *The Lady Eve* (1941). And today the low-comedy artistry of Stan & Ollie lives on in countless ways (see Chapter 2).

Finally, the Goldstein interview offers standard variations on a number of Laurel & Hardy subjects examined elsewhere, from the different personal interests of these teammates to their unrealized plans for TV. It is a broadly based interview meriting attention, though it lacks the knowing artistry of the Lisa Mitchell essay, "Laurels for Laurel," examined below.

On February 28, 1961, Associated Press movie writer James Bacon did an interview/article with Laurel that also featured French mime Marcel Marceau, who had made a pilgrimage to the comedian's Santa Monica home. Marceau observed, "I learned my art from watching Laurel & Hardy movies." (See also "Marcel Marceau on Stan Laurel: KUSF Interview, Early 1966," reprinted in the 1974 *Pratfall*, vol. 1, no. 11.) While Bacon's piece is entitled "Stan Laurel at 70: 'I'm All Washed Up,' " the comedian comes across in a much more upbeat mood. The negative title is merely Laurel's bald observation that because of ill health, which includes diabetes, he will not work again. Yet at the same time he mentions perpetual visitor Jerry Lewis, who is after Laurel to be a comedy consultant.

The interview rehashes a number of standard topics, from the team's greater popularity outside the United States to their lack of financial reimbursement for the great 1950s popularity of their old films on television. When asked about Chaplin's (then) omission from Hollywood Boulevard's "Walk of Fame" project, Laurel was even stronger than usual in his praise for him, "I think it's shocking . . . to omit the greatest [movie] artist of all . . . You can't rewrite history."

The interview is a broader overview than most. It closes with reference to a possible TV biography of the duo. Casting possibilities included Jackie Gleason or Jonathan Winters for Hardy, and a trio of choices for Laurel: Art Carney, Tony Perkins, or Dick Van Dyke. Not surprisingly, Laurel thought Van Dyke would best play him, but he was quite comfortable with either Gleason or Winters as Hardy.

On May 2, 1961 the *New York Morning Telegraph* ran the interview, "Laurel to Help Prepare TV Scripts on Team." The comedian was to look over scripts for a television cartoon series based on Stan & Ollie. Fittingly, he observed, "Some of the things we [Laurel & Hardy and company] did in those [old live-action] movies could be done in cartoons."

Laurel hoped the cartoons would not recycle previous Stan & Ollie storylines— "Bits and pieces of our old pictures won't be the way to attack it."

The comic highlight of the piece is the comedian's comment on Stan & Ollie dialogue, which was to be his primary focus on the cartoon scripts—"Ours was a special dialogue. It was the same dialogue all the time." Laurel went on to say his screen persona's lines were not that simple. Yet, his off-handed remark rang true. Like the patented "Here's another fine mess . . . " of Oliver, or Stanley's tearful scratching of his head with occasional variations on "I'm sorry," the Laurel & Hardy fan neither needed nor expected much dialogue— let alone variety.

Several interviews, including the Bacon piece, mention the team's greater popularity abroad. But there are obviously some U.S. devotees as fanatical as any in the world. A classic 1960s example of this was the Huntington, West Virginia, TV engineer Mike Polacek, about whom the February 1964 *8mm Collector* devoted two pieces: "My hobby, laurel & hardy" and "of mr. laurel and mr. hardy: Huntington Man Their No. 1 Fan." For Polacek, as for many others, Laurel & Hardy was an obsession. Years before the home video revolution Polacek had collected nearly a hundred films by the duo. The flip side of the super fan syndrome was that Laurel was equally loyal to these people. Whatever demons had once plagued the comedian through the messy marriages and bouts with the bottle were either gone or forever banished from public awareness. Not only did Laurel try to answer all his own fan mail, super fan Polacek was actually invited by the comedian to come visit for a week! (See Chapter 1 for a more detailed visit description.) "Regular guy" gestures such as these merely reinforce that fierce fan loyalty that makes it very difficult to be critical of an earlier Laurel.

The February 1964 issue of *8mm Collector* also boasted the short Laurel interview, "Meet a Gentleman! Stan Laurel!" The comedian had originally been approached to do an article for the journal, but he declined politely, saying writing was not "my cup of tea." (The admission itself is of special interest, since rare is the Laurel byline.) What eventually appeared was a rather basic interview (via correspondence) on the production side of the team's films.

In October 1964 the Hal Roach–authored essay "Living with Laughter" appeared in *Film and Filming*. The catalyst for the article was the completion of a season of Roach movies at the Cinematheque Francaise (Paris) and the National Film Theatre (London). (The following year the Gallery of Modern Art in New York put on "A Tribute to Hal Roach.") Because Roach discusses comedy in the context of his lengthy career, only a short section is devoted to Laurel & Hardy.

After a shaky opening on the duo, where he takes credit for their teaming and curiously describes them both as "English comedians," Roach has some interesting things to say. For instance, he noted how they complemented each other and increased the laugh ratio for a given bit: if "Hardy fell in the mud puddle, you would cut to his expression of disgust . . . then you cut to the bewildered Laurel looking at Hardy in the puddle, then back to Hardy." Consequently, there were three laughs instead of the one a solo comedian would have produced. Moreover, Roach might have added that with Ollie's direct-address tendencies (where he looks at the camera and thus makes direct connection with the viewer), he has a better opportunity to milk a bit for laughs, playing (as he does) off Stan's inspired stupidity.

Roach's comment that "The more ridiculous the situation the funnier they were" would seem to go against the Laurel & Hardy axiom of keeping things realistic. But Roach then describes the most realistic of situations—getting hay from a barn loft for a mule. It is only in the comically faulty reasoning of the duo that things become ridiculous. They decide it would be easier to take the mule to the loft and eliminate their hay-tossing chores. One is immediately reminded of their realistic carrying of a crated piano up a flight of stairs in *The Music Box* (1932) and the eventually ridiculous act of taking the box back down those seemingly endless steps because they have found an easier way to get to their destination.

Finally, there are some general Roach comments not specifically earmarked for Laurel & Hardy but that apply just the same. For example, Roach emphasized "as little dialogue as possible," reminiscent of McCarey's "do it visually" motto. And at an earlier point Roach has observed, "Great comedians are great pantomime artists and that goes from what we call the low comedian to the 'class' comedian like Cary Grant." Fittingly, despite the appropriate speaking voices of Laurel & Hardy, the meat of their comedy is visual. (For more on the physical comedy skills of Cary Grant, see my *Screwball Comedy A Genre of Madcap Romance*, 1986.)

In 1972, *Pratfall* (vol. 1, no. 9) reprinted an excerpt from an earlier Hal Roach interview on the team. Titled "H.R. on L. & H.," it is a revealing and blunt look at the volatile relationship between Roach and Laurel. A key focus concerns their falling out over *Babes in Toyland* (1934), with the comedian rejecting the producer's adaptation of the original play. Eventually Laurel got his way, but Roach was bitterly disappointed at how the film came out, claiming it was a commercial failure hurt by a condemnation from the "Parent Teachers Association of America" over storyland violence—"Instead of being a picture for children, it was condemned!" Period critics, however, praised the film.

Characterizing Hardy as someone who "did what he was told," Roach saves his wrath for Laurel. He found the comedian obsessed with being the total auteur, as was Charlie Chaplin. But even here, Roach finds Chaplin's work as very derivative, and warns that French comedian Tati was also trying to do too much. Fittingly, Roach later observes, "I never relied solely on one man on anything I did."

Other standard Roach comments include his fundamental belief in the inherently childlike nature of all comedy personae, his great respect for Laurel as a gagman but not a storyteller, and his theory that comedy should not be used to sustain a feature-length film.

The death of Laurel produced numerous career-in-review tributes and obituaries. The most methodically thorough is from the *New York Herald Tribune*, though its companion piece from the *New York Times* (both February 24, 1965) is equally effective because it is liberally peppered with quotes from the late comedian. Indeed, the *New York Times* piece is as if Laurel were narrating a review of his life. *The Times*'s obituary (February 24, 1965) is the most analytically poetic, with comments such as, Stan & Ollie were a "single unit, an expression of well-intentioned muddle-headedness in a harsh and practical world." These pieces are nicely complemented by Art Berman's *New York Journal-American* tribute "Great Comic's Epitaph: 'It's Been a Great Life' " (February 24), which spends more time on Laurel's retirement years (1955–1965), as well as literally his last days, using quoted remarks from his private physician, Dr. James Parrott.

Three separate items also helped make Laurel's funeral a media event—the ever-increasing cult status of the team, delivery of the eulogy by TV star Dick Van Dyke (a Laurel friend and fan), and the Laurel & Hardy comedy colleagues in attendance, from Buster Keaton and Patsy Kelly to Pat Buttram and Tim

Conway. Ironically, the most moving account of the funeral uncovered was an uncredited one found in the Laurel & Hardy clipping file of the Billy Rose Theatre Collection at the New York Public Library (Lincoln Center). Simply entitled "Film Comics at Funeral of Stan Laurel," it provided numerous excerpts from Van Dyke's eulogy, including the comically poignant gag Laurel made minutes before his death (quoted at the close of Chapter 1). For a thorough traditionally straightforward account of the funeral and eulogy, see the *New York Times*'s "Van Dyke Delivers Stan Laurel Eulogy" (February 27, 1965). (When McCabe's *Mr. Laurel & Mr. Hardy* was reissued in 1966, the foreword, "A Tribute by Dick Van Dyke," was drawn from his funeral eulogy for Laurel.)

Later in the year (November 23), Dick Van Dyke emceed an hour-long CBS special, *A Salute to Stan Laurel*. While the tribute was flawed by the top-heavy appearance of too many celebrity guests, publicity interviews before the event were the perfect opportunity for Van Dyke to reminisce about the comedian. An excellent example of this is Kay Gardella's *New York Daily News* piece (November 14), "Van Dyke to Emcee Stan Laurel Tribute."

See also the Bob Thomas interview of Van Dyke that appeared in the *New York Journal-American* (August 14, 1965). Done three months prior to Gardella's Van Dyke interview, as plans were just being put together for the Laurel special, it provides an early vantage point for the planned event. For instance, Van Dyke revealed: "The whole thing [the tribute] started at Stan Laurel's funeral . . . Gene Lester, the photographer, suggested it would be a good idea to have a tribute to the team on television, with proceeds to go to the Motion Picture Relief Fund." As the word quickly spread it became obvious the industry was "wild for the idea" and a special was born.

Despite the death of Laurel, Stan & Ollie had a highly visible 1965. In fact, it had already begun prior to his death. The team's Sons of the Desert fan club had been formed shortly before Laurel's death, and with his blessing. Moreover, the February 1965 issue of *Cahiers du Cinéma* contained the Serge Daney and Jean-Louis Noames interview with Leo McCarey, "Leo et les aléas." *Cahiers* later published this in its English series (January 1967) as "Taking Chances: Interview with Leo McCarey." The piece is at times very similar to author/director/interviewer Peter Bogdanovich's later unpublished "Leo McCarey Oral History" for the American Film Institute, which can be examined *only* at its Los Angeles library. (See both Chapter 1 and my earlier book, *Leo McCarey and the Comic Anti-Hero in American Film*.)

Part of the impetus for the Daney and Noames interview seems to have been the previous year's (1964) season of Roach films at the Cinémathèque Francaise (and the National Film Theatre). *Cahiers*'s opening comments note that the Laurel & Hardy short subjects shown in the Cinémathèque Francaise had been "supervised" by McCarey.

Since the interview attempts to cover McCarey's long career, references to Laurel & Hardy represent only one segment of the piece. However, the interview is most famous for McCarey's comments on Laurel's early attitude of superiority toward Hardy (again, see Chapter 1). Regardless, there is a wealth of Laurel & Hardy material here, from his many duties as team supervisor to his crucial role in putting together the pivotal *Putting Pants on Philip* (1927), when "no one wanted to make it." While McCarey's memory is not without flaws, such as minimizing Hardy's previous film acting experience, no history of the team is complete without his inclusion.

While McCarey himself died in 1969, old Laurel & Hardy related commentary from the director occasionally still surfaced—the most important being Bogdanovich's AFI-sponsored "Oral History" (1972). See also Bogdanovich's February 1972 *Esquire* piece, "Hollywood," which chronicles McCarey's amusing discovery of what would become a Stan & Ollie staple: the tit-for-tat routine.

Earlier articles on McCarey sometimes briefly feature the director's thoughts on his Laurel & Hardy period. For example, see Edward Fischer's *Ave Maria* (Catholic journal) piece "Leo McCarey Comes Our Way" (November 19, 1955), where the director discusses the pie-throwing birth of *The Battle of the Century* (1927). As an added side note on McCarey references, several Catholic journals paid attention to his career because of his strong Catholic faith, one that became the core of such celebrated films as *Going My Way* (1944) and *The Bells of St. Mary's* (1945). In addition to *Ave Maria*, articles can be found in the *Catholic Digest*, *Extension*, and *Sign: A National Catholic Monthly Magazine*.

Even McCarey articles that spend little or no time on the team can have value to Laurel & Hardy study, be it the rare McCarey-authored piece "Comedy and a Touch of Cuckoo" (*Extension*, November 1944) or a comic essay about McCarey with the run-on title, "Everything Happens to McCarey: During Those Sparse Times When He Isn't Breaking His Valuable Neck, Leo McCarey Does Direct Some Extraordinary Pictures" (by Sidney Carroll, *Esquire*, May 1943). The former piece finds McCarey revealing some of his thoughts on comedy, as applied to a scene from his *The Awful Truth* (1937). The latter essay (besides nicely connecting McCarey's real ties with the comic antihero world so often portrayed in his work) is also an amusing look at his professional career. And this overview includes an entertaining account of McCarey leaving the Roach company because the producer was just too healthy—no room for advancement by McCarey (see Chapter 1; for more on McCarey see my *Leo McCarey and the Comic Anti-Hero in American Film*, 1980.)

The spring 1967 issue of *The Cinemeditor* included an interview with Laurel & Hardy editor Bert Jordan. Entitled "A Life of Comedy," it was later reprinted (Spring 1968) in *Classic Film Collector*.

When one's subject is Laurel & Hardy, it is fitting that the most valuable item in the Jordan interview accidently surfaces in a comic anecdote the film editor means merely as a joke on himself. Like Laurel, Jordan is from England, but he has not mastered all the nuances of English . . . American style. Thus, when the comedian refers to a scene's "dumb waiter," Jordan assumes the focus is truly on a stupid waiter. It is a funny story that Laurel so enjoyed that he needled Jordan about it throughout their lengthy friendship.

In telling the anecdote, however, Jordan reconstructs some editing directions from Laurel: "Now, Bert, play the scene so that I leave the table in the long shot then go over to the dumb waiter and so on and so on." Though unfortunately brief, it does provide one with an idea of Laurel as the total filmmaker, because Jordan implies this is a typical example of Laurel's editing directions.

The first issue of *Pratfall* (1969) contained the interview "Babe London Visits Tent." Comedienne and long-time Laurel friend London appeared in the team's 1931 short subject *Our Wife*. The thrust of the piece concerned how pleasant the team was to work with, how Laurel was *Our Wife's* real director (instead of credited James Horne), and what a witty gentleman Laurel was during his last years—when London became especially close to him and his wife Ida.

Without trying to include every *Pratfall* first-person account with direct ties to Laurel & Hardy, the majority of the remaining pieces in this section are drawn from this journal's very rich pages.

The second issue of *Pratfall* (April 1969) contained an interview with character actor Mantan Moreland, best known for his role as chauffeur Birmingham Brown in the Charlie Chan films. Moreland appeared in Laurel & Hardy's *A-Haunting We Will Go* (1942), though he knew the team from the early 1930s. His comments on the movie are somewhat vague because he was simultaneously part of another film production (not an unusual situation for a popular supporting player during the studio era). Though *A-Haunting We Will Go* is an unintentionally sad film, produced during a sad part of the team's screen career, Moreland remembers Laurel as constantly being on: "Stan had people laughing all the time."

Moreland also recalls some flexibility with the script: "If they had something in the script that wasn't really funny, Stan would say, 'Wait a minute. Why don't you try this?' see, and we'd try to get something out of it."

An interesting link between the London and Moreland interviews is the similar descriptions of Hardy, though they concern production periods separated by over a decade. London observes, "I think Hardy took himself a little more seriously than Stanley did." Moreland states, "most of the time you'd see him [Hardy] serious." Moreland adds that when rehearsing, Hardy "didn't want any fooling at all and Stan wanted to play all the time. Like they'd be bawling each other out in the picture? That's the way they'd [entertainingly] be all the time."

This possibly provides a clue to any friction that might have existed in the first days of the team (see McCarey's comments in Chapter 1). By most accounts, including those of London and Moreland, Laurel & Hardy got along fine. Still, the teaming of a serious performer with a kidder (who was also the dominant behind-the-scene partner) might have initially generated some sparks in the beginning McCarey days. Moreover, as even the interview with film editor Bert Jordan revealed, Laurel could be relentless in his kidding once he was given a comic opening (as in the "dumb waiter"). However, none of these pieces mention what former Laurel wife Ruth called his "temperamental" nature (see "Ruth Laurel Remembers," in both Chapter 1 and later in this chapter).

Producer Joe Rock's "The Way It Was" piece appeared in *Pratfall*'s March 1970 issue (vol. 1, no. 4). Rock knew both members of the duo before they were teamed (he produced twelve of Laurel's silent comedies), and this is the period on which he focuses.

The fall 1971 edition of the *Classic Film Collector* contained the Jeannette Mazurki piece "Stan Laurel's Daughter Recalls Comic." This short, eclectic interview, pasted together as one rambling monologue, is capable of being quite moving: "As a child I wasn't impressed [with my father's fame]. I only resented that when we would go someplace he would be completely mobbed and I could never have him to myself." Other observations range from Laurel's favorite Stan & Ollie film (*Way Out West*, 1937), to the comedian's enjoyment of his boat and fishing.

The woman Lois came to know as a second mother also gave a 1971 interview—"Ruth Laurel Remembers" (*Pratfall*, vol. 1, no. 5). It is long for *Pratfall*, covering parts of five pages. And while she obviously still feels great affection for the comedian, her comments are direct. For instance, she describes a "good relationship" between Laurel and Hardy, yet one not helped by her husband's "temperamental" nature. She also nicely captures the comedian's sometime roller-coaster emotional state with a story from the production of *Sons of the Desert* (1933). During the wet and cold middle-of-the-night shooting of the film's roof rain scene, Ruth had been in attendance, at Laurel's request. At its completion she helped get him to his dressing room and provided the comedian with a good hot toddy, whereupon Laurel started to cry. When asked why, he replied, "You're the only woman that's ever seemed to care about my personal health."

She also provides a simple hypothesis (that sounds borrowed from Laurel) on why Chaplin so wanted to be the social climber and her husband was simply content to make comedy: Chaplin's early poverty differed from the economic freedom, even relative affluence, of Laurel's upbringing.

These observations and others make this a most recommended article. Moreover, like a good entertainer, she also manages to come up with a very strong close: "Stan had a changeable temperament. If he wanted to do something, he might change in 15 minutes. I'm the same way. We got along great. Through *three* marriages we got along great!"

The last line was added as comedy, but it beautifully summarizes that "changeable temperament," and how the comedian could be such an altar boy, especially with kindred spirit Ruth Laurel.

Joining the Ruth Laurel interview in this *Pratfall* issue is Robert Durden's brief account of attending an August 22, 1940 Red Cross benefit show that featured Laurel & Hardy. Taking place on San Francisco Bay's Treasure Island (which is also the title for the piece), Durden quotes from a memo to himself written immediately after the team's fifteen-minute sketch "How to Get a Driver's License." These recorded impressions and additional Durden thoughts make for a modest time capsule of an event that was a catalyst for Laurel & Hardy's 1940s tours.

In 1972 *Pratfall* (vol. 1, no. 8) featured a short piece entitled "Babe's Night Out," which featured Hardy's mid-1940s Hollywood supper-club habits at his preferred Granada Club. The material, in part, is drawn from a *Savannah Evening News* column by Todd Thomey (date uncited), which uses entertainer Jerry Wilson as its window on the Granada, where he was the young piano playing talent. Though interesting, it is all too brief and rather vague, beyond mentioning that Hardy enjoyed singing a song after his supper.

In the following *Pratfall* (vol. 1, no. 9), however, Wilson himself pens a follow-up essay, "Return of Babe's Night Out." This is longer and more informative than the first installment and corrects errors made in the earlier article. Though there is nothing earthshattering here, it is an entertaining peek at the private world of Hardy—about which so little is known.

Hardy sang two of his favorite songs the first time Wilson played for him in the Granada, "You Are the Ideal of My Dreams" and "Shine on Harvest Moon." Hardy's horse-betting habits frequently kept him broke, and it is gently implied that he sang for his supper that night, after club owner Al Quodbach had met him at the golf course earlier in the day.

Hardy, moreover, enjoyed the singing attention he received from Granada's Hollywood crowd, which included William Frawley and Ida Lupino that first night. It was also probably a pleasant throwback to his early career days as a nightclub singer.

Wilson interacted with Hardy on many other Granada nights and was always impressed with the modest sameness of the comedian. Two interesting final Wilson asides concern Hardy's gambling habit and his partner.

Though no specific time is given, Wilson states that a worried Hardy once had betting debts of $50,000 paid by a rich admirer. And Wilson asked Hardy "once why he never brought Stan in with him and he said that they had had a little squabble and also that Stan did not go out as much as he did."

Lee Patrick, the gangster's moll Dorcas of Laurel & Hardy's best post–Roach studio film, *Jitterbugs* (1943), was interviewed in the June 1973 issue of *Film Fan Monthly*. Though little space is devoted to the film, she proves provocative in her attack on critics praising the team for its improvisation. She does this out of respect for the work Laurel & Hardy put into making their comedy look spontaneous—"Their timing, their finesse, their reactions—were as carefully worked out and rehearsed as a Fred Astaire dance routine." Of course, one heard variations of this, as it related to 1950s television, in the later Laurel interviews, especially when addressing the team's shock at being thrust unprepared upon the live broadcast of "This is Your Life."

The 1974 *Pratfall* (vol. 1, no. 11) included a dialogue with pioneer filmmaker Jess Robbins (by Jordan Young), who directed Hardy in a number of Vitagraph shorts, as well as the *accidental* first Laurel & Hardy film, *Lucky Dog* (1919), where Hardy was merely a supporting player. The Robbins quote, "Nobody Knew Much About Anything Then," serves as the piece's title and a commentary on these early filmmaking days.

There is an interview, simply entitled "Ellinor Van Der Veer," with this minor Laurel & Hardy supporting player in a 1977 *Pratfall* (vol. 2, no. 2). Interviewer Robert Satterfield likens her to a modest (and generally unbilled) version of what Margaret Dumont was to the Marx Brothers—the high society straight woman. In the interview Van Der Veer is charming but at nearly ninety years of age she remembers little that is specific to the seven Laurel & Hardy films in which she appeared, besides the very pleasant working conditions on the Roach lot. As a provocative side note, her measuring stick for such working conditions are her unpleasant experiences under director Cecil B. DeMille, about whom she is most blunt: "He was a bastard."

Lisa Mitchell's July 1977 *Westways* essay, "Laurels for Laurel," is the best-written, most-poignant reminiscence I have encountered on the team, though the primary focus is on Laurel. Other pieces might provide more raw data, but Mitchell, like the good biographer, is able both to bring her character to life and genuinely give feelings to the facts. In writing about an artist, she has created something artistic.

"Laurels for Laurel" brings to mind the excellent Ray Bradbury 1987 short story, "The Laurel and Hardy Love Affair." But for the biographer, Mitchell's loving chronicle is the more important, simply because it really occurred.

Mitchell first met the comedian in 1956 when she was sixteen. While her classmates followed the career of contemporary performers like Elvis, she continued to visit and correspond with Laurel until his death. Like the couple in Bradbury's story, the duo "played Laurel and Hardy." Reenacting scenes from the team's films, Mitchell was Laurel while the comedian played Hardy. (As a child Mitchell had also used the nickname Stan—anticipating the Bradbury piece.)

Even when their many talks cover old ground, Mitchell generally manages to provide something extra. For instance, like Babe London and others, Mitchell mentions Laurel's ongoing wit during his retirement years, and provides examples. Thus, if the comedian were mildly ill, he would say, "I'm just so busy! I have to iron my bra and peel the olives." Or, once when Laurel declined candy because of his diabetes, he observed, slipping into his Stan persona, "I can't have any candy dear . . . I'm *diabolic*, you know!"

Like a classic comedy star, therefore, Mitchell successfully kept pathos from becoming bathos, even when she describes neighborhood children coming to his door to meet the forever-young Stan they knew from television. Not wanting to shock young fans who did not recognize the elderly Laurel as their hero, the comedian would tell them, "He's not home now, dears. He's away at the studio making pictures, but I'll tell him you came by."

Mitchell is also good about mentioning an occasional reference of interest, be it the 1959 *Films in Review* Laurel interview, or Paul Conrad's 1965 cartoon at the time of Laurel's death, where Stan has now joined Ollie in heaven . . . only to immediately drop his angel's harp on his partner's foot.

The essay is further complemented by the framing device with which it opens

and closes: an eight-year-old Mitchell's wonderful introduction to Laurel & Hardy via a Los Angeles theatre fittingly named The Laugh Movie. Thanks to Mitchell, it is now a memory for the ages.

Jerry Lewis's 1982 autobiography, *Jerry Lewis: In Person* (with Herb Gluck), devotes several pages to his Stan Laurel friendship in the "Book Six" section of the volume. The two met late in Laurel's life (1960), with Lewis playing comedy disciple. As was his nature, Laurel freely shared his memories (including his father's comedy influence) and his (Laurel's) thoughts on comedy theory— such as avoid imposing "moral lessons." Lewis freely acknowledges a great comedy debt to Stan Laurel.

A short joint interview with Laurel's daughter Lois and Hardy's widow Lucille Price appears in a 1982 *Pratfall* (vol. 2, no. 5). Again, Lois provides a moving memory, but this time about Hardy: "When I'd come down to the studio and I'd come through the door he'd always sing . . . ['Shine on Harvest Moon']. I always called him 'Uncle Babe.' He was a marvelous, marvelous man, and he and my father were very close."

Gilbert Salachas came up with a truly "imaginative" Laurel & Hardy interview in the August 3–9, 1985 issue of *Telerama*. Entitled "Laurel et Hardy: 'Impossible n'est pas anglais,' " the piece is a mixture of real quotes by the team (drawn from Roland Lacourbe's *Laurel et Hardy*) and questions by Salachas (plus a comic running commentary by this "creative" interviewer). It is a fun but valuable exercise in Laurel & Hardy, which by its very nature encourages readers to reconsider their own image of the team.

In the August 1986 issue of *Bowler Dessert* the Laurel & Hardy memories of Steve King are featured in Philip Sheard's "Laurel and Hardy Visit Any Old Port." Drawn from the team's December 1953 music hall visit to the port town of Hull, England, a young Steve King was able to meet and talk with the team, as well as closely follow their backstage activities. What surfaces is another valentine to the comedians' thoughtfulness, from Laurel's views on answering fan mail to Hardy's democratic politeness in getting supporting performer signatures for the team's autograph book. (For more on the 1953 tour, see "Laurel and Hardy in Nottingham," from the Spring 1988 *Bowler Dessert*. It contains rare commentary on Laurel's sister Beatrice Olga.)

In contrast to the sublime *Bowler Dessert* pieces, Joan MacTrevor's "Laurel et Hardy: la triste histoire des rois du rive morts dans la misère" from the June 11, 1987 *Cine Revue*, overemphasizes the sad side of their final years. While there were obviously many problems, MacTrevor's essay and occasional Laurel & Hardy quote (and those of actor/fan Dana Andrews) turn the comedians' last years into total melodrama. As if to demonstrate the fallacy of this position, MacTrevor inexplicably includes Laurel's upbeat joke about the caveman preferring hard labor to marriage (see Chapter 1).

Laurence Reardon's "Laurel & Hardy in Coventry" (1988) is a brief monograph affectionately detailing the team's 1947 and 1952 touring stops in the city. By talking to numerous fans who were there, Reardon manages to regenerate a sense of the excitement sparked by the team. Programs for both shows are reproduced, as well as some photographs.

As these closing entries reiterate, even including MacTrevor's maudlin article, the Laurel & Hardy heritage is as much one of love as laughter.

LAUREL & HARDY ARCHIVAL HOLDINGS

There are a number of libraries that provide extensive holdings on Laurel & Hardy, including one devoted exclusively to the team—the small but ambitious archive run by curator Bill Cubin in Ulverston (England), the town in which Laurel was born.

The British Film Institute (London-BFI) has extensive holdings on the team, from stills to clipping files. BFI provides excellent print coverage of the duo's British tours—something seriously lacking in U.S. archives. Moreover, of all the major research libraries in which I have studied (on this project and other books), BFI is easily the most professionally thorough in its assistance.

Invaluable material from abroad was also found at the Cinémathèque Francaise in Paris.

Within the United States, libraries of central importance are the New York Public Library at Lincoln Center, which houses the Billy Rose Theatre Collection; the Margaret Herrick Library at the Academy of Motion Picture Arts and Sciences (Beverly Hills); and the American Film Institute (AFI-Beverly Hills).

The academy library contains several all-important clipping files on the team, besides numerous other files on people of special interest to the student of the duo. In addition, the academy also offers pertinent script and stills collections.

The Billy Rose Theatre Collection also contains several invaluable Laurel & Hardy clipping files, complemented as at the academy by relevant files and stills. Furthermore, there is an excellent collection of recorded material. The New York Public Library system has, appropriately, an outstanding collection of former New York City newspapers on microfilm; these were very helpful in tracing a number of nearly forgotten Laurel & Hardy articles. (While the files in the Billy Rose Theatre collection are invaluable, many articles have only partial reference citations and/or are in a deteriorating or incomplete state. Thus, the microfilm collection [housed in the library's 43rd street "Newspaper Annex"] is pivotal, as one needs to play detective more often than even the traditional researcher.)

As related to Laurel & Hardy, the American Film Institute's most valuable holding is the unpublished Leo McCarey Oral History, which can only be examined in its library. AFI also offers clipping files and a stills collection.

Three other libraries proved helpful in this study. The University of Iowa's (Iowa City) main library, with its outstanding periodical collection, furnished a large number of Laurel & Hardy articles. UCLA's Theatre Arts Library (Los Angeles), housed in the University Research Library, provided access to several more clipping files on the duo. The Museum of Modern Art (New York City) offered both another source of stills and some very helpful screening arrangements.

5

Bibliographical Checklist of Key Laurel & Hardy Sources

BOOKS ABOUT LAUREL & HARDY

Barr, Charles. *Laurel & Hardy*. London: Studio Vista, 1967; repr. Berkeley: University of California Press, 1974.

Borde, Raymond, and Charles Perrin. *Laurel et Hardy*. Lyon, France: Serdoc (Premier Plan series), September 1965.

Coursodon, Jean-Pierre. *Laurel et Hardy*. Paris: Anthologie du Cinéma (publisher as well as name of series in which this study appeared), October 1965.

Crowther, Bruce. *Laurel and Hardy: Clown Princes of Comedy*. London: Columbus Books, 1987.

Everson, William K. *The Films of Laurel & Hardy*. Secaucus, New Jersey: Citadel Press, 1967; repr. 1972.

Giusti, Marco. *Laurel & Hardy*. Venice: Castora Cinema series (vol. 57), September 1978.

Guiles, Fred Lawrence. *Stan: The Life of Stan Laurel*. New York: Stein and Day, 1980.

Jones, Lori S., ed. *Laurel and Hardywood* (special quadruple edition of *Pratfall* magazine). Universal City, California: Pratfall, 1985.

Lacourbe, Roland. *Laurel et Hardy: au l'enfance de l'art*. Paris: Seghers Ed. Cinema Club, 1975.

Leeflang, Thomas. *The World of Laurel and Hardy*. Translated by Phil Goddard. Netherlands: Unieboek B.V., 1986; repr. Leicester, England: Windward, 1988.

McCabe, John. *The Comedy World of Stan Laurel*. Garden City, New York: Doubleday & Company, Inc., 1974.

———. *Mr. Laurel & Mr. Hardy*. New York: Doubleday and Company, Inc., 1961; new edition, New York: Grosset and Dunlop, 1966.

McCabe, John, Al Kilgore, and Richard W. Bann. *Laurel & Hardy*. London: W. H. Allen, 1975; repr. New York: Ballantine Books, 1976.

McCabe, John. *BABE: The Life of Oliver Hardy*. London: Robson Books, 1989.

Maltin, Leonard, ed. *The Laurel & Hardy Book*. New York: Curtis Books, 1973.

Nollen, Scott Allen. *THE BOYS: The Cinematic World of Laurel and Hardy*. Jefferson, North Carolina: McFarland & Company, Inc., 1989.

Owen-Pawson, Jenny, and Bill Mouland. *Laurel Before Hardy*. Kendal, England: Westmorland Gazette, 1984.

Scagnetti, Jack. *The Laurel & Hardy Scrapbook*. Middle Village, New York: Jonathan David Publishers, 1976.

Skretvedt, Randy. *Laurel and Hardy: The Magic Behind the Movies*. Beverly Hills, California: Moonstone Press, 1987.

Smith, Leon. *Following the Comedy Trail*. Bellflower, California: G. J. Enterprises, 1984.

————. *A Guide to Laurel and Hardy Movie Locations*. Bellflower, California: G. J. Enterprises, 1982.

SHORTER WORKS ABOUT LAUREL & HARDY

Agee, James. "Comedy's Greatest Era" (from *Life*, September 3, 1949). In *Agee on Film*, vol. 1, New York: Grosset and Dunlap, 1969, pp. 2–19.

Ainsworth, Katherine. "A Captive of a Comic Cult Confesses," *Los Angeles Times* ("Calendar" section), July 20, 1980, p. 3.

A. J. Jefferson's Diary During His 1935–36 Visit with Son Laurel, unpublished family document.

Alley, Homer. "of mr. laurel and mr. hardy: Huntington Man Their No. 1 Fan," *Herald-Advertiser* (Huntington, West Virginia), August 4, 1963 (n.p. cited); repr. in *8mm Collector*, February 1964, p. 8.

Anderson, Janice. "Laurel and Hardy." In *History of Movie Comedy*. New York: Exeter Books, 1985, pp. 89–95.

"Babe Hardy, the Fat Boy with Vim," *Florida Metropolis* (Jacksonville newspaper), February 20, 1916, p. 5–c.

Babes in Toyland review, *Variety*, December 18, 1934, p. 12.

Bacon, James. "Stan Laurel at 70: 'I'm All Washed Up.' " AP piece that appeared in *Pittsburgh Post Gazette*, February 26, 1961 (n.p. cited); repr. in *8mm Collector*, Spring 1965, p. 10.

Barnes, Peter. "Cuckoo," *Films and Filming*, August 1960, pp. 15, 32.

Benet, Lorenzo. "Bozo Stuck on Paying Tribute to Laurel & Hardy," *Los Angeles Daily News*, October 30, 1985 (n.p. cited). In "Laurel & Hardy Files," Special Collections, Margaret Herrick Library, Academy of Motion Picture Arts and Sciences, Beverly Hills, California.

Berman, Art. "Great Comic's Epitaph: 'It's Been a Great Life,' " *New York Journal-American*, February 24, 1965, p. 16.

Bermel, Albert. Chapter 8, "The Talking Thirties." In *Farce*. New York: Simon and Schuster, 1982, pp. 213–16.

Best, Natalie. "Popularity Rains on Laurel & Hardy: An Exclusive Interview," *TV Time Magazine*, September 8, 1951 (n.p. cited); repr. in *Pratfall* (vol. 2, no. 5), 1982, pp. 12–13.

Blanche, Ed. "Laurel and Hardy Make the Top Ten," *Los Angeles Times*, February 18, 1976, Section 4, p. 11.

Blyth, Jeffrey. "The Twilight of Clowns," *London Daily Mail*, November 13, 1959 (n.p. cited). In the "Laurel & Hardy Files," British Film Institute (London).

Boehnel, William. *Block-Heads* review, *New York World-Telegram*, August 30, 1938 (n.p. cited). In "*Block-Heads* File," Billy Rose Theatre Collection, New York Public Library at Lincoln Center.

———. *Way Out West* review, *New York World-Telegram*, May 4, 1937 (n.p. cited). In "*Way Out West* File," Billy Rose Theatre Collection, New York Public Library at Lincoln Center.

Bogdanovich, Peter. "Hollywood," *Esquire*, February 1972, pp. 8–10.

———. "Leo McCarey Oral History." Los Angeles: American Film Institute, 1972.

Bradbury, Ray. "The Laurel and Hardy Love Affair" (fiction), *Playboy*, December 1987, pp. 76–78, 210–11; repr. in condensed form in *Reader's Digest*, September 1988, pp. 149–52, and included in Bradbury book collection, *The Toynbee Convector*. New York: Alfred A. Knopf, 1987, pp. 83–92.

Britain, Jim (transcribed by). "This Is Your Life" (broadcast December 1, 1954), *Pratfall* (vol. 1, nos. 8 and 9), 1972, pp. 8–11 and 9–11.

Brooks, Leo. "Fan Or Buff," *Shifting Sands*, October 1988, n.p.

———. "Felix Knight and the Boys," *Shifting Sands*, December 1988, pp. [8–9].

———. "The Forties—a Retrospect" (three-part 1987 series), *Shifting Sands*, October, p. [6], November, p. [2], and December, p. [5].

———. "Hardy and Rogers: (*What Might Have Been)*", *Shifting Sands*, December 1988, pp. [11–12].

———. "Hardy Takes Charge," *Shifting Sands*, February 1988, p. [5].

———. "Mae Charlotte Dahlberg," *Shifting Sands*, December 1988, pp. [3–5].

———. "Scripts," *Shifting Sands*, February 1988, pp. [4–5].

———. "Teamwork," *Shifting Sands*, December 1988, p. [12].

———. "Vaudeville," *Shifting Sands*, January 1988, pp. [1–2].

———. "Worth a Thousand Words," *Shifting Sands*, October 1988, p. [5].

Burgeon, Vivien. "THE BIG SNEEZE: A Visit with Billy Gilbert," *Pratfall* (vol. 1, no. 3), 1969, pp. 4–7.

Byrd, Larry. "Babe London Visits Tent," *Pratfall* (vol. 1, no. 1), 1969, pp. 6–7.

Byrd, Larry, and Lee Blackburn. "Pratfall Interview: Mantan Moreland," *Pratfall* (vol. 1, no. 2), 1969, pp. 9–11.

Calder, Ritchie. "Laurel in Shirt Sleeves Holds Family Party," *London Daily Herald*, July 25, 1932, p. 9. (This issue also featured a front-page picture of the comedian with his father and stepmother.)

Canby, Vincent. "Slapstick That Sticks," *New York Times*, October 12, 1969, pp. 1, 13; repr. in *The National Society of Film Critics on Movie Comedy*, ed. by Stuart Byron and Elisabeth Weis. New York: Penguin Books, 1977, pp. 45–47.

Carlisle, John C. "Babes in Toyland (March of the Wooden Soldiers)." In *Magill's Survey of Cinema: English Language Films* (second series, vol. 1), ed. by Frank Magill. Englewood Cliffs, New Jersey: Salem Press, 1981, pp. 137–140.

Carroll, Kathleen. *Laurel & Hardy's Laughing '20s* review, *New York Daily News*, November 18, 1965 (n.p. cited). In *Collections of Newspaper Criticism*, Billy Rose Theatre Collection, New York Public Library at Lincoln Center.

Carroll, Sidney. "Everything Happens to McCarey: During those sparse times when he isn't breaking his valuable neck, Leo McCarey does direct some extraordinary pictures," *Esquire*, May 1943, pp. 57, 140–42.

Chavance, Louis. "Stan Laurel et Oliver Hardy," *La Revue du Cinema* (no. 7), pp. 28–36.

Christon, Lawrence. "The Discreet Charm of Laurel & Hardy," *Los Angeles Times* ("Calendar" section), January 10, 1988, pp. 4–5, 72.

Chump At Oxford, A review, *Variety*, February 21, 1940, p. 12.

Cohen, John S., Jr. *Sons of the Desert* review, *New York Sun*, January 1, 1934 (n.p. cited). In "*Sons of the Desert* File," Billy Rose Theatre Collection, New York Public Library at Lincoln Center.

Cooper, Ron. "Ollie and Stan: Two Minds without a Single Thought," *Saturday Evening Post*, Fall 1971, pp. 94–97, 114.

Creelman, Eileen. *Jitterbugs* review, *New York Sun*, June 5, 1943 (n.p. cited). In "*Jitterbugs* File," Billy Rose Theatre Collection, New York Public Library at Lincoln Center.

Crist, Judith. *Laurel and Hardy Laughing 20's* review, *New York Herald Tribune*, November 18, 1965 (n.p. cited). In *Collections of Newspaper Clippings of Moving Picture Criticism*. Billy Rose Theatre Collection, New York Public Library at Lincoln Center.

Crowther, Bosley. *A Chump at Oxford* review, *New York Times*, February 20, 1940, p. 17.

———. *Swiss Miss* review, *New York Times*, June 4, 1938, p. 18.

Daney, Serge and Jean-Louis Noames. "Leo et les aléas," *Cahiers du Cinéma*, February 1965, pp. 11–20; *Cahiers* English series published it as "Taking Chances: Interview with Leo McCarey," January 1967, pp. 43–54.

Dean, Loretta K. "THOSE FUNNY BOYS: A Few Inside Facts About the Screen's Funniest Pair of Comedians and the Man Who Has Photographed Most of Their Pictures," *American Cinematographer*, October 1929, pp. 4–5, 39; repr. as "The Screen's Funniest Comics" in *8mm Film*, February 1964, p. 8.

"Deepest Cut," *Theatre Arts*, September 1957, p. 14.

DuBrow, Rick. "Stan Laurel, Now 70, Rips Modern Hollywood Practices," *New York Morning Telegraph*, August 1, 1960 (n.p. cited). In "Laurel & Hardy Files," Billy Rose Theatre Collection, New York Public Library at Lincoln Center.

Durgnat, Raymond. Chapter 14, "Beau Chumps and Church Bells." In *The Crazy Mirror: Hollywood Comedy and the American Image*. Plymouth, England: Latimer Trend & Co., 1969; repr. New York: Dell, 1972, pp. 93–96.

"Edgar Kennedy: The Slow Burn," *Pratfall* (vol. 1, no. 2), 1969, pp. 4–5.

Everson, William. "The Crazy World of Laurel," *Take One*, no. 9, 1968, pp. 16–19.

Farber, Manny. "White Elephant Art Versus Termite Art," *Film Culture*, Winter 1962–63, pp. 9–13.

Fellner, Chris. "L & H Hit the Charts," *Pratfall* (vol. 2, no. 2), 1977, p. 3.

"Fiddle and the Bow, The," *New York Times*, August 9, 1957, p. 18.

"Film Comedians in Leeds: Whirlwind Tour of the Provinces by Laurel and Hardy," August 3, 1932 (n.p. and source cited), in the Laurel & Hardy Museum, (Ulverston, England).

"Film Comics at Funeral of Stan Laurel" (n.p. and source cited). In "Laurel & Hardy Files," Billy Rose Theatre Collection, New York Public Library at Lincoln Center.

Fischer, Edward. "Leo McCarey Comes Our Way," *Ave Maria*, November 19, 1955, p. 26.

Fox, Ian. "Laurel High-hats Hardy," *Film Weekly* (England), July 29, 1932, p. 17.

Frank, Elizabeth. "Laurel and Hardy Find New Fame," *Nottingham Chronicle* (England)

October 14, 1953 (n.p. cited). In the "Laurel & Hardy Files," British Film Institute (London).

"Funny Mr. Hardy's UNFUNNY Alimony Troubles," *The American Weekly*, January 27, 1946, p. 4.

"Funny Mr. Laurel Who Keeps on Getting Married," *New York Journal-American*, February 23, 1941, p. 5.

"Fun with Laurel and Hardy: Seeking the Fool-proof Job," *London Times*, March 16, 1961, p. 18.

Gardella, Kay. "Van Dyke to Emcee Stan Laurel Tribute," *New York Daily News*, November 14, 1965, Section 2, p. 30.

Garland, Robert. *Way Out West* review, *New York American*, May 4, 1937 (n.p. cited). In *"Way Out West* File," Billy Rose Theatre Collection, New York Public Library at Lincoln Center.

Gehring, Wes D. "Film's First Comic Anti-Heroes: Leo McCarey's Laurel and Hardy," *Ball State University Forum*, Autumn 1979, pp. 46–56.

———. "Leo McCarey: The Man Behind Laurel & Hardy," *Films in Review*, November 1979, pp. 543–49.

Gifford, Denis. "Laurel and Hardy," *Classic Film Collector*, Summer 1968, p. 36. See also, Gifford's "Flavor of the Month," *Films and Filming*, October 1984.

———. "The Latter Days of Laurel and Hardy," *Classic Film Collector*, Fall/Winter 1968, pp. 46, 53.

Glaze, Ann. "No Laughs in Laurel Home-Life, So Comedian and Wife Separate," *Movie Classic*, February 1933, p. 28.

Goldstein, Larry. "An Interview with Stan Laurel"(originally printed in 1961/1965); repr. without full citation in *Pratfall* (vol. 2, no. 2), 1977, pp. 8–9.

Great Guns review, *New York Times*, October 3, 1941, p. 27.

Greene, Graham. *A Chump at Oxford* review, *The Spectator*, February 23, 1940, p. 248.

Grierson, John. "Clowns of the Screen," *Everyman*, October 29, 1931, p. 430.

———. "The Logic of Comedy" and "Summary and Survey: 1935." In *Grierson on Documentary*, ed. by Forsyth Hardy. New York: Harcourt, Brace and Company, 1947, pp. 28–37 and pp. 125–43. Laurel & Hardy excerpts reprinted as "GRIERSON on Laurel & Hardy," *Pratfall* (vol. 2, no. 3), 1978, pp. 12–13.

Halliwell, Leslie. Chapter 7, "I'll bet you eight to five that we meet Dorothy Lamour: AMERICAN FILM COMEDY, 1930–45." In *Double Take and Fade Away*. London: Grafton Books, 1987, pp. 125–30.

———. "On the Trail of the Lonesome Pine: *Way Out West.*" In *Halliwell's Hundred: A Nostalgic Choice of Films from the Golden Age*. London: Granada, 1982, pp. 389–93.

———. "Our Dear Old Friends: *Sons of the Desert.*" In *Halliwell's Hundred: A Nostalgic Choice of Films from the Golden Age*. London: Granada, 1982, pp. 326–30.

Hall, Mordaunt. *The Devil's Brother* review, *New York Times*, June 10, 1933, pp. 16.

"Hardy of Laurel and Hardy Dies with Last Message to Wife Unspoken," *News Chronicle*, August 8, 1957 (n.p. cited). In the "Laurel & Hardy Files," British Film Institute (London).

Harmetz, Aljean. "Hal Roach to Receive Special Oscar," *New York Times*, March 12, 1984 (Arts/ Entertainment section), p. C 13.

Heath, Wes. "A Critique of the Critics," *Pratfall* (vol. 2, no. 2), 1977, pp. 12–13.

Herridge, Frances. "Laurel & Hardy Slapstick at Beekman," *New York Post*, November 18, 1965, p. 52.

Herring, Robert. ["On Laurel & Hardy"], *Close Up*, May 1930, pp. 364–68.

Hewson, David. "West End Opening for Laurel and Hardy Play," *The Times* (London), June 14, 1984, p. 3.

Hoffman, Allan. "The Twilight Years" (series, from his "dick and doof" column), *Classic Film Collector*, Summer 1969–Spring 1971.

Hogbin, John. "Laurel and Hardy Retain Their Appeal," *Eltham and Kentish Times* (England), August 18, 1961, p. 3.

"H.R. on L & H" ("Hal Roach on Laurel & Hardy"—excerpt from an interview). Reprinted without full citation in *Pratfall* (vol. 1, no. 9), 1972, pp. 4–6.

"I'll Never Work Again—Laurel," *Evening News* (London), August 8, 1957 (n.p. cited). In the "Laurel & Hardy Files," British Film Institute (London).

Interview with Lois Laurel and Lucille Hardy, *Pratfall* (vol. 2, no. 2), 1982, p. 11.

Jefferson, Joseph. "My Lad Laurel by Stan's Father," *Picturegoer Weekly*, January 9, 1932, pp. 16–17; repr. in *Pratfall* (vol. 1, no. 4), 1970, pp. 4–6.

Jenkinson, Philip. "In the Picture," *Radio Times*, September 16–23, 1988, p. 42.

Johaueson, Blaud. *Way Out West* review, *New York Daily Mirror*, May 4, 1937 (n.p. cited). In "*Way Out West* File," Billy Rose Theatre Collection, New York Public Library at Lincoln Center.

Johnson, Timothy W. "Big Business." In *Magill's Survey of Cinema: Silent Films* (vol. 1), ed. by Frank Magill, Englewood Cliffs, New Jersey: Salem Press, 1982, pp. 209–11.

Jones, Hank. "Here's to Finn!" *Pratfall* (vol. 1, no. 1), 1969, pp. 4–5.

Kanin, Garson. "Another Fine Mess: Laurel and Hardy." In *Together Again!: Stories of the Great Hollywood Teams*. Garden City, New York: Doubleday & Company, Inc., 1981, pp. 42–57.

Kennaugh, Alan. "Stan is Home," *TV Times*, August 6–12, 1983, pp. 10–11.

Kerkhoff, Jim (compiler). "Stan on Stage," *Pratfall* (vol. 1, no. 8), 1972, p. 7.

Kerr, Walter. Chapters 33 and 34, "Laurel and Hardy: The First Turnaround," and "Laurel and Hardy: The Saving Turnaround." In *The Silent Clowns*. New York: Alfred A. Knopf, 1975, pp. 318–35.

"The L. & H. Cult," *Time*, July 14, 1967, pp. 74–75.

Lahue, Kalton C. Chapter 6, "Hal Roach and the Rolin Phunphilms"; Chapter 7, "Comedy and the Independents, 1915–19"; Chapter 9, "Silver Screen and Golden Comedy." In *World of Laughter: The Motion Picture Comedy Short, 1910–1930*. Norman: University of Oklahoma Press, pp. 93–94, 104–7, 138–40.

[Laurel & Hardy and TV], *London Daily Express*, October 10, 1953 (n.p. cited). In the "Laurel & Hardy Files," British Film Institute (London).

"Laurel and Hardy: Au Revoir," *Philadelphia Bulletin*, February 28, 1965. Reprinted in *8mm Collector*, Spring 1965, p. 11.

"Laurel and Hardy: Enthusiastic Admirers in the North," *Kinematograph* (England), August 4, 1932, p. 12.

[Laurel & Hardy in 1947 London], *Daily Star* (London), February 12, 1947; in the "Laurel & Hardy Files," British Film Institute (London).

"Laurel and Hardy in Nottingham," *Bowler Dessert*, Spring 1988, pp. 14–15.

"Laurel and Hardy $10,000 in Dayton," *Billboard*, February 7, 1942, p. 17.

"Laurel & Hardy: The Above Have Arrived," *Evening News* (London), February 10, 1947; in the "Laurel & Hardy Files," British Film Institute (London).

"Laurel & Hardy to Broadcast To-night," *Daily Herald* (London), July 26, 1932, p. 3.

"Laurel and Hardy Top Chi[cago] With $18G [Thousand] . . . ," *Billboard*, January 24, 1942, p. 24.

"Laurel-Hardy Clown Way to London Kudoes," *Variety*, March 19, 1947, p. 48.

"Laurel, Hardy Set for Command Show," *New York Times*, October 22, 1947, p. 38.

Laurel, Stan. "My Eccentric Room-mate." In *The Legend of Charlie Chaplin*, ed. by Peter Haining. London: W. H. Allen, 1982, pp. 27–28.

"Laurel Smiling Again But Not for the Films," *New York Daily News*, November 16, 1958, p. 86.

Laurel, Stan, and Oliver Hardy. "You, Too, Can Be a Comedian!" *Hollywood Reporter*, September 1935 (n.p. or specific date cited); repr. in *The Hollywood Reporter: The Golden Years*, ed. by Tichi Wilkerson and Marcia Borie. New York: Coward-McCann, Inc., 1984, pp. 77–78.

"Laurel to Help Prepare TV Scripts on Team," *New York Morning Telegraph*, May 2, 1961 (n.p. cited). In "Laurel & Hardy Files," Billy Rose Theatre Collection, New York Public Library at Lincoln Center.

["Lee Patrick Interview"], *Film Fan Monthly*, April 1972 (incomplete citation). In "*Jitterbugs* File," Billy Rose Theatre Collection, New York Public Library at Lincoln Center.

LeGuay, Philippe. "laurel et hardy: une allégorie de la catastrophe," *Positif*, July-August 1978, pp. 20–26.

Leon, Darren. "A Search for a Cinematic Bag of Gold," *Los Angeles Times*, January 11, 1983, Section 6, p. 4.

Lewis, Jerry. "Book Six." In *Jerry Lewis: In Person*. New York: Atheneum, 1982, pp. 225–32.

"London Palladium," *Variety*, March 19, 1947, p. 20.

MacColl, Rene. "Hardy (The Fat Half of Laurel & Hardy) Dies—To Stay Fat," *London Daily Express*, August 8, 1957. In the "Laurel & Hardy Files," British Film Institute (London).

Mack, Paul. Untitled interview with Lois Laurel and Lucille Hardy, *Pratfall* (vol. 2, no. 5), 1982, p. 11.

MacTrevor, Joan. "Laurel et Hardy: la triste histoire des rois du rive morts dans la misère . . . ," *Cine Revue*, June 11, 1987, pp. 42–43.

Maltin, Leonard. Chapter 1, "Laurel and Hardy." In *Movie Comedy Teams*, 1970; repr. New York: A Signet Book, 1974, pp. 11–68.

———. Chapter 10, "Laurel & Hardy." In *The Great Movie Comedians: From Charlie Chaplin to Woody Allen*. New York: Crown Publishers, 1978, pp. 102–11.

———. "Laurel and Hardy." In *The Great Movie Shorts: Those Wonderful One- and Two-Reelers of the Thirties and Forties*. New York: Bonanza Books, 1972, pp. 47–56.

"Marcel Marceau on Stan Laurel: KUSF Interview, Early 1966" (title is the extent of reprint citation). See *Pratfall* (vol. 1, no. 11), 1974, p. 11.

Masters, Dorothy. *Way Out West* review, *New York Daily News*, May 4, 1937 (n.p. cited). In "*Way Out West* File," Billy Rose Theatre Collection, New York Public Library at Lincoln Center.

Mast, Gerald. Chapter 12, "More Fun Shops." In *The Comic Mind: Comedy and the*

Movies, 2d edition. 1973; repr. Chicago: University of Chicago Press, 1979, pp. 190–93.

————. Chapter 6, "Movie Czars and Movie Stars." In *A Short History of the Movies*, 3d edition. 1971; rpt. Indianapolis: Bobbs-Merrill, 1981, pp. 118–19.

Mazurki, Jeannette. "Stan Laurel's Daughter Recalls Comic," *Classic Film Collector*, Fall 1971, p. 53.

McCaffrey, Donald W. Chapter 5, "Duet of Incompetence." In *The Golden age of Sound Comedy: Comic Films and Comedians of the Thirties*. New York: A. S. Barnes and Company, 1973, pp. 89–103.

McCarey, Leo. "Comedy and a Touch of Cuckoo," *Extension*, November 1944, p. 5.

McKnight, Gerald. "Sad Reunion of Two Men Made World Laugh," *London Dispatch*, November 11, 1956 (n.p. cited). In the "Laurel & Hardy Files," British Film Institute (London).

McPherson, Colvin. "The Funny Men Have Their Big Inning," *St. Louis Post Dispatch*, November 3, 1940 (n.p. cited). In "Laurel & Hardy Files," Billy Rose Theatre Collection, New York Public Library at Lincoln Center.

"Meet a Gentleman! Stan Laurel," *8mm Collector*, February 1964, p. 9.

Miller, Henry. "The Golden Age." In *The Cosmological Eye*. Norfolk, Connecticut: New Directions, 1939, pp. 47–62.

"Mr. Oliver Hardy: Fat Man in Slapstick" (obituary), *London Times*, August 8, 1957, p. 8e.

"Mr. Stan Laurel: A Great Comedy Partnership" (obituary), *London Times*, February 24, 1965, p. 15a.

Mitchell, Lisa. "Laurels for Laurel," *Westways*, July 1977, pp. 38, 40–41, 78.

Mitchell, Robert. "Way Out West." In *Magill's Survey of Cinema: English Language Films* (first series, vol. 4), ed. by Frank Magill. Englewood Cliffs, New Jersey: Salem Press, 1980, pp. 1823–25.

Moak, E. R. "Tear-Stained Laughter," *Photoplay*, June 1933, pp. 40–41, 106–7.

Montgomery, John. Chapter 16, "The Eccentrics." In *Comedy Films: 1894–1954*, 2d edition. 1954; repr. London: George Allen & Unwin, 1968, pp. 231–32.

Mooring, W. H. "With MacLaurel & MacHardy in Bonnie Scotland," *Film Weekly* (England), June 28, 1935, pp. 8, 9, 28.

Nelson, Richard Alan. "Before Laurel: Oliver Hardy and the Vim Company, A Studio Biography." In *Current Research in Film* (vol. 2), ed. by Bruce A. Austin. Norwood, New Jersey: Ablex Publishing Corporation, 1986, pp. 136–55.

Nemy, Enid. "Broadway: A Musical About Laurel and Hardy Due Next Season," *New York Times*, June 8, 1984, p. C–2.

"Newest Upheaval in the Not-So-Private Life of Sad-Faced Mr. Laurel," *New York Journal-American*, December 10, 1939 (n.p. cited). In "Laurel & Hardy Files," Billy Rose Theatre Collection, New York Public Library at Lincoln Center.

Nizer, Alvin. "Laurel and Hardy," *Liberty* (cover story), Summer 1975, pp. 34–35, 37–39.

Noames, Jean-Louis. "L'art et la manierede de Leo McCarey," *Cahiers du Cinema*, February 1965, pp. 24–30. Translated under the title of "Taking Chances: Interview with Leo McCarey" in *Cahiers du Cinéma in English*, January 1967, pp. 43–54.

"No Laughing Matter: Laurel & Hardy Find Themselves on TV . . . for Free," *TV Guide*, April 23, 1955, pp. 14–15. Reprinted in *Pratfall* (vol. 2, no. 4), 1980 (n.p.).

Nugent, Frank S. *Block-Heads* review, *New York Times*, August 30, 1938, p. 14.

———. *Way Out West* review, *New York Times*, May 4, 1937, p. 29.

"Oliver Hardy Dies at 65; In 380 Films [sic] with Laurel," *New York Herald Tribune*, August 8, 1957 (n.p. cited). In "Laurel & Hardy Files," Billy Rose Theatre Collection, New York Public Library at Lincoln Center.

"Oliver Hardy of Film Team Dies; Co-Star of 200 Slapstick Movies," *New York Times*, August 8, 1957, p. 23.

"One More Crash in Love Can Not Sour Stan Laurel," *Milwaukee Journal*, July 6, 1943 (n.p. cited). In "Laurel & Hardy Files," Billy Rose Theatre Collection, New York Public Library at Lincoln Center.

Our Relations review, *Variety*, November 18, 1936, p. 13.

Palmer, Jerry. Chapter 2. "The Semiotics of Humour: The Logic of the Absurd." In *The Logic of the Absurd: On Film and Television Comedy*. London: British Film Institute, 1987, pp. 39–58.

Parish, James Robert, and William T. Leonard (with Gregory W. Mank and Charles Hoyt). "Laurel & Hardy." In *The Funsters*. New Rochelle, New York: Arlington House Publishers, 1979, pp. 406–18.

Parker, Eleanor. "Two Prize Idiots," *Playgoer*, October 1929. Reprinted in *Pratfall* (vol. 1, no. 3), 1969, pp. 10–12.

Paul, William. "Film: *Way Out West*," *Village Voice*, January 29, 1970, p. 58.

Pelswick, Rose. *Jitterbugs* review, *New York Journal-American*, June 5, 1943 (n.p. cited). In "*Jitterbugs* File," Billy Rose Theatre Collection, New York Public Library at Lincoln Center.

Polacek, Mike. "my hobby, laurel and hardy," *8mm Collector*, February 1964, p. 9.

Pope, Dennis. "Dennis Pope on Stanley LAUREL & Oliver Norvell HARDY," *Film*, Autumn 1967, pp. 32–34.

Presbys, Henry J., and James L. Limbacher. "L. & H. & Henry Ford," *Pratfall* (vol. 1, no. 11), 1974, pp. 4–5.

Reardon, Laurence. "Laurel & Hardy in Coventry." Macclesfield, England: privately published in conjunction with the Multiple Sclerosis Society, 1988.

Rense, Rip. "Pies Will Be Flying at Premier of Laurel and Hardy Treasures," *Los Angeles Herald Examiner*, July 11, 1983, p. C2.

———. "Stumbling Upon the Lost Films of Laurel and Hardy," *Los Angeles Herald Examiner*, December 9, 1982 (n.p. cited). In "Laurel & Hardy Files," Special Collections, Margaret Herrick Library, Academy of Motion Picture Arts and Sciences, Beverly Hills, California.

———. "They Haven't Deserted Stan and Ollie," *Los Angeles Examiner*, October 19, 1981 (n.p. cited). In "Laurel & Hardy Files," Special Collections, Margaret Herrick Library, Academy of Motion Picture Arts and Sciences, Beverly Hills, California.

Roach, Hal. "Living with Laughter," *Films and Filming*, October 1964, pp. 23–25.

Robinson, David. "Laurel and Hardy, W. C. Fields." In *The Great Funnies: A History of Film Comedy*. New York: E. P. Dutton, 1969, pp. 90–97.

———. "The Lighter People," *Sight & Sound*, July-September 1954, pp. 39–42, 52.

Robinson, Jeffrey. "Laurel & Hardy." In *Teamwork: The Cinema's Greatest Comedy Teams*. New York: Proteus, 1982, pp. 26–40.

Rock, Joe. "The Way It Was," *Pratfall* (vol. 1, no. 4), 1970, pp. 7–9.

Rohauer, Raymond. "A Tribute to Hal Roach" (program). New York: Gallery of Modern Art, pp. 1–12.

Rothstein, Mervyn. "A Filmic Bouquet of Laurel and Hardy Rarities," *New York Times*, December 15, 1984, p. 16.

"Ruth Laurel Remembers," *Pratfall* (vol. 1, no. 5), 1971, pp. 4–7, 12.

"Saddest Man in Hollywood, The," *Look*, June 21, 1938, p. 36.

"Sad-Pan Stan's Comic Wife Troubles," *New York Journal-American*, January 29, 1938, p. 4.

"Sad Pan, [Wife's] Frying Pan Met, Says Stan Laurel," *New York Daily News*, October 26, 1938 (n.p. cited). In "Laurel & Hardy Files," Billy Rose Theatre Collection, New York Public Library at Lincoln Center.

Salaches, Gilbert. "Laurel et Hardy: 'Impossible n'est pas anglais,' " *Telerama*, August 3–9, 1985, pp. 8, 10.

Satterfield, Robert B. "Ellinor Vanderveer," *Pratfall* (vol. 2, no. 2), 1977, pp. 10–11.

Schelly, William. Chapter 16, "Stan, Ollie and Harry." In *Harry Langdon*. Metuchen, New Jersey: Scarecrow Press, Inc., 1982, pp. 177–89.

Scheuer, Philip K. "Comics Famous 'By Accident,' " *Los Angeles Times*, December 29, 1929, Section 3, pp. 11, 18.

———. "Hardy Perennials Win Laurels; Rosy Bids Bud From Comics' Europe Work," *Los Angeles Times*, July 8, 1951, Section 4, pp. 1, 3.

Sennwald, Andre. *Babes in Toyland* review, *New York Times*, December 13, 1934, p. 28.

———. *Sons of the Desert* review, *New York Times*, January 12, 1934, p. 29.

Shadduck, Jim. "The Ku-Ku Song Man!" *Pratfall* (vol. 1, no. 7), 1972, pp. 6–10.

Sheard, Philip. "Laurel and Hardy Visit Any Old Port," *Bowler Dessert* (Scotland), August 1986 (no. 23), pp. 10–11.

"Shooting Script for Laurel and Hardy's *The Fixer Uppers*," *Classic Images*, March 1986, pp. 14–16.

Silver, Charles. "Leo McCarey: From Marx to McCarthy," *Film Comment*, September 1973, pp. 8–11.

Sons of the Desert review, *New York American*, January 8, 1934 (n.p. cited). In "*Sons of the Desert* File," Billy Rose Theatre Collection, New York Public Library at Lincoln Center.

Spensley, Dorothy. "Those Two Goofy Guys," *Photoplay*, July 1930, pp. 72, 136; repr. in Chapter 3 of this text.

"Stan Laurel Dies; Movie Comedian," *New York Times*, February 24, 1965, p. 41.

"Stan Laurel est Mort," *Cinema*, 1965 (no. 95), pp. 25–26.

"Stan Laurel Is Dead at 74—8 Years after Oliver Hardy," *New York Herald Tribune*, February 24, 1965 (n.p. cited). In "Laurel & Hardy Files," Billy Rose Theatre Collection, New York Public Library at Lincoln Center.

"Story of a Fat Boy," *Motography: Exploiting Motion Pictures*, November 25, 1916, p. 1211.

Taylor, Simon Watson. " 'HERE'S ANOTHER FINE MESS!': A dissertation on Laurel and Hardy—the ambassadors of the unprivileged," *Film Survey*, Spring 1947, pp. 21–24; repr. in *Pratfall* (vol. 2, no. 2), 1977, pp. 6–7.

"têt-à-tête avec deux têtes de pioche," *L'Ecran Francais*, November 25, 1947 (no. 126), pp. 8–9.

Thomas, Bob. "Comedy Veterans Plan Comeback," July 1956 AP article; repr. without full citation in *Pratfall* (vol. 2, no. 5), 1982, p. 13.

————. "Stan Laurel, Ill at 67, Can't Bear Old Films," *New York World-Telegram and Sun*, December 5, 1957 (n.p. cited). In "Laurel & Hardy Files," Billy Rose Theatre Collection, New York Public Library at Lincoln Center.

————. "Tip of Derby for Laurel and Hardy," *New York Journal-American*, August 14, 1965 (n.p. cited). In "Laurel & Hardy Files," Billy Rose Theatre Collection, New York Public Library at Lincoln Center.

Thomey, Todd. "Babe's Night Out" (originally part of a *Savannah Evening News* column); repr. without full citation in *Pratfall* (vol. 1, no. 8), 1972, p. 5.

Tildesley, Alice L. "Funny Film Faces: How They Got That Way" [1930]. Laurel & Hardy segment reprinted in *Pratfall* (vol. 1, no. 8), 1972, p. 13.

"Together Again," *Daily Express* (London), May 7, 1950 (n.p. cited). In "The Laurel & Hardy Files," British Film Institute (London).

Trubo, Richard. "Ollie and Stan: They Bore Life's Burdens with Courage," *Southland Sunday* magazine (*Long Beach Independent Press-Telegraph*), November 10, 1974, pp. 14–18.

Usher, Shaun. "The People's Clowns," *Daily Mail* (London), November 26, 1987, p. 30.

"Van Dyke Delivers Stan Laurel Eulogy," *New York Times*, February 27, 1965, p. 25.

Verb, Boyd. "Laurel Without Hardy," *Films in Review*, March 1959, pp. 153–58.

Vonnegut, Kurt. "Prologue." In *Slapstick*. New York: Delacorte Press/Seymour Lawrence, 1976, pp. 1–19.

Walker, Helen Louise. "Ka-Plop and Ka-Bloop: Laurel and Hardy Reveal What Makes You Hear Such Funny Things," *Motion Picture Classic*, June 1930, pp. 70, 103, 105; repr. in Chapter 3 of this text.

Walls, Trevor. "Stan Gets a Tan by Computer," *Daily Star* (London), April 22, 1980 (n.p. cited). In "The Laurel & Hardy Files," British Film Institute (London).

Wardle, Irving. *Block-heads* (the play) review, *The Times* (London), October 18, 1984, p. 8.

Warwick, Robert. "*A Life of Comedy*," *Cinemeditor*, Summer 1967, pp. 20–22; repr. in *Classic Film Collector*, Spring 1968, p. 10.

"Who's Who This Week in Pictures," *New York Times*, October 2, 1932, Section 9, p. 4.

Wilson, Jerry. "Return of Babe's Night Out," *Pratfall* (vol. 1, no. 9), 1972, p. 15.

Winston, Archer. *Jitterbugs* review, *New York Post*, June 5, 1943, p. 10. In "*Jitterbugs*" File, Billy Rose Theatre Collection, New York Public Library at Lincoln Center.

Wright, Basil. "Blest Pair of Sirens," *World Film News*, June 1937, p. 3.

————. *Block-heads* review, *The Spectator*, September 16, 1938, p. 439.

————. Chapter 3, "All Talking, All Singing, All Dancing." In *The Long View*. New York: Alfred A. Knopf, 1974, pp. 128–29.

————. "The Last of Laurel," *World Film News*, October 1938, p. 265.

Young, Jordan. "Early Ollie: The Plump and Runt Films," *Pratfall* (vol. 1, no. 12), 1975, pp. 3–7.

————. "Laurel & Hardy Meet the Pink Panther," copyright 1978. Reprinted in *Pratfall* (vol. 2, no. 5), 1982, pp. 4–5.

————. "Nobody Knew Much About Anything Then," *Pratfall* (vol. 1, no. 11), 1974, pp. 6–8.

————. "Popularity Grows on Borrowed Roots," *Pratfall* (vol. 1, no. 5), 1971, pp. 7–9.

Chronology

Constructing a chronology necessitates using all of one's sources. Laurel & Hardy time lines are, moreover, relatively rare in team literature. (For an earlier example see Roland Lacourbe's French text, *Laurel et Hardy*, 1975.)

A time line is a very subjective project. For instance, because of the high number of film short subjects the team made and the text's inclusion of a Laurel & Hardy filmography, not every less-than-feature length movie is noted. However, an effort has been made to cite some of the most central short subjects. But even here, there is no uniform listing of most pivotal short subjects.

Still, the time line—biography at a glance—should be ambitious enough to serve as a solid starting point for the interested reader. For a more fleshed out look at the duo return to this book's opening chapter.

March 19, 1884	Laurel's parents marry: Arthur Jefferson ("A. J.") and Margaret ("Madge") Metcalfe. His father found success as an actor, writer, and theater manager. His mother became an accomplished actress. At the time of Laurel's birth, both parents were struggling performers.
June 15, 1884	Harry Langdon is born.
1886	Laurel's older brother Gordon is born.
Aug. 27, 1887	Jimmy Finlayson is born.
April 16, 1889	Charlie Chaplin is born.
March 12, 1890	Hardy's parents marry: Oliver Hardy, Sr. was in poor health and managed a hotel, while Emily had four children from a former marriage.
April 26, 1890	Edgar Kennedy is born.

June 16, 1890	Stan Laurel is born, though he is christened Arthur Stanley Jefferson. His birth is in Ulverston, England, at the home of his maternal grandparents, George and Sarah Metcalfe. This is his home until age six or seven. Besides Laurel there were three other children: older brother Gordon and younger siblings Olga Beatrice and Edward Everett (''Teddy''). Another brother, Sydney, died in infancy.
Jan. 14, 1892	Hal Roach is born.
Jan. 18, 1892	Oliver Hardy is born in Harlem, Georgia, though he is christened Norvell (his mother's maiden name). He will later take his father's first name. After the elder Hardy's death, Oliver's mother owned and operated various small hotels. Hardy had two half brothers and two half sisters from his mother's former marriage.
Nov. 22, 1892	Hardy's father dies (born Dec. 5, 1841).
Sept. 12, 1893	Billy Gilbert is born.
Dec. 1894	Laurel's sister Olga Beatrice is born.
Jan. 20, 1897 (?)	Mae Busch is born.
Oct. 3, 1898	Leo McCarey is born.
April 30, 1899	Laurel's brother Sydney dies in infancy.
May 1900	A 9-year-old Laurel makes his stage debut.
April 1, 1901	Laurel's younger brother Edward Everett (''Teddy'') Jefferson is born. It is a difficult delivery and Madge is in poor health until her death in 1908.
1901	An eleven-year-old Laurel, overhearing his mother, first learns of his father's extramarital affairs.
Dec. 18, 1904	George Stevens is born.
April 3, 1905	Hal Roach musical director T. Marvin Hatley is born. His compositions include Laurel & Hardy's theme song, ''The Dance of the Cuckoos.''
May 1906	Sixteen-year-old Laurel makes stage debut.
1907–1909	Laurel becomes member of the Levy and Cardwell Juvenile Pantomimes Company (members range in age from six to eighteen).
Sept. 1, 1908	Laurel's mother, talented actress Madge Metcalfe, dies.
September 1910	Discovered by British music hall legend Fred Karno earlier in the year, Laurel leaves on a Karno troupe tour of America as an understudy to Charlie Chaplin. However, Laurel later breaks with the tour and returns to Britain.

1910	Hardy becomes a film theatre projectionist, a position he holds for the next three years.
October 1912	Laurel returns to Karno troupe for a second American tour. Again he is Chaplin's understudy.
1913	Hardy marries film pianist Madelyn Saloshin and also begins working in the Jacksonville, Florida, movie industry. Hardy and Madelyn later divorce.
May 1913	Chaplin accepts an offer from the New York office of Kessel and Bauman, the parent organization for Mack Sennett's Keystone Comedy Company, but his Karno commitment will hold him until November.
December 1913	Chaplin arrives at the Keystone Studio in California.
1913	The second American Karno tour fails after Chaplin's defection. Laurel decides to stay in the United States and finds vaudeville success in the sketch *The Nutty Burglars*.
Feb. 7, 1914	Chaplin's second film, *Kid Auto Races at Venice*, opens. It marks the first appearance of the tramp character. Chaplin makes thirty-three more films in 1914.
1914	Laurel's vaudeville act *The Nutty Burglars* is reworked to cash in on the amazing popularity of Chaplin. Laurel played his role as Charlie the Tramp.
April 15, 1915	Laurel's grandpa George Metcalfe dies. He was seventy-eight.
1915–1917	"The Stan Jefferson Trio" tours vaudeville in the sketch *The Crazy Cracksman*. Laurel's stage persona continues to be that of Chaplin's Tramp.
Dec. 16, 1916	Laurel's grandma Sarah Metcalfe dies. She was eighty-five.
1916	Hardy (Plump) and Billy Ruge (Runt) are teamed in thirty-five one-reeler comedies called the "Plump and Runt" series. Producing company Vim Comedies shot them in Jacksonville, Florida, during the winter and New York City in the summer.
Early 1917	Hardy begins appearing in the King Bee comedies of Billy West—the best of the Chaplin imitators.
Spring 1917	Hardy and the Billy West comedies move to New York City.
April 1917	The United States enters World War I; Hardy attempts to enlist while in New York City, but he is refused.

October 1917	Hardy and Billy West troupe head west to Hollywood (just prior to this there had been a brief production stop in New Jersey).
1917	Laurel meets vaudeville performer Mae Dahlberg. Though often a stormy relationship, they remain in a common-law marriage until 1925. When the comedian, still known as Stan Jefferson, expresses interest in a new stage name, Mae suggests Laurel. Shortly after this Laurel appears in his first film, *Nuts in May*.
1918	Production of the King Bee comedies of Billy West (and supporting Hardy) stop.
1918–1921	Hardy free-lances in a number of film productions, from Jim Aubrey comedies to Buck Jones westerns.
1918	Laurel stars in the film *Lucky Dog*, briefly sharing screen time with supporting player Hardy. But their teaming is still years away. (This film is sometimes mistakenly listed with a 1917 release date.)
1919–1921	His film market all but dried up, Laurel makes only *The Rent Collectors* (1921). The 1919 Laurel shorts released by Roach had actually been shot in 1918. He works sporadically in vaudeville with Mae but a film career has become his goal. There are other hard times before a 1922 break.
1921–1925	Hardy appears in a number of Larry Semon films. While Hardy's free-lance work with Roach begins in 1924, there are still additional Semon projects that include Hardy; for example, Semon's 1925 feature film adaptation of *The Wizard of Oz*.
1921–1922	Fatty Arbuckle is involved in scandal.
Nov. 24, 1921	Hardy marries second wife Myrtle in Los Angeles.
January 1922	Hardy supports Semon in *The Sawmill*, sometimes considered the latter's best film.
1922–1923	"Bronco Billy" Anderson produces and directs Laurel in six films, including the popular parody of Valentino's *Blood and Sand* (1922), entitled *Mud and Sand* (1922). Other spoofs follow, such as the 1923 take-off of *When Knighthood Was in Flower* called *When Knights Were Cold* (1923).
1923–1924	Roach rehired Laurel; the focus is on more parodies.

1924–1925	Film producer Joe Rock temporarily brings Laurel personal and professional stability at a time when the comedian's problems threatened his career. Besides rekindling Laurel's film career, he engineered the comedian's break from his difficult common-law wife, Mae Dahlberg. While parodies continue, such as the 1924 *West of Hot Dog* spoof of *West of Pecos* (1922), Laurel also now generates good reviews in straight comedies like *Half a Man* (1925).
1924	Hardy begins to do free-lance work for Roach. In the years prior to the 1927 teaming of Laurel & Hardy, Hardy has minor supporting roles in some Leo McCarey-directed Charley Chase films, as well as some directed by his future partner.
1925	*Paperhanger's Helper*, from Hardy's solo career, is released. According to Hardy, of all his extensive pre-Laurel work, this film most anticipates the later duo. (It is sometimes mistakenly listed with a 1915 release date.)
1925	Laurel returns to Roach, but Rock questions the comedian's exit. The producers begin a 1926 legal battle over Laurel's services. Roach wins, but Laurel largely confines his talents to off-screen film activities during the controversy.
July 1926	A Hardy cooking accident puts Laurel back on the screen—director Laurel had to sub for Hardy in *Get 'em Young*.
August 13, 1926	Laurel marries Lois Neilson. Roach had arranged their 1925 blind date to take Laurel's mind off Dahlberg's exit.
Dec. 26, 1926	*45 Minutes from Hollywood* is released. Not yet teamed, Laurel and Hardy both appeared but had no shared scenes.
1927	McCarey teams Laurel & Hardy.
Jan. 13, 1927	*Duck Soup* (Laurel & Hardy version) is released.
Oct. 8, 1927	*The Second Hundred Years* is released.
Dec. 3, 1927	*Putting Pants on Philip* is released. The first ''official'' Laurel & Hardy film.
Dec. 10, 1927	Lois, Jr. is born to Lois and Stan Laurel.
December 1927	Because of his great success with Laurel & Hardy, McCarey is made a Roach corporation vice-president.
Dec. 31, 1927	*The Battle of the Century* is released.
Jan. 28, 1928	*Leave 'em Laughing* is released.

February 1928	After the last quarter figures of 1927 showed it to be the most profitable Roach period to date, McCarey is given a new contract in which he receives a percentage of the Laurel & Hardy film profits.
March 24, 1928	*From Soup to Nuts* is released.
June 16, 1928	On Laurel's 38th birthday, he buys a new Beverly Hills home.
Nov. 3, 1928	*Two Tars* is released.
Dec. 29, 1928	*We Faw Dawn* is released.
1928	Laurel takes Alyce Ardell as a mistress. Hardy also takes a mistress in the late 1920s—Viola Morse.
Jan. 26, 1929	*Liberty* is released.
April 20, 1929	*Big Business* is released.
May 4, 1929	*Unaccustomed as We Are*, Laurel & Hardy's first dialogue film, is released. Note the tongue-in-cheek title.
May 18, 1929	*Double Whoopee* is released.
July 1929	Oliver and Myrtle Hardy separate, but reconcile before the year's end.
Aug. 10, 1929	*A Perfect Day* is released.
October 1929	Fred Karno is signed by Roach to write and produce.
Nov. 23, 1929	*The Hollywood Revue of 1929* (feature) is released. Laurel & Hardy contribute a magic art sketch to what is essentially a M-G-M all-star variety show.
Dec. 14, 1929	Laurel & Hardy's last nontalking film, *Angora Love*, is released.
Jan. 4, 1930	*Night Owls* is released.
Jan. 17, 1930	*The Rogue Song* (feature) is released. Laurel & Hardy comic relief scenes are added after the initial shooting is completed.
February 1930	Roach fires Karno, later claiming he is unhappy with the British vaudeville legend's gag-writing abilities.
March 22, 1930	*Brats* is released.
May 7, 1930	A premature son, Stanley Robert, lives little more than a week after his birth to Lois and Stan Laurel.
May 31, 1930	*Hog Wild* is released.
Nov. 29, 1930	*Another Fine Mess* is released.

February 1931	Charlie Chaplin makes a second triumphant return to England, which eventually takes him around the world.
Aug. 15, 1931	*Pardon Us* (feature) is released.
Nov. 15, 1931	Will Rogers's weekly article calls Laurel & Hardy the comedy team "favorites with all of us movie folks, as well as the audiences . . . "
Jan. 23, 1932	*Helpmates* is released.
April 16, 1932	*The Music Box* is released.
July 23, 1932	Laurel & Hardy (plus the latter's wife Myrtle) dock at Southhampton, England. They are met by Laurel's father and stepmother, Venitia, who traveled to London with them. A mob scene of fans occurs in both Southhampton and London, where a well-attended press conference takes place at the Savoy Hotel (their temporary London residence).
July 24, 1932	Laurel has a family tea at the Savoy Hotel.
July 25–Aug. 21, 1932	Capitalizing on Laurel & Hardy's visit to Great Britain, M-G-M British distributors were encouraged to declare this period "Laurel & Hardy Month."
July 25, 1932	After appearing on stage at London's Empire Theatre of Leicester Square (in support of their film *Any Old Port*, 1932), Laurel & Hardy's exit requires seven policemen to keep back the crowds.
July 26, 1932	Laurel & Hardy, rarely on radio, do a guest spot on BBC.
July 29, 1932	Eight thousand Laurel & Hardy fans give the duo a midnight welcome at Glasgow's Central Station. Twenty people are hurt, nine seriously.
Aug. 18, 1932	The duo cut a commercial record at London's Columbia Gramophone Studios. Entitled "Laurel and Hardy Visit London," it is an amusing thank you for their reception.
Aug. 30, 1932	Laurel & Hardy and the latter's wife Myrtle return from Britain, docking in New York City.
Sept. 17, 1932	*Pack Up Your Troubles* (feature) is released.
Nov. 5, 1932	*Their First Mistake* is released.
Nov. 18, 1932	*The Music Box* wins an academy award for the "Best Live Action Comedy Short Subject of 1931–32."
May 1933	Lois Laurel files for divorce.
May 5, 1933	*The Devil's Brother* (feature; also known as *Fra Diavolo*) is released.

June 1933	Hardy files for divorce from Myrtle.
Oct. 3, 1933	The Hardys reconciliation is a well-publicized "new start."
Dec. 17, 1933	Laurel's younger brother Everett ("Teddy") dies. He had been living with Laurel and working as a chauffeur at a local hotel. He was thirty-three.
Dec. 29, 1933	*Sons of the Desert* (feature) is released.
February 1934	*Oliver the Eighth* is released.
February 1934	Laurel was said to be leaving the country and breaking up the team to avoid any further divorce-related attachments to his income. This was merely a Laurel strategy to safeguard his salary.
Early 1934	The comedian legally changes his name to Laurel prior to exchanging vows with Virginia Ruth in April.
April 3, 1934	Laurel "courts" controversy by marrying Virginia Ruth in Mexico while his divorce from Lois is not yet official. He acknowledges this by announcing that until his divorce is final Laurel and Ruth will not live together.
June 23, 1934	*Going Bye-Bye!* is released.
July 21, 1934	*Them Thar Hills* is released.
October 1934	Laurel's divorce decree from Lois becomes official.
Nov. 30, 1934	*Babes in Toyland* (feature) is released.
Dec. 8, 1934	*The Live Ghost* is released.
March 15, 1935	Laurel is fired by Roach. "Laurel & Hardy Separate" run the news stories.
April 4, 1935	The team is reunited when Laurel and Roach patch up their differences and the comedian signs a new contract.
Circa Aug. 6, 1935	*Thicker Than Water* is released, the team's final starring two-reeler.
Aug. 23, 1935	*Bonnie Scotland* (feature) is released.
September 1935	Laurel legally marries Virginia Ruth. They divorce in late 1936 and marry and divorce again in the 1940s.
Christmas 1935	Laurel's father ("A. J.") and his second wife Venitia come over for the holidays and stay until spring.
January 1936	*Tit for Tat* is nominated for the "Best Short Subject— Comedy" Oscar. However, in March Robert Benchley's *How to Sleep* takes the prize.
Feb. 14, 1936	*The Bohemian Girl* (feature) is released.

Oct. 30, 1936	*Our Relations* (feature) is released.
November 1936	Myrtle Hardy sues her husband for separate maintenance; the suit is eventually dismissed.
Dec. 24, 1936	Virginia Ruth divorces Laurel.
Jan. 16, 1937	Laurel files a court answer that he is not now, or ever was, the husband of Mae Dahlberg, who is suing him for $1,000 monthly separate maintenance. She claims they entered a common-law marriage June 18, 1919. She is unsuccessful.
April 16, 1937	*Way Out West* (feature) is released.
May 18, 1937	Hardy and Myrtle are divorced.
May 21, 1937	*Pick a Star* (feature) is released. Laurel & Hardy appear in two scenes.
October 1937	Laurel and Roach come to a contract arrangement, after the comedian's unofficial strike since early in the year. But Laurel had incorporated, and Roach's contract is with Stan Laurel Productions.
Dec. 31, 1937	Laurel receives final decree of divorce from Virginia Ruth.
Jan. 1, 1938	Laurel marries third wife Vera Shuvalova (stage name Illeanna). Second wife Virginia Ruth follows new couple to Yuma, Arizona, where Laurel and Illeanna have eloped. Virginia Ruth claims her divorce from the comedian was illegal.
Jan. 11, 1938	Laurel requests a court restraining order against Virginia Ruth (applied in April).
Feb. 27, 1938	To forestall Virginia Ruth's bigamy charges, Laurel and Illeanna repeat their vows in another Yuma civil ceremony.
April 1938	Laurel and Illeanna go through still another ceremony (in her Russian Orthodox faith).
May 20, 1938	*Swiss Miss* (feature) is released.
July 6, 1938	Laurel's wife Illeanna is both fined and sentenced to five days in jail for driving recklessly and without a license. Laurel observed, ''If she'd only kept out of the car like I told her to.''
Aug. 18, 1938	Harry Langdon is signed by Roach Studios to team with Hardy, replacing the fired Laurel.
Aug. 19, 1938	*Block-Heads* (feature) is released.
August 1938	Roach fires Laurel, just days after the August 19 release of *Block-Heads*.

Sept. 28, 1938	Laurel is arrested for drunk driving. He nearly hit a police car while driving on the wrong side of the road. Shirtless and "badly" bleeding, he tells authorities his wife hit him with a frying pan. He spends the night in jail. In the October trial the jury fails to arrive at a verdict. The charges are dropped in December.
1938	A mystery person, probably Virginia Ruth, keeps calling the police and fire departments, hospitals, funeral parlors and other places, reporting all manner of fictitious mayhem taking place at the Laurel home.
December 1938	Laurel sues Roach's studio for nearly three-quarters of a million dollars, citing breach of contract.
February 1939	The Roach studio elaborates on the causes for Laurel's firing.
April 1939	All charges are dropped and Laurel is back under contract to Roach.
May 1939	Laurel and wife Illeanna are divorced.
May 1939	*Zenobia*, the one-film teaming of Oliver Hardy and Harry Langdon, is released.
October 1939	The team incorporates as "Laurel and Hardy Feature Productions."
Oct. 20, 1939	*The Flying Deuces* (feature) is released.
Nov. 24, 1939	The court dismisses former Laurel wife Illeanna's attempt to have their May divorce set aside.
Feb. 16, 1940	*A Chump at Oxford* (short version feature) is released. The long version is released in the United States in early 1941.
March 7, 1940	Hardy marries third wife, script girl Lucille Jones, in Las Vegas.
April 1940	Laurel & Hardy's concurrent but separate contracts with Roach end, and the team forever breaks with him.
May 3, 1940	*Saps at Sea* (feature) is released.
June 1940	Hardy's school-teacher sister Emily Crawford dies. She had been a Los Angeles resident since the late 1920s.
Aug. 22, 1940	Laurel & Hardy perform the sketch "How to Get a Driver's License" at a San Francisco Red Cross benefit. The response is so good that it is the catalyst for a tour.
Late September 1940	Laurel & Hardy begin a ten-week, twelve-city stage tour.
Oct. 11, 1940	Hal Roach's wife Margaret sues him for separate maintenance.

Jan. 11, 1941	Laurel remarries Virginia Ruth but they separate before the year is half over. They officially divorce in 1946.
April 1941	The team is the guest of Mexico's president at a major film festival in Mexico City.
April 23, 1941	Laurel & Hardy secure a film contract with 20th Century-Fox.
Sept. 22, 1941	*Time* magazine reports the U.S. government has sued Hardy for $96,757 in income taxes.
Oct. 10, 1941	*Great Guns* (feature) is released.
November 1941	Laurel & Hardy play a tour of American Army bases in the Caribbean.
January and February 1942	Laurel & Hardy have another successful stage tour.
Spring 1942	Laurel & Hardy take part in the three-week *Hollywood Victory Caravan* tour.
Aug. 7, 1942	*A-Haunting We Will Go* (feature) is released.
Circa April 4, 1943	*Air Raid Wardens* (feature) is released.
Early 1943	Laurel & Hardy make appearance in the one-reel government film *The Tree in a Test Tube*.
June 11, 1943	*Jitterbugs* (feature) is released.
Nov. 19, 1943	*The Dancing Masters* (feature) is released.
September 1944	*The Big Noise* (feature) is released.
December 1944	Harry Langdon dies.
March 1945	*Nothing But Trouble* (feature) is released.
May 18, 1945	*The Bullfighters* (feature) is released.
January 1946	Hardy's second wife Myrtle attempts to obtain more alimony.
April 19, 1946	Mae Busch dies.
May 6, 1946	Laurel marries Ida Kitaeva Raphael in Yuma, Arizona.
March 11, 1947	Laurel & Hardy receive a rousing reception at their London Palladium opening. Originally booked for two weeks, they are held over an additional week.
Nov. 3, 1947	Royal Command Performance at the Palladium Theatre.
1947	Laurel's last visit to his Ulverston birthplace.
Nov. 9, 1948	Edgar Kennedy dies.

1949	Hardy plays a part in the charity production of *What Price Glory?* The cast also includes John Wayne.
Sept. 3, 1949	Critic James Agee's essay, "Comedy's Greatest Era," appears in *Life* magazine.
September 1949	Hardy provides strong comic support in the John Wayne feature *The Fighting Kentuckian*.
1949	Laurel's father Arthur ("A.J.") Jefferson dies.
April 1950	Hardy has a comic cameo in Frank Capra's *Riding High*.
April 1, 1951	Laurel and his wife depart from France to America. Production has ended on *Atoll K*. One almost wonders if the April Fool's Day exit was self-deprecatingly planned.
Nov. 21, 1951	*Atoll K* (feature) is released in France. It will also be known as *Robinson Crusoeland* and *Utopia*.
1952	A shorter *Atoll K* is released in the United Kingdom as *Robinson Crusoeland*.
1952	Last family reunion between Laurel and his cousins.
1952	The team plays an extended stage tour of Britain. Laurel writes a new tour sketch, based on their short subject *Night Owls*.
Oct. 9, 1953	Jimmy Finlayson dies.
Fall 1953	The team returns again for a stage tour of Britain. Laurel writes another new sketch, *Birds of a Feather*. It is during the 1953 portion of the tour (at Birmingham) that they meet graduate student and future pivotal biographer John McCabe.
May 1954	What proves to be their last British stage tour is cut short by Hardy's health problems.
December 1954	*Atoll K* is released in the United States as *Utopia*.
1955	Laurel suffers a stroke.
September 15, 1956	Hardy suffers a massive stroke from which he never recovers.
Aug. 7, 1957	Oliver Hardy dies.
Aug. 9, 1957	Hardy's funeral in Los Angeles. Laurel's doctor forbids his attendance. His wife Ida, however, is with Hardy's widow Lucille during the services.

April 17, 1961	Laurel is honored at the Academy Awards with an Oscar "for creative pioneering in the field of cinema comedy." Poor health prevents him from attending, and the award is accepted by Danny Kaye. For unknown reasons, the Academy had turned down Laurel's original request to have Jerry Lewis accept the Oscar.
1961	Larry Harmon (the original Bozo the Clown) receives the exclusive publicity rights to the likenesses of Laurel & Hardy. The arrangements were made through Laurel and Lucille Hardy.
1961	John McCabe's *Mr. Laurel & Mr. Hardy* is published.
Dec. 20, 1962	Hal Roach Studios is sold to a real estate developer. Everything is leveled in 1963.
July 27, 1964	Laurel returns home after a 10-day stay in the hospital. The comedian has been given tests to correct his insulin dosage for diabetes. He has been well remembered by fans with cards and letters.
1964	Chaplin's *My Autobiography* is published. Somehow, no mention is made of Karno understudy and roommate Laurel.
Feb. 23, 1965	Stan Laurel dies.
Nov. 23, 1965	CBS television has a star-studded salute to Laurel hosted by Dick Van Dyke.
July 14, 1967	*Time* magazine does an article on the Laurel & Hardy cult movement—something that actually has been going on for years.
July 5, 1969	Leo McCarey dies.
Sept. 23, 1971	Billy Gilbert dies.
March 8, 1975	George Stevens dies.
Dec. 25, 1977	Charlie Chaplin dies.
Jan. 26, 1980	Laurel's widow, Ida, dies of natural causes in Sherman Oaks, California. (Her age is unreported).
April 9, 1984	Hal Roach is given an honorary Academy Award "in recognition of his unparalleled record of distinguished contributions to the motion picture art form."
Autumn 1984	*Block-Heads*, a musical about Laurel & Hardy, opens at a London West End theatre, the Mermad.

November 1985	The postal department decides to honor Laurel & Hardy with a commemorative stamp in 1987—the 60th anniversary of their teaming. Unfortunately, differences occurred between the postal department and Larry Harmon (the catalyst for the honor) and the stamp has yet to appear.
Aug. 23, 1986	T. Marvin Hatley dies.
January 1987	A Los Angeles judge rules that Harmon owns exclusive marketing rights to Laurel & Hardy—barring Lois Laurel (the comedian's daughter) and her husband, Anthony Hawes, from using likenesses of the team to sell shirts and mugs. The Haweses had hoped to use a new California Celebrity Rights Law to usurp the earlier claim.
1989	John McCabe's *BABE: The Life of Oliver Hardy* is published.

Filmography

Every Laurel & Hardy text with a film listing was at some time consulted in the compiling of the following filmography. But the most helpful were the definitive one by Richard Bann in the McCabe/Kilgore/Bann *Laurel & Hardy* (1975), and those in Randy Skretvedt's *Laurel and Hardy: The Magic Behind the Movies* (1987) and Bruce Crowther's (with the assistance of Glenn Mitchell) *Laurel and Hardy: Clown Princes of Comedy* (1987).

This filmography is limited to films in which *both* Laurel & Hardy appeared, including the early accidental joint credits—*A Lucky Dog* (1918, brief scene together; frequently incorrectly dated 1917 or 1919), and *45 Minutes from Hollywood* (1926, no scenes together). There is also a selected compilation list of films made up in part or in toto of original Laurel & Hardy work. As a historical footnote, when the team was still in mid-career their short subjects were sometimes edited into feature-length compilations overseas—especially in France.

METRO

1918 *A Lucky Dog* (2 reels).*
     Producer: Gilbert M. Anderson (Bronco Billy). Director: Jess Robbins. With: Florence Gillet.

HAL ROACH—PATHE

1926 *45 Minutes from Hollywood* (2 reels).
     Producer: Hal Roach. Director: Fred L. Guiol. Story: Hal Roach. Titles: H. M. Walker. With: Glen Tryon, Charlotte Mineau, Rube Clifford, Sue O'Neil (Molly O'Day), Theda Bara, Edna Murphy, Jerry Mandy, Ham Kinsey, Ed Brandenberg, Jack Hill, Al Hallet, "Tiny" Sandford, Our Gang, The Hal Roach Bathing Beauties.

*Two reels run approximately twenty minutes.

1927 *Duck Soup* (2 reels).
Producer: Hal Roach. Director: Fred L. Guiol. Story: From a sketch by Laurel's father, Arthur "A. J." Jefferson. Titles: H. M. Walker. With: Madeleine Hurlock, William Austin, Bob Kortman.

Slipping Wives (2 reels).
Producer: Hal Roach. Supervisor: F. Richard Jones. Director: Fred L. Guiol. Story: Hal Roach. Camera: George Stevens. Editor: Richard Currier. Titles: H. M. Walker. With: Priscilla Dean, Herbert Rawlinson, Albert Conti.

Love 'Em and Weep (2 reels).
Producer: Hal Roach. Director: Fred L. Guiol. Story: Hal Roach. Titles: H. M. Walker. With: Mae Busch, James Finlayson, Charlotte Mineau, Vivien Oakland, Charlie Hall, Mae Wallace, Ed Brandenberg, Gale Henry.

Why Girls Love Sailors (2 reels).
Producer: Hal Roach. Director: Fred L. Guiol. Story: Hal Roach. Titles: H. M. Walker. With: Viola Richard, Anita Garvin, Malcolm Waite.

With Love and Hisses (2 reels).
Producer: Hal Roach. Director: Fred L. Guiol. Story: Hal Roach. Titles: H. M. Walker. With: James Finlayson, Frank Brownlee, Chet Brandenberg, Anita Garvin, Eve Southern, Will Stanton, Jerry Mandy, Frank Saputo, Josephine Dunn.

HAL ROACH—M-G-M

Sugar Daddies (2 reels).
Producer: Hal Roach. Director: Fred L. Guiol. Camera: George Stevens. Titles: H. M. Walker. With: James Finlayson, Noah Young, Charlotte Mineau, Edna Marian, Eugene Pallette, Charlie Hall, Jack Hill, Sam Lufkin, Dorothy Coburn, Ray Cooke.

HAL ROACH—PATHE

Sailors, Beware! (2 reels).
Producer: Hal Roach. Director: Hal Yates. Story: Hal Roach. Titles: H. M. Walker. With: Anita Garvin, "Tiny" Sandford, Viola Richard, Mae Wallace, Connie Evans, Barbara Pierce, Lupe Velez, Will Stanton, Ed Brandenberg, Dorothy Coburn, Frank Brownlee, Harry Earles, Charley Young.

HAL ROACH—M-G-M

The Second Hundred Years (2 reels).
Producer: Hal Roach. Director: Fred L. Guiol. Story: (Everson filmography credits Leo McCarey). Editor: Richard Currier. Titles: H. M. Walker. With: James Finlayson, Eugene Pallette, "Tiny" Sandford, Ellinor Van Der Veer, Alfred Fisher, Charles A. Bachman, Edgar Dearing, Otto Fries, "Mazooka" O'Conor, Frank Brownlee, Dorothy Coburn, Charlie Hall, Rosemary Theby.

Call of the Cuckoos (2 reels).
Producer: Hal Roach. Supervisor: Leo McCarey. Director: Clyde A. Bruckman.

Camera: Floyd Jackman. Editor: Richard Currier. Titles: H. M. Walker. With: Max Davidson, Lillian Elliott, Spec O'Donnell, Charley Chase, James Finlayson, Frank Brownlee, Charlie Hall, Charles Meakin, Leo Willis, Lyle Tayo, Edgar Dearing, Fay Holderness, Otto Fries.

Hats Off (2 reels).
Producer: Hal Roach. Supervisor: Leo McCarey. Director: Hal Yates. Editor: Richard Currier. Titles: H. M. Walker. With: James Finlayson, Anita Garvin, Dorothy Coburn, Ham Kinsey, Sam Lufkin, Chet Brandenberg.

HAL ROACH—PATHE

Do Detectives Think? (2 reels).
Producer: Hal Roach. Director: Fred L. Guiol. Story: Hal Roach. Titles: H. M. Walker. With: James Finlayson, Viola Richard, Noah Young, Frank Brownlee, Will Stanton, Charley Young, Charles A. Bachman.

HAL ROACH—M-G-M

Putting Pants on Philip (2 reels).
Producer: Hal Roach. Supervisor: Leo McCarey. Director: Clyde A. Bruckman. Camera: George Stevens. With: Sam Lufkin, Harvey Clark, Ed Brandenberg, Dorothy Coburn, Chet Brandenberg, Retta Palmer, "Mazooka" O'Conor, Eric Mack, Jack Hill, Don Bailey, Alfred Fisher, Lee Phelps, Charles A. Bachman.

The Battle of the Century (2 reels).
Producer: Hal Roach. Supervisor: Leo McCarey. Director: Clyde A. Bruckman. Story: Hal Roach. Camera: George Stevens. Editor: Richard Currier. Titles: H. M. Walker. With: Dick Gilbert, George K. French, Sam Lufkin, Noah Young, Gene Morgan, Al Hallet, Anita Garvin, Eugene Pallette, Lyle Tayo, Charlie Hall, Dorothy Coburn, Ham Kinsey, Bert Roach, Jack Hall, "Mazooka" O'Conor, Ed Brandenberg, Dorothy Walbert, Charley Young, Ellinor Van Der Veer. (The Crowther filmography credits Lou Costello as being a crowd extra.)

1928 *Leave 'Em Laughing* (2 reels).
Producer: Hal Roach. Supervisor: Leo McCarey. Director: Clyde A. Bruckman. Story: Hal Roach. Camera: George Stevens. Editor: Richard Currier. Titles: Reed Haustis. With: Edgar Kennedy, Charlie Hall, Viola Richard, Dorothy Coburn, "Tiny" Sandford, Sam Lufkin, Edgar Dearing, Al Hallet, Jack V. Lloyd, Otto Fries, Jack Hill.

HAL ROACH—PATHE

Flying Elephants (2 reels).
Producer: Hal Roach. Director: Fred Butler. Story: Hal Roach. With: Dorothy Coburn, Leo Willis, "Tiny" Sandford, Bud Fine.

HAL ROACH—M-G-M

The Finishing Touch (2 reels).
Producer: Hal Roach. Supervisor: Leo McCarey. Director: Clyde A. Bruckman.

Camera: George Stevens. Editor: Richard Currier. Titles: H. M. Walker. With: Edgar Kennedy, Dorothy Coburn, Sam Lufkin.

From Soup to Nuts (2 reels).
Producer: Hal Roach. Supervisor: Leo McCarey. Director: Edgar Kennedy. Story: Leo McCarey. Camera: Len Powers. Editor: Richard Currier. Titles: H. M. Walker. With: Anita Garvin, "Tiny" Sandford, Otto Fries, Edna Marian, Ellinor Van Der Veer, George Bichel, Dorothy Coburn, Sam Lufkin, Gene Morgan.

You're Darn Tootin' (2 reels).
(United Kingdom title: *The Music Blasters*.) Producer: Hal Roach. Supervisor: Leo McCarey. Director: Edgar Kennedy. Story: Leo McCarey. Camera: Floyd Jackson. Editor: Richard Currier. Titles: H. M. Walker. With: Sam Lufkin, Chet Brandenberg, Christian Frank, Rolfe Sedan, George Rowe, Agnes Steele, Ham Kinsey, William Irving, Charlie Hall, Otto Lederer, Dick Gilbert, Frank Saputo.

Their Purple Moment (2 reels).
Producer: Hal Roach. Supervisor: Leo McCarey. Director: James Parrott. Camera: George Stevens. Editor: Richard Currier. Titles: H. M. Walker. With: Anita Garvin, Kay Deslys, Jimmy Aubrey, Fay Holderness, Lyle Tayo, Leo Willis, Jack Hill, Retta Palmer, "Tiny" Sandford, Sam Lufkin, Ed Brandenberg, Patsy O'Byrne, Dorothy Walbert.

Should Married Men Go Home? (2 reels).
Producer: Hal Roach. Supervisor: Leo McCarey. Director: James Parrott. Story: Leo McCarey and James Parrott. Camera: George Stevens. Editor: Richard Currier. Titles: H. M. Walker. With: Edgar Kennedy, Edna Marian, Viola Richard, John Aassen, Jack Hill, Dorothy Coburn, Lyle Tayo, Chet Brandenberg, Sam Lufkin, Charlie Hall, Kay Deslys.

Early to Bed (2 reels).
Producer: Hal Roach. Supervisor: Leo McCarey. Director: Emmett Flynn. Camera: George Stevens. Editor: Richard Currier. Titles: H. M. Walker. With: simply, Laurel & Hardy.

Two Tars (2 reels).
Producer: Hal Roach. Supervisor: Leo McCarey. Director: James Parrott. Story: Leo McCarey. Camera: George Stevens. Editor: Richard Currier. Titles: H. M. Walker. With: Thelma Hill, Ruby Blaine, Charley Rogers, Edgar Kennedy, Clara Guiol, Jack Hill, Charlie Hall, Edgar Dearing, Harry Bernard, Sam Lufkin, Baldwin Cooke, Charles McMurphy, Ham Kinsey, Lyle Tayo, Lon Poff, Retta Palmer, George Rowe, Chet Brandenberg, Fred Holmes, Dorothy Walbert, Frank Ellis, Helen Gilmore.

Habeas Corpus (2 reels).
(Synchronized music and sound effects.)
Producer: Hal Roach. Supervisor: Leo McCarey. Director: James Parrott. Story: Leo McCarey. Camera: Len Powers. Editor: Richard Currier. Titles: H. M. Walker. With: Richard Carle, Charles A. Bachman, Charley Rogers.

We Faw Down (2 reels).
(United Kingdom title: *We Slip Up.*)
(Synchronized music and sound effects.)
Producer: Hal Roach. Director: Leo McCarey. Editor: Richard Currier. Titles: H. M. Walker. With: George Kotsonaros, Bess Flowers, Vivien Oakland, Kay Deslys, Vera White, Allen Cavan.

1929   *Liberty* (2 reels).
(Synchronized music and sound effects.)
Producer: Hal Roach. Director: Leo McCarey. Story: Leo McCarey. Camera: George Stevens. Editor: Richard Currier and William Terhune. Titles: H. M. Walker. With: James Finlayson, Tom Kennedy, Jean Harlow, Harry Bernard, Ed Brandenberg, Sam Lufkin, Jack Raymond, Jack Hill.

Wrong Again (2 reels).
(Synchronized music and sound effects.)
Producer: Hal Roach. Director: Leo McCarey. Story: Leo McCarey (Crowther and Skretvedt filmographies credit just McCarey; Bann adds Lewis R. Foster). Camera: George Stevens. Editor: Richard Currier. Titles: H. M. Walker. With: Del Henderson, Harry Bernard, Charlie Hall, William Gillespie, Jack Hill, Sam Lufkin, Josephine Crowell, Fred Holmes.

That's My Wife (2 reels).
(Synchronized music and sound effects.)
Producer: Hal Roach. Supervisor: Leo McCarey. Director: Lloyd French. Story: Leo McCarey. Editor: Richard Currier. Titles: H. M. Walker. With: Vivien Oakland, Charlie Hall, Jimmy Aubrey, William Courtwright, Sam Lufkin, Harry Bernard.

Big Business (2 reels).
Producer: Hal Roach. Supervisor: Leo McCarey. Director: James Wesley Horne. Story: Leo McCarey. Camera: George Stevens. Editor: Richard Currier. Titles: H. M. Walker. With: James Finlayson, "Tiny" Sandford, Lyle Tayo, Retta Palmer, Charlie Hall.

Unaccustomed As We Are (2 reels).
(Talking picture.)
Producer: Hal Roach. Director: Lewis R. Foster. Story: Leo McCarey. Dialogue: H. M. Walker. Camera: George Stevens, Len Powers, John McBurnie, Jack Roach (Skretvedt Filmography). Editor: Richard Currier. With: Mae Busch, Thelma Todd, Edgar Kennedy.

Double Whoopee (2 reels).
(Silent.)
Producer: Hal Roach. Director: Lewis R. Foster. Story: Leo McCarey. Camera: George Stevens and Jack Roach. Editor: Richard Currier. Titles: H. M. Walker. With: John Peters, Jean Harlow, "Tiny" Sandford, Charlie Hall, Ham Kinsey, Rolfe Sedan, Sam Lufkin, William Gillespie, Charlie Rogers, Ed Brandenberg.

Berth Marks (2 reels).
(Talking Picture.)

Producer: Hal Roach. Director: Lewis R. Foster. Story: Leo McCarey. Story Editor: H. M. Walker. Camera: Len Powers. Editor: Richard Currier. With: Harry Bernard, Baldwin Cooke, Charlie Hall, Pat Harmon, Siles D. Wilcox. (The Crowther filmography lists Paulette Goddard as being an extra.)

Men of War (2 reels).

(Talking picture.)

Producer: Hal Roach. Director: Lewis R. Foster. (The Everson filmography credits the story to McCarey.) Dialogue: H. M. Walker. Camera: George Stevens and Jack Roach. Editor: Richard Currier. With: James Finlayson, Harry Bernard, Anne Cornwall, Gloria Greer, Pete Gordon, Charlie Hall, Baldwin Cooke.

Perfect Day (2 reels).

(Talking picture.)

Producer: Hal Roach. Director: James Parrott. Story: Hal Roach and Leo McCarey. Story Editor: H. M. Walker. Editor: Richard Currier. With: Edgar Kennedy, Kay Deslys, Isabelle Keith, Harry Bernard, Clara Guiol, Baldwin Cooke, Lyle Tayo, Charley Rogers.

They Go Boom (2 reels).

(Talking picture.)

Producer: Hal Roach. Director: James Parrott. Story: Leo McCarey. Story Editor: H. M. Walker. Editor: Richard Currier. With: Charlie Hall, Sam Lufkin.

Bacon Grabbers (2 reels).

(Synchronized music and sound effects.)

Producer: Hal Roach. Director: Lewis R. Foster. Story: Leo McCarey. Camera: George Stevens and Jack Roach. Editor: Richard Currier. Titles: H. M. Walker. With: Edgar Kennedy, Jean Harlow, Charlie Hall, Bobby Dunn, Harry Bernard, Sam Lufkin, Eddie Baker.

The Hoose-Gow (2 reels).

(Talking picture.)

Producer: Hal Roach. Director: James Parrott. Story: Leo McCarey. Story Editor: Elmer R. Raguse. Camera: George Stevens, Len Powers, Glen Robert Kershner. Editor: Richard Currier. Title Editor: Nat Hoffberg. With: James Finlayson, "Tiny" Sandford, Leo Willis, Dick Sutherland, Ellinor Van Der Veer, Retta Palmer, Sam Lufkin, Eddie Dunn, Baldwin Cooke, Jack Ward, Ham Kinsey, John Whiteford, Ed Brandenberg, Chet Brandenberg, Charles Dorety, Charlie Hall.

M-G-M

The Hollywood Revue of 1929 (feature—120 minutes).

Producer: Harry Raft. Director: Charles F. Riesner. Laurel & Hardy contribute an eight-minute magic sketch to what is essentially an early sound variety show. With Jack Benny as emcee, other talent includes: Conrad Nagel, Joan Crawford, Marian Davies, Buster Keaton, Norma Shearer, John Gilbert, Lionel Barrymore, Ann Dvorak, Marie Dressler. The Laurel & Hardy routine steals the show.

HAL ROACH—M-G-M

Angora Love (2 reels).
(Synchronized music and sound effects.)
Producer: Hal Roach. Director: Lewis R. Foster. Story: Leo McCarey. Camera: George Stevens. Editor: Richard Currier. Titles: H. M. Walker. With: Edgar Kennedy, Charlie Hall, Harry Bernard, Charley Young.

1930   *Night Owls* (2 reels).
Producer: Hal Roach. Director: James Parrott. Story: Leo McCarey. Story Editor: Richard Currier. With: Edgar Kennedy, James Finlayson, Anders Randolph, Harry Bernard, Charles McMurphy, Baldwin Cooke.

Blotto (2 reels).
Producer: Hal Roach. Director: James Parrott. Story: Leo McCarey. Dialogue: H. M. Walker. Camera: George Stevens. Editor: Richard Currier. With: Anita Garvin, "Tiny" Sandford, Baldwin Cooke, Charlie Hall, Frank Holliday, Dick Gilbert, Jack Hill.

Brats (2 reels).
Producer: Hal Roach. Director: James Parrott. Story: Leo McCarey and Hal Roach. Dialogue: H. M. Walker. Camera: George Stevens. Editor: Richard Currier. Title Editor: Nat Hoffbert. With: Laurel & Hardy in dual roles.

Below Zero (2 reels).
Producer: Hal Roach. Director: James Parrott. Story: Leo McCarey. Dialogue: H. M. Walker. Camera: George Stevens. Editor: Richard Currier. Title Editor: Nat Hoffberg. With: Charlie Hall, Frank Holliday, Leo Willis, "Tiny" Sandford, Kay Deslys, Blanche Payson, Lyle Tayo, Retta Palmer, Baldwin Cooke, "Bobby" Burns, Jack Hill.

M-G-M

The Rogue Song (feature—115 minutes).
(Two-color Technicolor.)
Producer/Director: Lionel Barrymore. Laurel & Hardy (directed by Roach) do eight scenes, to be inserted as comic relief in grand opera singer Lawrence Tibbett's already completed debut film for M-G-M.

HAL ROACH—M-G-M

Hog Wild (2 reels).
(United Kingdom title—*Aerial Antics*.)
Producer: Hal Roach. Director: James Parrott. Story: Leo McCarey. Dialogue: H. M. Walker. Camera: George Stevens. Editor: Richard Currier. With: Fay Holderness, Dorothy Granger, Charles McMurphy.

The Laurel and Hardy Murder Case (3 reels).
Producer: Hal Roach. Director: James Parrott. Dialogue: H. M. Walker. Camera: George Stevens and Walter Lundin. Editor: Richard Currier. With: "Tiny" Sand-

ford, Fred Kelsey, Bobby Burns, Del Henderson, Dorothy Granger, Frank Austin, Lon Poff, Rosa Gore, Stanley Blystone, Art Rowlands.

Another Fine Mess (3 reels).
Producer: Hal Roach. Director: James Parrott. Story: Based on sketch by Laurel's father, A. J. Jefferson. Dialogue: H. M. Walker. Camera: George Stevens. Editor: Richard Currier. With: Thelma Todd, James Finlayson, Eddie Dunn, Charles Gerrard, Gertrude Sutton, Harry Bernard, Bill Knight, Bob Mimford, Bobby Burns, Joe Mole.

1931 *Be Big* (3 reels).
Producer: Hal Roach. Director: James Parrott. Dialogue: H. M. Walker. Camera: Art Lloyd. Editor: Richard Currier. With: Anita Garvin, Isabelle Keith, Charlie Hall, Baldwin Cooke, Jack Hill, Ham Kinsey, Chet Brandenberg.

Chickens Come Home (3 reels).
Producer: Hal Roach. Director: James W. Horne. Dialogue: H. M. Walker. Camera: Art Lloyd and Jack Stevens. Editor: Richard Currier. With: Mae Busch, Thelma Todd, James Finlayson, Frank Holliday, Elizabeth Forrester, Norma Drew, Patsy O'Bryne, Charles French, Gertrude Pedlar, Frank Rice, Gordon Douglas, Ham Kinsey, Baldwin Cooke, Dorothy Layton.

PARAMOUNT & NATIONAL SCREEN SERVICE

The Stolen Jewels (2 reels).
(United Kingdom title—*The Slippery Pearls*.)
Producer: Pat Casey. Director: William McGann. Cameo appearance by Laurel & Hardy in a star-studded cast, from Buster Keaton to Irene Dunne.

HAL ROACH—M-G-M

Laughing Gravy (2 reels).
Producer: Hal Roach. Director: James W. Horne. Dialogue: H. M. Walker. Camera: Art Lloyd. Editor: Richard Currier. With: Charlie Hall, Harry Bernard, Charles Dorety.

Our Wife (2 reels).
Producer: Hal Roach. Director: James W. Horne. Dialogue: H. M. Walker. Camera: Art Lloyd. Editor: Richard Currier. With: Jean "Babe" London, James Finlayson, Ben Turpin, Charlie Rogers, Blanche Peyson.

Pardon Us (feature—56 minutes).
(United Kingdom title—*Jailbirds*.)
Producer: Hal Roach. Director: James Parrott. Dialogue: H. M. Walker. Camera: George Stevens. Editor: Richard Currier. With: Walter Long, James Finlayson, June Marlowe, Charlie Hall, Sam Lufkin, Harry Bernard, "Tiny" Sandford, Bobby Burns, Baldwin Cooke, Charlie Rogers, and others, including "extras" Hal Roach and James Parrott.

Come Clean (2 reels).
Producer: Hal Roach. Director: James W. Horne. Dialogue: H. M. Walker. Cam-

era: Art Lloyd. Editor: Richard Currier. With: Gertrude Astor, Linda Loredo, Mae Busch, Charlie Hall, Eddie Baker, "Tiny" Sandford, Gordon Douglas.

One Good Turn (2 reels).
Producer: Hal Roach. Director: James W. Horne. Dialogue: H. M. Walker. Camera: Art Lloyd. Editor: Richard Currier. With: Mary Carr, Billy Gilbert, Lyle Tayo, Dorothy Granger, Snub Pollard, Gordon Douglas, Dick Gilbert, Baldwin Cooke, George Miller, Ham Kinsey, Retta Palmer, Charley Young, William Gillespie.

Beau Hunks (4 reels).
(United Kingdom title—*Beau Chumps*.)
Producer: Hal Roach. Director: James W. Horne. Dialogue: H. M. Walker. Camera: Art Lloyd and Jack Stevens. Editor: Richard Currier. With: Charles Middleton, Charlie Hall, "Tiny" Sandford, Harry Schultz, Gordon Douglas, Sam Lufkin, Marvin Hatley, Jack Hill, Leo Willis, Bob Kortman, Baldwin Cooke, Dick Gilbert, Oscar Morgan, Ham Kinsey, Broderick O'Farrell, James W. Horne.

On the Loose (2 reels).
Producer/Director/Story: Hal Roach. Dialogue: H. M. Walker. Camera: Len Powers. Editor: Richard Currier. With: Laurel & Hardy making a cameo in the ZaSu Pitts—Thelma Todd series.

1932   *Helpmates* (2 reels).
Producer: Hal Roach. Director: James Parrott. Dialogue: H. M. Walker. Camera: Art Lloyd. Editor: Richard Currier. With: Blanche Payson, Bobby Burns, Robert Callahan.

Any Old Port (2 reels).
Producer: Hal Roach. Director: James Parrott. Dialogue: H. M. Walker. Camera: Art Lloyd. Editor: Richard Currier. With: Walter Long, Julie Bishop, Harry Bernard, Charlie Hall, Bobby Burns, Sam Lufkin, Dick Gilbert, Eddie Baker, Will Stanton, Jack Hill, Baldwin Cooke, Ed Brandenberg.

The Music Box (3 reels).
Producer: Hal Roach. Director: James Parrott. Dialogue: H. M. Walker. Camera: Walter Lundin and Len Powers. Editor: Richard Currier. With: Billy Gilbert, William Gillespie, Charlie Hall, Gladys Gale, Sam Lufkin, Lilyan Irene.

The Chimp (3 reels).
Producer: Hal Roach. Director: James Parrott. Dialogue: H. M . Walker. Camera: Walter Lundin. Editor: Richard Currier. With: Billy Gilbert, James Finlayson, "Tiny" Sandford, Charles Gamora, Jack Hill, Bobby Burns, George Miller, Baldwin Cooke, Dorothy Layton, Belle Hare, Martha Sleeper.

County Hospital (2 reels).
Producer: Hal Roach. Director: James Parrott. Dialogue: H. M. Walker. Camera: Art Lloyd. Editor: Bert Jordan and Richard Currier. With: Billy Gilbert, Sam Lufkin, Baldwin Cooke, Ham Kinsey, May Wallace, Frank Holliday, Lilyan Irene, Belle Hare, Dorothy Layton, William Austin.

Scram! (2 reels).
Producer: Hal Roach. Director: Raymond McCarey. Dialogue: H. M. Walker. Camera: Art Lloyd. Editor: Richard Currier. With: Arthur Housman, Rychard Cramer, Vivien Oakland, Sam Lufkin, Charles McMurphy, Baldwin Cooke, Charles Dorety.

Pack Up Your Troubles (feature—68 minutes).
Producer: Hal Roach. Directors: George Marshall and Raymond McCarey (though the codirector credit for Leo's brother is now in question). Dialogue: H. M. Walker. Camera: Art Lloyd. Editor: Richard Currier. With: Donald Dillaway, Jacquie Lyn, Mary Carr, James Finlayson, Rychard Cramer, Adele Watson, Tom Kennedy, Charles Middleton, Muriel Evans, Grady Sutton, C. Montague Shaw, Billy Gilbert, and others.

Their First Mistake (2 reels).
Producer: Hal Roach. Director: George Marshall. Editor: Richard Currier. With: Mae Busch, Billy Gilbert, George Marshall.

Towed in a Hole (2 reels).
Producer: Hal Roach. Director: George Marshall. Camera: Art Lloyd. Editor: Richard Currier. With: Billy Gilbert.

1933 *Twice Two* (2 reels).
Producer: Hal Roach. Director: James Parrott. Camera: Art Lloyd. Editor: Bert Jordan. With: Laurel & Hardy each in two roles, Baldwin Cooke, Charlie Hall, Ham Kinsey.

Me and My Pal (2 reels).
Producer: Hal Roach. Directors: Charles Rogers and Lloyd French. Camera: Art Lloyd. Editor: Bert Jordan. With: James Finlayson, James C. Morton, Eddie Dunn, Charlie Hall, Bobby Dunn, Carole Borland, Mary Kornmand, Charles McMurphy, and others.

The Devil's Brother (*Fra Diavolo*, feature—90 minutes).
Producer: Hal Roach. Directors: Roach and Charles Rogers. Adaptation from the Daniel F. Auber comic opera: Jeanie MacPherson. Camera: Art Lloyd and Hap Depew. Editor: Bert Jordan and William Terhune. With: Dennie King, Thelma Todd, James Finlayson, Lucille Brown, Lane Chandler, Arthur Pierson, Henry Armetta, Matt McHugh, Nina Quartaro, Wilfred Lucas, and others.

The Midnight Patrol (2 reels).
Producer: Hal Roach. Director: Lloyd French. Camera: Art Lloyd. Editor: Bert Jordan. With: Robert Kortman, Charlie Hall, Walter Plinge, Harry Bernard, Frank Brownlee, James C. Morton, "Tiny" Sandford, Edgar Dearing, and others.

Busy Bodies (2 reels).
Producer: Hal Roach. Director: Lloyd French. Camera: Art Lloyd. Editor: Bert Jordan. With: "Tiny" Sandford, Charlie Hall, Jack Hill, Dick Gilbert, Charley Young.

Wild Poses (2 reels).

Producer/Director: Robert F. McGowan. Camera: Francis Corby. Editor: William Terhune. With: Laurel & Hardy cameo in an Our Gang film.

Dirty Work (2 reels).
Producer: Hal Roach. Director: Lloyd French. Camera: Kenneth Peach. Editor: Bert Jordan. With: Lucien Littlefield, Sam Adams.

Sons of the Desert (feature—68 minutes).
(United Kingdom title—*Fraternally Yours.*)
Producer: Hal Roach. Director: William A. Seiter. Story: Frank Craven. Camera: Kenneth Peach. Editor: Bert Jordan. Song: "Honolulu Baby," by Marvin Hatley. With: Mae Busch, Dorothy Christie, Charley Chase, Lucien Littlefield, and others.

1934   *Oliver the Eighth* (3 reels).
Producer: Hal Roach. Director: Lloyd French. Camera: Art Lloyd. Editor: Bert Jordan. With: Mae Busch, Jack Beaty.

M-G-M

Hollywood Party (feature—68 minutes).
Producers: Harry Rapf and Howard Dietz. Directors: Richard Boleslawski and Allen Dwan. Laurel & Hardy, with Lupe Velez, contribute a sketch to another variety show-like feature supposedly set at a Hollywood party. Other talent includes: Jimmy Durante, Ted Healy, and his Stooges (Moe, Larry, and Curly), and Walt Disney Technicolor sequences.

HAL ROACH—M-G-M

Going Bye-Bye! (2 reels).
Producer: Hal Roach. Director: Charles Rogers. Camera: Francis Corby. Editor: Bert Jordan. With: Walter Long, Mae Busch, Sam Lufkin, Harry Dunkinson, Ellinor Van Der Veer, Baldwin Cooke, and others.

Them Thar Hills! (2 reels).
Producer: Hal Roach. Director: Charles Rogers. Camera: Art Lloyd. Editor: Bert Jordan. With: Billy Gilbert, Charlie Hall, Mae Busch, Bobby Dunn, Sam Lufkin, Dick Alexander, and others.

Babes in Toyland (feature—79 minutes).
Producer: Hal Roach. Directors: Charles Rogers and Gus Meins. Screenplay: Nick Grinde and Frank Butler. Adapted from the musical comedy by Victor Herbert and Glen MacDonough. Camera: Art Lloyd and Francis Corby. Editor: William Terhune and Bert Jordan. With: Charlotte Henry, Felix Knight, Henry Brandon, Florence Roberts, Ferdinand Munier, William Burress, Virginia Karns, and others.

The Live Ghost (2 reels).
Producer: Hal Roach. Director: Charles Rogers. Camera: Art Lloyd. Editor: Louis MacManus. With: Walter Long, Mae Busch, Arthur Houseman, Harry Bernard, Charlie Hall, Sam Lufkin, Baldwin Cooke, and others.

1935   *Tit for Tat* (2 reels).
Producer: Hal Roach. Director: Charles Rogers. Camera: Art Lloyd. Editor: Bert

Jordan. With: Charlie Hall, Mae Busch, James C. Morton, Bobby Dunn, Baldwin Cooke, and others.

The Fixer Uppers (2 reels).
Producer: Hal Roach. Director: Charles Rogers. Camera: Art Lloyd. Editor: Bert Jordan. With: Mae Busch, Charles Middleton, Arthur Houseman, Bobby Dunn, Noah Young, and others.

Thicker Than Water (2 reels).
Producer: Hal Roach. Director: James W. Horne. Story: Stan Laurel. Camera: Art Lloyd. Editor: Ray Snyder. With: Daphne Pollard, James Finlayson, Ed Brandenberg, Charlie Hall, Bess Flowers, Lester Dorr, and others.

Bonnie Scotland (feature—80 minutes).
Producer: Hal Roach. Director: James Wesley Horne. Screenplay: Frank Butler and Jeff Moffitt. Camera: Art Lloyd and Walter Lundin. Editor: Bert Jordan. With: June Lang, William Janney, Anne Grey, James Mack, James Finlayson, David Torrence, Maurice Black, Daphne Pollard, and others.

1936　*The Bohemian Girl* (feature—70 minutes).
Producer: Hal Roach. Directors: James W. Horne and Charles Rogers. Based on the Michael W. Balfe opera. Camera: Art Lloyd and Francis Corby. Editors: Bert Jordan and Louis McManus. With: Antonio Moreno, Jacqueline Wells, Darla Hood, Mae Busch, James Finlayson, William P. Carleton, Thelma Todd, and others.

On the Wrong Trek (2 reels).
Producer: Hal Roach. Directors: Charles Parrott (Charley Chase) and Harold Law. Camera: Art Lloyd. Photographic Effects: Roy Seawright. Editor: William Ziegler. With: Laurel & Hardy cameo in a Charley Chase film.

Our Relations (feature—74 minutes).
Producer: Stan Laurel. Supervisor: L. A. French. Director: Harry Lachman. (Suggested by the William Wymark Jacobs short story, "The Money Box.") Screenplay: Richard Connell and Felix Adler. Adaptation: Charles Rogers and Jack Jevne. Camera: Rudolph Meté. Photographic Effects: Roy Seawright. Editor: Bert Jordan. With: Daphne Pollard, Betty Healy, Sidney Toler, James Finlayson, Iris Adrian, Lona Andre, Alan Hale, Sr., Arthur Houseman, Ralf Harolde, Noel Madison, and others.

1937　*Way Out West* (feature—65 minutes).
Producer: Stan Laurel. Director: James W. Horne. Original Story: Jack Jevne and Charles Rogers. Screenplay: Charles Rogers, Felix Adler, and James Parrott. Camera: Art Lloyd and Walter Lundin. Photographic Effects: Roy Seawright. Editor: Bert Jordan. With: Sharon Lynne, James Finlayson, Rosina Lawrence, Stanley Fields, Vivien Oakland, Avalon Boys Quartet (includes Chill Wills), and others.

Pick a Star (feature—70 minutes).
Producer: Hal Roach. Director: Edward Sedgwick. Laurel & Hardy appear in two short scenes of this musical starring Patsy Kelly, Jack Haley, and Rosina Lawrence.

1938   *Swiss Miss* (feature—72 minutes).
Producer: Hal Roach. Director: John G. Blystone. Story: Jean Negulesco and Charles Rogers. Screenplay: James Parrott, Felix Adler, and Charles Melson. Camera: Norbert Brodine and Art Lloyd. Photographic Effects: Roy Seawright. Editor: Bert Jordan. With: Della Lind (Grete Batzier), Walter Woolf King, Eric Blore, Adia Kuznetzoff, Charles Judels, Ludovico Tomarchio, Jean de Briac, George Sorel, Charles Gamora, and others. (Music: Scoring receives an Academy Award nomination.)

Block-Heads (feature—58 minutes).
Producer: Hal Roach. Director: John G. Blystone. Story and Adaptation: Charles Rogers, Felix Adler, James Parrott, Harry Langdon, and Arnold Belgard. Camera: Art Lloyd. Photographic Effects: Roy Seawright. Editor: Bert Jordan. With: Patricia Ellis, Minna Gombell, Billy Gilbert, James Finlayson, and others. (Marvin Hatley receives an Academy Award nomination for best original score.)

RKO—RADIO PICTURES

1939   *The Flying Deuces* (feature—69 minutes).
Producer: Boris Morros. Director: A. Edward Sutherland. Original Story and Screenplay: Ralph Spence, Alfred Schiller, Charles Rogers, and Harry Langdon. Camera: Art Lloyd. Photographic Effects: Howard Anderson. Editor: Jack Dennis. With: Jean Parker, Reginald Gardner, Charles Middleton, Jean Del Val, Clem Wilenchick (Crane Whitley), James Finlayson, and others.

HAL ROACH—UNITED ARTISTS

1940   *A Chump at Oxford* (feature—63 minutes overseas; original American release was 42 minutes, but longer version released in America during early 1941).
Producer: Hal Roach. Director: Alfred Goulding. Original Story and Screenplay: Charles Rogers, Felix Adler, and Harry Langdon. Camera: Art Lloyd. Photographic Effects: Roy Seawright. Editor: Bert Jordan. With: Forrester Harvey, Wilfred Lucas, Forbes Murray, Frank Baker, Eddie Borden, and others.

Saps at Sea (feature—57 minutes).
Producer: Hal Roach. Director: Gordon Douglas. Original Story and Screenplay: Charles Rogers, Felix Adler, Gil Pratt, and Harry Langdon. Camera: Art Lloyd. Photographic Effects: Roy Seawright. Editor: William Ziegler. With: James Finlayson, Ben Turpin, Rychard Cramer, and others.

20th CENTURY-FOX

1941   *Great Guns* (feature—74 minutes).
Producer: Sol M. Wurtzel. Director: Montague "Monty" Banks. Story and Screenplay: Lou Breslow. Camera: Glen MacWilliams. Editor: Al de Gaetano. With: Sheila Ryan, Dick Nelson, Edmund MacDonald, Ludwig Stossel, Kane Richmond, Mae Marsh, Ethel Griffies, and others.

1942   *A-Haunting We Will Go* (feature—67 minutes).
Producer: Sol M. Wurtzel. Director: Alfred L. Werker. Story: Lou Breslow and

Stanley Rauth. Screenplay: Lou Breslow. Camera: Glen MacWilliams. Editor: Alfred Day. With: Dante the Magician (Harry A. Jansen), Sheila Ryan, John Shelton, Don Costello, Elisha Cook, Jr., Edward Gargan, Mantan Moreland, Willie Best, and others.

UNITED STATES GOVERNMENT

1943   *The Tree in a Test Tube* (1 reel).
Producer: Department of Agriculture (Forest Service)—at 20th Century-Fox. Director: Charles McDonald. Laurel & Hardy make a brief appearance in this war-effort production.

M-G-M

Air Raid Wardens (feature—67 minutes).
Producer: B. F. Zeidman. Director: Edward Sedgwick. Original Screenplay: Martin Rackin, Jack Jevne, Charles Rogers, and Harry Crane. Camera: Walter Lundin. Editor: Irvine Warburton. With: Edgar Kennedy, Jacqueline White, Horace McNally, Nella Walker, Donald Meek, Henry O'Neill, and others.

20th CENTURY-FOX

Jitterbugs (feature—74 minutes).
Producer: Sol M. Wurtzel. Director: Malcolm St. Clair. Screenplay: Scott Darling. Camera: Lucien Andriot. Special Photographic Effects: Fred Sersen. Editor: Norman Colbert. With: Vivian Blaine, Robert Bailey, Douglas Fowley, Noel Madison, Lee Patrick, Robert Emmett Keane, and others.

The Dancing Masters (feature—63 minutes).
Producer: Lee Marcus. Director: Malcolm St. Clair. Screenplay: W. Scott Darling. Suggested by a George Bricker story. Camera: Norbert Brodine. Special Photographic Effects: Fred Sersen. Editor: Norbert Brodine. With: Trudy Marshall, Robert Bailey, Matt Briggs, Margaret Dumont, Allan Lane, Charlie Rogers, and others.

1944   *The Big Noise* (feature—74 minutes).
Producer: Sol M. Wurtzel. Director: Malcolm St. Clair. Screenplay: W. Scott Darling. Camera: Joe MacDonald. Special Photographic Effects: Fred Sersen. Editor: Norman Colberts. With: Doris Merrick, Arthur Space, Veda Ann Borg, Bobby Blake, Frank Fenton, James Bush, and others.

M-G-M

1945   *Nothing But Trouble* (feature—70 minutes).
Producer: B. F. Zeidman. Director: Sam Taylor. Screenplay: Russell Rouse and Ray Golden. Additional Dialogue: Bradford Ropes and Margaret Gruen. Camera: Charles Salerno, Jr. Editor: Conrad A. Nervig. With: Mary Bolard, Philip Merivale, Henry O'Neill, David Leland, John Warburton, Matthew Boulton, Connie Gilchrist, and others.

20th CENTURY-FOX

The Bullfighters (feature—69 minutes).
Producer: William Girard. Director: Malcolm St. Clair. Screenplay: W. Scott Darling. Camera: Norbert Brodine. Special Photographic Effects: Fred Sersen. Editor: Stanley Rabjohn. With: Margo Woode, Richard Lane, Carol Andrews, Diosa Costello, Frank McCown, Ralph Sanford, and others.

FILMS SIRIUS/FRANCO-LONDON/FORTEZZA FILM

1951   *Atoll K* (feature—French release at 98 minutes; 1952 release in United Kingdom as *Robinson Crusoeland* at 82 minutes; 1954 release in United States as *Utopia* at 82 minutes).
Producer: Raymond Eger. Director: Leo Joannon. Screenplay: John Klorer, Frederick Kohner, Rene Wheeler, and Pierro Tellini, from an idea by Leo Joannon. Camera: Armand Thirard and Louis Nee. Editor: Raymond Isnardon. With: Suzy Delair, Max Elloy, Adriano Rimoldi, Felix Oudart, and others.

SELECTED COMPILATIONS

1957   *The Golden Age of Comedy*
(Robert Youngson Production/DCA)

1960   *When Comedy Was King*
(Robert Youngson Production/20th Century-Fox)

1963   *Days of Thrills and Laughter*
(Robert Youngson Production/20th Century-Fox)

1964   *M-G-M's Big Parade of Laughs*
(Robert Youngson Production/M-G-M)

1965   *Laurel & Hardy's Laughing Twenties*
(Robert Youngson Production/M-G-M)

1966   *The Crazy World of Laurel and Hardy*
(Jay Ward Production)

1967   *The Further Perils of Laurel & Hardy*
(Robert Youngson Production/20th Century-Fox)

1970   *Four Clowns*
(Robert Youngson Production)

Selected Discography

The starting point for this section was the collection of the New York Public Library. It has been supplemented by the discographies from Bruce Crowther's *Laurel and Hardy: Clown Princes of Comedy* and Roland Lacourbe's French text *Laurel et Hardy*. A final source has been the private collections of both friends and colleagues. Because Laurel & Hardy material has been, and continues to be, released in a number of packaging arrangements, this alphabetized list is not complete. But with the foundation established here, the list illustrates the ongoing interest in Laurel & Hardy. (LP albums, unless otherwise noted.)

"Another Fine Mess" (with the Boston Barbers)/"The Stan and Ollie Serenade" (with the Boston Serenaders) (45 rpm record) (United Artists UP36107).

Babes in Toyland (soundtrack album). 1974 (Mark 56 Records 577).

Film Star Parade (ASV Living Era 5020).

The Golden Age of Comedy (Charisma PCS 11).

Hal Roach and MGM Present Laurel and Hardy (78 rpm). 1932 (Columbia DX 370).

In Trouble Again! 1972 (Mark 56 Records 600).

Laurel & Hardy. 1975 (Mark 56 Records 688).

Laurel & Hardy: Another Fine Mess. 1973 (Mark 56 Records 579).

Laurel and Hardy, Naturally High. 1970 (Douglas 10).

Laurel & Hardy: No-U-Turn. 1973 (Mark 56 Records 601).

Laurel and Hardy on the Air. (Radiola MR 1104).

Laurel and Hardy: The Golden Age of Hollywood Comedy. 1975 (United Artists Records UAG 29676).

The Movie Collection. (Deja Vu DVLP 2054).

A Nostalgia Trip to the Stars—Vol. 2. 1973 (Monmouth-Evergreen MES 7031).

The Rogue Song (soundtrack album). 1980 (Pelican Records LP 2019).

This Is Your Laff. 1963 (Peter Pan Record 8018). "Shine on, Harvest Moon"/"The World Is Waiting for the Sunrise" (45 rpm). (Columbia DB 9145).

Sons of the Desert (soundtrack album) (Mark 56 Records 689).

''The Trail of the Lonesome Pine''/''Honolulu Baby'' (45 rpm record). 1976 (Mark 56 Records 303).

Voices from the Hollywood Past (Laurel interview). 1975 (Delos DEL F25412).

Voices of the Stars (78 rpm). (Regal-Zonophone MR 1234). ''You Are the Ideal of My Dreams''/''Let Me Call You Sweetheart'' (45 rpm record). (United Artists UP 36164).

Index

Abbott & Costello, 24, 34, 95–96, 102–3, 137, 180, 182, 184, 211–12

Academy of Motion Picture Arts and Sciences (Beverly Hills), 81

Adventurer, The (Chaplin, 1917), 133

Aerial Antics. See Hog Wild

Agee, James, 89–90, 91, 171, 178, 183, 184–85, 186, 189, 270

A-Haunting We Will Go (1942), 93, 101, 103, 241, 269

Ainsworth, Katherine, 216

Air Raid Wardens, 93, 101, 192, 269

Allen, Steve, 36

Allen, Woody, 59, 96, 196

All Night Long (1924), 45

Amander, Charles (Charles Aplin), 12

American Cinematographer, 220

American Vaudeville as Ritual (McLean), 46

Anderson, Gilbert M. ("Broncho Billy"), 22–23, 24, 262

Anderson, Janice, 213

Andrews, Carol, 103

Angora Love (1929), 264

Animal Crackers (stars Marx Brothers, 1930), 93, 130, 174

"An Interview with Stan Laurel" (Goldstein), 234–35

Another Fine Mess (1930), 6, 58, 264

Any Old Port (1932), 3, 56, 264

Arbuckle, Fatty, 22, 115, 180, 196, 262

Ardell, Alyce, 40, 264

Are Parents People? (St. Clair, 1925), 103

"Artful Antics of Baby Hardy, The," 20

Astaire, Fred, 163

Atlantic Constitution, 47, 48

"At Laurel's Father's Home Suburb," 224

"At Laurel's Home Suburb," 57–58

Atoll K (1951), 93, 104, 105, 108–9, 113, 182, 270

Aubrey, Jimmy, 10, 18, 262

Austin, Bruce, 213

Ave Maria, 240

Awful Truth, The (1920s Broadway play by Arthur Richman), 51

Awful Truth, The (McCarey film, 1937), 29, 51, 52 (illus.), 206, 240

"Babe Hardy, The Fat Boy with the Vim," 9–10, 198

"Babe London Visits Tent," 241

Babes in Toyland (1934), 65, 67, 79, 80 (illus.), 87, 171, 172–73, 210–11, 238, 266

"Babe's Night Out," 243
Babe: The Life of Oliver Hardy (Mc-
  Cabe), 30, 158, 272
Bacon, James, 235–36
Balázs, Béla, 90
Ball State University Forum, 209
Bancroft, George, 88
Bank Dick, The (stars Fields, 1940), 192,
  205
Bann, Richard, 165, 167
Bara, Theda, 1, 40
Barber Shop, The (stars Fields, 1933),
  113
Barnes, Peter, 189
Barr, Charles, 33, 51, 63, 162–63, 164,
  188, 200
Battle of the Century, The (1927), 27,
  37, 134, 143, 149, 151, 184, 222,
  240, 263
BBC, 56, 265
Bears and Bad Men (1918), 18
"Beau Chumps and Church Bells"
  (Durgnat), 193–94
Beau Hunks (1931), 96
Beckett, Samuel, 137, 139, 194, 197
"Before Laurel: Oliver Hardy and the
  Vim Company, A Studio Biography"
  (Nelson), 213
Behind the Screen (Chaplin, 1916), 196
Below Zero (1930), 150
Benchley, Robert, 46, 130, 131, 134,
  266
Benny, Jack, 73
Bergman, Ingrid, 28, 76
Bergson, Henri, 168, 204, 235
Berman, Art, 238
Bermel, Albert, 212
Big Business (1929), 37–38, 125, 207,
  264; comic violence in, 6, 97, 135,
  175, 206; the cop in, 98, 132, 134
Big House, The (1930), 23
Big Noise, The (1944), 93, 186, 269
"Big Sneeze, The: A Visit with Billy
  Gilbert" (Burgeon), 198
Big Store, The (stars Marx Brothers,
  1941), 93
Billboard magazine, 101, 102, 185, 198

Birds of a Feather (Laurel & Hardy
  sketch), 110, 157, 270
Birthmarks (1929), 220
Blackbeard, Bill, 47
Blacksmith, The (Keaton, 1922), 103
Blaine, Vivian, 99, 101, 102
Blair, Walter, 130
Blanche, Ed, 209
"Blest Pair of Sirens" (Wright), 175,
  186, 187
Block Heads (1938), 77, 79, 87, 96, 171,
  172, 173, 177 (illus.), 188, 267; gas
  stove in, 4; inspired dumbness in, 17;
  Harry Langdon and, 45, 88–89, 106;
  swan song nature of, 175, 176
Block-Heads (1984 musical play based on
  Laurel & Hardy), 86, 205, 219, 271
Blood and Sand (stars Valentino, 1922),
  22–23, 262
Blotto (1930), 133
Blyth, Jeffrey, 234
Boehnel, William, 89, 179
Bogdanovich, Peter, 32, 50, 107, 239,
  240
Bohemian Girl, The (1936), 77, 79, 152,
  266
Bonnie Scotland (1935), 65, 79, 81, 87,
  96, 152, 189–90, 225, 266
Borde, Raymond, 44, 79, 163, 167–68
Bostock, Gordon, 13, 15
Bow, Clara, 37
Bowler Dessert (Scotland), 161, 199, 245
"Box to Hide In, A" (Thurber), 85
*Boys: The Cinematic World of Laurel and
  Hardy, The* (Nollen), 164
"Bozo Stuck on Paying Tribute to Laurel
  & Hardy," 218
Bradbury, Ray, 138, 214, 244
Brats (1930), 50, 132, 166, 200, 264
"Bringing Up Father" (McManus comic
  strip), 46
Britain, Jim, 230
"Broadway: A Musical About Laurel and
  Hardy Due Next Season" (Nemy), 219
Brooks, Leo M., 9, 21, 47, 84, 91, 94,
  95, 199
Bruce, Lenny, 167

Buck Benny Rides Again (stars Benny, 1940), 73

Buck Privates (stars Abbott & Costello, 1941), 95–96, 102–3

Bullfighters, The (1945), 77, 93, 104, 182, 203, 227, 269

Bunny, John, 46, 180

Burgeon, Vivien, 198

Busch, Mae, 60, 65–66, 137, 165, 260, 269

Busy Bodies (1933), 200

Butler, David, 95

Butler, Frank, 29, 30

Byrd, Larry, 196, 206

Cagney, James, 101–2

Cahiers du Cinéma, 34, 207, 239

Calder, Ritchie, 223

Campbell, Eric, 10, 19

Canby, Vincent, 199

Candy, John, 138

Canton Film Appreciation Group of Cardiff (film series planned, in part, by Laurel), 195

Capra, Frank, 33, 45, 74, 164, 270

"Captive of a Comic Cult Confesses, A" (Ainsworth), 216

Carney, Art, 136–37, 233, 236

Carroll, Kathleen, 194

Carroll, Sidney, 48, 240

Carson, Johnny, 137

Carter, Jimmy, 216

Caruso, Enrico, 6

Caught in the Draft (stars Hope, 1941), 96

Cavalcanti, Alberto, 44, 63, 176

Chaplin, Charlie, 110, 189, 196, 210, 236, 238, 259; autobiography of, 16, 271; comparing Laurel and/or Hardy to, 17, 133–34, 139, 163, 172, 175, 190, 198, 209, 242; Karno and, 36, 105–6, 147, 224, 260, 261; Laurel kids, 76; Laurel praises, 233, 236; McCarey praised by, 33; phenomenal popularity of, 12, 13, 14, 21–22, 54, 55, 125, 261, 265; West, the best impersonator of, 9, 10; women and, 18, 81, 107

Chase, Charley, 27, 29, 31, 38, 40, 51, 68, 146

Chavance, Louis, 168, 170–71

Chickens Come Home (1931), 58

Christie, Dorothy, 66

Christon, Lawrence, 214–16

Chump at Oxford, A (1940), 66, 79, 91, 134, 173, 268

Cinema (France, 193

Cinemeditor, 240

Cine Revue, 245

City Lights (Chaplin, 1931), 164

Classic Film Collector. See *Classic Images*

Classic Images, 191–93, 227, 236–37, 240, 242

Close Up (Herring), 170

"Coburn's Minstrels," 2

Coconuts (stars Marx Brothers, 1929), 130

Cohen, John S., Jr., 69

Colbert, Claudette, 74, 101

Coleman, Dabney, 66

College (Keaton, 1927), 64, 79, 139

College English, 207

Columbia, 192

"Comedy and a Touch of Cuckoo" (McCarey), 240

"Comedy's Greatest Era" (Agee), 89, 171, 183, 184–85, 186, 190, 270

"Comedy Veterans Plan Comeback" (Thomas), 230

Comedy World of Stan Laurel, The (McCabe), 34, 154, 157, 158, 160

"Comic Couple Now a Cult," 193

"Comics Famous 'By Accident' " (Scheuer), 221–22

Conklin, Chester, 13

Connally, Marc, 64

Conrad, Paul, 244

Cooke, Alice, 14, 15, 22

Cooke, Baldwin "Baldy," 14, 15, 22

Cooper, Ron, 205

Cops (Keaton, 1922), 79, 139

Costello, Lou, 275. See also Abbott & Costello

Cramer, Rychard, 165

"Crazy Cracksman, The," 14, 15, 261

"Crazy World of Laurel, The," (Everson), 33, 195–96
Creelman, Eileen, 181
Crist, Judith, 194
"Critique of the Critics, A" (Heath), 171, 197
Crosby, Bing, 95, 96, 107
Crowther, Bosley, 98, 171–72
Crowther, Bruce, 63, 163–64, 199
Cubin, Bill, 219, 246
"Cuckoo" (Barnes), 189
Cuckoo: A Celebration of Stan Laurel and Oliver Hardy (BBC, 1974), 3, 9

Dahlberg, Mae (Laurel's common-law wife), 21, 267; background on, 15; Joe Rock's influence on, 24–25, 263; Laurel's stormy relationship with, 22, 28, 81, 83; naming of "Laurel" by, 16, 262; softer image of, 199
Daily Express (London), 94, 228, 232
Daily Herald (London), 35, 56, 57, 77, 160, 223–24
Daily Mail (London), 105, 213, 234
Daily Star (London), 104, 219, 228
"Dance of the Cuckoos" (Laurel & Hardy's theme song), 57, 68, 110, 125, 159, 198, 260
Dancing Masters, The (1943), 93, 191, 269
Daney, Serge, 239–40
Dan Leno Hys Booke (Leno), 47, 79
Darling, Scott, 103
Davies, Marion, 24
Day, Clarence, 46, 130
Day at the Races, A (1937), 24, 64
Daydreams (Keaton, 1922), 208
Day of the Locust, The (West), 135
Days of Thrills and Laughter (Youngson, 1961), 189
Dean, Loretta, 220
"Deepest Cut," 232
DeHavilland, Olivia, 101
Delfont, Bernard, 113
Dempsey, Jack, 27
DeNiro, Robert, 138–39
"Dennis Pope on Stanley LAUREL &

Oliver Norvell HARDY" (Pope), 194–95
Dent, Vernon, 19
Detroit News, 38
Devil's Brother, The (1933, also known as Fra Diavolo), 65, 66, 172, 175, 233, 265
"Discreet Charm of Laurel & Hardy, The" (Christon), 214–15
Disney, Walt, 53 (illus.), 172
Double Whoopee (1929), 48, 50, 217, 264
Dressler, Marie, 38
"Drivers' License Sketch, The," 92, 104, 157, 185, 242, 268
DuBrow, Rick, 234
Duck Soup (1927), 6, 32, 58, 217
Duck Soup (McCarey, stars Marx Brothers, 1933), 29, 44, 128, 172, 206, 226, 263
"Duet of Incompetence" (McCaffrey), 205–6
Dumont, Margeret, 24, 128, 181, 244
Durante, Jimmy, 160
Durden, Robert, 242
Durgnat, Raymond, 193–94

"Early Ollie: The Plump and Runt Films" (Young), 10, 198
L'Ecran Francais, 105–7, 168, 228
"Edgar Kennedy: The Slow Burn," 198
Edwards, Blake, 194, 197
Edwards, Ralph, 9, 230
8mm Collector. See Classic Images
"Ellinor Van Der Veer" (Satterfield), 244
Eltham and Kentish Times, 190
"Encore: An Interview/Article Collage," 30
Esquire, 48, 240
Evening News (London), 104, 228, 231
Everett, Eldon K., 227
Everson, William, 33, 89–90, 98, 166–67, 194, 195–96, 199
Everyman (England), 173
"Everything Happens to McCarey: During those sparse times when he isn't breaking his valuable neck, Leo Mc-

Carey does direct some extraordinary pictures'' (Carroll), 48, 240
Extension, 240

Fairbanks, Douglas, Sr., 144, 149
Farber, Manny, 190
"Far Side, The" (Larson), 140
Fatty at Coney Island (Arbuckle, 1917), 196
"Felix Knight and the Boys'' (Brooks), 199
Fellner, Chris, 209
Ferguson, Otis, 178
Fibber McGee and Molly (radio program), 42
"Fiddle and the Bow, The,'' 189, 231
Fields, W.C., 18, 41, 68, 73, 125, 188, 200; antiheroic persona of, 46, 65, 181, 205; copyrighted Library of Congress sketches of antiheroic, 46; huckster persona of, 128; McCarey as drinking companion of, 40; meshing surrealistic scenes into the movie realism of, 90, 113; mistress's book on, 156; Otis Ferguson on, 178; Universal on, 192
Fighting Kentuckian, The (stars Wayne, 1949), 107, 270
"Fight to Greet Actors," 224
Film (Beckett, 1946), 139
Film (England), 194
"Film Comedians in Leeds: Whirlwind Tour of the Provinces by Laurel & Hardy," 57
Film Culture, 190
Film Daily, 69
Film Fan Monthly, 243
"Filmic Bouquet of Laurel and Hardy Rarities, A'' (Rothstein), 217
Films and Filming (England), 189, 192, 193, 237
"Film's First Comic Antiheroes: Leo McCarey's Laurel and Hardy'' (Gehring), 209
Films in Review, 33, 157, 168, 209, 233
Films of Laurel and Hardy, The (Everson), 166–67, 194
Film Survey, 183

"Film: Way Out West'' (Paul), 200
Film Weekly (England), 35, 61, 97–98, 224, 225
The Finishing Touch (1928), 37, 143
Finlayson, James, 6, 24, 73, 98, 135, 165, 198, 270
"First Turnaround, The'' (Kerr), 206
Fischer, Edward, 240
Fisher, Bud, 47–48
Florida Metropolis, 9–10, 198
Flying Deuces, The, (1939), 69–70, 79, 91, 96, 268
Following the Comedy Trail (Smith), 169, 200
Fonda, Jane, 66
Ford, John, 73, 88, 187
45 Minutes from Hollywood (1926), 21, 262
Four Clowns (Youngson, 1970), 189
Fox, Ian, 35
Fra Diavolo (1933, also known as *The Devil's Brother*), 90, 188
Frank, Elizabeth, 111, 228
Frauds and Frenzies (1918), 18
From Soup to Nuts (1927), 222, 264
Front Row, 199
Frozen North, The (Keaton, 1922), 23
"Funny Film Faces: How They Got That Way'' (Tildesley), 144, 222–23
"Funny Mr. Laurel Who Keeps on Getting Married," 226
Fun on the Tyrol, 7
"Fun with Laurel and Hardy: Seeking the Fool-proof Job,'' 190
Further Perils of Laurel and Hardy (Youngson, 1967), 189

Gable, Clark, 74
Gardella, Kay, 239
Garland, Robert, 75, 179
Garvin, Anita, 165
Gershwin, George, 64
Get 'em Young (1926), 28, 263
Gifford, Dennis, 192
Gilbert, Billy, 61, 77, 198, 202, 209, 260, 271
Gilford, Jack, 139–40
Giusti, Marco, 163

Glaze, Ann, 224–25
Gleason, Jackie, 14, 136–37, 233, 236
Goat, The (Keaton, 1921), 103
Godard, Jean-Luc, 31
Goddard, Paulette, 278
Goddard, Phil, 161
Going Bye-Bye! (1934), 79, 266
Going My Way (McCarey, 1944), 29, 95
Golden Age of Comedy, The (Youngson, 1958), 189
"Golden Eye, The" (Miller), 176, 178
Goldstein, Larry, 234–35
Golf (1922), 19
Good Soldier Schweik (Hasek), 60
Gordon, Pete, 40
Go West (Keaton, 1925), 73
Go West (stars Marx Brothers, 1940), 73
Granada Club, 243
Grant, Cary, 42, 101, 238
"Great Comic's Epitaph: 'It's Been a Great Life' " (Berman), 238
Great Guns (1941), 93, 95–98, 103, 182–83, 192, 229, 269
Great Race, The (Edwards, 1965), 194
Greene, Graham, 134, 176
Green Pastures (Connally), 64
Grierson, John, 44, 130, 173–75, 178, 186, 191
Grodin, Charles, 138–39
Guide to Laurel and Hardy Movie Locations, A (Smith), 169, 200
Guiles, Fred Lawrence, 7, 17, 23, 30, 40, 54–55, 58, 62–63, 156, 158–60, 164

Habeas Corpus (1928), 217
Half a Man (1925), 27, 263
Hall, Charlie, 165
Hall, Mordaunt, 172
Hallelujah (Vidor, 1929), 64
Halliwell, Leslie, 213–14
"Hal Roach to Receive Special Oscar," 219
"Happy Hooligan" (Opper comic strip), 47
Hardy, Elizabeth (half sister), 2, 9
Hardy, Emily (half sister), 2, 268
Hardy, Henry (half brother), 2

Hardy, M. Emmie (mother), 2, 3, 225, 259, 260
Hardy, Madelyn Saloshin (first wife), 8, 10, 261
Hardy, Myrtle Lee Reeves (second wife), 28–29, 40–41, 54, 91, 93, 108, 262, 264, 265, 266, 267, 269
Hardy, Oliver (father of the comedian), 2, 3, 16, 17, 259, 260
Hardy, Oliver Norvell, frontispiece (illus.), 11 (illus.), 39 (illus.), 43 (illus.), 53 (illus.), 71 (illus.), 80 (illus.), 100 (illus.), 112 (illus.), 126 (illus.), 177 (illus.), 201 (illus.); company man, 92; gambling of, 40–41, 107, 226, 243; gold and, 4, 19, 27, 41, 228; name, 17; newspaper comics and, 47–48, 49 (illus.); parallels between McCarey and, 27; praise and/or preference for, 170–71, 173–74, 184, 205; Semon and, 18–20, 262; singer, 2–3, 6, 8, 9, 10, 12, 17, 64, 74–75, 147, 208–9; teaming of Laurel and, 34; weight of, 8–9, 10, 17, 104, 111, 113, 228, 229, 230, 231, 232; women and, 28, 40–41, 62, 91–92, 261, 264, 266, 267, 268, 269. *See also* Laurel, Stan; Stan & Ollie
Hardy, Lucille (third wife), 117 n.14, 127, 159, 218, 245, 270, 271; BBC documentary and, 3, 9; Hardy on comedy via, 67; his weight and, 9, 12, 232; in-laws and, 91–92, 199; marriage of the comedian and, 91, 108, 268. *See also* Hardy, Oliver Norvell
Hardy, Sam (half brother), 2
"Hardy and Rogers: *What Might Have Been*" (Brooks), 199
"Hardy of Laurel and Hardy Dies with Last Message to Wife Unspoken," 232
"Hardy Perennials Win Laurels: Rosy Bids Bud from Comics' Europe Work," (Scheuer), 109–10, 228–29
Harlow, Jean, 50
Harmon, Larry, 127, 218–19, 272
Harris, Joel Chandler, 65
Hasek, Jaroslav, 60
Hatley, T. Marvin, 68, 159, 198, 260,

272, 285. *See also* "Dance of the Cuckoos"

Hats Off (1927), 62–63, 223

Heath, Wes, 171, 197

"Helpful Henry" (comic strip), 47, 48

Helpmates (1932), 1, 4, 6, 63, 200, 265

" 'HERE'S ANOTHER FINE MESS!':
A Dissertation on Laurel and Hardy—
the ambassadors of the unprivileged"
(Taylor), 183–85, 197

"Here's to Finn!" (Jones), 198

Herman, Pee Wee, 180

Herridge, Frances, 174

Herriman, George, 46

Herring, Robert, 170

Hesse, Herman, 59–60

Hill, Hamlin, 133, 207

Hitchcock, Alfred, 210

Hoffman, Allan, 191–92

Hogbin, John, 190

Hog Wild (1930), 6, 132, 164, 166, 175,
176, 200, 215, 264

Hold That Ghost (stars Abbott & Costello, 1941), 103

"Hollywood" (Bogdanovich), 240

Hollywood Party (1934), 104

Hollywood Reporter, 225–26

Hollywood Review of 1929, 65, 264

"Hollywood Victory Caravan," 101–2,
269

Home from the Honeymoon (A.J. Jefferson), 6, 7, 58. *See also Duck Soup*

Honeymooners, 14, 136–37, 139

"Honolulu Baby" (Hatley), 68

Hoose-Gow, The (1929), 129, 150, 200

Hope, Bob (Leslie T. Hope), 13, 96,
101–2, 195, 196

Hope & Crosby, 24

Horne, James, 241

Horse Feathers (stars Marx Brothers,
1932), 61

Housman, Arthur, 165

Howard, Curly, 9. *See also* Three
Stooges, The

Howard, Kathleen, 65, 181

"How to Get a Driver's License." *See*
Drivers' License Sketch, The"

"H.R. on L & H," 238

Hubbard, Frank "Kin" (Abe Martin), 16

Hughes, John, 138

Huns and Hyphens (1918), 18

Hurley, Edgar, 13, 14

Hurley, Wren, 13, 14

"I'll Never Work Again," 231

"In the Blue Ridge Mountains of Virginia," 74. *See also* "Trail of the
Lonesome Pine, The,"

In the Night Kitchen (Sendak), 137

It Happened One Night (Capra, 1934), 74

It's a Gift (stars Fields, 1934), 65, 205

Jefferson, Arthur J. ("A.J."—Laurel's
father), death of, 270; diary of, 72–73;
essay on Laurel by, 58, 233; importance of *Home from the Honeymoon*,
by, 6–7, 58 (see *Duck Soup*, 1927; *Another Fine Mess*, 1930); Laurel helped
by, 5, 6, 7, 12; marriage of Metcalfe
and, 259; visiting Hollywood by, 58,
72–73, 223, 266; womanizing, 17–18,
57, 260

Jefferson, Arthur Stanley. *See* Laurel,
Stan

Jefferson, Beatrice Olga (Laurel's sister),
55, 111, 245, 260

Jefferson, Everett (Teddy—Laurel's
younger brother), 69, 260, 266

Jefferson, Gordon (Laurel's older
brother), 259, 260

Jefferson, Joseph, 2

Jefferson, Joseph III, 2

Jefferson, Sydney (Laurel's brother), 260

Jefferson, Venitia (Laurel's stepmother),
55, 57, 72, 165, 266

Jenkinson, Philip, 216

Jitterbugs (1943), 93, 98–99, 101, 102–
3, 179–81, 186, 191, 203, 243, 269

Joannon, Leo, 108–9

Johaueson, Blaud, 181, 182

Jones, Bobby, 54

Jones, Hank, 198

Jones, Lori S., 196

Jordan, Bert, 76, 240–41

Kanin, Garson, 211
"Ka-Plop and Ka-Bloop: Laurel and
  Hardy Reveal What Makes You Hear
  Such Funny Things," 42, 143–44,
  147–51
Karno, Fred, 7, 260, 264
Kaufman, George, 67
Kaye, Danny, 115, 116, 271
Keaton, Buster, 64, 103, 163, 192, 207–
  8, 209, 210; comedy pantheon in-
  cludes, 14, 190; dark comedy of, 79,
  139; decline of, 26, 160; Laurel fu-
  neral attended by, 238; parody and,
  23, 73
Kelly, Gene, 163
Kelly, Patsy, 88
Kennaugh, Alan, 219
Kennedy, Edgar, 31, 101, 133, 206, 259,
  269
Kerkhoff, Jim, 198
Kerr, Walter, 30, 129, 206–7
Keystone Kops, 234–35
"Keystone Trio, The," 13
Kilgore, Al, 165
Kinematograph (England, later called
  Kine Weekly), 55, 56, 57–58, 224
King Bee productions, 9, 10, 12, 261,
  262
Kinsey, Hamilton, 75–76
Knight, Arthur, 188
Kracauer, Siegfried, 131
"Krazy Kat" (Herriman comic strip), 46
"Ku-Ku Song Man!, The" (Shadduck),
  198

Lacourbe, Roland, 168–69, 259
Lady Eve, The (Sturges, 1941), 235
Laemmle, Carl, 16
Lahue, Kalton C., 14, 194
"L & H & Henry Ford" (Presbys and
  Limbacher), 197
"L & H Cult, The," 194
"L & H Hit the Charts" (Fellner), 209
"L & H: Just Like a Film," 105
Langdon, Harry, 19, 192, 193; birth of,
  259; comedy pantheon member, 14,
  106, 190; decline of, 106, 129; influ-
  ence on Laurel & Hardy of, 27, 45–46;

Laurel replaced by, 46, 79, 84, 87,
  88–89, 106, 267, 268
Larson, Gary, 140
"Last of Laurel, The" (Wright), 175,
  176
"Latter Days of Laurel and Hardy" (Gifford), 192
Laughing Gravy (1931), 174
Laughton, Charles, 92
Laurel, Ida Kitaeva Raphael (Laurel's last
  wife), 107–8, 114, 115, 116, 127,
  241, 269, 270, 271
"Laurel, Illeanna (Laurel's third wife),
  76, 81–85, 86, 87, 94, 107, 267, 268
Laurel, Lois, Jr. (Laurel's daughter), 3,
  38, 39 (illus.), 70, 72, 83, 85, 116,
  146, 242, 245, 263, 272
Laurel, Lois Neilson (Laurel's first wife),
  54, 69, 85, 93, 116, 146, 263, 264;
  early marriage stability of, 26, 38, 83;
  Laurel mothered by, 58–60
Laurel, Stan, frontispiece (illus.), 39 (illus.), 43 (illus.), 53 (illus.), 71 (illus.),
  78 (illus.), 80 (illus.), 100 (illus.), 126
  (illus.), 177 (illus.), 201 (illus.); comedy theory of, 221, 222, 223, 225,
  234–35, 245; dark humor of, 75–77,
  79, 83, 91, 110, 116, 137–38, 157,
  167, 174, 176; drinking of, 22, 25, 26,
  70, 81, 84; fishing of, 72–73, 77, 114,
  145, 228, 242; friction between Hardy
  and, 34–36, 241; instability of, 82, 83,
  84, 242; letter writing of, 35, 36, 102,
  115, 161, 232, 237; parody and, 22–
  24, 27, 48, 50, 73–75, 230; production
  control, loss of, 94–95; reincarnation
  and, 69–70; teaming of Hardy and, 34;
  trips to England by Hardy and, 28, 51,
  54, 55, 92, 104, 112 (illus.), 157,
  223–24; wit of, 72, 76, 84, 85–86,
  114, 116, 161, 226, 227, 244; woman
  problems of, 15, 25, 40, 58–59, 81,
  114, 116, 153, 165; workaholic nature
  of, 4, 15, 38, 159, 220. See also
  Hardy, Oliver Norvell; Stan & Ollie
Laurel, Stanley Robert Jefferson (Laurel's
  son), 38, 264
Laurel, Virginia Ruth (Laurel's second

wife), 88, 93, 94, 107, 116, 153, 156, 159–60, 266, 267, 269; A.J. Jefferson on, 72–73; comedian's early relationship with, 70; eccentric, 81–82, 83–84, 85–86, 268; Laurel's temperamentality according to, 35, 241; *Way Out West* inspired by, 73

Laurel & Hardy (Barr), 162–63, 188, 200

"Laurel & Hardy" (Gifford), 192

Laurel & Hardy (Giusti), 163

Laurel & Hardy (McCabe), 29, 158, 166–67

"Laurel and Hardy" (Nizer), 208

"Laurel and Hardy: Au Revoir," 193

"Laurel and Hardy: Big European Itinerary," 55

Laurel & Hardy Book, The (Maltin), 164–66

Laurel & Hardy: Clown Princes of Comedy (Crowther), 163–64, 199

"Laurel and Hardy: Enthusiastic Admirers in the North," 56, 224

Laurel and Hardy Feature Productions, 92, 93

"Laurel and Hardy Find New Fame: But It Hasn't Brought Them a Cent" (Frank), 111, 228, 268

Laurel & Hardy in Coventry (Reardon), 105, 245–46

"Laurel and Hardy in Nottingham," 245

"Laurel and Hardy Love Affair, The" (Bradbury), 138, 214, 244

Laurel & Hardy Magazine, The, 199

"Laurel and Hardy Make the Top Ten" (Blanche), 209

"Laurel & Hardy Meet the Pink Panther" (Young), 197

"Laurel and Hardy Retain Their Appeal" (Hogbin), 190

Laurel & Hardy Scrapbook, The (Scagnetti), 161–62

"Laurel & Hardy Slapstick at Beekman" (Crist), 194

Laurel and Hardy's Laughing Twenties (Youngson, 1965), 189, 194

"Laurel & Hardy: The Above Have Arrived," 228

Laurel and Hardy: The Golden Age of Hollywood (album), 208–9

Laurel and Hardy: The Magic Behind the Movies (Skretvedt), 36, 165–66

"Laurel & Hardy to Broadcast Tonight," 224

"Laurel and Hardy Visit Any Old Port" (Sheard), 199, 265

"Laurel and Hardy Visit London" (record), 57

Laurel Before Hardy (Owen-Pawson and Mouland), 17, 155, 160–61

Laurel et Hardy (Borde and Perrin), 44, 167–68

"Laurel et Hardy" (Chavance), 168, 170–71

Laurel et Hardy (Coursodon), 167–68

"Laurel et Hardy: Impossible n'est pas anglais" (Salachas), 245

"Laurel et Hardy: la triste histoire des rois du rive morts dans la misère" (MacTrevor), 114–15, 245

Laurel et Hardy: Ou l'enfance de l'art (Lacourbe), 168–69

"laurel et hardy: una allegorie de la castrophe" (Guay), 209

"Laurel, Hardy Legacy: A Victory for Widows' Rights," 127

"Laurel High-hats Hardy" (Fox), 35, 224

"Laurel in Shirt Sleeves Holds Family Party" (Calder), 223

"Laurels for Laurel" (Mitchell), 244

"Laurel Smiling Again But Not for the Films," 233

"Laurel to Help Prepare TV Scripts on Team," 236

"Laurel Weds No. 3 as No. 2 Gives Chase," 81–82

"Laurel Without Hardy," 33, 233

Lawrence, Rosina, 73, 181

Leave 'Em Laughing (1928), 64, 69, 263

Leeflang, Thomas, 161

"Legend Grows, The" (Atherton), 113

LeGuay, Philippe, 209

Lemon Drop Kid, The (stars Hope, 1951), 96

Leno, Dan, 2, 47, 79, 83, 103, 115, 161, 186
"Leo et les aléas" (Daney and Noames), 239–40
"Leo McCarey Comes Our Way" (Fischer), 240
"Leo McCarey: From Marx to McCarthy" (Silver), 206
"Leo McCarey Oral History," 30, 33, 51, 165, 239–40, 246
"Leo McCarey: The Man Behind Laurel & Hardy" (Gehring), 209
Leon, Darren, 218
Leonard, William, 209
Lewis, Jerry, 96, 105, 114, 115, 116, 161, 236, 245, 271
Liberty (1928), 37, 208, 214, 217, 264
Liberty (magazine), 208
Life, 183
Life in a Putty Knife Factory (Smith), 28
"Life of Comedy, A," 193, 240–41
"Lighter People, The" (Robinson), 185–88
Limbacher, James, 197
Linder, Max, 180
Live Ghost, The (1934), 79, 266
"Living with Laughter" (Roach), 237–38
Lloyd, Harold, 13–14, 24, 37, 38, 79, 190
"Logic of Comedy, The" (Grierson), 173–76, 186, 191
Lombard, Carole, 81
London Daily Star, 73
London Dispatch, 231
Long, Walter, 65, 165
Look (magazine), 84, 199, 227
Los Angeles Daily News, 218
Los Angeles Examiner, 216
Los Angeles Herald Examiner, 217, 218
Los Angeles Record, 38
Los Angeles Times, 50, 109, 127, 214, 216, 218, 221, 228
Low Man on a Totem Pole (Smith), 28
Lubin Motion Pictures, 9
Lucas, Wilfred, 65
Lucky Dog (1918), 21, 243, 262
Ludin, Walter, 101
Lynne, Sharon, 74, 75, 181

McCabe, John, 9, 17, 83, 164, 165, 168; *Babe: The Life of Oliver Hardy* by, 4, 282; books on Laurel and/or Hardy, 156–60; *Comedy World of Stan Laurel, The* by, 34; *Laurel & Hardy* by, 29; *Mr. Laurel and Mr. Hardy* by, 29–30, 118 n.43, 203, 271; "Songs of the Desert" and, 116; team meets, 110–11, 270
McCaffrey, Donald W., 66, 205–6
MacCall, Rene, 232
McCarey, Leo, 52 (illus.), 157, 159, 162, 203, 205; antiheroic life of, 6, 48, 50–51, 85, 161, 217, 239–40; birth of, 260; career background, 29, 95, 161; charisma of, 27–28; comic realism of, 32, 42, 50, 61, 80, 90; death of, 271; motto of, 41, 238; moving to features by, 44–45, 63; pacing of, 30, 41, 118 n.43, 129–30, 166; stories by, 27, 44–45, 48, 88, 110, 166; supervisor, 27, 32–33, 62–63, 64, 222; teaming by, 3, 29–30, 263; tit-for-tat routine by, 31–32, 50, 129; W.C. Fields drank with, 40
McCarey, Stella Martin, 51
MacFarland, Spanky, 88
McIntyre, William A., 199
McKnight, Gerald, 231
MacLaine, Shirley, 69
McLean, Albert F., Jr., 46
McLeish, Kenneth, 137
McMannus, George, 46
McPherson, Calvin, 185
MacTrevor, Joan, 245
MacWilliams, Glen, 99
Madame Mystery (1926), 28
"Mae Charlotte Dahlberg" (Brooks), 199
Magill, Frank, 210–11
Maginot Line, 86
Maltin, Leonard, 164–66, 202–4, 211
Mamoulian, Rouben, 64
Man on the Flying Trapeze, The (stars Fields, 1935), 14
"Man Who Corrupted Moonbaum, The" (Thurber), 50, 51
Marceau, Marcel, 115, 167, 236

"Marcel Marceau on Stan Laurel: KUSF
Interview, Early 1966," 236
March of the Wooden Soldiers. See
Babes in Toyland
Martin, Pete, 48
Martin, Steve, 73, 85, 138, 139
Martin & Lewis, 23, 34, 96. *See also*
Jerry Lewis
Marx, Betty, 58
Marx, Chico, 4, 58, 74, 93, 130, 161,
226
Marx, Groucho, 24, 29, 44, 61, 67, 130,
161, 181, 196, 225, 235
Marx, Harpo, 29, 61, 64, 130, 171, 174,
206
Marx Brothers, 18, 24, 34, 44, 54, 73,
172, 202, 244; critically praised, 125;
dark comedy of the, 174; Laurel &
Hardy, W.C. Fields, and the, 68, 128,
181, 188, 200; McCarey and the, 29;
verbal slapstick of the, 129–30
Mast, Gerald, 33, 132, 133, 204
Masters, Dorothy, 75, 181–82
Mazurki, Jeanette, 242
Meadows, Audrey, 136–37
"Meet a Gentleman! Stan Laurel!," 237
Men O'War, (1929), 96
Metcalfe, George (Laurel's maternal
grandfather), 26, 76, 260, 261
Metcalfe, Madge (Laurel's mother), 1,
17–18, 40, 259, 260
Metcalfe, Sarah (Laurel's maternal grand-
mother), 161, 260, 261
M-G-M (Metro-Goldwyn-Mayer), 38, 54,
65, 93, 101, 189, 192, 265; comedy
shortsightedness of, 26, 118 n.32, 235
M-G-M's Big Parade of Fun (Youngson),
1964), 189
Midnight Run (Brest), 138–39
Miller, Henry, 176, 178
Milwaukee Journal, 226
Min and Bill (stars Dressler, 1930), 38
Mr. Hulot (Jacques Tati), 207
Mr. Laurel & Mr. Hardy (McCabe), 29–
30, 110–11, 156, 157, 158, 159, 168,
174, 203, 271
Mitchell, Lisa, 244–45
Moak, E.R., 34, 225

Model-T Ford, 135, 138, 226
Monsieur Beaucaire (stars Valentino,
1924), 27
Monsieur Don't Care (1924), 27
Montgomery, John, 188
Monty Python's Flying Circus, 109, 202
Mooring, W.H., 225
Morecambe & Wise, 137, 163
Moreland, Mantan, 241
Morros, Boris, 91
Morse, Viola, 40, 91–92, 264
Motion Picture Classic, 143, 147, 222
Motion Picture Exhibitors Herald-World,
36–38, 69, 169–70
Motion Picture Herald Tribune. See *Mo-
tion Picture Exhibitors Herald-World*
Motography: Exploiting Motion Pictures,
10
Mouland, Bill, 17, 155, 160–61
Movie Classic, 59–60, 224
Mud and Sand (1922), 22–23, 211, 262
Mumming Birds, 7
Murnau, F.W., 18
Music Box, The (1932), 28, 77, 87, 131,
138, 176, 187, 195; Basil Wright and,
61; Leo McCarey and, 62–63; Oscar
for, 53 (illus.), 54, 205; realism and,
89–90, 193–94, 237; Sisyphus, 208,
209
"Mutt and Jeff" (Fisher comic strip),
47–48
My Autobiography (Chaplin), 16, 271
My Favorite Brunette (stars Hope, 1947),
96
"my hobby, laurel and hardy" (Polacek),
115, 236–37
"My Lad Laurel by Stan's Father" (Jef-
ferson), 58, 223
My Life with Chaplin (Grey, with
Cooper), 156
My Little Chickadee (stars Fields and
West, 73, 192

Nation, The, 178
Native American Humor (Blair), 130
Neilson, Lois. *See* Laurel, Lois Neilson
Nelson, Richard Alan, 213
Nemy, Enid, 219

Never Give a Sucker an Even Break
  (stars Fields, 1941), 90, 192
"Newest Upheaval in the Not-So-Private
  Life of Sad-Faced Mr. Laurel," 81,
  226
Newhart, Bob, 139
New Republic, 178
News Chronicle, 231–32
Newsweek, 102, 104
New York American, 75, 179. See also
  New York Journal-American
New York Daily Mirror, 181
New York Daily News, 75, 81–82, 181,
  194, 226, 239
New Yorker, The, 46, 130
New York Evening Post, 68
New York Herald Tribune, 88, 189, 194,
  238
New York Journal-American, 81, 98,
  226–27, 229, 239
New York Morning Telegraph, 234, 236
New York Post, 75, 88–89, 98, 180, 182,
  194
New York Sun, 69, 179, 181
New York Times, 56, 165, 199, 219; ac-
  colades for team by, 69, 75, 89, 98,
  171–72, 182–83, 188–89, 197, 217;
  counterview of, 171, 197; Laurel &
  Hardy coverage in death by, 231, 238,
  239
New York World-Telegraph, 69, 89, 179
New York World Telegraph and Sun, 232
Nickelodeon (Bogdanovich, 1976), 50
Night at the Opera, A (stars Marx Broth-
  ers, 1935), 44, 67, 128, 226
Night in an English Music Hall, A, 7
Night in the Show, A (1915), 7
Night Owls (1930), 110, 147, 264, 270
"1937—An Interview with L & H," 227
9 to 5 (stars Fonda), 66
Nizer, Alvin, 208
Noames, Jean-Louis, 239–40
"Nobody Knew Much About Anything
  Then" (Young), 243
"No Laughing Matter: Laurel & Hardy
  Find Themselves on TV . . . for Free,"
  230
"No Laughs in Laurel Home-Life, So

Comedian and Wife Separate" (Glaze),
  59–60, 224–25
Nollen, Scott Allen, 164
Normand, Mabel, 13, 31, 180
Nosferatu (Murnau, 1922), 18
Nothing But Trouble (1944), 93, 192
Nottingham Chronicle (England), 11, 228
Nugent, Frank S., 75, 89, 171
Nuts in May (1917), 15, 16, 262
Nutty Burglars, The, 14, 261
Nutty Professor, The (Lewis), 96

"Obliging Oliver" (comic strip), 48, 49
  (illus.)
"of mr. laurel and mr. hardy: Huntington
  Man Their No. 1 Fan" (Alley), 115,
  236–37
Oliver the Eighth (1934), 66, 69, 266
"Ollie and Stan: They Bore Life's Bur-
  dens with Courage" (Trubo), 206
"Ollie and Stan: Two Minds Without a
  Single Thought" (Cooper), 205
One Good Turn (1931), 215
"One More Crash in Love Can Not Sour
  Stan Laurel," 226
Opper, Fred, 47
Oranges and Lemons (1923), 21
"Our Gang" series, 22, 24, 29, 38, 88
Our Relations (1936), 79, 173, 188, 205,
  267
Our Wife (1931), 241
Owen-Pawson, Jenny, 17, 155, 160–61

Pack Up Your Troubles (1932), 65, 96,
  265
Palmer, Jerry, 214
Pangborn, Franklin, 90
Paperhanger's Helper, The (1925), 10,
  198, 263
Pardon Us (1931), 5, 23, 64, 66, 265
Parish, Robert, 209
Parker, Eleanor, 144, 221, 230
Parrott, Charles. *See* Chase, Charley
Parrott, James, 40, 73
Parsons, Louella, 93
Part-Time Wife (McCarey, 1930), 51
Patrick, Lee, 243
Paul, William, 200

Pelswick, Rose, 98, 179–80
Pembroke, Perce, 25
"People's Clowns, The" (Usher), 213
Perelman, S.J., 46, 130
Perfect Day, A (1929), 50, 77, 133, 135, 147, 264
Perrin, Charles, 44, 79, 163, 167–68
Peters, John, 48, 50
Photoplay, 34, 64, 143, 145, 222, 225
Pick a Star (1937), 79, 267
Pickford, Mary, 144, 149
Picturegoer Weekly (England), 58, 223
Pie-eyed (1925), 25
"Pies Will Be Flying at Premier of Laurel and Hardy Treasures" (Rense), 217
Planes, Trains and Automobiles (Hughes, 1987), 138–39
Playboy, 214
Playgoer, 221
Play It Again, Sam (Allen, 1972), 59, 96
Playtime (Tati, 1967), 208
"Plump and Runt" series, 10
Polacek, Mike, 115, 236–37
Pope, Dennis, 194
"Popularity Grows on Borrowed Roots" (Young), 137, 197
"Popularity Rains on Laurel & Hardy: An Exclusive Interview," 229
Porgy and Bess (Gershwin), 64
Positif, 209
Poston, Tom, 139
Powers, Len, 220
Pratfall, 10, 34–35, 167, 169, 196–98, 222, 230, 235, 236, 238, 241–45
Presbys, Henry, 197
Price, Kate, 10
Purple Rose of Cairo (Allen, 1985), 196
Putting Pants on Philip (1927), 62, 240, 263

Radio Times, 216
Ramish, Adolph, 15
Raphael, Ida Kitaeva. *See* Laurel, Ida Kitaeva Raphael
Ray, Bobby, 10, 198
Raynor, Dan, 8
Reardon, Laurence, 105, 245–46
Reeves, Alf, 7

Reeves, Myrtle Lee. *See* Hardy, Myrtle Lee Reeves
Rense, Rip, 216–18
"Return of Babe's Night Out" (Wilson), 104–5, 243
Richie, Billie, 12
Richman, Arthur, 51
Riding High (1950), 107, 270
"Ripley's Believe It or Not" (newspaper panel), 54, 128
Roach, Hal, 29, 31, 34, 45, 147; birth of, 260; businessman, 24, 26, 36, 38; comedy according to, 67, 237–38; conflict between Laurel and, 22, 46, 59, 77, 79, 86–87, 88, 127, 238, 226, 267, 268; lifetime achievement Oscar for, 219, 271
Roach, Hal, Jr., 113
Road to Morocco (stars Hope and Crosby, 1942), 24
Robbins, Jess, 243
Robin Hood, 104
Robinson, David, 157, 185–88
Robinson, Jeffrey, 211
Robinson Crusoeland. See *Atoll K*
Rock, Joe, 16, 22, 24–26, 27, 28, 197, 242, 263
Rogers, Charley, 101
Rogers, Virginia Ruth. *See* Laurel, Virginia Ruth
Rogers, Will, 24, 32, 63, 200, 265
Rogue Song, The (1930), 145, 222, 264
Rothstein, Mervyn, 217
Roughing It (Twain, 1872), 73
Ruge, Billy, 10, 198, 261
Ruggles of Red Gap (McCarey, 1935), 92
Rum 'Uns from Rome, The, 7
Runyon, Damon, 96
"Ruth Laurel Remembers," 197, 242
Ryskind, Morrie, 67

"Saddest Man in Hollywood is a Comedian: Stan Laurel," 84, 227
"Sad Pan, Frying Pan Met, Says Stan Laurel," 82, 226
"Sad-Pan Stan's Comic Wife Troubles," 226

"Sad Reunion of Two Men Made World
Laugh" (McKnight), 231
Safety Last (stars Lloyd, 1923), 14, 37
Sailors, Beware!, 274
St. Clair, Malcolm, 103
St. Louis Post Dispatch, 185
Salachas, Gilbert, 245
Saloshin, Madelyn. *See* Hardy, Madelyn
Saloshin
"Salute to Stan Laurel, A," 239
Sandburg, Carl, 8
Sandford, Tiny, 132, 134, 165
Sandrich, Mark, 101
San Francisco Examiner, 92
Saps at Sea (1940), 66, 79, 91, 268
Satterfield, Robert, 244
Saturday Evening Post, 48, 205
"Saving Turnaround, The," (Kerr), 206–
7
Sawmill, The (1922), 19, 262
Scagnetti, Jack, 161–62
Schelly, William, 106, 212–13
Scheuer, Philip K., 221, 228–29
"Search for a Cinematic Bag of Gold"
(Leon), 218
Seawright, Roy, 75
Second Hundred Years, The (1927), 32,
147, 263
Seiter, William, 196
Sellers, Peter, 115
"Semiotics of Humor, The: The Logic of
the Absurd" (Palmer), 214
Semon, Larry, 10, 18–19, 40, 83, 144,
150, 262
Sendak, Maurice, 137
Sennett, Mack, 7, 8, 13, 19, 22, 103,
133–34, 151
Sennwald, Andre, 60, 171
Shadduck, Jim, 198
Sheard, Philip, 199
Shifting Sands, 84, 199
Shipman, Ben, 40, 93, 94, 107
Shoulder Arms (Chaplin, 1917), 96
Should Married Men Go Home? (1928),
131, 133
Shriek of Araby, The (1923), 23
Shuvalova, Vera. *See* Laurel, Illeanna
Sight and Sound (England), 157, 185–86

Silver, Charles, 206
Sisyphus, 207, 208, 209
Skretvedt, Randy, 28, 32, 36, 64, 69,
87, 95, 98, 165
Slapstick (Vonnegut), 138, 215
"Slapstick that Sticks" (Canby), 199
Slipping Wives (1927), 32
Smith, H. Allen, 28, 85
Smith, Leon, 169, 200
Snow Hawk (1925), 25
Soilers, The (1923), 24
Soldier Man, The (1926), 45
Somewhere in Wrong (1925), 25
Sons of the Desert (fan club), 116, 137,
157, 160, 165, 167, 194, 198–99,
216–17
Sons of the Desert, The (1933), 43 (il-
lus.), 60, 196, 205, 212, 242, 266;
greatest feature was, 42, 44, 65–69,
73, 75, 171, 203, 205; Virginia Ruth
Laurel inspired, 73
Soup to Nuts (1928), 37
Speak Easily (Keaton, 1932), 208
Spectator, The (England), 89, 175, 176
Spensley, Dorothy, 64, 144–47
Spoilers, The (1923), 24
Spoor, George K., 22
Spot of Trouble, A (Laurel & Hardy
sketch), 110
Stagecoach, The (Ford, 1939), 73, 88
Stan & Ollie (screen character trade-
marks), affection between, 24, 62, 97,
204, 205; crying and, 23, 62, 71 (illus.), 103, 127, 132, 137, 145, 146,
147, 167; direct address and, 10, 177
(illus.), 195–96, 200, 237; dumbness
of, 31, 47, 54, 74, 129, 162, 170,
187; puddles and, 73–74, 144, 147,
149, 150; realism of, 32, 42, 44, 129,
147, 151–52, 163, 191, 203, 222–23,
225–27; slower pacing of, 30–31, 129,
203, 206–7, 211–12, 215, 221–22,
225; tie-twiddling and, 20 (illus.), 103,
132, 137, 138, 167, 214; tit-for-tat
and, 6, 31–32, 42, 97, 103–4, 130,
134, 135, 170, 209; women and, 15,
22, 26, 60, 83, 98, 131. *See also*
Hardy, Oliver Norvell; Laurel, Stan

"Stan Gets a Tan by Computer" (Walls), 219
"Stan Is Home" (Kennaugh), 219
"Stan Laurel at 70: 'I'm All Washed Up' " (Bacon), 236
"Stan Laurel est Mort," 193
"Stan Laurel, Ill at 67, Can't Bear Old Films" (Thomas), 232
"Stan Laurel, Now 70, Rips Modern Hollywood Practices" (DuBrow), 234
"Stan Laurel Pouts Out, Hardy to Solo," 88
Stan Laurel Productions, 88, 267
"Stan Laurel's Daughter Recalls Comic (Mazurki), 242
"Stan, Ollie and Harry" (Schelly), 212–13
"Stan on Stage" (Kerkhoff), 198
Stan : The Life of Stan Laurel (Guiles), 156, 158–60
Steamboat Bill, Jr. (Keaton, 1928), 208
Steppenwolf (Hesse), 59–60
Stevens, George, 33, 203, 260, 271
Stick Around (1925), 10, 198
"Story of a Fat Boy," 10
"Stumbling Upon the Lost Films of Laurel and Hardy" (Rense), 218
Sturges, Preston, 108, 235
"Summary and Survey: 1935" (Grierson), 174
Swiss Miss (1938), 67, 79, 88, 89–91, 171–72, 176, 184, 188, 203, 267

Take One, 33, 195
Taming of the Shrew, The (stars Fairbanks and Pickford, 1929), 144, 149
Tati, Jacques, 207, 208, 238
Taylor, Simon Watson, 183–85, 197
"Teamwork" (Brooks), 199
"Tear-Stained Laughter" (Moak), 34, 225
Telerama, 245
Temple, Shirley, 72
"têt-à-tête avec deux têtes de pioche," 105–7, 228
That's My Wife (1929), 133, 136
Theatre Arts, 232

Their First Mistake (1932), 60, 61–62, 65, 265
Their Purple Moment (1928), 22, 133
Them Thar Hills (1934), 61, 66, 90, 135, 266
"They Haven't Deserted Stan and Ollie" (Rense), 216
Thicker Than Water (1935), 79, 81, 266
Thirer, Irene, 88
This Is Your Life, 8–9, 152, 230
Thomas, Bob, 230–31, 232, 239
Thomas, Dylan, 202
Thomey, Todd, 243
"THOSE FUNNY BOYS: A Few Inside Facts About the Screen's Funniest Pair of Comedians and the Man Who Has Photographed Most of Their Pictures" (Dean), 220–21
"Those Two Goofy Guys" (Spensley), 64, 104, 144–47
¡Three Amigos! (stars Martin, Chase, and Short, 1986), 73
Three Stooges, The, 9, 24, 42, 125, 127, 184, 212, 234–35. See also Howard, Curly
Three Week Ends (stars Bow, 1928), 37
Thurber, James, 46, 50, 77, 85, 130
Tibbett, Lawrence, 65
Tildesley, Alice L., 144, 222–23
Time, 194, 269, 271
Times, The (London), 60, 86, 129, 188, 190, 219, 238
Tit for Tat (1935), 266
"Together Again," 228
Topper (stars Grant, 1937), 67
Toto the Clown (Arnold Nobello), 21, 22
"Trail of the Lonesome Pine, The" (record), 3, 57, 208–9
Tree in a Test Tube, The (1943), 93, 269
"Tribute to Hal Roach, A" (Gallery of Modern Art), 194, 237
Trubo, Richard, 206
Tugboat Annie (stars Dressler, 1933), 38
Tunney, Gene, 27
Turpin, Ben, 23
TV Guide, 230
TV Times (England), 219, 229
Twain, Mark, 73

20th Century-Fox, 92, 93, 94, 95, 99, 101, 102, 104, 192, 235, 269
"20 Hurt in Laurel and Hardy Stampede," 224
Twice Two (1933), 136
"Twilight of Clowns, The" (Blyth), 234
"Twilight Years, The" (Hoffman), 191–92
Twins (1925), 25
"Two Prize Idiots" (Parker), 221, 230
Two Tars (1928), 31, 37, 96, 134–35, 170, 206, 264

Unaccustomed As We Are (1929), 41–42, 88, 264
Uncle Remus stories (Harris), 65
Under Two Flags (1922), 24
Under Two Jags (1923), 24
Universal, 16, 192
"Universal Appeal of Laurel and Hardy, The" (Gifford), 192
Usher, Shaun, 213
Utopia. See *Atoll K*

Valentino, Rudolph, 22–23
Van Dyke, Dick, 51, 115, 116, 137, 156, 161, 231, 236, 238–39, 271
"Van Dyke to Emcee Stan Laurel Tribute" (Gardella), 239
Variety, 20, 69, 75, 88, 98, 138, 165, 172–73, 178–79, 185, 194
Verb, Boyd, 44, 233
Vidor, King, 64
Village Voice, 200, 202
Vim Studios, 9–10, 213, 261
"Virginia Lucille Jones Hardy Price" (Brooks), 199
Vitagraph, 18, 20, 40
Vonnegut, Kurt, 137–38, 215, 218
Von Stroheim, Eric, 48, 50

Waiting for Godot (Beckett), 137, 139, 197
Walker, Helen Louise, 5, 143–44, 147–51
Wallace, Richard, 28
Walls, Trevor, 219
Wandering Papas (1925), 28

Wardle, Irving, 86, 219
Warshow, Robert, 178
Warwick, Robert, 76
"Way It Was, The," 197, 242
Wayne, John, 73, 107, 270
Way Out West (1937), 44, 77, 79, 100 (illus.); critics on, 171, 172, 173, 175, 176, 181–82, 188, 200, 205, 210, 213; Laurel's favorite film was, 242; parody in, 23, 73–76, 182; stagecoach scene in, 152, 227; "The Trail of the Lonesome Pine" and, 3, 57, 74, 208; Virginia Ruth Laurel inspired, 73; "white magic" in, 60, 66, 201 (illus.)
W.C. Fields & Me (Monti and Rice), 156
Weber & Fields, 212
Weekend (Godard, 1967), 31
We Faw Down (1928), 69, 133, 264
West, Billy, 9, 10, 12, 18, 261, 262
West, Mae, 41, 73, 128, 200
West, Nathanael, 135
"West End Opening for Laurel and Hardy Play," 219
West of Hot Dog (1924), 27, 263
West of Pecos (1922), 27, 263
Westways, 244
"What the Picture Did For Me" (review section of *Motion Picture Exhibitors Herald-World*), 36–38
Wheeler and Woolsey, 216
When Comedy Was King (Youngson, 1960), 189
When Knighthood Was in Flower (stars Marion Davies, 1922), 24, 262
When Knights Where Cold (1923), 24, 262
"White Elephant Art Versus Termite Art" (Farber), 190–91
"white magic," 60–61, 66, 157–58, 190, 201 (illus.), 202, 204
White Wings (1923), 21
"Who's Who This Week in Pictures," 224
Wilder, Billy, 107, 109–10
Wile E. Coyote, 20
Williams, Robin, 139
Wilson, Jerry, 104–5
Winsten, Archer, 75, 180, 182

Winters, Jonathan, 236
With Love and Hisses (1927), 32, 96
"With MacLaurel & MacHardy in Bonnie Scotland" (Mooring), 225
"Wizard of Id, The" (Hart and Parker), 128
Wizard of Oz, The (1925), 20, 262
Woollcott, Alexander, 171
World Film News, 175
World of Laurel and Hardy, The (Leeflang), 161
"Worth a Thousand Words" (Brooks), 84, 199

Wow-Wows, The, 7
Wright, Basil, 61, 89, 175–76, 178, 186
Wrong Again (1929), 203

Yes, Yes Nanette (1925), 28
Young, Jordan R., 10, 137, 197, 198, 213, 243
Youngson, Robert, 189, 194, 199, 202–3
You're Darn Tootin' (1928), 217
"You, Too, Can Be a Comedian!" (Laurel & Hardy), 225–26

Zenobia (1939), 46, 88, 212, 268

About the Author

WES D. GEHRING is a Professor in the Department of Communications at Ball State University. He was named BSU Outstanding Young Faculty, 1982–1983 and Outstanding Researcher, 1985–1986.

Recent Titles in
Popular Culture Bio-Bibliographies: A Reference Series

Knute Rockne: A Bio-Bibliography
Michael R. Steele

John Henry: A Bio-Bibliography
Brett Williams

Charlie Chaplin: A Bio-Bibliography
Wes D. Gehring

Hank Williams: A Bio-Bibliography
George William Koon

Will Rogers: A Bio-Bibliography
Peter C. Rollins

Billy the Kid: A Bio-Bibliography
Jon Tuska

Errol Flynn: A Bio-Bibliography
Peter Valenti

W.C. Fields: A Bio-Bibliography
Wes D. Gehring

Elvis Presley: A Bio-Bibliography
Patsy Guy Hammontree

Charles A. Lindbergh: A Bio-Bibliography
Perry D. Luckett

The Marx Brothers: A Bio-Bibliography
Wes D. Gehring

Mae West: A Bio-Bibliography
Carol M. Ward

The Beatles: A Bio-Bibliography
William McKeen